Primary Circulation Area

Secondary Circulation Areas

D1242791

THE CHARLOTTE OBSERVER

The Daily Carolina Observer.

"ONWARD AND UPWARD---TRUE TO THE LINE."

VOL. 1.   CHARLOTTE, N. C., MONDAY MORNING, JANUARY 25, 1869.   **NO. 1.**

Attorneys at Law.

Vance & Dowd, Office at Court House.
Brown & Hutchison,   do.
Burwell & Tyler,   do.
J. H. Wilson, Office at Residence.
Osborne & Barringer, next building to Court House.
Jones & Johnston, over Express Office.
W. F. Davidson, over Koopman's Store.
R. P. Waring.
S. P. Smith.
S. W. Davis.
R. D. Osborne.
W. M. Shipp.

Physicians.

J. M. Miller,   J. P. McCombs,
C. J. Fox,   J. P. Jones,
R. Gibbon,   S. E. Bratton,
W. W. & R. K. Gregory,   P. P. Medlin.

Dentists.

Traywick & Blant,   J. H. Waytt,
A. W. Alexander,   W. E. Carr.

Druggists.

Dr. F. Scarr, Trade Street.
Dr. J. H. McAden, Northwest corner Trade and Tryon Streets.
Drs. Kilgore & Cureton, Northeast corner Trade and Tryon Streets.
Drs. Smith & Brem, Southwest corner Trade and Tryon Streets.
Dr. J. N. Butt, corner Trade and College Streets.

Banking Houses.

City Bank, Trade Street—Col. W. A. Williams, Cashier; C. N. G. Butt, Teller.
T. W. Dewey & Co., Tryon Street—T. W. Dewey, Cashier; E. Dewey, Teller.
First National Bank, Tryon Street—R. Y. McAden, President; W. P. Pegram, Cashier; L. S. Riddle, Teller.

Express and Telegraph Office.

W. P. Hill, Agent Southern Express.
G. H. King, Operator W. U. T. Co.

Railroad Officers.

N. C. R. R. H. M. Pritchard, Agent.
C. & S. C. R. R. Wm. Pegram, Agent.
W. C. & R. R. T. S. Whisnant, Agent.

Hotels.

Mansion House, W. P. Moore.
Matthews House, (formerly Charlotte Hotel) near N. C. R. R. Depot, Mrs. Rowe.
Trotter House, nearly opposite Tryon St. Methodist Church, Joshua Trotter.
Farmers' Hotel, Springs Corner, up stairs, Mr. Rich.

Architects.

Allen & Gregory.

Fire and Life Insurance.

Hutchison, Burroughs & Co., Trade Street.
W. A. Williams, City Bank.
Caldwell & Brenizer, old Charlotte Bank.
Chas. E. Bradshaw, at Haltom & Gray's.

Commission Merchants.

M. L. Wriston & Co., Mansion House building.
R. M. Oates & Co., Northeast corner trade and College streets.
Stenhouse, Macaulay & Co., Southwest corner Trade and College Streets.
J. Y. Bryce & Co., Trade Street.
Coit & Sims, Oates Building, Trade Street.

Booksellers and Stationers.

Tiddy & Bro. Tryon Street, Springs' Building.
Wade & Gunnels, Tryon Street, Meacham's old stand.

Watchmakers & Jewellers.

John T. Butler, Tryon Street.
A. Hales, Trade Street.
T. W. Davis, Tiddy & Bro's old stand, Trade Street.

Founderies, Factories, &c.

Mecklenburg Foundry and Machine Shop, on N. C. R. R.
Rock Island Factory, on N. C. R. R.
North State Washing Machine Co., near Lutheran Church.
Charlotte Foundry, Tatem, Sykes & Co.
Cook & Ellyson, Manufacturers and Dealers in all kinds of Farming Tools, in old Navy Yard.

Crockery Dealer.

Jas. Harty, near Court House, Trade Street.

Boot and Shoe Dealers.

S. B. Meacham, McAden's Iron Front Building, Tryon Street.
S. P. Smith next door to Dewey's Bank, Tryon Street.

Tinners and Dealers in Stoves, &c.

D. H. Byerly & Co., Trade St., under Mansion House.
Wiley & Gaston, Trade Street, near Court House.

Hardware.

Brem, Brown & Co., Trade Street.
Oates, Walter Brem & Co., corner store under Mansion House.
Taylor & Duncan, Trade Street.

Dry Goods.

TRADE STREET.

Brem, Brown & Co.,   J. Roessler, Agent,
Wittkowsky & Rintels,   B. Koopmann,
Asher & Mayer,   H. M. Phelps,
Baxbaum & Lang,   Elias & Cohen,
E. Lowengard,   J. H. Henderson,
J. R. Heckscher,   H. & B. Emanuel,

TRYON STREET.

Elias & Cohen,   Barringer & Wolfe,
A. Frankenthal,   C. M. Query.

Groceries.

TRADE STREET.

W. J. Black,   Stenhouse, Macaulay & Co.
Wm. H. Gregory,   B. M. Presson & Co.,
A. Berryhill,   Frazier, Scarlet & Co.,
S. Gross,   H. E. Hammond & Co.,
M. D. L. Moody,   McMurray, Davis & Co.,
W. A. Hannon,   J. S. Means & Sons,
W. S. Wearn,   W. Richards & Co.,
Walker & Bro.,   I. H. McGinn,
J. M. Sims,   Grier & Alexander,
T. Gifford,   H. B. McAllister,
  Jas. Platt.

TRYON STREET.

Carson & Grier,   Duls & Hilker.

Saddle and Harness Maker.

R. Shaw & Son, Tryon Street, opposite McAden's Iron Front Building.

Boot and Shoemakers.

E. H. White, Trade Street, opposite Bryce's Building.
C. Roediger, Trade Street, nearly opposite Presbyterian Church.
T. A. Hannon, Tryon Street, nearly opposite Matthews House.

Bar Rooms and Restaurants.

TRADE STREET.

Our House,   J. F. Alexander,
Wm. Dunn,   W. W. Hart,
Kinzel & Johnston,   F. M. Squires,
  J. D. Palmer.

TRYON STREET.

W. R. Cochrane,   Rigler & Horrah,
R. Morrison,   Geo. Cross,
Bryant & Co., College Street.

Cigar Manufacturer.

Thos. Kenny, Tryon Street.

Distillers.

Groot, Kuck & Co., Tryon Street.

Barbers.

Frank Schillinger, Trade Street.
Gulon & Gray,
Jerry Bethel, Tryon Street.
Span & Turner.

JACK CLAIBORNE

THE CHARLOTTE OBSERVER

ITS TIME AND PLACE, 1869–1986

The University of North Carolina Press
Chapel Hill and London

Library of Congress Cataloging-in-Publication Data

Claiborne, Jack.

The Charlotte observer.

Includes index.

1. Charlotte observer (Charlotte, N.C. : 1916)

I. Title.

PN4899.C335C433   1986   071′.5676   86-40026

ISBN 0-8078-1712-0

This book is dedicated to the memory of all
those men and women whose daily labors
through the years as carriers, truck drivers,
technicians, clerks, printers, pressmen,
salesmen, writers, photographers, editors and
publishers have made the Observer a
welcome messenger to generations of readers.

CONTENTS

ACKNOWLEDGMENTS

Nearly two years ago, when editors at the *Observer* asked if I could write a history of the newspaper in time for its 1986 centennial, without hesitating I said, "Sure." I had witnessed nearly half of that history and assumed that researching the other half would be a breeze. Only later, after surveying the change the paper had undergone over the past century, did I fully appreciate the scope of my assignment. Then I learned the worst: other than microfilm copies of the newspapers themselves, there were no records of the *Observer*'s operations, policies, personnel or profits for most of the years prior to 1955. In researching and writing the paper's history, I was going to need the memories and resources of many other people. Fortunately, there were a great many generous people willing to help.

I am especially grateful to William S. Price, Jr., director of the North Carolina Division of Archives and History; to his assistant, Suellen Hoy; and the division's director of publications, Jeffrey Crow, for their advice, encouragement, and assistance in locating valuable sources of information. It was Price who urged me to go beyond telling the *Observer*'s "inside story"—the newsroom lore that is handed down from one generation of reporters and editors to the next. He suggested that I broaden the focus by putting the *Observer* in the context of its times, in Charlotte, in North Carolina, and in the South. That is what I have tried to do.

I got similar advice from Margaret Blanchard and Donald L. Shaw, who teach journalism and communications history at UNC–Chapel Hill. Both steered me to valuable sources for understanding the history of journalism and other media, including Edwin and Michael Emery's *The Press and America: An Interpretive History of the Mass Media*, which provided a valuable backdrop for my research into the *Observer*'s history. Robert Banzhaf, who teaches printing production and management at Appalachian State University, was helpful in providing information about the development of printing technology.

Much of my understanding of events in North Carolina was gained from *North Carolina: The History of a Southern State*, by Hugh Talmadge Lefler and Albert Ray Newsome. Similarly, for background about the South after the Civil War, I consulted *The Desolate South*,

1865–1866, by John T. Trowbridge, and *The South During Recon-struction, 1865–1877*, by E. Merton Coulter. For background on the South after Reconstruction, I relied on C. Vann Woodward's *Origins of the New South, 1877–1913*, Paul M. Gaston's *The New South Creed*, and George B. Tindall's *The Emergence of the New South, 1913–1946*. For background on national affairs I turned to Samuel Eliot Morison's *Oxford History of the American People*.

Much of my information about Charlotte before the Civil War and during Reconstruction came from Dr. John Brevard Alexander's *Reminiscences of the Past Sixty Years* and from *Hornets' Nest: The Story of Charlotte and Mecklenburg County*, by LeGette Blythe and Charles Raven Brockmann. For many details relating to medical developments in Charlotte, I am indebted to Janette Greenwood, who shared with me portions of her manuscript on the history of Pres-byterian Hospital. Much of my understanding of Cameron Morri-son's career and campaign for governor was derived from Douglas Carl Abram's "A Progressive-Conservative Duel: The 1920 Demo-cratic Gubernatorial Primaries in North Carolina," which appeared in the *North Carolina Historical Review* for Autumn 1978.

I am also grateful to *Observer* editors and reporters whose past historical sketches provided a broad framework for my inquiries. Among them were Peter McLauchlin, Col. Charles R. Jones, Joseph P. Caldwell, James H. Parham, Julian S. Miller, Ernest B. Hunter, and Thomas G. Fesperman.

The bulk of the newspaper research for this volume was done in the Carolina Room of the Charlotte-Mecklenburg Public Library, where microfilm files include not only all available issues of the two *Observer*s and of the *Charlotte News*, but also copies of other Char-lotte newspapers which offer an insight into the *Observer*'s develop-ment. I am grateful to the late Charles R. Brockmann, who started the Carolina Room collection; to Mary Louise Phillips, its retired director who devoted years to building it up; and to director Bob Anthony and his staff, Anne Dugger, Rosemary Lands, and Jim Chapman, who made its resources available to me.

Other research was done in the *Observer*'s own library, directed by Sara Klemmer. To her and her staff—Eddie Owens, Norma Blunk, Dee Davis, Evelyn Helle, Kathie Gimla, and Carol Smith—I am grateful for much kind assistance.

Much of the information about *Observer* purchases of land, build-ings, and equipment and about sales and mortgages of its property came from trusts and deeds filed in the office of the Mecklenburg County Register of Deeds. The current supervisor of that office,

Charles E. Crowder, was personally helpful in making those documents available to me.

For biographical information on printer-editor Harper Elam, I am indebted to his son, J. H. Elam, Jr., of Greensboro, and for biographical information on the four Confederate veterans who founded the 1869 *Observer*, I am thankful to Mrs. Sam Presson, an *Observer* feature writer in the 1930s who briefly sketched their careers. Mrs. Presson's father-in-law ran the grocery over which the four veterans established their second-floor print shop. For additional information on each of the four veterans, I am indebted to Horace Rudisill of the Darlington, South Carolina, Public Library; to Alexia J. Helsley of the Reference and Research Division of the South Carolina Department of Archives and History; to Sarah McMaster of the Fairfield County Public Library in Winnsboro, South Carolina; to Anne Williams and Edith Clark of the Historic Salisbury Foundation; and to Irene Seago of the Anson County Public Library.

For information on the career of Johnstone Jones, who succeeded the four printers as the *Observer*'s editor and publisher, I am grateful to Ruth Byers of the York County Public Library in Rock Hill, South Carolina, and to Susanna Shuster, research librarian of the *Los Angeles Times*.

My research included several weeks spent in the North Carolina Collection of the Louis Round Wilson Library at UNC–Chapel Hill, tracing the personal histories of dozens of North Carolinians who figured in the *Observer*'s development. I am grateful to H. G. Jones, director of the North Carolina Collection, and to his staff, particularly Alice Cotten and Linda Lloyd, for their kind assistance.

Information on the background of William S. Hemby came from the will of his father, Thomas Hemby, which my sister Anne Overcash located in the Union County Courthouse in Monroe. Further information about Hemby came from his niece, Mrs. Kathleen Gurley of Charlotte, and her cousins, W. D. Henley and Beverly Leahy, and from Mrs. Peggy Jemison of Memphis, Tenn., a candidate for a Ph.D. in history.

Much of the information about *Observer* editor J. P. Caldwell came from *Joseph Pearson Caldwell: A Biographical Sketch*, published in 1933 by H. E. C. ("Red Buck") Bryant and Rufus R. Clark. Other information came from Josephus Daniels's memoir, *Editor in Politics*, and from Thad Stem, Jr.'s history, *The Tar Heel Press*.

Other information on Caldwell and his *Observer* partner, D. A. Tompkins, came from the private papers of Daniel A. Tompkins, which are preserved in the Southern Historical Collection at UNC's

Wilson Library. For assisting my review of those and other documents, I am grateful to Carolyn A. Wallace, director of the collection, and to her staff.

For many details concerning D. A. Tompkins's relations with Ambrose Gonzales, Word Wood, George Stephens, and J. C. Hemphill, I am indebted to Lewis Pinckney Jones of Wofford College, whose 1952 Ph.D. dissertation, *Carolinians and Cubans: The Elliotts and Gonzales, Their Work and Their Writings*, is in the Wilson Library at Chapel Hill, and to Willard B. Gatewood, Jr., of the University of Arkansas, whose 1954 master's thesis, *James Calvin Hemphill in the Presidential Campaign of 1912*, is in the Perkins Library at Duke University.

Information about events leading to Curtis B. Johnson's purchase of the *Observer* came from the late Kenneth Whittsett, whose memory of those events was tape-recorded by Katherine Cogswell in 1979 and graciously made available to me. Other details of Johnson's purchase came from Fred W. Hunter, a former *Observer* carrier and circulation agent who allowed me to tape-record his rich memory of events from 1911 to the mid-1950s. I owe much of my information about circulation manager M. H. Brandon to his son, Gilbert, in Memphis, Tennessee.

I am grateful to Eudora Garrison for answering many questions about Curtis Johnson's policies in publishing the newspaper, and to her husband, Wilton, for supplying valuable details about the administration of the paper's sports department. Both allowed themselves to be interviewed for this history, as did many other former *Observer* carriers and employees, including T. D. Kemp, Jr., Dick Banks, Frank Trull, the late Leary Adams, Granbery Ward, Bruce Rogers, David Cauble, Bill Friday, Paul Stroup, Arnold Jones, Carlos Kumpe, Hazel Trotter, Mabel Biggers, Sam Miller, Marjorie Dumbell, Frank Vita, Kays Gary, Bill Johnson, Harry Golden, Jr., Randolph Norton, and LeGette Blythe.

For valuable insights into problems posed by the will of Curtis Johnson, I am indebted to his widow, the late Mrs. Curtis Johnson, who consented to be interviewed just prior to her death, and to attorney Fred B. Helms, who represented the American Trust Company in litigation about the will. Mrs. Johnson was also helpful in describing events leading up to and resulting from Ralph Nicholson's tenure as editor and publisher.

Other details of Ralph Nicholson's administration came from the memory of C. A. ("Pete") McKnight, who at the time was editor of the *Charlotte News* and a correspondent for *Time* magazine. Though blind and confined to a wheelchair as a result of crippling strokes, McKnight kindly consented to be interviewed often about his own tenure as editor of the *Observer* and offered many valuable insights into general changes affecting the newspaper industry.

Others whose interviews contributed to my understanding of the Knight-McKnight years were James L. Knight, Lee Hills, Don Oberdorfer, Larry Jinks, Dwayne Walls, Jim Batten, Dorothy Ridings, Jane Rogers Davis, Whitey Kelley, Joy Walker, David Gillespie, Fred Sheheen, David McCullough, Victor McElheny, Mebane Dowd, Beverly Carter, Jim Hardin, M. S. Van Hecke, and Frank Barrows.

A number of other present and former *Observer* editors and writers kindly wrote reminiscences that proved to be highly valuable in enriching my understanding of the newspaper. They were Stan Brookshire, Earl Heffner, Bunny Harris Stevenson, Eva Saunders, Rolfe Neill, Harriet Doar, Jay Jenkins, John York, John Eslinger, Nancy Brachey, Gerry Leland, Jean Vandiver Leland, Bill Lamkin, Fran Burg, Ron Moore, Don Sturkey, Don Seaver, Joe Doster, Walter Damtoft, Larry Tarleton, Judge James B. McMillan, Jake Simms, Susan Jetton, Reese Cleghorn, Tom Fesperman, Jimmy Dumbell, Carl Stepp, Laura Sessions Stepp, W. Davis Merritt, Jr., John C. Gardner, Mike Soper, Sam S. McKeel, Dale Allen, Joan Behrmann, Erwin Potts, Charles M. Hauser, Ned Cline, Malcolm Scully, Senator Jesse Helms, Rita Adams Simpson, and Rich Oppel.

In addition, I am grateful to three former *Charlotte News* staffers, reporter Emery Wister and photographers Tommy Franklin and Jeep Hunter, whose memories contibuted to my understanding of the rivalry between the *Observer* and the *News*.

At a crucial point in my research I had the valuable assistance of Stephen and Christian Stemkowski, Cynthia B. Oates, and Ellyn Ritterscamp, all in the history department at UNC-Charlotte. I appreciate their willingness to put aside their own studies and assist me.

David R. Goldfield, Robert Lee Bailey Professor of History at UNCC, kindly read each of the thirteen chapters and made many timely suggestions for their improvement, a service that enriched my own understanding and greatly enlarged the scope of the book. To him I am especially grateful. Others who read one or more chapters and helped me avoid embarrassing errors were Dan Morrill, Oak Winters, Walter Spearman, Dwayne Walls, Bob Anthony, Harriet Doar, Carlos Kumpe, Eudora Garrison, Hazel Trotter, Marjorie Dumbell, M. S. Van Hecke, Kays Gary, Rolfe Neill, and Richard Maschal. Pete McKnight kindly listened as all thirteen chapters were read to him and offered valuable suggestions.

Acknowledgments

I am especially indebted to *Observer* publisher Rolfe Neill and editor Rich Oppel for their patient support and encouragement throughout the writing of the book. It became a longer project than either they or I bargained for. The technical assistance of Bob De Piante, James Braswell, and Hank Durkin in helping me write the history on a computer was invaluable. I could not have written anything this long and complex on a typewriter.

I am also deeply grateful to Jerry Shinn, editor of the *Observer* editorial pages, who offered advice and guidance throughout, and to my colleagues Ed Williams, Tom Bradbury, Frye Gaillard, Carol Dykers, Jane McAlister, and Doug Marlette, for generously assuming my share of the daily editorial chores for the better part of eighteen months. They deserve a special thanks. So does my wife, Margaret, who listened indulgently to my concerns about this project and, as usual, offered wise counsel.

My earnest hope is that the finished product is worthy of the contribution of all those good people.

*A bright, enterprising, influential daily press, in
any town, is a centralizing power. . . . The press
advertises the locality—is the exponent of its life
and spirit—is the center of its moral, political and
social influence, and does more, perhaps, than
any other agency to attract the organized industry
of its near and remote neighborhood.*

Dr. J. G. Holland in
Scribner's Monthly, March 1874

THE
CHARLOTTE
OBSERVER

INTRODUCTION

The critical moment occurs every night about ten o'clock. The warning bell rings, the danger light blinks, a deep hum rises from the fifty-horsepower motors, and the huge gray machine groans and squeaks and slowly gathers momentum. Its initial thump-thump-thump swells to a steady throb, then a high whine, and finally a deafening roar. The presses of the *Charlotte Observer* are printing another day's edition.

On this Friday evening in April 1986, eighteen of the thirty-six printing units are running in unison, printing 47,000 copies an hour of a sixty-page Saturday morning paper in black and white and eight colors. The presses will stop and start five more times over the next six hours as they take on new plates and print, fold, cut, count, and deliver 237,865 copies before 4:22 a.m.

As fast as they surge from the mouths of the machine, the freshly printed papers are pinned in the springs of a conveyor belt and whisked in a continuous stream into the overhead mailroom, where they are automatically stacked, wrapped, bundled, and shunted into waiting trucks bound for Myrtle Beach, Wilmington, Raleigh, and Florence. As those trucks depart, they are replaced by others headed for Asheville, Fayetteville, Wilkesboro, Lexington, Hickory, and Boone. Behind those come others going to the nearer communities of Shelby, Albemarle, Gastonia, Statesville, Monroe, Rock Hill, and Lancaster. Finally, as the big presses slow, trucks are loaded with bundles to be distributed across Mecklenburg County and dropped on street corners in the nearest neighborhoods of Charlotte: in Dilworth, Biddleville, and Fourth Ward.

Over the previous twenty-four hours, much of the work done in the block-long building that houses the *Charlotte Observer* was focused toward that moment when the huge presses would unleash their power: John Cleghorn's interview with a dairy farmer north of Statesville, Elizabeth Leland's account of a Lions Club proposal to induct women, Jim Morrill's profile of a candidate for the United States Senate, Tammy Joyner's report on the governor's reception for Japanese businessmen, Foon Rhee's digest of a love-triangle murder in Lenoir, Valerie Reitman's summary of a Michigan firm's plans for a plant in Salisbury, Polly Paddock's column from a peach orchard in

Filbert, South Carolina, Tom Higgins's yarn about a fishing-tackle swap in Morganton, Kathy Haight's review of a sold-out concert at the Coliseum, the placing of 200 columns of classified ads, the listing of fifteen columns of stock-market quotations, the recording of forty-six obituaries, the preview of thirty-four channels of TV shows, and much more of interest to readers and advertisers in the sixty-five Carolinas counties served by the *Observer*.

The presses are the nexus of the news gathering–news disseminating operation, the waist of the hourglass through which everything flows. They symbolize the *Charlotte Observer*'s role in the daily life of the Piedmont Carolinas. Every night, all the news and information collected from around the world and surrounding counties is evaluated, interpreted, and organized in the newspaper's editorial and advertising offices, then funneled through the presses to be packaged and redistributed back to the surrounding region. Much of the time, even the very newsprint on which the paper is printed is a part of that collecting-processing-redistributing system. Until its manufacture into wood pulp at the Bowater plant in Catawba, South Carolina, maybe sixty to ninety days earlier, the paper was standing as pine trees in the many forests that dot the Carolinas.

The newspaper reflects the region, and the region reflects the newspaper. Through the *Observer*, the region gives and receives an image of itself and becomes a community. Its people gain a shared experience that builds a common bond. The banker in Charlotte finds a kinship with the textile worker in Belmont, the mechanic in Richfield, and the teacher in Clover. The paper provides a platform for understanding and controversy, and a forum for consensus or dissent. It highlights both accomplishments and shortcomings, inspires hope and satisfaction, records disappointment and defeat. It reinforces tradition and stimulates change. And the rhythm of its publication, morning after morning, year after year, builds a sense of direction and continuity.

The *Charlotte Observer* is deeply embedded in the life of its city and region and has been for more than 100 years, since the paper was a four-page, single-sheet publication, printed and folded by hand, and distributed by train. Its history is the history of Charlotte and the surrounding counties. It has grown as they have grown, from rolling farms and cotton fields to a dispersed urban region devoted to manufacturing, distribution, communications, and finance.

Over those 100-plus years, the pages of the *Observer* have recorded that evolution in the region's life and economy. Event by event they have chronicled the progress that accompanied the harnessing of electricity, the extension of the telephone, the laying of water and sewer lines, the building of schools and colleges, the coming of automobiles, trucks, and highways, the rise of cities and suburbs, the expansion of housing, the growth in advertising, the burgeoning of athletics and recreation, the rising status of blacks and women, the shifting emphasis on religion, and, through it all, the tumult of politics.

Like the region itself, which was shaped by men like Zeb Vance, James Duke, Daniel Tompkins, Henry Belk, Cameron Morrison, and Max Gardner, the newspaper bears the imprint of many personalities: Joseph Caldwell, Adelaide Williams, Wade Harris, Hazel Trotter, Pete McKnight, Kays Gary, all sons and daughters of the region.

In a startling way, the *Observer*'s history parallels that of the newspaper industry itself. It reflects the steady evolution of newspapering from a printer-oriented enterprise to one dominated by editors, then by publishers, and finally by corporations and huge conglomerates. But in important ways, the *Observer*'s history is also unique to the Piedmont Carolinas. In part, it has become the newspaper it is because of the region, and the region has become the place it is because of the newspaper. In so far as the two are one and inseparable, this is their story.

CHAPTER 1

FOUNDING THE OLD *OBSERVER*

1869–1872

At the end of the Civil War, the South lay shattered and spent. The plantation system it fought to defend was bankrupt. The wealth invested in slaves was gone. The bonds bought from the Confederacy were worthless. There wasn't a bank that was solvent or a currency that was sound. All around was wreckage left by four years of war and neglect.

One could trace the course of conflict by following the line of splintered trees, littered fields, smashed fences, and wrecked railroads. In many towns and cities, whole blocks had been leveled or burned. Roofs had been torn from houses, and walls demolished by exploding shells. Once-aristocratic Charleston wept amid ashes and weeds. In Atlanta, where the entire business district had been burned, people sought shelter in hovels built of scrap lumber and tin.

In Virginia, some men lived by selling uniforms they had stripped from the dead. At the edge of the Spotsylvania battlefield, an old woman and two girls moved silently among trees and trenches, scavenging for bullets to sell for salvage. In Richmond, people lined up outside offices of the Relief Commission, awaiting a daily ration of food and the tools and seeds for a garden.

Even the people who had food or valuables were not confident of keeping them. Burglary and theft were widespread. In many cities, there was the added threat of smallpox. In a letter to his brother, Georgia poet Sidney Lanier lamented, "Pretty much the whole of life has been merely not dying."

Not only had the South lost the war, it also had lost its sense of order and purpose. The abolition of slavery had destroyed the plantation system that was the region's organizing principle. Something new, some other economic and social framework, would have to be established to take its place. But established how? With what capital? Under whose leadership?

Compounding those questions were others of more immediate import. How long would the South be occupied by federal troops? What price would it be asked to pay for its rebellion? When would it be left to manage its own affairs? The clemency proposed by Lincoln was being overridden by a punitive Congress.

There was still another question of even greater moment: what would become of the freed slaves? Waves of northern reporters and writers traveled the South in search of solutions to that riddle. They encountered a wide variety of opinion. Many white southerners assumed that blacks, once beyond the care of their white masters, would die of starvation and disease—though many ex-slaves seemed to be faring better than poor whites. Other white southerners saw blacks as undesirables to be returned to Africa—and in the next breath complained about a shortage of hands to work the fields. Still other southern whites thought blacks should be educated and, perhaps in time, granted limited citizenship.

No matter where the visiting writers and reporters went in the South, one fact was abundantly clear: most whites regarded blacks as inferiors and were determined to keep them subservient. Nothing the North could do in punishing the South was likely to alter that. In fact, much that had been done served to strengthen it.

Amid the desolation and despair, a few places showed signs of renewed activity and the promise of recovery. In burned-out Richmond, black and white workmen were clearing wreckage and repairing buildings in a restoration that would soon make Richmond one of the South's most industrial cities. In Nashville, supply merchants were doing a brisk business in cotton seed. On the fertile plains of West Tennessee, new cotton nodded in the fields. And on the wharves at Memphis, black laborers loaded bales of cotton onto barges.

Among the reviving places was the town of Charlotte, North Carolina, which had escaped the ravages of battle and, despite losses in money and manpower, emerged from the war with greater resources than most southern communities. Though it had been founded a century earlier, Charlotte was little more than a country crossroads, a place of wooden storefronts where miners brought gold to be assayed, farmers brought cotton to be sold, and trains from North Carolina met those from South Carolina and Georgia. It was obviously a trading center, as opposed to a political or manufacturing town. In the decade before the war it had enjoyed a spurt of growth and welcomed the establishment of its first daily newspaper, the *Evening Bulletin*.

The war had given Charlotte a larger potential. It wasn't thriving, but it projected a spirit of enterprise that attracted people and inspired optimism. To its mining and farming base was added a munitions factory, a quartermaster depot, and, when the port of Norfolk was under siege, a Confederate navy yard employing several hundred mechanics. After Appomattox, that promise brought people from surrounding counties surging into the town. The presence of 6,000 federal troops suggested hard money might be available there, and an office of the Freedmen's Bureau offered a haven for former slaves. Gold mining had been resumed, farmers were again bringing cotton to be weighed and sold, and merchants had restocked their stores. By 1867, a minor building boom was under way; one bank had been revived and a new one organized. The *Evening Bulletin* had died, but two other dailies had risen to take its place, first the evening *Daily News* and later the morning *Carolina Times*.

People who could see past the ruin and poverty said all that Charlotte and other southern communities needed was a little time and fresh supplies. The weather was still kind, the land was still fertile. Cotton at strong prices, plus good harvests of rice, tobacco, sugar, and corn, should produce a recovery. Southerners looked to the North for capital and to Europe for labor.

Others saw the need for more than mere seed and sustenance. They called for a profound change in strategy and attitude. The South would have to put aside its reliance on land alone, they said; it would have to find the means to engage in manufacture. In addition to fields and forests, it needed cities and factories like those in the North. It needed to develop its mines and ports, to stimulate commerce and promote trade. Such people urged the building of another kind of South, an aggressive, opportunistic, entrepreneurial region.

In 1866, New Orleans magazine publisher J. D. B. DeBow began urging the South to industrialize, to diversify its one-crop agriculture, and to pursue commerce. Though he knew the region lacked capital and labor, DeBow was convinced that if the South told its story persuasively and documented its potential, money and manpower would come.

Another publisher who saw the need for southern reform was Gen. Daniel Harvey Hill of Charlotte. A West Point graduate, Hill had taught mathematics and military science at Davidson College and, just before the war, founded Carolina Military Institute at East Morehead and Brevard streets (in buildings later known as the "D. H. Hill School"). During the war, at Big Bethel Church, Virginia, he led southern troops to their first major victory and was later cited for gallantry in several engagements. He came home as Charlotte's most honored Confederate hero and began publishing *The Land We Love*, a magazine devoted to the virtues of the Old South and a southern view of the Civil War.

The first issue of Hill's magazine appeared about the time of *DeBow's Review* and was almost as forward-looking. It contained an editorial advocating a dramatic change in southern education. "The old plan of education in the palmy days of the South gave us orators and statesmen but did nothing to enrich us, nothing to promote material greatness," Hill said. "The South must abandon the aesthetic and ornamental for the practical and useful." He said the South needed men who could use the plane, the saw, the anvil, the loom, and the mattock. "The everlasting twaddle about politics is giving place to important facts in history, in the mechanic arts, in morals, in philosophy," he suggested.

General Hill would soon retreat from that stance and would ridicule the materialism that it implied. But a rising generation of younger editors and writers, unburdened by Old South loyalties, would take up the theme and expand and promote it into an article of faith. Slowly the image of a new South rising from the ashes of the old began to win converts across the region. By the mid-1870s, the term "New South" was beginning to appear in the news and editorial columns of southern newspapers, especially the Atlanta *Constitution*, edited by Henry W. Grady, and the Louisville *Courier-Journal*, edited by Henry Watterson.

The term had a variety of meanings, but as used by Grady and Watterson it implied a move away from the Old South's emphasis on land and agrarian values. As advocates of a New South they urged the pursuit of industry and commerce and the development of an assertive, entrepreneurial spirit. One southern editor suggested the shift required "a liberalizing state of mind which recognized that a new order of things has come."

In the years before the establishment of chambers of commerce, cotton councils, boards of trade, and other organizations that speak for business, the job of articulating and promoting that shift in aspirations fell to the newspapers. They were the one organizing force available to the region and the voice of the popular culture. Without book publishers or a book-buying public to appeal to, southern writers, poets, essayists, and historians wrote and sold their ideas to newspapers. Thus newspapers not only reflected the tenor and drift of New South thinking; many of them added substance and direction to that thought.

Implicit in the developing New South creed was a change in the pace and style of southern living, which previously had been overwhelmingly rural. The pursuit of industry and commerce would require the building of cities, the establishment of an urban setting where people could come together to manufacture and process goods, operate warehouses, make sales, run trains, generate power, and carry on commercial enterprises. It would also require the development of an urban middle class composed of directors, managers, engineers, accountants, shopkeepers, inspectors, and dozens of other functionaries whom the plantation system had managed to get along without.

Altering southern attitudes was not easy. The region clung tenaciously to its old ways, and the occupation by federal troops, a confiscatory federal tax policy, and the presence of carpetbag governments helped to distract southern thinking. But by the 1880s, the editorials of Henry Grady in Atlanta and Henry Watterson in Louisville, trumpeting the New South's potential, were being read and discussed throughout the region and were influencing the thought of other southern leaders.

Across the old Confederacy, faith in the New South would soon create a crescent of new cities, strung out along the railroad lines like baubles on a necklace. Ultimately, the new centers of commerce and industry, built to take advantage of water power available in the upland South, would replace the older port cities as the focus of southern life and commerce.

What follows is the story of a newspaper that grew up to serve one of those emerging cities of the New South. Like many other southern institutions, the *Charlotte Observer* struggled to life in the gritty, threadbare days after the Civil War and Reconstruction. Like many newspapers, it followed the development pattern of the newspaper industry itself, moving from the enterprise of the printer to the era of the editor, to the age of the publisher, and finally to the dominance of corporate chains and conglomerates. In one form or another, and under a succession of printers, editors, and publishers, the *Observer* became a true believer and loyal apostle of the New South creed.

When the first *Observer* died in the 1880s, another sprang up to take its place and, over the next century, grew to express and enhance Charlotte's restless quest for New South prominence. That *Observer* would prosper and grow beyond Charlotte to become the business voice of the Piedmont region of North Carolina and South Carolina, with a circulation that exceeded the population of its home city. In North Carolina, it became the voice of western enterprise, as opposed to eastern agriculture. It would encourage thrift, applaud industry, promote education, and enrich the culture.

Like other newspapers of its day, it would also endorse white supremacy, approve a cruel segregation, and join the campaigns that disfranchised blacks. But as the years passed and passions cooled, the editors of the *Observer* began to sense the depth of black suffering and slowly learned to appreciate black aspirations. After the depression of the 1930s, the newspaper softened its racial views and, at a critical moment in the mid-twentieth century, became a leader in the movement for racial justice.

Slowly, painfully, the *Observer* also struggled to free itself from a repressive political party that demanded absolute loyalty. Later, it struggled again to throw off the oppressive influence of a business community that overweighed the paper's judgment and compromised its objectivity. In time, it developed a social conscience and learned to stand above the marketplace and comment honestly on the forces that were shaping life in Charlotte and the Carolinas.

Though it grew to huge size and gained great wealth and power, the newspaper had humble origins. It was not begun out of a grand design to create a new economic and social order; like so many other institutions of the New South, it was, instead, a product of chance circumstance and human need.

In the spring of 1868, handsome, dark-haired Harper J. Elam reached the age of twelve, when a boy was expected to declare his intentions in life, and decided to cast his lot with the printing trade. It was an honored calling, one that had boosted other boy-printers to fame and fortune. It helped Benjamin Franklin achieve international renown, propelled Horace Greeley to national political prominence, and raised editor William W. Holden of Raleigh's *North Carolina Standard* to the office of governor.

For Harper Elam, becoming a printer was a step up the journalistic ladder. Since moving from Rock Hill, South Carolina, to Charlotte in the dying days of the Civil War, he had been a newspaper carrier, delivering Capt. R. P. Waring's *Carolina Times* to First Ward readers. When he was ready for larger responsibilities, he walked to the *Times* offices overlooking Independence Square and signed on as an apprentice in its print shop. As a "printer's devil," he would run errands and do the dirty work while learning to set type.

Harper Elam had no way of knowing it, but he was part of a broad movement under way in American journalism. It was still the age of the printer in the newspaper industry, and throughout the 1860s and 1870s, hundreds of other boys about his age were making similar commitments to the nation's newspapers and magazines. They included Charles H. Taylor, who would revive a dying *Boston Globe*; Adolph Ochs of Knoxville, who would rescue a sinking *New York Times*; and John A. Cockerill, a tough, hard-driving Ohio farm boy who would lead the St. Louis *Post-Dispatch* and the New York *World* to national acclaim.

For such young men, apprenticing in the printing trade was the avenue to an education and an entrance to the middle class. And in the 1860s and 1870s, that entryway was wide open. The Civil War's battles and casualty lists had converted millions of ordinary Americans into readers of newspapers, which previously had appealed only to the elite. Newspapers in turn needed men who could report and write and set type.

The war's end brought an upheaval in American life. The slaves were freed, Lincoln was shot, women pushed for equal rights, industries expanded, farms were mechanized, and railroads opened the West. That upheaval and discontent bred a vigorous press. For a few hundred dollars and a hand-operated printing press, ambitious printers—or lawyers aspiring to public office—could launch their own newspapers and, on the strength of their own labor and ingenuity, attempt to shape public opinion in their favor. Left to their own devices, printers put out newspapers in all shapes and sizes, and adhered to a wide variety of journalistic standards.

In that post-war era, newspapers were regarded as instruments of power, a means of forwarding the hopes of people caught in economic and cultural change. Every organization sought to have its own printer and publication as a friendly link to the larger public. Between 1870 and 1900, while the national population was doubling, the number of weekly newspapers tripled and the number of dailies quadrupled. In Charlotte alone in that period, more than fifty newspapers were started, sixteen of them dailies, most of them operated by printers. Only a few survived more than a month. The risks of publishing were very high.

Among the casualties was Capt. R. P. Waring's *Carolina Times*, which suspended publication in the fall of 1868. It wasn't because the paper was unpopular. Its suppression by Union officials during the federal occupation of Charlotte assured it a special affection among southern readers. Shortly after the federal troops arrived, Captain Waring, a Confederate veteran, complained editorially that the South was "under a more grinding despotism" than any nation in history. As if to validate the charge, federal soldiers arrested him on Christmas Eve, imprisoned him in Raleigh, convicted him of sedition, and fined him $300. Waring paid the fine—a dear sum in those days—and came home to an adoring public.

But, in the deflated southern economy, Waring found it impossible to keep his paper afloat. With little hard money in circulation and local banknotes being exchanged for a fraction of their face value, most firms did business on the barter system. The *Carolina Times* paid apprentice Harper Elam half his $4 weekly wages in cash and asked him to take out the rest in trade with merchants who advertised in the paper. In the fall of 1868, when the paper ceased publication, young Elam was left with no wages at all.

Harper Elam was not alone in his straitened circumstances. Charlotte's unpaved streets were lined with idle blacks and whites looking for jobs. Among them were four journeyman printers, all Confederate veterans, who had come to town to work for General Hill in publishing *The Land We Love*. The magazine had a national circulation of 12,000, but too few readers had paid for their subscriptions, and in the fall of 1868 the magazine was sold to its backers in Baltimore, leaving the four Confederate veterans out of work.

They were encouraged to pool their resources and start another morning newspaper. Among the encouragers were James T. Tate, president of the Bank of Mecklenburg, and Thomas W. Dewey, the bank's cashier (in whose offices the Confederate cabinet held one of its last meetings). Having seen the impact of Charlotte's three previous dailies, the bankers knew what a newspaper could do for the town in promoting business and stimulating growth. But all previous dailies had ceased publication. E. H. Britton's *Evening Bulletin* had enjoyed popularity before the war, but died afterward. It was succeeded by the *Daily News*, owned and edited by Hamilton C. Jones and Robert D. Johnston, a pair of politically ambitious lawyers who had moved from Salisbury to Charlotte after the war. Their law practice flourished, but their newspaper lived only a few months. The third paper was Waring's *Carolina Times*, which for a second time had ceased publication and was presumed dead.

Knowing that history, bankers Tate and Dewey didn't offer to invest in the four printers' venture, but promised to extend a loan if one was needed. Word of their personal support was passed among other business leaders, and late that fall the project was begun. Harper Elam and three others—fourteen-year-old Charles Moore, a black drayman named Alfred Hawshaw, and Peter McLauchlin, one of the four unemployed printers—met at a dim storage shed near the corner of Trade and Brevard streets to gather equipment for the new newspaper. On their hands and knees, they sifted through the dust and cobwebs for scattered pieces of used type, which they sorted and returned to the appropriate type cases.

The storage shed was behind the home of Col. William R. Myers, the town's largest landowner who earlier that year had published the *Union Republican*, a campaign newspaper that helped the Grand Old Party sweep the 1868 elections. Afterward, Colonel Myers had no further use for the printing equipment, so he sold it, presumably at below-market prices, to the four printers. The purchase included 1,000 pounds of long primer (the equivalent of ten-point type), 200 pounds of brevier (the equivalent of eight-point type), and seventy-five pounds of nonpareil (the equivalent of six-point type). It also included a dozen fonts of display type, some office furniture, and an antique hand-operated Washington press.

The equipment was loaded on wagons and hauled up East Trade to a building about a half-block from the Square (where the Radisson Plaza would later build a service entrance). There, over B. M. Presson's grocery, the four printers set up shop. From there, on Monday, January 25, 1869, under the slogan "Onward and Upward, True to the Line," they issued the first edition of the *Daily Carolina Observer*, a single sheet, four-page newspaper later renamed the *Charlotte Observer*.

Like many other people, the four printers had moved to Charlotte from surrounding Carolina towns at the close of the war. They did business under the name "Smith, Watson & Co., An Association of Printers." The Smith was James H. Smith, thirty, a slight, sad-eyed son of Winnsboro, South Carolina, who had apprenticed on the Fairfield County *Herald*. When the war broke out, he joined the South Carolina infantry, but proved to be too frail for soldiering and was soon discharged. On the *Observer*, he managed the paper's business affairs and lived with his wife and son in rooms off the second-floor print shop.

The Watson was John M. Watson, thirty-three, a Marylander who migrated to Rowan County. He had served the Confederate army in Mississippi, returned home to set type for the Salisbury *Gazette*, married Mary Smith of Rowan, and moved to Charlotte. A genial, self-educated man, he was the *Observer*'s first editor, though he was hardly a polished writer.

The other partners were Peter McLauchlin, twenty-five, and Gaston Paul, thirty. McLauchlin was the son of Scotch immigrants who settled in Darlington, South Carolina. After serving in the Confederate army, he married and moved to Charlotte. On the *Observer* he was foreman of the composing room. Paul was a friendly, dark-haired Anson County native who was a printer in Wilmington when the war started. He joined the North Carolina infantry, saw action throughout Virginia, returned to Wadesboro to marry Addy Mc-Craney, and moved to Charlotte. He ran the *Observer's* job shop, which supplemented the paper's income by printing business cards, legal forms, stationery, invitations, announcements, invoices, etc.

In their opening editorial, the four printers acknowledged that journalism had not previously proved profitable in Charlotte, but they hoped the city's improving commerce would soon support a morning daily. The South, they said, had not had been on "so sound a footing" since the war, "nor has business worn so encouraging an aspect." Like others they believed the South's recovery awaited only "a few more cotton crops." They cited "the hum of stirring life upon our streets . . . the sound of the hammer, the ring of the anvil, the puff of the engine, and the roar of machinery." They took comfort in the fact that "every civilized community, or at least every growing, re-fined and prosperous city must have, and must encourage, a pros-perous daily paper; and we are not without hope that our unremit-ting efforts may obtain for us that encouragement and secure for us that prosperity."

Indeed, as the year 1869 dawned, the business outlook was im-proving. Trade was increasing, the two railroads serving the city were repaired, and efforts were under way to repair and build two more. Col. William Johnston, a Charlotte lawyer and railroad finan-cier, was overseeing construction of a line from Atlanta to Charlotte. Another company had resumed construction of a line from the port at Wilmington. The prospect of a Wilmington-to-Charlotte link was already inspiring rivalry between the two cities.

Wilmington was the state's largest municipality, but Charlotte was again showing a tendency to grow. It ended the 1860s with twice the population of the previous decade and had the momentum to double again in the next ten years. General Hill was predicting that Charlotte would become "the London of the South," a forecast that was widely reprinted and commented on, sometimes with jeers. The favorable prospects prompted Zeb Vance, North Carolina's wartime governor, to move to Charlotte and establish a law office with Colonel Johnston and Maj. Clement Dowd, who served as mayor of the town from 1869 to 1871.

By 1869, Charlotte's 4,400 residents (42 percent of them black) oc-cupied an area bounded roughly by Twelfth Street on the north, McDowell Street on the east, Morehead Street on the south, and Cedar Street on the west. From one side of the town to the other was about a thirty-minute walk. Everything beyond was farmland.

The town contained seven churches for white people and at least three for blacks. It had two major hotels, the Central on the Square (where NCNB stands) and the Charlotte Hotel on North Tryon (where the Belk store stands). It also had three smaller hotels, several boarding houses, and thirteen bars and restaurants. Offering their services were eighteen lawyers, thirteen doctors, five dentists, five druggists, twenty-one manufacturers, three banks, three insurance agencies, twenty-eight dry-goods merchants, sixteen grocers, seven confectioners, five jewelers, two bookshops, three tailors, three milliners, and one livery stable. The town also included two colleges—Charlotte Female Institute (later Queens College) and Biddle Institute (later Johnson C. Smith University)—and three preparatory schools—Charlotte Male Academy, Charlotte Female Academy, and Bronson's School (supported by St. Peter's Episcopal Church). Beyond the town limits were sixteen gold mines employing several hundred people, and in the fourth block of West Trade Street, the United States Mint was again doing business as an assay office.

Missing from that mix were many enterprises whose advertising would later be essential to a successful newspaper. For instance, there were no men's or women's clothing shops and nothing to compare with a modern department store. The day of mass-produced clothing, furnishings, and appliances was dawning elsewhere in the country, but its promise was yet to be felt in the South. Steam engines were still a novelty; electricity had yet to be harnessed; and the telephone was still a decade away. Even with the railroads, a creaking stage coach still left at seven o'clock each morning, bound for Wadesboro and points east.

The four printers promised to devote their newspaper to "news of the day, literature, science, art, agriculture & etc." and pledged to "commit our columns to no party." They were, they said, "practical printers" trying to supply citizens of Mecklenburg and adjoining counties with a daily paper "worthy of their patronage." To promote the community and the opportunities it offered—and, no doubt, to encourage advertising—the four printers listed most of the town's businesses in a "Business Directory of The City Of Charlotte" that filled two columns of type on the front page of each day's paper. On page four, another three-and-a-half column "Directory" listed most of the federal and state officials in North Carolina.

Unlike other journals, which were usually founded to promote a political point of view, the *Observer* was politically independent and tended to play down politics. It did not even cover meetings of the Charlotte aldermen or the Mecklenburg commissioners. In the turmoil of the times, it may have been difficult to know whose politics to espouse. Across the South, Reconstruction had blurred the old lines between Whigs and Democrats. Some Whigs had joined the Democrats in forming a Conservative party opposed to the radical Republicans. Other Whigs, usually those who had opposed secession, had become Republicans. The latter included Charlotte's three wealthiest citizens, Colonel Myers, industrialist Rufus Barringer, and John M. Morehead (for whom Morehead Street is named).

An *Observer* editorial for July 19, 1869, offered an example of the cynicism that permeated Reconstruction politics. Noting that Virginia voters had united under the Conservative banner, the editorial complained, "Old principles have ceased to have any practical application; old issues have passed away, and the Southern people must of necessity adapt themselves to the altered condition of things. . . . In adopting political platforms now we have to frame them with reference not to what we wish but what we cannot possibly avoid. When we adopt a platform embracing universal suffrage or equality of political rights between the races, we do not mean to endorse them in principle, but to accept them as part of the Constitution of the State until we can get rid of them in a constitutional manner, if we ever can."

But in downplaying politics, *Observer* editors made it clear that they didn't approve of Reconstruction, didn't like being forced to liberalize the North Carolina Constitution, resented the Fourteenth and Fifteenth amendments making blacks equal to whites, and loathed the policies of North Carolina's Reconstruction governor, William W. Holden. Their paper was clearly a white man's publication and often used crude slurs in referring to blacks. Blacks who had voted for the first time in the 1868 elections were referred to as "Fifteenth Amendments."

The *Observer* for June 6, 1869, included a note that "respectable darkies want to go into Washington theaters on a perfect equality with the white people and not be compelled to go into the part occupied by the riff raff of common niggers. With cheap niggers they will not associate. This is their idea of equality and distinction of color."

Though one of the city's twelve aldermen was black, and blacks were running successful churches and businesses, the early *Observer* rarely covered their activities. As far as the paper was concerned, Biddle Institute, the black churches, and the local office of the Freedmen's Bureau were invisible. That attitude was common among most white newspapers, in the North as well as the South, and did not change until blacks began publishing newspapers of their own.

The content of the early *Observer* was not well organized, and it was hard to tell what was news, what was editorial, and what was advertising—a failing common to other newspapers as well. The front and back pages were devoted almost entirely to advertising, leaving the two inside pages for news and editorial matter, much of it clipped from other newspapers. Telegraph news was available from several news services organized during the Mexican and Civil wars, but the *Observer* of 1869 could not afford it.

In fact, for the first six months the fledgling paper carried very little original material. Its national and state news and most of its editorials were reprinted from other journals. The local news consisted of market reports, one-sentence personals about the comings and goings of townspeople, and the names of travelers registered at local hotels or arriving on trains. Other items were mild stuff about storms that damaged crops or uprooted trees, new construction projects, the opening of a new business, or "new goods" that had arrived at local stores: "R. M. Miller & Co. has received a new shipment of salt. Now is a good time to buy salt."

For the first seven months, the paper was published six days a week and skipped Sundays. Beginning in August 1869, it adopted a Tuesday-Sunday schedule and skipped Mondays, allowing its employees to take Sundays off. In that, the *Observer* was probably ahead of its time. The norm among newspapers was not to publish on Sundays, out of deference to wishes of religious groups. As late as 1883, there were still only about 100 Sunday newspapers published in the country.

In addition to the morning paper, Smith, Watson and Company also produced a semiweekly and, beginning in August 1869, a weekly. Those were important to the paper's success, for the weeklies and semiweeklies used much of the same material that had been published in the daily and brought in extra revenue at little additional cost. On many newspapers, the weekly edition had a larger circulation than the daily and its revenues subsidized the daily.

The *Observer*'s publication schedule was enough to tax the energies of its small work force. In June 1869, the Raleigh *Standard* complained that the *Observer* had not had an original editorial "in more than two months." The *Observer* replied, "But, Mr. *Standard*, we have to work—set type and attend to other duties connected with the office—from early morning to dewy eve and have no time to write long-winded editorials."

That was probably the truth. At that time, the paper had no designated reporters or editorial writers. Its staff consisted of the four printer-publishers, a salaried compositor named J. M. George, the apprentice Harper Elam, and a seventeen-year-old pressman named Anthony Rivers, who apparently was a prodigious worker. Sixty years later, looking back on his printing career, Harper Elam remembered Anthony Rivers as "the best pressman I ever saw."

Rivers came to Charlotte as a slave in 1862, accompanying the Confederate navy yard from Norfolk. Big, strong, and taciturn, he could stand for hours beside the hand-run Washington press and pull the heavy lever that printed the newspaper. Printing one side of a single sheet required twenty-two movements of the hands and twenty-seven movements of the feet, but at a rhythmic pace Anthony Rivers could pull 250 impressions an hour. At that rate, he could print a thousand copies of the four-page paper in about eight hours: four hours to print one side of the sheet (pages one and four) and four hours to print the other side (pages two and three).

Pages one and four, which contained ads, train schedules, the city (and later the county) directory, and other promotional matter, changed little from day to day and could be printed early. The two inside pages, which contained news and editorial matter, were printed last. At about midnight, Rivers would let himself into the print shop and, working alone, methodically print the last two pages. He had to finish before dawn to get the papers on the early mail trains and to distribute them to carriers.

The *Observer* had four carriers, one for each of the city's four wards. They included Harper Elam and his brother, Richard, who would also become a printer. They also included the two Moore brothers, Charles C. and Walter W., sons of a widowed schoolteacher. Both of the Moore boys would grow up to achieve distinction. Charles was Mecklenburg clerk of court from 1910 to 1922. Walter finished Davidson College and Union Seminary at Richmond, taught Hebrew and Old Testament, and was president of Union Seminary from 1904 to 1926.

Years later, when he was clerk of court, Charles Moore recalled his "happy days" as an *Observer* carrier. "We were made much of," he said, "and it was a regular thing for each of us to be invited in to Christmas breakfast" at homes along the delivery route. "I always took Christmas breakfast with Col. William R. Myers, one of the subscribers on my East Trade route," he said. "My brother W. W. took breakfast with Mr. W. J. Yates, proprietor of the [weekly] *Charlotte Democrat*, who lived at the corner of Tryon and Morehead." He recalled that Harper Elam, who carried the Fourth Ward route, usually ate Christmas breakfast with Mayor Dowd, who lived near the corner of Sixth and Tryon.

Besides delivering the paper, running errands, and doing the shop dirty work, Harper Elam's duties as printer's devil included chopping wood for the fire that heated the newspaper office and going to the pump halfway down the next block for pails of water. Years later, Wilton Capps, who was Harper Elam's successor as printer's devil, wrote that anyone who thought *Observer* printers were averse to drinking anything as mild as water never had to go to the well for them. "They were a thirsty lot," he recalled. The "devil's" duties also included maintaining a supply of wicks and tallows because the printers not only set type by hand but also by candlelight. Only wealthy people could afford gas lamps, and electric lights were at least eighteen years away.

In addition to the work of the regular staff, the publishers acknowledged the editorial contributions of at least two local writers, Col. Hamilton C. Jones, the lawyer who had founded and later folded the evening *Daily News*, and Mrs. Fanny M. Downing, an author who fled to Charlotte during the siege of Norfolk. By the time the *Observer* was founded, Jones had been elected to the North Carolina Senate and was becoming a power among state and local Democrats. He often wrote political editorials for the *Observer*, including, no doubt, the one that appeared on November 3, 1869, under the headline "The Governor and the Ku Klux." It jeered at Governor Holden's effort to put down Klan terror that discouraged blacks from voting. Opening with the assertion that he who governs least governs best, the editorial argued that Governor Holden was violating that maxim by intervening in local affairs. It suggested that if left alone, "the people . . . *will* right themselves. . . . Every member of society who has either character or property to lose is a friend of law and order." Such sophistry was unlikely to have come from an unlettered printer like John Watson.

The influence of Fanny Downing, a mother, poet, and novelist who also wrote for General Hill's *The Land We Love*, was often apparent in the *Observer*. She was not the first or only newspaper woman in North Carolina, but women in newspaper offices were still rare. In fact, women working outside the home were rare. They were yet to be employed as secretaries—a reliable typewriter had not been invented—or even as store clerks. The influence of Mrs. Downing probably accounts for the *Observer*'s early emphasis on women's education, women's suffrage, and women's rights, which were lively national issues until the mid-1880s. She may have helped select the poetry and short stories that the early *Observer* published. Occasionally the paper also carried fashion notes and household tips that Mrs. Downing may have written. The May 29, 1869, issue included this advice on how to clean kid gloves: "Put them on and rub them well with corn meal. This persisted in for a few minutes will render them nearly as good as new."

Mrs. Downing probably wrote the lead editorial in that same issue, rebuking a local speaker for making jokes about women. "Of all the evils prevailing among young men, we know of none more blighting in its moral effects than the tendency to speak slightly of the virtue of women," the editorial said. It went on to warn: "Let young men remember that their chief happiness in life depends upon their utter faith in women. No worldly wisdom, no misanthropic philosophy, no generalization can cover or weaken this fundamental truth." Those sentiments, too, were unlikely to have come from printer-editor Watson.

Somehow the paper managed to survive, perhaps because of the all-out dedication of its small staff and the fact that nearly everything the printers owned was riding on the outcome. By stressing business and eschewing politics, it avoided offending readers. The loans and good will of bankers Tate and Dewey no doubt helped, as did the consistent advertising of such merchants as watchmaker John T. Butler, shoemaker S. B. Meacham, grocer D. G. Maxwell, and the English-born Tiddy brothers, stationers and booksellers who were subscription agents for the *Observer* and also suppliers of its paper. The Tiddy brothers' daily ads on the front page may have been trade-outs in exchange for newsprint.

The *Observer*'s survival was made more difficult by the rise of competing newspapers. No sooner had the new paper appeared in January 1869 than Captain Waring revived the *Daily Times* and published it until November 30. For a few months in the fall of 1869, E. H. Britton also resumed the *Daily Bulletin*. In 1870, after the *Times* and the *Bulletin* had again collapsed, Maj. W. A. Hearn moved to Charlotte from Goldsboro and established the *Daily Dispatch*, but it failed within a year. In addition, there were two weeklies, W. J. Yates's *Western Democrat*, a fixture in Charlotte for many years, and the *Southern Home*, which D. H. Hill edited after the demise of *The Land We Love*. It was a crowded field and was to remain so for thirty years. As soon as one competitor collapsed, another took its place, often using the same offices, machinery, and printers. That situation would continue until increased technology made the cost of starting a newspaper high enough to discourage casual competition.

As the weeks passed, the *Observer*'s owners began to invest their profits in improving the looks and content of the paper. On July 9, 1869, they changed its name from the *Daily Carolina Observer* to the *Charlotte Observer*, in a crisp, black, old English masthead similar to that of the modern *Observer*. In incorporating the city's name in its title, the paper strengthened its identity and increased its promotional value to the community. Two weeks later the publishers expanded their coverage of local news by making Gaston Paul the local reporter, an assignment that Paul accepted hesitantly. Under the column head bearing his name and new title, he wrote, "It will be seen . . . that one of the publishers has taken charge of the Local Department of the *Observer* and hereafter more time and attention will be devoted to collecting items for this hitherto neglected but most looked-to column of our paper. . . . Any inadvertence must be attributed to inexperience in the business, as this is his first attempt" at reporting.

What followed were several items from the previous morning's mayor's court where people accused of misdemeanors were tried. In one case, a man named Moses Cruse was excused for selling liquor on Sunday after he claimed he didn't know that it was against the law. Reporter Paul summarized the hearing and then added, "We hope [Cruse], for the sake of good order, will sell no more liquor on the Sabbath and [will] subscribe to the *Observer*, in which he will find all such ordinances ventilated from time to time." In another case, two men were found guilty of kicking down the door to a house occupied by Sue McClure. They were fined the costs of court and ordered to pay for a new door, prompting reporter Paul to moralize: "If Sue would repair her morals, she would have less call for money to repair her broke [*sic*] doors."

Within a few days, the local report was filling from one and a half to two columns a day and giving the paper a newsy quality. On August 17, the editors called attention to the fact that "reading matter"—in this case, a story on improved farming methods—had been added to the otherwise sterile front page. The next day the front page included the first installment of a serialized romance, a sure sign the paper was trying to increase circulation.

On August 20, 1869, under the heading "A Word for Ourselves," the printer-publishers issued this editorial plea:

From the day the first number of the *Observer* was launched upon the sea of popular favor . . . we have received *words* of encouragement and praise. . . . We have striven and worked hard to *deserve* and *retain* this expression of approbation from our people—and have at times been subject to the greatest straits to procure the wherewith to keep bread for our families and meet the expenses of the office. . . .

We now make an appeal to our friends to exert themselves a little in our behalf. . . . We feel we *deserve* more than we are getting. . . . If our citizens wish to see the paper *continue* to improve, they must come forward to our support. We know it is the desire of every merchant in Charlotte to see a *first-class* paper emanate from their city—and this we have promised if they will but stand by us, and we think we have come nearer to it than anyone else could under the same circumstances. But still, we are a long way from *first-class* yet, and are likely to remain so . . . unless better patronized.

When a significant rise in patronage did not result, the partnership began to break up. In January 1870, Gaston Paul sold out to his colleagues and began running an independent job shop (which soon produced *Our Weekly*, another competitor for the *Observer*). Two years later, Peter McLauchlin sold out and became a partner in the *Lantern*, a new weekly in Rock Hill.

Also in January 1870, editor John Watson suffered the first of several illnesses that put him out of work for much of the next two years. He was succeeded by a pair of lawyer-editors recently arrived from surrounding counties. The first was Francis Justice, a Confederate veteran from Cleveland County. The second was Julian W. Wright of Goldsboro, who had graduated from the University of North Carolina in 1858, served in the Confederate army, surrendered in Greensboro, and moved to Charlotte. Regrettably, no *Observer*s for 1870 and 1871 have been preserved, and only one for the year 1872, so we have little way of measuring their impact on the paper. That is unfortunate because critical decisions were made in those years in North Carolina and across the South affecting the course of politics and economics for the remainder of the century. It would be instructive to know how the *Observer* viewed those developments.

In state after state in the old Confederacy, Democrats were "redeeming" governments from radical Republicans, only to deliver them to exploitive financial interests in the North and perpetuate the South's colonial status. That happened in North Carolina, as Democrats regained control of the legislature in 1870, abandoned the state aid to railroads that had produced prewar prosperity, and began leasing—and later selling—the state's rail network to northern investors. Some of the bitter fights over freight rates and railroad routes, which continued well into the twentieth century, resulted from those leases and sales.

The one surviving 1872 issue of the *Observer*, for March 31, indicates the paper hadn't changed much in size, layout, or content. But it contained three portents of change. One was that the *Observer* was being published by James H. Smith and Company, indicating that John M. Watson, since demoted to local editor, had also sold his share of the company. Another was a brief item announcing that lawyer-editor Julian W. Wright had moved to Statesville and joined Col. Charles R. Jones in publishing a new weekly known as the *Intelligencer*. The third was that James H. Smith and Company was the advertising and subscription agent for the *Lantern*, the Rock Hill weekly published by McLauchlin and Johnstone Jones. Before long, John Watson would be editing the *Lantern*, and Johnstone Jones—and later Charles R. Jones—would be editing the *Observer*.

In four years, the four Confederate veterans had launched the paper, established its identity, linked it to the fortunes of Charlotte, and successfully fought off competitors. Though in time the old *Observer* would fold and be replaced by another, the early paper established some precedents that its successor would follow for most of the next century. One was its strong ties to the Piedmont Carolinas. Most of the people who worked on the old *Observer* were migrants from surrounding towns and counties. That pattern would continue, assuring the paper a steady supply of Carolinas talent and a strong regional flavor. Another precedent was the paper's character as a commercial rather than a political enterprise. That too was to remain the case. Though future editors and publishers would take vigorous roles in politics, they would continue to publish a business rather than a political paper. Charlotte was a business town, and the *Observer* would remain a business newspaper.

CHAPTER 2

THE *OBSERVER* GAINS A VOICE
1872–1874

In September 1872, as his consumptive lungs weakened, James H. Smith, the last of the four founding printers to retain an interest in the *Observer*, sold the paper to a different kind of journalist, a young man with an aristocrat's background and an optimist's point of view. He was Johnstone Jones, a twenty-four-year-old lawyer who, according to a colleague, "knew nothing of the printer's art and always had that spic and span appearance entirely foreign to the average country editor." But Jones made up in talent what he lacked in experience, and in a brief, twenty-five-month tenure made a lasting impact on the paper.

Under Johnstone Jones, the *Observer* entered the second phase of newspaper development. It moved from the control of printers to the leadership of an editor. Following an example set in New York by editors James Gordon Bennett in the 1830s, Horace Greeley in the 1840s, and Henry Raymond in the 1850s, Johnstone Jones set out to win the respect of readers with an *Observer* that reflected his talent, vision, and personality. Under his leadership, the paper acquired an editorial voice and became a progressive influence in community and state affairs. He brought to the paper Joseph P. Caldwell, a young reporter whose vigorous writing and eye for news enlivened the paper's coverage. Caldwell was later to become an *Observer* editor and a force in North Carolina journalism for nearly forty years. Johnstone Jones also introduced telegraphic news that put *Observer* readers in closer touch with events around the world and enhanced Charlotte's potential as a marketplace. Had the panic of 1873 not intervened, he might have led the old *Observer* to a different fate.

Jones took over during a period of transition in the city, the state, and the nation. Life was changing fast, and people were grabbing greedily at the fruits of change. Mark Twain called it "the Gilded Age," an era of the swindle, the hustle, the fraud, and the fast buck.

The Crédit Mobilier scandal that rocked the Grant administration was but one evidence of widespread corruption in and out of government. The Tweed Ring was being exposed in New York. Jay Gould was watering the stock of the Erie Railroad; Cornelius Vanderbilt was looting the New York Central; Collis P. Huntington was buying the California legislature; and John D. Rockefeller was elbowing rivals aside to create Standard Oil.

After seven years of political turmoil and the expense of occupying the old Confederacy, the North was weary of Reconstruction and was about ready to return the South to southerners. A book by ex-abolitionist James Pike of Maine, *The Prostrate South,* had shocked northern readers, like an *Uncle Tom's Cabin* in reverse. Slowly, Whig-Democrats, operating as the Conservative party, were regaining control of southern legislatures and rescinding the acts of radical Republicans. In North Carolina, the state university at Chapel Hill, closed since the onset of Reconstruction, was being returned to the supervision of trustees appointed by the legislature and would soon reopen. Elsewhere in North Carolina, farming was regaining prewar levels, manufacturing was setting production records, and the gospel of industrialization was being preached across the land.

Among the preachers were Johnstone Jones and the *Observer.* Jones did not write about the New South—that term had yet to gain acceptance—but he envisioned a reviving South and expressed the forward-looking spirit that the term *New South* would soon symbolize. Though federal troops were still occupying some southern states and Republican governors elected with the support of black votes were still sitting in most southern capitals, he could see positive change coming. "We are not among those who take this dark view of the destiny of the Southern states," he said in an editorial dated May 30, 1873. "We belong to the youth of the country . . . whose childhood was passed amid exciting scenes of the great civil war, and who have come to manhood's estate under the new order of things. . . . We see many encouraging signs in the now gloomy sky of our future." He encouraged people in Charlotte and the South to put aside "dead things of past ages" and prepare for the future by industrializing, improving schools, welcoming immigration, and developing the South's mineral and forest resources.

For six months Jones's partner in publishing the *Observer* was Peter McLauchlin, another of the paper's four founders. When they assumed ownership, Jones became editor and McLauchlin supervised the printing. Their partnership lasted until March 1873, when Jones borrowed $1,000 to buy out McLauchlin and become sole owner. McLauchlin stayed on as composing-room foreman. The buy-out may have resulted more from printer McLauchlin's need for cash than from Jones's desire for added status. The new editor did not need titles to identify him as a leader and a thinker.

Johnstone Jones came from a patrician family with deep roots in North Carolina history. His maternal grandfather was James Iredell of Edenton, a former governor of North Carolina and one of George Washington's appointees to the first group of judges on the United States Supreme Court. A grandfather on his father's side had been an aide to Lafayette in the American Revolution. Johnstone Jones's father, Col. Cadwallader Jones of Orange County, North Carolina, and later of York County, South Carolina, was one of the few men to serve in the legislatures of both Carolinas—in the North Carolina House of Commons before the Civil War and in the South Carolina Senate during Reconstruction.

During the Civil War, Johnstone Jones was a cadet at the Arsenal, a military school in Columbia, South Carolina. In the fall of 1864, when he was barely sixteen, he enlisted with his classmates in the Confederate army and was sent to the coast to defend South Carolina against an invasion by Sherman. The cadets were no match for Sherman's marauders and steadily retreated—across South Carolina to Columbia, northeast to Camden, across the state line to Fayetteville and Goldsboro, and then west to Raleigh and Greensboro, where they surrendered.

After the war, Jones clerked for the North Carolina Supreme Court, read law under William K. Ruffin of Hillsborough, was admitted to the bar in 1870, and began practicing law in Raleigh. Two years later, as radical Republicans were dominating the South Carolina legislature, he returned to his father's York County plantation and, with his brother, Iredell Jones, and printer Peter McLauchlin, founded the weekly Rock Hill *Lantern* as a voice for the Conservatives (later to become Democrats). Their purpose, they said, was "to shed light in dark places." The paper was a forerunner of the modern Rock Hill *Evening Herald*. Eight months later, Jones and McLauchlin moved to Charlotte, borrowed $700 from Col. William R. Myers, and bought the *Observer*.

Jones immediately began to give *Observer* editorials a healing tone and a hopeful outlook. They addressed state issues more forth-rightly—though from a partisan point of view—and gave the paper a more consistent character and identity. In January 1873, as another Republican administration was taking office in Raleigh, Jones told readers that its leaders might serve the state better than their radical predecessors. The new officers might be "thoroughly Republican," he said, but "they are not thoroughly corrupt and unprincipled, as are most Radical officials who have proven curses to the South since the war."

Though he counseled others to put aside fetters of the past, Jones had trouble doing so himself. When Gov. Tod Caldwell pledged in an inaugural address to conduct a less partisan government, Jones responded, "Let him stick close to his commendable resolution . . . and he will do much towards restoring peace and harmony among all the people." Then Jones added a gibe that revealed his own partisan spirit. Noting that Caldwell proposed to appoint Republicans only where he could do so without detriment to public service, Jones observed, "As there are comparatively few good, honest men in the Republican party of this State, the Governor will necessarily have a small lot of fellows to pick from." It was a charge that North Carolina Democrats, once they regained control of state government, would use against Republicans for a century.

When Governor Caldwell kept his pledge and began naming Democrats to some offices, Jones and the *Observer* sputtered their praise. The first instance came when Caldwell asked Dr. Charles Phillips, a UNC mathematician temporarily teaching at Davidson College, to become the state's superintendent of public instruction, a position of crucial importance in reviving the public schools. Phillips declined the appointment—the salary was too low, he said—but editor Jones called the offer "gratifying evidence" of the governor's sincerity. Later, when Governor Caldwell gave the superintendency to Raleigh Democrat Kemp P. Battle, Jones applauded, "It is a good sign when a Republican Governor has the moral courage to disappoint . . . office-seekers in his own party and appoint a man from the ranks of his political opponents."

Jones's political bias also led him to oppose moves to merge the state's railroads into one system, a dream of the progressives who conceived the state network in the 1840s. The merger called for extending rails into the mountains and uniting the state, east and west. Jones acknowledged the merits of a consolidation, but feared its political implications. "There is not a right-minded man in North Carolina who would oppose the consolidation scheme if there was assurance that it would be entrusted to men who would honestly and faithfully carry out the purposes of the General Assembly," his editorial said. The consolidation would create "a gigantic corporation that must inevitably become the controlling power in the State. There is danger in it. In the hands of a Radical railroad ring, it will become a vast engine of evil. . . . The traders and farmers of North Carolina will feel some of the grinding oppressions that have made railroad combinations odious in the states of the West."

Jones feared monopolies and supported the formation of farmer organizations "to check . . . the growth and power of mammoth railroad corporations and secure a reduction in freight tariffs." He noted that no opposition to railroads had arisen in the Carolinas, but he predicted that "if the railroad companies do not act wisely . . . and abandon that harsh, grasping, monopolizing policy which is being pursued by some of them," Carolina farmers would also revolt. Within a few years, North Carolina farmers did just that.

Partisan feelings also colored the *Observer*'s endorsement of bills to repudiate a large portion of the state debt because more than half of it was incurred under Republicans. A few years earlier, when a radical Congress forced southern states to renounce their Confederate debt, southerners objected because renunciation meant financial ruin for many families and institutions, among them the University of North Carolina and Davidson College, which had invested their endowments in Confederate bonds. But times had changed, and in January 1874 the *Observer* advocated the repudiation of radical Republican debts, saying, "The State . . . stands with its people in one and the same boat; this, the world knows, has been disabled—scuttled by pirates in such vital parts, that it requires the utmost exertions of crew, pilot and all to keep the good old ship above water." The debt amounted to more than $40 million, about one-half the value of the state's lands and nearly one-third the value of all taxables. "To pay such a debt is simply impossible," the editorial said.

Ultimately the state did repudiate much of the debt, in an act later overturned by the United States Supreme Court. Fortunately, only a few holders of repudiated bonds tried to redeem them; otherwise, the state might have faced financial ruin. But the long debate over repudiation left a lasting scar on state politics by creating a climate for cutting costs, reducing taxes, and discouraging expenditures. That climate later led to the defeat or delay of many essential and progressive programs.

That did not deter Johnstone Jones. When it came to public expenditures, he was rarely on the side of the tightfisted. He chastised Congress for delaying a $5,000 appropriation to operate the United States Mint in Charlotte for another year. In response to contentions that the mint was useless, he argued that it would stimulate mining and create wealth to benefit the whole country. "There is no reason why North Carolina should not rank with California, Montana and

Colorado in . . . gold production," Jones said, and pointed out that federal grants were supporting mints and assay offices in those states. "It is our gold and silver, more than anything else we have, that will attract the eye of the foreigner and the capitalist and will induce immigration and investments . . . in our midst."

Closer to home, the *Observer* accused the Conservative (Democrat) controlled North Carolina legislature of false economy in failing to appropriate a small sum to send a representative North Carolina product to a world's fair in Vienna. "As long as a short-sighted, *rigidly* economical policy prevails in our government, no rapid progress in the material and industrial progress and development of our state need be expected," Jones wrote. He expressed the same view when Charlotte merchants failed to underwrite the Fair of the Carolinas, which brought visitors to town and showed off products of surrounding farms and factories.

Jones also lamented the North Carolina legislature's failure to invest more in the public schools and build the labor force needed for an industrial economy. "That the cause of education languishes in this State is apparent to the most casual observer," said an editorial on January 18, 1873. "Schools are few and far between; a small proportion only of the boys and girls of the country are being educated, and the rising generation are [sic] for the most part growing up in ignorance." To remedy that, he said, "the Legislature should not hesitate to apply double or even treble the amount now appropriated for public instruction. . . . The advantage—aye, the necessity—of education in this enlightened age is felt and duly appreciated by all sensible people."

Such appeals in behalf of education were to become a constant theme of *Observer* editors, though they rarely got results. The oligarchs who controlled state and local governments could afford to educate their children in private schools and considered educating the poor and the blacks a waste of money. That attitude would prevail until the turn of the century, when, with blacks no longer a political threat, Gov. Charles B. Aycock could lead a successful crusade for education.

Jones pelted Charlotte and Mecklenburg County officials with similar arguments in behalf of education, frequently calling on them to increase local support for public schools. That campaign got results in October 1873, when Charlotte opened one of the state's first graded schools, headed by the Reverend J. B. Boone, pastor of what would become the First Baptist Church. But the school was not entirely supported by public money. Part of its income came from the national George Peabody Fund and part from tuitions. Even so, it set an example that soon persuaded Charlotteans to tax themselves in support of public schools and helped to make aid to education a cornerstone of Charlotte's quest for New South status.

Unlike the *Observer* of 1869–72, when the paper rarely said anything critical about the community, the paper under Johnstone Jones was full of suggestions for building and improving the city. It helped to teach people moving to town from nearby farms what life in an urban community could be. In January 1873, when the streets were muddy enough to be treacherous, the paper noted that while such mire might have deterred Sherman from marching here, the future "London of the South" deserved better. A few months later, when the streets were dry and dusty, the paper called for the public purchase of a water sprinkler, saying, "A city without a water sprinkler is like a house without a broom." The paper called for higher pay for police, tighter enforcement of sanitation rules to prevent cholera, resurfacing the wagon-rutted South College Street which led to the platform where cotton was received and weighed, and an expansion of the cotton platform, where wagons often had to wait in long lines. "The interest of the cotton trade, which is Charlotte's most vital interest, demands this increase of facilities," the paper said.

Johnstone Jones's progressive editorials were consistent with the philosophies of other urban editors in the New South. Henry Grady in Atlanta, Henry Watterson in Louisville, and Francis Dawson in Charleston often expressed similar views. But the progressive outlook was not shared by people in rural places, where political attitudes were shaped by harsh poverty and a virulent racism.

Under Johnstone Jones the *Observer* toned down its previous racist sentiment. Crude jokes and jeering references to blacks all but disappeared. But in keeping with what would become the New South spirit, the paper continued to regard blacks as semibarbarians and continued to promote white supremacy. An editorial on December 11, 1873, said: "We believe that all the highest and noblest destinies of mankind are entrusted to the keeping of the white race and that they [members of the white race] have a God-given right to subdue and control and civilize and Christianize, all inferior races of men." Such feelings were apparently shared by most *Observer* readers and helped lay the foundation for the segregated society that arose in the 1890s and early 1900s.

Like most other males, Johnstone Jones was also contemptuous of politically active feminists, especially those who sought the right to vote. When suffragette Susan B. Anthony, in an effort to create a test case for her cause, was arrested in New York for voting illegally, Jones called her a "fiery termagant" who "ought to be condemned to the 'shower bath' at Sing Sing, until she is cooled off and sobered down."

As lively as *Observer* editorials were, anyone reading the paper in those days had to be impressed with the vigor of its local news columns where young Joseph P. Caldwell was holding forth in a compelling style. His hiring, in November 1872, proved to be the best of many things that Johnstone Jones did to improve the paper.

Born Joseph Pearson Caldwell in Statesville on June 16, 1853, he was the son of a two-term Whig congressman also named Joseph Pearson Caldwell. The elder Caldwell died fourteen days after his son's birth, a misfortune that deeply marked the younger Caldwell's life and character. He grew up to become a soft touch for boys, orphans, and unfortunates of every kind and often had to be restrained from aiding down-and-out printers. On his mother's side, he was descended from Col. Thomas Polk, the surveyor and legislator who founded Charlotte and called the militia meeting that was said to have adopted the disputed Mecklenburg Declaration of Independence. That kinship may have contributed to Caldwell's loyal defense of the Mecklenburg Declaration throughout his career.

Young Caldwell grew up working on his mother's farm and studying at home under the tutelage of his older sister, Jennie, a gifted teacher. He had hopes of going to college until the "storm and distress" of Reconstruction closed the university and wiped out the family's savings. Most of his education came from working on newspapers and private reading. He was well versed in Shakespeare, the Bible, and Emerson's essays.

At age fourteen he signed on as a printer's devil at the weekly *Iredell Express* in Statesville. During Reconstruction, the paper shifted its political loyalties from Whig to Republican and immediately provoked opposition. Col. Charles R. Jones, an Iredell farmer, teacher, and justice of the peace, started the *Intelligencer* as a Democratic alternative and hired away young Caldwell by raising his pay from five dollars to six dollars a week. Colonel Jones also gave Caldwell an opportunity to report and write, something at which the young man proved to be highly gifted.

In the fall of 1872, while attending Charlotte's Fair of the Carolinas, Caldwell visited the *Observer* office and met Johnstone Jones, who had just taken over as editor and was looking for someone to handle local reporting. He offered Caldwell thirty dollars a month to become "city editor." Caldwell accepted and reported for duty on November 1. He was nineteen years old.

A tall man of medium build, with a long face, sandy hair, and a bushy mustache, Caldwell made a favorable impression on Charlotteans. He looked them in the eye when he talked, and displayed a sincerity that inspired trust. Capt. Sam Ashe, a Raleigh editor and historian, met Caldwell at about that time and described him as " . . . not spare, but without any surplus flesh. His hair was light with an observable reddish tinge. His complexion was bright with some color over his face, and he had the appearance somewhat of a Scotch lad. . . . He moved briskly, always as if in full possession of his thoughts and with a calm purpose to do what he had in mind. . . . Indeed, he had a pleasing personality: fresh, vigorous, and like most others who dabble in the printings' ink, he had a fondness for his work."

What Caldwell wrote was usually aimed right at his readers. He often said he tried to write with an Iredell County farmer in mind, believing that what would interest him would also interest other readers, many of whom were right off the farm. He had a talent for compressing a lot in a few words. Few of his stories were long, but their number and variety indicated that he spent his days walking the town, recording what he saw and heard. Like other newsmen of the day, he wrote with pad and pencil—typewriters were still several years away—and in a handwriting that would become legendary for its illegibility.

Among those who admired his talent was Harper Elam, the printer's devil who was nearing the end of his apprenticeship and winning prizes for typesetting speed. Fifty years later Elam remembered Caldwell as "the best city editor I have ever seen" and marveled at his ability to produce two and a half to three columns of news day after day.

Perhaps no story better displayed his young talents than a three-and-a-half-column account of a January 1874 hanging in the jail yard at Sixth and Tryon streets (later the site of Discovery Place museum). Prior to 1910, when the state prison introduced the electric chair, executions in North Carolina took place at county jails. Caldwell's story not only shows off his powers of observation and writing skills, but also offers a candid assessment of racial attitudes in the community.

The condemned man was Joe Baker, a semiliterate, twenty-nine-year-old white man convicted of murdering a black man at a westside bar. The fact that the courts of North Carolina would execute a white man—and a Confederate veteran, at that—for killing a black man made the case of exceptional interest.

The story, which filled almost an entire page, is even more remarkable for having been written in pencil and sent to typesetters a paragraph or two at a time. It was already in type before Caldwell got a chance to review what he had written. By then he might make minor changes, but the story's basic tone and structure could not be altered. The story said, in part:

Yesterday afternoon Joseph Baker expiated the crime of murder upon the gallows. Perhaps no execution which ever took place in this county has excited such universal interest, nor has any man ever before executed here had so entirely the sympathy of the good people of the community.

The history of the crime for which he paid the awful penalty... is briefly this: One Saturday afternoon last March, Baker, in common with a number of other persons, was at the grog shop of Henry C. Severs about one mile northwest of Charlotte, when Newton Wilfong, a negro and an entire stranger to his slayer, came into the house. He was drunk and was disposed to be boisterous; so much so that Severs, the proprietor, ordered him out of the house. The negro refused to go, and Severs, seizing an axe handle, caught him and forced him out, striking him twice with the handle while ejecting him from the door. At this stage Baker, who had taken offense at some general remark made by Wilfong... stepped between him and Severs and stabbed him to the heart with a pocket knife. The negro died in a very few moments, and Baker, who had gone to his house nearby, was arrested a short time afterward... and was committed to jail....

A mother's love for a desperately wicked and wayward son was never more beautifully shown than in this case. The old and ignorant mother of the murderer caused a petition to be circulated asking His Excellency the Governor to spare her son the ignominy of the scaffold and send him to the Penitentiary for life.... He listened to her plea and respited her son two weeks from the 2nd of January, promising to commute the sentence if he could find anything to justify him in taking that step. Last Friday night, Gov. Caldwell came to Charlotte on a visit and among his callers were the wife and mother of Joe Baker. The mother was particularly importunate, but notwithstanding her appeals, and notwithstanding the fact that he was approached on the subject by a delegation of the most prominent gentlemen of the city, the Governor remained inexorable, determined that the course of the law of the land should not be stayed...

Reporter Caldwell told of visiting Baker's cell the previous day and finding that the prisoner "fully appreciated the fact that his earthly career was near its close. He had been reading his Bible and praying during most of the day, and had been prayed with by several ministers. Yet his mind was far from easy, and he told us at sundown that he had no hope . . . "

The scaffold had been erected just in the rear of the jail. A high fence had been erected on all sides, so as to exclude the victim from the public gaze. Crowds had congregated around the jail door all the morning, and negroes smiled significantly to each other as the hour for the execution drew near. . . . The fences in all the vicinity were filled with persons anxious to see the death of a fellow being . . . and some had even climbed to the very top of the steeple of the Tryon Street Methodist Church [on the southwest corner of Sixth and Tryon], from which they could get a view of the jail yard.

At about 1:15 p.m., Baker, accompanied by Sheriff Alexander, Deputy Sheriff Caldwell and others came upon the scaffold. Baker wore a downcast look, but stepped out upon the scaffold with a firm and steady step. . . . [He] was asked if he would like to pray for himself; he said, "Yes," and knelt down upon the scaffold. His words were clear and ringing and were distinctly heard by all those around. . . . There was a deep earnestness and a rough eloquence in the words he uttered. . . . With one accord the spectators uncovered their heads. . . .

At 1:30 o'clock, the prayers being over with, Deputy Sheriff Caldwell stepped forward and drew the black cap over the face and head of the culprit . . . [who] bade adieu to Sheriff Alexander, Deputy Caldwell and the Rev. J. F. Butt, grasping each of them warmly by the hand. . . . At the end of this, Baker asked the Sheriff if he was not almost ready, and received in reply, "Yes." He thereupon straightened himself up and stood firm and erect.

Then the axe fell; the rope was severed; the platform was dropped, and the soul of Joseph Baker was launched out into the Great Unknown.

Caldwell could also write with a sense of humor, as he did in September 1875 in describing the first typewriter in Charlotte:

The principle of its working is the same as that employed in playing a piano. All the keys are marked. They look like the end of the spools, when you first open a box of Coates's thread

. . . . When you touch the right key (and experienced machine writers, we are told, do sometimes touch the right one), a little piece of wire, which acts like the leg of a "limber jack," flies up and hits the ribbon and both hit the paper. . . . Then you raise the top of the machine and look at the letter, and if it is the right one you close up the machine and make another one. If it is the wrong one, you get up and take out that sheet of paper and get a new one and start again.

Once he had acquainted himself with Charlotte, Caldwell branched out to win friends in surrounding towns. His visits to Lincolnton, Newton, Concord, Monroe, and Gastonia, none of which had a daily paper, produced stories designed to gain a wider audience for the *Observer* and increase its circulation in those communities. The stories were among the *Observer*'s earliest efforts to link itself to the region.

Johnstone Jones was also involved in expanding the paper's regional influence. When railroad service was begun between Charlotte and Spartanburg, he joined a delegation of Charlotte merchants, bankers, lawyers, and government officials on the first southbound train and wrote a three-and-a-half-column story describing the towns they passed through. Though the story was intended to increase circulation, it may have offended some people, especially those in towns that didn't get a favorable mention. In Gaston County, for instance, Jones noted that the road might have gone through the town of Dallas, then the county seat, but residents there had failed to buy their quota of railroad stock, and the line went through Gastonia instead. As a result, Gastonia grew but Dallas didn't.

Five months later, Jones wrote another long story heralding the start of railroad service between Charlotte and Atlanta. The $8 million route, known then as the Airline Railroad, was financed in part by $300,000 in stock purchased by Charlotte and Mecklenburg County. It promoted Charlotte's growth as a railroad junction and added a new dimension to the *Observer*'s reach. Trains going south each morning could deliver the paper to readers along the way.

Growth was the *Observer*'s constant theme, and Johnstone Jones and Joseph Caldwell were unstinting in their support of projects that would promote Charlotte's development. In April 1873 the paper listed the city's thirty-six manufacturing establishments by name, owner, and product, and commented: "It is true that some of them are quite small, but they give promise of better things. . . . We may

confidently look forward to a day when one of the most distinguish-
ing features in the enterprise of Charlotte will be its thriving industries." In September 1873, reporter Caldwell analyzed the 1870 Census and noted that Mecklenburg's 13,578 whites and 10,721 blacks
made it the third most populous county in the state, behind New
Hanover (Wilmington) and Wake (Raleigh). "This section of North
Carolina is just entering upon an era of great and swiftly growing
prosperity; if our people will only seize hold of the golden opportunities now presented, a future pleasant to contemplate awaits them."

The *Observer* not only encouraged people to seize those opportunities; it openly promoted the sale of stock in ventures that might
make those opportunities possible. Without a wealthy family or industry to draw upon, Charlotteans had to pool their resources to
provide community amenities. In February 1873, the *Observer*
urged people to buy stock in a $7,000 icehouse that would help make
summers more bearable. By mid-July, the paper was embarrassed to
report that the company's machinery had failed to produce ice. When
a drive was launched to sell stock to build a civic auditorium, the *Observer* gave the effort daily coverage. "A hall in keeping with the dignity, character and dimension of the city is needed for the accom-
modation of the public on the occasion of lectures, operatic and
dramatic performances, art exhibitions, musical entertainments,
feasts and festivals and etc. Let us have a building that will be an or-
nament to the city," an editorial said. When the drive was oversub-
scribed, the paper observed, "We have lost in not having this hall in
the past eight years twice as much as it will require to build it."
Again, the paper was educating readers to the opportunities—and
obligations—of living in a city.

The hall was completed in the summer of 1874. It sat on the east
side of South Tryon, a few doors south of East Fourth Street (later the
site of BarclaysAmerican) and was known as the Opera House. Its
second-floor auditorium contained 1,500 seats; the first floor was
devoted to retailing. Among its early sellouts were touring shows by
comedian Josh Billings and a Shakespearean troupe headed by actor
Edwin Booth. Among early conventions held there was one by the
North Carolina Press Association, of which *Observer* editor Johnstone Jones had been a founding member.

Other promotions in which the *Observer* participated included a
drive to organize the Second Presbyterian Church (forerunner of
Covenant Presbyterian), the formation of the YMCA, the organization of volunteer fire departments (whose members included several
Observer employees, among them Harper Elam), a campaign that

resulted in a new jail, a rising temperance movement, and an unsuccessful effort to get a union station built to serve all railroads. It also cheered the chartering of Commercial National Bank, Charlotte's second national bank and a forerunner of NCNB.

In addition to giving the *Observer* an editorial voice and hiring Joseph Caldwell, Johnstone Jones made other improvements. He changed the paper's name to the *Daily Charlotte Observer*—to distinguish it from the weekly and semiweekly editions. He commenced regular coverage of Charlotte's board of aldermen and Mecklenburg's county commissioners, and ran daily summaries of state legislative proceedings. He tightened the paper's management by hiring M. A. Park as business manager and appointing J. M. George as the first circulation manager.

He also accelerated production by abandoning the weary Washington hand press in favor of a more modern rotary press that rolled sheets of paper over a flatbed of inked type. The rotary press belonged to the *Southern Home*, a weekly newspaper owned by D. H. Hill. It was housed on the second floor of the Springs Building on the north side of East Trade, one door off Independence Square (later the site of Eckerd's Drugs). For several months, Jones and his colleagues set the paper in type in their print shop on the south side of East Trade and carried it across the street to the Springs Building to be printed. In December 1873, when D. H. Hill moved out, Jones moved the *Observer* offices and print shop into the Springs Building.

With the faster press the paper improved its format, content, and production routine. News that had been confined to the inside pages could be published on page one, and the paper could be printed later. To go with the improved printing, in March 1873 Johnstone Jones added the telegraph service of the American Press Association. It gave the *Observer* immediate access to national news, including reports from major cotton and financial markets. The reports enabled merchants and farmers in the Charlotte area to make their prices competitive with those elsewhere in the country. With telegraph news, Johnstone Jones, Joseph Caldwell, and their typesetters began working past midnight to get the latest dispatches into print. What previously had been a daytime job became night-time. The *Observer* became truly a morning paper and was rapidly registering circulation gains.

In September 1873, a national disaster interrupted the success. Just as the *Observer* was beating drums to raise capital for the city's first cotton mill, banks and investment houses began to collapse in

New York and other financial centers, destabilizing markets and money supplies across the country. It was the panic of 1873, a depression as shocking to Americans of that generation as the stock market crash of 1929 would be to Americans of the 1930s. The depression that followed changed the political climate and deeply influenced the 1874 and 1876 elections.

For a few weeks *Observer* readers could follow the unfolding drama through the paper's daily telegraph reports. In the panic's first few days Johnstone Jones and Joseph Caldwell tried to assure their readers that "the danger is past, the storm is subsiding, and Charlotte is unhurt." But as the collapse continued, Charlotte-area farmers, merchants and bankers, as well as the *Observer* itself, began to feel its impact. The price of cotton, which had been eighteen cents a pound, fell to fourteen cents in the first week and continued to drop. On October 30, Joseph Caldwell reported the price was "ruinous to the producer. . . . The best grades sold yesterday for 12 cents—not much more than enough to pay for its production." Prices inched down by fractions until November 8, when they hit eleven cents. That meant farmers who had expected to get $95 a bale would get only $55 instead.

The loss in income was soon crimping the Carolinas' economy. If farmers had less money to spend, so did the people with whom they traded. Increasingly, the *Observer* complained that "tight money" was strangling economic activity. Charlotte's hopes of raising capital for a cotton mill vanished. The town would have to wait nearly ten years to cross that New South threshold. A number of local businesses tottered and a few failed. The most spectacular collapse was by the Bank of Mecklenburg, headed by James Tate and Thomas Dewey, the *Observer*'s original patrons. Its closing wiped out the savings of its depositors.

As the economy slowed, the *Observer*'s circulation and advertising declined also, and Johnstone Jones was forced to cut costs. On November 12, the telegraph news disappeared. There was no announcement, no apology; it simply was not there anymore. It was restored in March 1874, but by then the paper's circulation had fallen to about 300 to 400 a day.

Charlotte and the rest of the country needed three to five years to recover from losses caused by the panic. Almost every fall thereafter, farmers, merchants, bankers, and investors grew uneasy, lest the disaster strike again. In the fall of 1884, there was another tremor, though on a smaller scale. And in 1893, there was a panic to rival that of 1873. Such panics were dramatic evidence that the South, while enjoying few of the benefits of the national economy, was suffering from most of its burdens.

The panics were products of financial dislocations that helped make national monetary policy—whether to deflate the economy by making gold the basis of all currency or whether to inflate it by permitting the free coinage of silver—the raging political issue of the rest of the nineteenth century. Expanding the monetary base was an issue of critical importance to the agricultural West and the reviving South.

A letter reprinted in the *Observer* on January 20, 1874, analyzed the problem from the Carolinas' point of view. The letter was from Col. William Johnston, a Charlotte lawyer, real estate man, and railroad financier who helped build the Airline Railroad to Spartanburg and Atlanta and would later serve two terms as Charlotte's mayor. It said in part:

> In North and South Carolina, we had $20 million in banking capital chartered before the war. These banks had authority to issue three [dollars in loans] for every one [dollar in deposits], and hence could supply nearly $60 million in currency for industrial pursuits. Now they have only $3,455,460 of national bank capital and with the reserve restrictions upon their issues [banks] can scarcely furnish three millions of currency. This contrast shows the great destitution of means in the South.
>
> As with North and South Carolina, so with many other states, except New York, Pennsylvania and the New England states, which have relatively more than their proportion of bank capital. The government's requiring a large reserve to be kept, and the rates of interest paid by the New York banks, cause the currency to center there. . . . The temptation to loan it at high rates to wild speculative objects contributes with the scarcity of it to produce the panics. These panics generally occur in September, when the money is needed in the South and West to move cotton, grain and other productions. Then it cannot be controlled; the borrowers fail, the collaterals prove worthless, the banks totter, confidence is impaired, depositors make a run, a panic ensues, suspensions take place, and the country suffers.

While the *Observer* was reporting the panic's impact, it was also noting a steady decline in the health of its founder and former publisher, James H. Smith. After selling the paper to Jones, Smith went home to Winnsboro, South Carolina, to rest. Six months later, he resumed newspaper work on the *Progress*, a weekly in Lincolnton. He suffered a relapse, returned to Winnsboro and died there of consumption on December 4, 1874. He was thirty-five.

During much of the panic, the *Observer* lacked the services of apprentice Harper Elam. From April to December 1874, the seventeen-year-old Elam was serving as composing room foreman for the *Sun*, a new weekly being published in Concord. There he became friends with the publisher's fifteen-year-old nephew, Wade Hampton Harris, and taught him to set type. Young Harris, another aspiring printer-editor, would later move to Charlotte as an *Observer* reporter, found the *Charlotte News*, and spend the last twenty-three years of his life as editor of the modern *Charlotte Observer*.

Though it was brief, Johnstone Jones's leadership of the *Observer* was significant, for he demonstrated to people in Charlotte and the surrounding region what a daily newspaper could do in providing news, promoting commerce, and encouraging public improvements. He stabilized the *Observer*, enlivened its commentary and news coverage, and extended its influence into surrounding counties. Jones gave the newspaper a personality and a voice and, with the assistance of Joseph Caldwell, might have raised it to great prominence. Like Charlotte, the *Observer* was growing steadily and, with a breakthrough in cotton manufacturing, would have been on the threshold to even greater growth. But the panic of 1873 and the depression that followed exhausted the paper's reserves and left it vulnerable to any publisher with hard cash.

CHAPTER 3

TRIUMPH AND TRAGEDY UNDER CHAS. R. JONES
1874–1887

In the depths of the depression caused by the panic of 1873, the *Observer* was sold to a quick, contentious, contradictory man whose energy and talent would raise the paper to impressive heights, then plunge it to ruin. The man was Col. Charles R. Jones, an Iredell County editor who had the grit and tenacity to be a successful newspaper manager, but fell victim to exaggerated ambition and erratic judgment. He promoted education, industrialism, and commercial growth, but refused to follow the dictates of a tightly controlled and increasingly repressive Democratic party dominated by railroad and industrial interests. In time his defiance would cost him his newspaper and ultimately his life.

Except for a brief interim, Jones owned the *Observer* from the spring of 1874 until the fall of 1887, a convulsive period in the life of the South and the nation. During the period, the disputed Hayes-Tilden presidential election threatened to revive the Civil War. Reconstruction ended, federal troops were withdrawn from the South, railroads were extended to the Pacific, and the nation endured a succession of Indian wars—including the massacre of Gen. George A. Custer at Little Big Horn. It was a time of national pride, highlighted by the centennial of the Declaration of Independence, and a time of national shame, marked by the assassination of President Garfield and the Haymarket Riot. A brief flicker of idealism, in the reform of civil service and the adoption of a major civil rights law, was snuffed out by laissez-faire economics and survival-of-the-fittest doctrines of the social Darwinists.

North Carolina itself experienced similar contradictions. In the election of 1876, the Democratic party "redeemed" the state from Republican governors, only to deliver it to reactionary interests, largely the railroads, which controlled much of its industry and finance. As a result, the Democratic party became unresponsive to rising demands for education and economic justice. While the state's cities prospered with new business and industry, people in the countryside, increasingly the victims of sharecropping, crop-lien financing and overproduction, sank deeper into debt. Freight and interest rates rose as farm prices fell. Farmers protested, but Democratic leaders ignored them.

During the period Charlotte experienced continued growth. The first blocks of Tryon and Trade streets were paved, a chamber of commerce was organized, St. Peter's Hospital was built, the city's first cotton mill was organized, telephones were installed, water and sewer lines were laid, and electric lights were hung. The city got a new hotel (the Buford, at Tryon and Fourth streets), a new railroad terminal, a system of horse-drawn streetcars, and, after several unsuccessful referenda, authority to spend tax money for schools and roads.

During those years Charlotte also got about 5,000 new residents, including three aggressive New South entrepreneurs: Edward D. Latta from Pendleton, South Carolina; W. J. F. Liddell from Erie, Pennsylvania; and Daniel A. Tompkins from Edgefield, South Carolina. Each would contribute significantly to the growth of Charlotte and the region. Latta, a clothing merchant and manufacturer, would enter the real estate business, electrify the streetcars, develop the suburb of Dilworth, and contribute much to the building of Charlotte and its environs. Liddell, an inventor and machinist, would organize a foundry for the design and manufacture of industrial machinery that was to boost Charlotte as the center of the southern textile industry. Tompkins, an engineer and economic visionary, would have a hand in organizing, building, or equipping more than 350 cotton mills throughout the Piedmont Carolinas and Georgia. In time he also published the *Charlotte Observer* and two other newspapers.

Liddell came to Charlotte after the panic of 1873 had wiped out his efforts to build a foundry in Wisconsin. He decided to try his luck in the South and was passing through Charlotte on May 20, 1875, when 75,000 people were in town to celebrate the centennial of the Mecklenburg Declaration of Independence. That throng and the excitement in the city persuaded him to stay.

Col. Charles R. Jones was responsible for attracting much of that crowd and generating much of that excitement. He was building the *Observer* into the largest and, arguably, the liveliest newspaper in the Carolinas, and promoting the 100th anniversary of the Mecklen-burg Declaration was just part of his drive to put Charlotte and his newspaper on the map. Under his management, the paper prospered and was expanded into an eight-page daily, twice its original size. Reinvesting the paper's profits, Jones steadily acquired better equipment and larger quarters. The paper hired its first Washington and Raleigh correspondents, became a member of the old Associated Press (a forerunner of the modern news cooperative of the same name), began running daily weather reports, and introduced class-ified advertising, sports coverage, and the use of photographs. It also began publishing "extras" on the occasion of dramatic news events.

Capitalizing on Charlotte's favorable railroad connections, Jones managed to get the *Observer*, then the only daily west of Raleigh, de-livered before breakfast to homes across a wide area of the Piedmont Carolinas. He made it so much a part of the region's daily life that even after the paper's death readers continued to call the morning paper from Charlotte "the *Observer*," no matter what its real name was.

Although the paper was popular among readers, its tactless editor and publisher was not. A proud, pretentious man who liked to refer to himself in the third person as "Chas. R.," Jones frequently bucked public sentiment with editorial stands that angered or embarrassed state and local leaders. Jones had a tendency to make himself, rather than the ideas he was advancing, the object of controversy. Unwilling to stand above the battle and comment on it, he became a combat-ant. That changed the focus of debate from issues to personalities and weakened his and the *Observer*'s effectiveness.

Jones's combativeness may have stemmed from the frustrations of his early life. He was born Charles Reynolds Jones on May 25, 1841, in Fayetteville, where his father, also named Charles Reynolds Jones, was editing the weekly *Carolinian*. When the Mexican War started, the elder Jones formed an infantry company and won distinction in the fighting around Vera Cruz. He came home a hero, moved his fam-ily to a plantation eighteen miles north of Statesville, and became a general in the state militia. He was politicking to win his son, young Charles R., an appointment to West Point when he died in 1857. A few weeks later, the congressman from that district gave the appoint-ment to another youth, mortifying young Jones. It may have been then that he resolved to avenge that slight by becoming a congress-man himself.

At age seventeen, the disappointed Jones went west, worked on a steamboat on the Mississippi, and clerked in a hotel in New Orleans.

In July 1859, he settled in northeast Texas, where he became a printer's devil on the weekly *Bonham Era*. He was learning the printing trade and enjoying the rough and tumble of Texas politics when the Civil War began. He returned to Statesville, joined an Iredell County infantry unit, and was sent to Virginia. He was later commissioned a lieutenant and served the rest of the war on various adjutant staffs. Among his commanders was Col. Alfred H. Belo, who afterward would found the *Galveston Times* and the *Dallas Morning News*.

After the war, Jones returned to Iredell and began teaching school, farming land that he inherited from his father, and taking an active role in politics. In January 1866, he married Mary E. Colvert, with whom he fathered four children.

In 1872, when the weekly *Iredell Express* changed its politics from Democrat to Republican, he joined real estate man Fred H. Pendleton in founding the *Statesville Intelligencer* as a Conservative (Democratic) alternative. That was when Jones hired young Joseph P. Caldwell as a printer and discovered his reporting and writing talent.

Jones made the *Intelligencer* a financial success, but constantly involved it in personal controversy. In the fall of 1873, during a joust with Republican revenue agents, Jones publicly called one of them a liar and was challenged to print a retraction or fight a duel. When Jones did neither, several agents waylaid him at his newspaper office and beat him up.

Six months after that encounter, Jones was in Charlotte arranging to buy the *Observer* from Johnstone Jones. Again his partner was Fred Pendleton. Records at the Mecklenburg County courthouse suggest that Jones and Pendleton bought the *Observer* by paying off the $1,700 in debts Johnstone Jones owed on it. If that was the total price, it was a bargain. At the time, $6,000 was considered the minimum investment for starting a daily newspaper. But after the panic of 1873, the *Observer* was at a low ebb, with a daily circulation of fewer than 400 copies a day. At the time, Colonel Jones was thirty-two.

The sale was announced on April 1, 1874. Charles Jones and Fred Pendleton became the publishers and Johnstone Jones remained as editor. Colonel Jones pledged to make the *Observer* "at least the equal of any paper in the state." Three weeks later, the paper appeared in a wider, seven-column format, printed on a new press with new typefaces. It also had a higher subscription rate, up one dollar to seven dollars a year.

The purchase united Colonel Jones with his protégé, Joseph Caldwell, whose work was being admired and reprinted across the state.

The young city editor had a job offer from a paper in Wilmington, then a larger city than Charlotte, but Jones raised Caldwell's pay and persuaded him to stay. Other members of the *Observer* staff included Harper Elam, now a journeyman printer; Peter McLauchlin, the printing foreman; journeyman J. M. George, the circulation director; apprentice Wilton Capps; and laborer-pressman Anthony Rivers. To that crew, Colonel Jones added twenty-three-year-old pressman Asbury Brown and several printers who had worked for him in Statesville.

At about the same time, Colonel Jones moved the *Observer* offices out of the Springs Building on the Square and into the second floor of Oates Hall on the northwest corner of Trade and College streets, where the paper had more room. Before the Opera House was built, Oates Hall's second floor was Charlotte's auditorium and concert hall. The Oates brothers operated a cotton brokerage on the first floor.

Though Colonel Jones improved the *Observer*'s facilities, he did not promote harmony within the organization. Editor Johnstone Jones was soon scouting Raleigh for other employment, and Fred Pendleton was preparing to return to Statesville. On September 6, 1874, Colonel Jones became sole owner. His announcement was a sample of the inflated rhetoric that Charlotteans would come to expect from him. It said: "To be sole possessor of a fearless, outspoken, independent journal, published in the 'cradle of liberty,' in the midst of the best people on the green earth, enjoying the good will, friendship and patronage of the businessmen of the liveliest city in the South; to greet the public this morning with such a reputation as we possess is such an honor as we are hardly able to appreciate. Chas. R. Jones."

Fred Pendleton stayed another week, then left. Johnstone Jones left two weeks later to become secretary of the North Carolina Senate, editor of the Raleigh *News* (before its merger with the *Observer* to form the *News and Observer*), and in 1877 state adjutant general, an appointment he held for twelve years. He later practiced law in Morganton and Asheville, served a term in the North Carolina House, and moved to California, where he was elected a district attorney and practiced law until his death in July 1922, at age seventy-three.

When Johnstone Jones left, the *Observer* not only lost his talent as an editorial writer but in time also lost the services of its star reporter, Joseph Caldwell. After two years in Raleigh, Jones persuaded Caldwell to join him as city editor of the *News*, a job Caldwell kept only ten months. He quit in a dispute over stockholder interference with daily production of the paper. The experience soured Caldwell on the idea of editing a newspaper in a state capital and sent him back to Charlotte.

Meanwhile, Colonel Jones had replaced Caldwell on the *Observer* by hiring twenty-year-old J. Lenoir Chambers as city editor. Born in Burke County, but raised in Iredell, Chambers was educated at Davidson College, learned newspapering on the *Statesville Landmark*, and spent five years on the *Observer*, first as a local reporter, then as an editorial writer. He left to manage the Liddell Company and later joined E. D. Latta in founding the Charlotte Consolidated Construction Company, which built Dilworth. In the latter role he become one of the town's most influential leaders. His son, Lenoir Chambers, also entered journalism and, as editor of Norfolk's *Virginian Pilot*, won a Pulitzer Prize in 1960.

For three years after Johnstone Jones's departure, Colonel Jones conducted the *Observer*'s editorial page and turned it into a toady for the Conservative (Democratic) party. His editorials referred to "our party," "our candidates," and "our platform." Much of his loyalty was based on the Conservatives' advocacy of white supremacy. In endorsing candidates for state and county offices in 1874, Jones said, "The chief argument for supporting the Conservative cause is to wipe out the negro party. . . . They would govern us with negroes and mean white men." On Election Day the paper carried a note saying, "*The Observer* will cast 11 votes today—for honesty, decency and intelligence." The item inspired visions of the *Observer* staff marching in file to the polling booth, led by the jaunty Jones.

When the elections in 1874 gave Conservatives control of the state legislature, the *Observer* celebrated by running a drawing of a crowing rooster, a symbol of Democratic supremacy predating the donkey. (Even after cartoonist Thomas Nast popularized the donkey, the rooster remained a Democratic emblem in many southern states, where it was considered a symbol of white supremacy.) To Colonel Jones, the 1874 victory meant that "the white people, the taxpayers, the men who bear the burdens of the government, who own the soil and possess the property are determined to rule." The election encouraged Conservatives (Democrats) to think they might win the presidency in 1876.

Apparently the colonel knew his weaknesses as an editorialist because he soon hired a succession of gifted writers to relieve him of the editorial chores. The first was Willoughby F. Avery, age thirty-two, son of a prominent Burke County family descended from Waightstill Avery, North Carolina's first attorney general, who was said to have signed the Mecklenburg Declaration of Independence. At the outbreak of the Civil War, young Avery was first in his class at the university at Chapel Hill but quit school to join the Confederate army. He was wounded at Sharpsburg, wounded again at Gettysburg, and almost killed at Spotsylvania. After the war he worked on newspapers in Hickory and Asheville before joining the *Observer* in March 1875.

That fall, Avery was sent to Raleigh to cover the constitutional convention that drafted amendments designed to reduce black participation in North Carolina politics. The amendments eliminated the popular election of county commissioners in favor of having them appointed by local justices of the peace, who were appointed by the legislature. The change meant that even in predominantly black counties, blacks were not likely to serve on county boards. The *Observer* cheered the convention's proposal, though it left local government in the control of close-knit, highly conservative courthouse cliques. It also discouraged the political participation of poor whites, leaving the Democratic party to become even more elitist.

While Avery was in Raleigh, Colonel Jones sold a share of the *Observer* to F. Brevard McDowell, a twenty-six-year-old lawyer from Statesville, and allowed McDowell to take over Avery's editorial duties. McDowell was a Davidson College graduate who studied law at the University of Virginia but wanted a career in journalism. He paid Colonel Jones $4,500 for a half interest in the paper and took over management of the news and editorial departments, leaving Jones to look after the business and mechanical operations. Each partner drew a salary of seventy-five dollars a month.

McDowell proved to be a facile writer with an interest in history and literature. But his presence crowded out Avery, who resigned thirty days later. Avery went home to Morganton and founded the weekly *Blue Ridge Blade* but was dogged by poor health and died in November 1876. His nephew, Isaac Erwin Avery, would later follow him to the *Observer* and attract a wide following as the paper's first local columnist.

McDowell's partnership with Jones lasted only twenty months. In May 1877 he sold out, accepting $500 in cash and Jones's notes for $4,000. Four weeks later it became clear why. An industrial school that later would become the University of Arkansas had appointed Gen. D. H. Hill as its president. McDowell succeeded General Hill as editor and publisher of the weekly *Southern Home*. He was elected to the board of aldermen, and became an influential figure in the Charlotte business community. He later sold the *Home*, joined the Liddell

Company, became a partner in Latta's Charlotte Consolidated Construction Company, and served four years as Charlotte's mayor. When McDowell Street was opened in the early 1890s, it was named for him.

Just as McDowell was leaving the *Observer* in May 1977, Joseph Caldwell was ending his stint with the *News* in Raleigh. He returned to Charlotte, married Maggie Spratt, daughter of an old Mecklenburg family, and became the third editorialist hired by Jones.

No matter who wrote *Observer* editorials under Colonel Jones, three policies remained constant: (1) the paper continued to boost Charlotte as a center of commerce and industry; (2) it continued to crusade for tax-supported graded schools in Charlotte and for public education generally; and (3) it continued its aggressive support of white supremacy. All three made the *Observer* a typical New South newspaper in the mold of Henry Grady's Atlanta *Constitution*.

When it came to promoting commerce and industry, what was good for Charlotte or the region was usually good for the *Observer*. When the long-stalled Carolina Central Railroad was completed from Wilmington to Charlotte, it retired the stagecoach and opened a whole new territory for expansion. The *Observer* celebrated for days and with good reason: the railroad could deliver the newspaper to thousands of new customers east of the city, from Monroe to Wadesboro to Rockingham, Hamlet, Laurinburg, and Lumberton. After a banquet at the Central Hotel honoring those whose investments had financed the completion (including Edward Matthews of New York, for whom the town of Matthews is named), the *Observer* ran the texts of speeches by every notable present. It was another example of the *Observer*'s regional consciousness.

The paper also continued to hammer at the need for a cotton mill to create jobs and make Charlotte less dependent on the industrial North. When the Lineberger brothers of Belmont opened a mill on the Catawba River, the *Observer* applauded and asked why Charlotte couldn't organize one. In a long story about a water-powered mill employing 350 workers at Randleman near Greensboro, the *Observer* suggested that a similar mill powered by steam might be even more profitable in Charlotte. Jones organized many meetings to promote financing for a local cotton mill.

Though he held cotton manufacturing to be of considerable consequence, Colonel Jones—and the *Observer*—put even greater energy into crusading for public education. "Of all the questions before the southern people at this day, that of education transcends all others in importance, for upon it depends the future progress, greatness and glory of our section," said an editorial of January 1, 1883. The paper even espoused educating blacks. "The negro race, if they [sic] are to be citizens, must be educated," the paper said. "They must have preachers and teachers of their own people. . . . The well-being of the community demands it."

The *Observer* was one of the few newspapers in the Carolinas to support the Blair Bill aimed at giving federal aid to public schools on the basis of the adult illiteracy. With one of the nation's highest illiteracy rates, North Carolina would have received $7 million to $10 million under the bill, enough to have doubled the size of its public school system. But in the rural South the Blair Bill was regarded as a threat to local and state control, and southern votes in Congress prevented its passage.

When North Carolina was trying to choose a location for a normal school for blacks, the *Observer* urged Charlotte to offer a site. Charlotte did not, and the school went to Fayetteville, instead, and became Fayetteville State University. Later, when the state invited cities to offer land for an agricultural and mechanical college for white students, the *Observer* pleaded with Charlotte to enter a strong bid, but the city did not. The school was finally built in Raleigh and became North Carolina State University.

Even though Jones opened the paper's news columns to more stories about black institutions, such as Biddle Institute, the *Observer* was unyielding in its defense of white supremacy. When Congress passed the Civil Rights Act of 1875, giving blacks access to white hotels, railroad cars, and other public accommodations, the *Observer* condemned it as another Reconstruction "iniquity" that would worsen race relations. In April 1875, the act was tested in Charlotte with near-disastrous results. A black man en route to Charleston with his wife and a child registered at the Central Hotel on the Square. They were shown to rooms, and while they were being served in the dining room, a crowd of forty to fifty angry whites gathered at the hotel's South Tryon entrance. When a manager barred the door, the crowd went around to a kitchen entrance on East Trade, poured into the dining room, surrounded the blacks, and ordered them to leave. As the frightened guests gathered their belongings, the hotel manager refunded their money, and the black headwaiter offered them rooms at his home, which they accepted.

The *Observer* reported the incident in a long front-page story and then commented, "We have no apologies to make for . . . those citizens who ordered him [the black man] from the hotel. In fact, it will be late in the day when the *Observer* advises its readers to eat any more dirt."

Despite improvements Jones made in the newspaper and the talent he recruited, the *Observer* remained limited in its ability to report large, complex national stories. Like most southern communities Charlotte lacked the libraries and scholars that a newspaper needed to analyze and interpret such events. A good example was the disputed Hayes-Tilden presidential election of 1876, which brought into conflict a welter of political, economic, and social forces from across the country.

Crowds gathered outside the *Observer* offices the night after the November 1876 election, anticipating a Democratic sweep. By early morning, it appeared that Democrat Samuel J. Tilden of New York might win the presidency. Two days later, he led Republican Rutherford B. Hayes of Ohio by more than 250,000 votes and was within one vote of victory in the Electoral College. He had to win only one of twenty contested electoral votes to claim the White House. The *Observer* ran headlines proclaiming "Victory! A Nation Redeemed," and every day for a week it printed a drawing of the crowing rooster. Not only was Tilden winning the presidency, but North Carolina Democrats had elected Charlottean Zeb Vance governor and regained control of the Council of State. North Carolina and the South appeared to be free from Reconstruction.

But hanging in the balance of the presidential election were more than the personal careers of Samuel Tilden and Rutherford Hayes. Also at stake were the banking, monetary, tariff, and railroad policies that had shaped the nation's business and industry since the Civil War. Those policies favored the industrial North over the agrarian South and West. Eastern money managers and industrial barons were not accepting defeat without exhausting every alternative. Months passed as Congress recounted votes and wrangled over which ballots were bona fide in four contested states. Gradually, the Republicans began turning things around. Relying on sketchy stories from its telegraph service, the *Observer* could do little more than editorially stamp its foot at what appeared to be an unfolding fraud. It lacked the resources to report the discreet negotiations under way between northern railroad interests and southern senators and congressmen.

The dispute was resolved in early March by a special commission of seven Republicans and six Democrats who, voting along party lines, awarded all four contested states to the Republicans, giving

Hayes the edge in electoral votes, 185 to 184. That news arrived in the *Observer* offices by telegram on Saturday morning, March 3. The editors didn't wait for the Sunday edition; they spread the word by publishing the paper's first "extra."

What the *Observer* didn't—and couldn't—report were the terms of the settlement, known as the Compromise of 1877. As reported by newspapers in Washington and New York (Joseph Pulitzer covered the story for the New York *Sun*), the election of 1876 was not stolen by northern Republicans as much as it was sold by southern Democrats. In accepting the compromise, southerners wrung from Hayes and an alliance of northern railroad financiers a list of concessions far exceeding the removal of federal troops from the South. They won federal aid for clearing southern harbors, for repairing southern levees, and for building railroads, chief among them the Southern Pacific. The southerners' goal was to make their region more attractive to northern capital, but what they did was assure the continuation of its colonial status. Among the southerners consenting to the compromise were such New South advocates as Henry Watterson of the Louisville *Courier-Journal*, Sen. L. Q. C. Lamar of Mississippi, and Sen. John B. Gordon of Georgia. In effect, the southern Democrats redeemed their region from Republican governments by delivering it into the hands of eastern capitalists. In doing so, they committed the Democratic party in most southern states to the interests of big business and the status quo.

After the Hayes election, Jones and the *Observer* settled down to a period of relative peace and prosperity. Jones became a man about town. At a gathering in the loft over E. D. Latta's clothing store, he helped to organize Charlotte's first chamber of commerce and was elected its secretary. He spoke at numerous meetings to devise strategy for attracting more railroads to Charlotte and visited Raleigh, Winston-Salem, and Wilmington to lobby railroad men in Charlotte's behalf. In speeches and editorials, he continued to advocate taxes to support graded schools; but, lacking support from the city's wealthiest citizens, a referendum on a school tax failed by ninety-two votes. He participated in drafting State Sen. S. B. Alexander's bill to let Mecklenburg County spend tax money for the construction and repair of roads, a measure that pioneered highway development in the state and gave Charlotte a big advantage over other cities.

As business improved, so did the *Observer's* advertising and circulation. E. D. Latta bought a big, three-column ad on page one every day. The Singer Company bought ads for its sewing machines, a sign that national manufacturers were beginning to see the reviving South as a market. Other national advertisers included the Procter & Gamble Company and the Royal Baking Powder Company. The paper had introduced classified ads in March 1876 and was still trying to educate the public to their effectiveness. It also began running results of local and major league baseball games, indicating that Charlotte, like other urban places, was developing a hunger for spectator sports.

The weekly *Observer*, which was circulated by mail to farmers and other readers in isolated places, was expanded to forty and fifty columns, making it the largest weekly in the Carolinas. Its circulation climbed past 1,500, exceeding that of the daily paper. With the help of the railroads, the daily continued to gain in circulation, and by September 1879, it was averaging 1,208 copies a day, four times the number sold when Jones bought the paper in 1874. Among the added subscribers was Zebulon B. Vance, formerly of Charlotte, who had been elected North Carolina's new governor. Vance wrote the paper on January 9, 1877, saying, "This is to inform you that I have recently removed to Raleigh and would be glad to have my paper sent here. Z. B. Vance." Two years later, when Vance was elected to the United States Senate, his son David signed on as an *Observer* reporter.

The prosperity soon began to show in the paper's looks and offices. In September 1878, the *Observer* appeared in fresh, clean typefaces, and a year later it moved diagonally across Trade Street, from Oates Hall to the J. L. Morehead Building, three doors from the corner of Trade and College (later the site of Charlotte's Convention Center). More than 200 townspeople attended an open house there between nine and eleven o'clock one Saturday night and drank toasts to the paper, described by ex-mayor Clement Dowd as "the pride of our city, an honor to our country, the best daily paper in North Carolina and one of the very best in the South." In April 1880, the paper became one of twenty-two subscribers to Charlotte's first telephone exchange.

Things were going so well, in fact, that the *Observer* could risk offending its white readers by publishing more news of the black community. To its coverage of Biddle Institute and an occasional black political meeting, it added stories about black churches. When a black Presbyterian congregation (now First United Presbyterian Church) built a $4,500 sanctuary on the northeast corner of College and Seventh, the *Observer* reported it. When a group broke from the black First Baptist Church to form Ebenezer Baptist, the *Observer* reported that. And when leaders of the A.M.E. Zion Church held a conference at Salisbury, the *Observer* ran summaries of each session and an editorial saying, "These people of North Carolina and the South are now enjoying a larger degree of peace and good feeling than they have known since the war." But the softer attitude on race did not change the *Observer*'s opinion of the women's movement. The paper remained adamantly opposed to what it jeeringly called "female suffrage."

Not all the news was good. Word came that the *Observer*'s first editor, John M. Watson, had died at age forty-one. That was followed by news that Gaston Paul, another of the four founders, had died near Wadesboro at age thirty-nine. That left Peter McLauchlin as the only survivor. He was still setting type in the composing room, but after the election of President Grover Cleveland in 1884 he would resign to take a job as a railway postal clerk.

The other bad news was that after nearly eight years on the *Observer*, Joseph Caldwell was leaving in January 1880 to buy the *Statesville Landmark* and turn it into one of North Carolina's most admired weeklies. His departure would deprive editor Jones not only of an editorial writer, but apparently of a stabilizing influence on the paper's politics as well.

Jones's troubles began in the spring of 1880, shortly after Caldwell's departure. Restless under the stand-pat policies of state Democrats, he wrote a long editorial applauding the rise of independent journals across the country and the advantage they enjoyed over party newspapers. That probably set suspicious minds to wondering. When he allowed his name to be entered as a candidate for mayor, readers had cause to doubt his judgment, for he was not popular. He asked to withdraw, but he was too late to avoid embarrassment: the leading candidate got 200 votes; Jones got twenty-five. Afterward he launched a strident campaign against the North Carolina congressional delegation for failing to secure a federal building for Charlotte, a criticism that provoked testy responses all around.

Capping those misjudgments was his harsh reaction to the shooting of President Garfield. The shooting occurred on Saturday, July 2, 1881, and news of it stunned Charlotteans the next morning. Crowds gathered in front of the *Observer* office where bulletins on the president's condition were posted. The next day citizens gathered at the courthouse at Trade and Church streets to pass resolutions expressing sympathy for the wounded leader. Jones helped to word the resolution that was sent to Washington.

To give employees Independence Day off, the *Observer* normally did not publish on July 5. But recognizing the public interest in the president's condition, Jones called in a skeleton staff on July 4 and the next morning published a two-page "extra" containing the latest medical advisories. He included an editorial that deplored the shooting, but in analyzing the causes of such treachery he recalled Garfield's role in negotiating the 1877 compromise that put Hayes in the White House ahead of the Democrat Tilden. Jones suggested that the assault on Garfield was just retribution. "They have sown the wind and they shall reap the whirlwind," he wrote.

The editorial provoked an uproar. That night there was another gathering at the courthouse, this time to censure Jones. Preachers, merchants, and business leaders expressed outrage. Samuel Wittkowsky, the town's leading merchant, said Jones should have a chance to defend himself. Jones appeared, agreed that perhaps he had been impolitic, but insisted that everything in the editorial had been said during the previous fall's election campaign. The gathering passed a resolution saying Jones's sentiments were not shared by other Charlotteans. The resolution was sent to other newspapers for publication.

In August 1881 came a censure of another type. When the legislature authorized a statewide referendum on prohibition, Jones disappointed friends by going all out to support the proposal. In addition to daily editorials, he published a special supplement—without advertising—pointing up the evils of alcohol. When the votes were counted, prohibition lost, three to one. It failed in the white community, the black community, the city, and the county.

In September came a third censure, this time from Charlotte businessmen. For three straight days, Jones published editorials blasting Senator Vance and other state politicians for allowing New York purchasers of the Western North Carolina Railroad to renege on pledges to complete the road and end the discrimination in freight rates. His tone was angry and insulting. Fearing that such criticism might damage Charlotte's standing among the powerful, local business leaders passed a resolution saying *Observer* editorials did not reflect their thinking. The resolution was sent to every major newspaper in the state, and many rival editors printed it in full. Business leaders also began discussing possibilities of starting a new Charlotte daily.

All of that should have shaken Jones, who knew the penalties for creating discord among Democrats. He himself had written of the thin edge that North Carolina Democrats held against Republicans and had warned that only a united party could prevent the return of blacks and carpetbaggers to office. Splitting the party was about the worst sin a Democrat could commit.

By early October 1881, rumors were circulating that Democrats had raised $6,000 to start a rival paper in Charlotte. Sam Ashe of

Raleigh, chairman of the Democratic Executive Committee and editor of the *News and Observer*, advised against such a move, predicting that "the money would probably be sunk within six months." People unhappy with the *Observer* would be wiser to pay Jones "a considerable price" for his paper, he suggested.

Jones seemed to enjoy the notoriety. Joseph Pulitzer's St. Louis *Post-Dispatch* was showing journalists all over the country how vigorous and liberating an independent newspaper could be, and Jones obviously prized that independence for himself. He wrote an editorial saying, "The independent newspaper will make enemies, but when it is bold enough to have opinions of its own based upon what it believes to be right, a sober second judgment of the public will set it right in the end. . . . It cannot afford to be dodging about to find out which is the popular side of any issue as it rises, and this paper at least will never do it." As if to prove his independence, Jones took out after the Democrats who dominated county government. The scheme allowing justices of the peace to appoint county commissioners—a practice he had earlier approved—was now termed "undemocratic" and indefensible. A party that entrusts its fortunes to cliques "disregards the people's wishes . . . [and] will find before long that the people will be heard," Jones said.

In mid-July 1882, Jones compromised his editorial objectivity by running for Congress as an independent, declaring that he had neither the time nor the inclination to court the county leaders who controlled the Democratic nominating convention—among whom he had no support, of course. Speaking for Democratic loyalists, the Raleigh *News and Observer* first urged Jones to reconsider, then read him out of the party. "As a matter of course, Democrats who have heretofore sustained *The Observer* will no longer support it. They do not want to contribute to the support of a paper that has betrayed their cause," the *News and Observer* said. A few days later, *News and Observer* editor Sam Ashe said he had changed his mind: perhaps the Democrats *should* start a rival daily in Charlotte.

In late July 1882, Joseph Caldwell visited the city, reportedly to explore the possibilities of starting another newspaper. In early August, it was announced that a new paper, the *Daily Journal*, would be issued on August 22, with ex-congressman Alfred M. Waddell of Wilmington, one of the Democratic party's most gifted writers and speakers, as editor. David Vance, who had left the *Observer* for a job in Baltimore, would be the local reporter. W. C. Wolfe, formerly of the *Monroe Enquirer*, would be business manager.

Jones's restlessness within the Democratic party was shared by a great many other people in the South. Many farmers, small merchants, and rural political leaders were upset by the Democrats' deafness to their concerns. A decade later, they would unite to create the Populist Revolt. But Jones never stepped back to inform his readers of the broad discontent that was building or to explain the economic and political issues behind it. Had he done so, his quest for political independence might have gained greater respect. Instead, he waged a narrow, personal fight, and by September 1 realized that his cause was doomed. If he was to remain a candidate, he would have to run as a Republican, something he was unwilling to do. He withdrew from the race, saying he could not risk splitting the Democrats and returning the Republicans to power. But by then, the damage was done; the competing *Daily Journal* was on the streets, touting itself as "the only first-class daily in Charlotte."

It was not the first time the *Observer* under Colonel Jones had faced competition from another daily. Over the previous eight years it had survived challenges from the *Daily Eagle*, the *Daily Age*, the *Daily Press*, and the *Daily Advertiser*, each of which had died. But this time the struggle was more than a newspaper battle; it was a political war. Though Jones resumed his Democratic loyalty after quitting the congressional race—won by former Charlotte mayor Clement Dowd—community attitudes toward him remained chilly. The big Latta Bros. ad that had graced *Observer* front pages for several years disappeared, as did ads for other prominent merchants. Jones was obviously being punished.

If Jones was hurt, he never let it be known. All fall and into the Christmas season, he boasted that the *Observer* was increasing circulation faster than ever. When two tax-supported graded schools were opened, one for whites and one for blacks, he claimed a large share of the credit. He hired Wade H. Harris of the Concord *Sun* as a reporter and sent him out to cover county fairs in the area. He also expanded the Sunday edition to eight pages, claiming that with increased advertising a larger paper was necessary. In December, he made the paper's first promotional use of Santa Claus and ran letters to Santa from area children.

The big news came in early November 1882, when Jones announced he had bought as offices for the *Observer* the three-story brick building at No. 2 Granite Row, on the southwest corner of Independence Square. For the first time, the paper would have a street-floor entrance where people could place advertising, buy subscriptions, or order job printing. Jones paid $7,000 for the building, $1,000 in cash and $6,000 in notes. Jones also bought a three-and-a-half-horsepower, gas-fed steam press that, at 1,020 impressions an hour, could complete the *Observer*'s daily press run (printing one side of a sheet at a time) in four hours. The *Observer* moved into its new quarters over New Year's. Jones celebrated with a long editorial, outlining the paper's history and listing a staff that included four writers and editors, eight printers, two pressmen, one janitor, five carriers, and correspondents in Raleigh, Washington, New York, Greensboro, Salisbury, Concord, Statesville, and Monroe. The implied message seemed to be, "If the *Daily Journal* is going to put the *Observer* out of business, it is going have to fight to do so."

For a while the *Observer* and the *Daily Journal* sniped at each other at some distance. Then, in February 1883, they fought at close range. P. A. Grimsley, a pressman for the *Daily Journal*, entered the *Observer* offices and attacked H. J. Stone, an *Observer* pressman, stabbing him in the chest, slashing his cheek, and slicing off half his ear. Colonel Jones dived into the fray to prevent further injury. The fight, which stemmed from an old grudge, was no doubt aggravated by rivalry between the two newspapers.

In the meantime, the *Journal* was showing signs of financial strain. Hugh W. Harris of Pineville, a young lawyer recently graduated from Columbia University, and his father, Robert H. Harris, a wealthy farmer, bought an interest in the paper, providing new capital and strengthening the paper's ties to Mecklenburg County. All of which made the March 27, 1883, announcement in the *Observer* even more startling. It said that Colonel Jones had sold the *Observer* to the *Daily Journal*, which would become the *Journal-Observer*. The *Journal-Observer* would move into the *Observer*'s new quarters and two *Observer* staffers, P. F. Duffy and Wade H. Harris, would join the *Journal-Observer* staff. "With this announcement, I retire from journalism in North Carolina, possibly forever," Jones said.

But, as in other matters involving Charles R. Jones, all was not what it appeared. Deeds filed at the courthouse indicate that Jones had driven a hard bargain. A. M. Waddell, Hugh Harris, and Robert Harris had agreed to pay $12,787.67 for the *Observer*, rent its building for $600 a year, and provide Jones an office from which to collect bills still owed him. Furthermore, the agreement stipulated that the *Observer* would remain in Jones's name until terms of the sale were fully satisfied. The terms required Waddell and the Harrises to put down $2,000 in cash and pay $1,248.42 plus 6 percent interest on October 1 and $3,179.75 plus 6 percent interest each January 1 from 1884 to 1886.

In agreeing to that, Waddell and the Harrises probably overestimated the *Journal-Observer*'s profit potential. The paper might earn enough in six months to cover the October payment of $1,248.42—

an amount equal to about a 20 percent annual return on investment. But in the next four months the paper was unlikely to earn the $3,179.75 due on January 1, 1884.

The *Journal-Observer* appeared under its new masthead on March 31, 1883, and dived into covering Charlotte's growth. On April 6, 1883, it reported that "Daniel A. Tompkins of Pennsylvania will open at an early date in Charlotte a Southern headquarters for the sale of machinery manufactured by the Westinghouse Machine Co." That notice must have rankled Tompkins, who was neither a Pennsylvanian nor a salesman. He was a South Carolinian, the son of a prominent doctor and planter in Edgefield County. He was also an engineer who burned with ambition to help the South realize its industrial potential. But in the South of the 1880s, a business affiliation in Pennsylvania was likely to command more respect than a pedigree from South Carolina. The Civil War defeat and Reconstruction poverty had left Southerners with an inferiority complex about their region. Tompkins intended to do something about that. He had spent the previous year traveling the South, looking for a favorable spot from which to launch his industrializing campaign. He chose Charlotte for its location, water-power potential, railroad connections, and general spirit of commerce.

At the same time the *Journal-Observer* was welcoming Tompkins, it was saying farewell to Harper Elam, the former apprentice boy who had grown up with the *Observer* but apparently felt estranged by the new name and new owners. He accepted a job as foreman on the *Greensboro Patriot*. News of his departure came in a brief item, written no doubt by Wade Harris, who had learned to set type at Harper Elam's instruction. "By long and steady connection with this paper, Harper came to be almost a part and parcel of the office and to see him go makes his old associates feel like they had lost something," the story said. "So strongly did this feeling prevail . . . that every now and then yesterday the printers would involuntarily feel about their pockets," in search of what was missing.

Elam found happiness in Greensboro, became a leader among volunteer firemen, was elected to the board of aldermen, helped to organize the first fire department, and in 1890, with fellow printer J. M. Reece, founded the *Daily Record*, for many years the city's evening newspaper. It was Elam who gave Greensboro the name "Gate City," because of its excellent railroad connections. It was also Elam who led a campaign to have the Guilford Courthouse battleground, scene of a pivotal Revolutionary War engagement, designated a national historic site. Elam Avenue in Greensboro is named for him. In

1969, his grandson Harper J. Elam III, a lawyer, was elected Greensboro's mayor.

The *Journal-Observer* was keeping a wary eye on Colonel Jones, who was in and out of the office and scurrying about Charlotte. The paper reported on April 15, 1883, that Jones had traded $750 in cash and 108 acres of land in Iredell County for a house and lot at Ninth Street and North Tryon, then occupied by E. D. Latta. After suffering Latta's political displeasure, the colonel probably got a measure of satisfaction out of becoming his landlord. Jones also ran again for mayor, finishing a poor third. A few days later he took off on a month-long train trip to California, to attend a Knights Templar convention in San Francisco. On his return, he wrote a long story for the *Journal-Observer* describing his journey.

In six months, the *Journal-Observer* never seemed to generate much momentum. It spent much of the time feeling out the town, like a stranger at a lawn party trying to strike up a conversation. It never caught the city's pace or attracted the advertising the *Observer* had enjoyed.

Even so, Charlotteans must have been startled on October 14, 1883, when they picked up their Sunday paper and found there the old masthead of the *Observer* and the old bluster of Colonel Jones. In buying back the paper, his only explanation was, "It was *business* to sell out *The Observer* on the 1st day of April," and business to buy it back in October.

Again, courthouse records tell a different story. They indicate that the owners of the *Journal-Observer* could not meet the payment schedule. It was not the $3,179.75 due in January that caused their default; it was the $1,248.42 due on October 1. When that date came and they could not pay, Colonel Jones apparently gave them a ten-day extension, then took action. By then, Waddell and the Harrises probably realized they were in a bind and asked for a settlement. Jones accepted their payment of $1,248.42, canceled the three remaining notes, returned $1,000 of their down payment, and took back his newspaper. A. M. Waddell went back to Wilmington, where he later became mayor and a leading figure in the campaign of 1900 to disfranchise blacks. Hugh Harris entered the practice of law in Charlotte and later served as a United States commissioner, a state legislator, and a city attorney.

Colonel Jones resumed publication of the *Observer* as if nothing had happened. Even the big Latta ad soon reappeared on the front page. He enjoyed two years of relative peace before his ambitions again got him in trouble. In November 1883, he expanded the daily edition to eight pages, making it the largest in the state. Jones filled the *Observer*'s extra columns with news and illustrated features about such things as oil gushers in Pennsylvania, the rise of Minneapolis and other new cities in the Midwest, the homes of famous people in Washington, D.C., and life in London. Through an expanded *Observer*, Charlotteans were getting a better look at the world and what it was like to live in a city.

In February 1884, when a string of tornadoes cut a swath through the Carolinas, laying waste to much of Richmond County and killing eleven people in a village near Rockingham, the *Observer* fulfilled another function of newspapers: it called for disaster relief. In the days before the Red Cross and similar agencies, newspapers were the chief organizers of emergency charity. Colonel Jones ran daily requests for money, food, and blankets for "cyclone" victims. A few weeks later, the *Observer* published a thank-you note from the mayor of Rockingham, a young lawyer named Charles W. Tillett, who would later move to Charlotte and become an important civic and political leader.

During that period of relative peace, Jones had the satisfaction of seeing the Supreme Court declare the Civil Rights Act of 1875 unconstitutional. He celebrated with a front-page editorial suggesting that the rest of the country was at last experiencing the excesses of Reconstruction. That decision by the court, and another a decade later authorizing separate-but-equal public facilities, laid the legal foundations on which the South would build a segregated society in the 1890s and early 1900s.

For a while, Jones was even in good graces with local and state Democratic leaders. He was a delegate to the party's county, district, and state conventions and a speaker with Senator Vance and ex-governor Jarvis at ceremonies marking the completion of the Western North Carolina Railroad. In 1884, when Grover Cleveland became the first Democrat to be elected president in twenty-eight years, the *Observer* rejoiced by printing a drawing of a crowing rooster five columns wide and a foot high.

The period also saw continued progress in Charlotte. The first cotton-seed-oil mill was built and later equipped with electric lights. Engineer D. A. Tompkins installed the engine that generated the electricity. Members of the Charlotte bar, led by Robert D. Johnston, Heriot Clarkson, and Hugh Harris, organized the Law Library. The *Observer* encouraged attorneys to buy shares in the library, claiming it would improve the practice of law in the community. Clement Dowd gave up his congressional seat to accept President Cleveland's appointment as district collector of internal revenue and moved the IRS offices from Statesville to Charlotte. And the Houston Thompson Electric Light Company offered to replace the gas lamps on downtown streets with electric lights. Though the gas suppliers were politically powerful, the *Observer* advocated the switch to electric lights. Despite a recession that had depressed prices and deflated currency, Colonel Jones greeted the year 1886 with a New Year's Day editorial full of optimism. But the year was to prove disastrous for Jones and the *Observer*.

Early in January, Jones's old ambition to be a member of Congress—and his antagonism toward Democratic leaders—surfaced again. When the *Observer* carried a story on the number of newspaper editors serving in the House of Representatives, it was a sign that Jones was contemplating another congressional race. He again charged that "fair weather friends" in Congress were ignoring Charlotte's needs. He attacked Sen. Zeb Vance as a political "dictator" who had put sixteen members of his family on the federal payroll. Other editorials accused Vance and Matt Ransom, North Carolina's other senator, of "stealing" from taxpayers by approving Senate expenditures for perfumed soap and other luxuries.

Such charges made friends of North Carolina's senators and congressmen furious, but when measured against the real grievances Jones might have cited, they seem petty. A more devastating indictment was made by Walter Hines Page, editor of the *State Chronicle* in Raleigh. Once a New South advocate in the style of Henry Grady, Page had begun pointing out that North Carolina's backwardness was the product of small men and small minds. For several years he had urged an end to the complacent conservatism that was blocking the state's progress. In giving up the fight and moving to New York, he wrote a farewell letter comparing North Carolina's leaders to Egyptian mummies: "It is an awfully discouraging business to undertake to prove to a mummy that it is a mummy. You go up to it and say, 'Old fellow, the Egyptian dynasties crumbled several thousand years ago; you are a fish out of water . . . ' The old thing grins that grin which death set on its solemn features when the world was young; and your task is so pitiful that even the humor of it is gone."

But, according to Page, North Carolina's "mummies" were a "solemn fact." If you want to know what's wrong with the state, "it is the mummies," he suggested. Among the men who held the highest places in the state or had the greatest influence on education, not one was a scholar, he complained. Not one of the state's five most influential editors could earn ten dollars a week on a metropolitan newspaper, he alleged. The editorial won Page many admirers, but also provoked outrage.

Among the offended was Jones, who failed to see the larger issues Page had raised and the opportunities they offered dissenters like himself. Instead of shouting "amen" to someone who shared his views, Jones assumed he was one of the editors Page had belittled. He pointed out that Page was a financial failure and that he, Jones, had succeeded with the *Observer*.

Again there was talk of founding a new daily in Charlotte to oppose Jones and discipline his politics. Within a few weeks, the *Observer* reported that William S. Hemby, "a young journalist of wide experience," had bought the old *Daily Journal* equipment and planned to start a newspaper in Oates Hall at East Trade and North College streets, once the home of the *Observer*. The new paper would be called the *Evening Chronicle* and would be Democratic in its politics. On March 23, the *Observer* reported, "*The Evening Chronicle* made its first appearance yesterday afternoon, and the first number is a very creditable one. Mr. W. S. Hemby is editor and proprietor and James Robinson is local editor. *The Chronicle* has a good display of advertisements, and is a newsy, sprightly and well-printed paper of 24 columns. *The Observer* gives it a cordial greeting."

Later in the year, after Jones had entered the race for Congress as one of eleven independents on the Mecklenburg ballot—a measure of the dissent building in the county—the *Chronicle* shifted to morning publication to compete head to head against the *Observer*. Day after day it aimed a stream of derision at "Chas. R.," and rallied support for the regular Democratic ticket. The *Chronicle* was not the only rival Jones had to worry about; two other newspapers, the daily *Evening Times* and the weekly *Carolina Gazette*, also entered the field and sapped the *Observer*'s strength. The eight-page *Observer* shrunk to four pages. By Election Day, when Jones was beaten by a margin of two to one, the paper was obviously going downhill. After the election, the *Chronicle* hired away Wade Harris and began to crow over the *Observer*'s decline.

On August 2, 1887, the *Chronicle* carried an item saying the *Observer* offices were closed and the paper had ceased publication. In the spring of 1888, Colonel Jones briefly revived the *Observer* as an afternoon daily, but he spent most of his time trying to collect more than $10,000 in back bills for advertising and subscriptions owed the morning *Observer*. The accounts represented all that was left of his once-enviable estate, and the threat of losing everything he had built began to affect his behavior. He became distracted and increasingly unstable and on February 6, 1889, was declared insane. But before he could be admitted to the state hospital at Morganton, he died of uremic poisoning at age forty-eight.

In an editorial in the *Statesville Landmark*, Joseph Caldwell said of him:

> Chas. R. Jones was so unlike other men that it is difficult to estimate him. He was what men call "a strange genius." There was never a man of his ability who had as many mental weaknesses. He was a perpetual contradiction. No man could ever say with confidence, "Jones will take this or that view of this or that question," for no one could ever tell in advance what he would say or do about any given matter. So it fell out that sometimes he proved himself to be a very wise man and at other times a very unwise one. But he had positive qualities and some of them very admirable qualities. He was not only an able business man, while he attended to his business, but a tireless one. His energy was a proverb. He was a kindly man—one so easily touched that he might almost have pleaded guilty to a charge of emotionalism. . . . We deeply deplore his untimely end; untimely because he died at an age when a man should be in the zenith of his powers and his usefulness. He was one distinct type of man, but his heart was right, and the world always saw his worst side. Peace to the ashes and to the memory of Chas. R.

Colonel Jones accomplished his goal of giving Charlotte a paper that was "at least the equal of any in the state." His *Observer* helped promote the city and the region, pushed for progress in business and education, and offered his readers a broader view of the world. But his ambitions and personal quirks cost him dearly in his efforts to free the paper from the dictates of an oppressive political situation and his desire to run the paper independent of business oligarchs. His paper left a deep impression on the region, however, and its name would later be revived by the very publication that put it out of business.

CHAPTER 4

THE *CHRONICLE* BECOMES THE *OBSERVER*
1886–1892

After forcing the old *Observer* out of business, the *Charlotte Chronicle* flourished briefly, then staggered to a near collapse. Without Colonel Jones to compete against, the paper lost energy and purpose. It had difficulty attracting readers and advertising and slipped into debt. Only a rescue by fifty of Charlotte's most prominent business leaders prevented its failure. But a newspaper controlled by the town's top businessmen inspired little credibility; almost everything it reported or commented on touched one or more of their personal or financial interests. Criticism from competing publications plus continued financial losses finally convinced the blue-chip backers that only someone independent could restore community trust and preserve the paper as a badge of Charlotte's urbanity. That was when D. A. Tompkins and Joseph P. Caldwell bought the *Chronicle* and converted it into what would become the modern *Charlotte Observer*.

The *Chronicle* lasted six years, from March 1886 until March 1892, and was a constant concern of Charlotte's business-political establishment, which had promoted its founding. Like other business leaders in the New South, members of the Charlotte power structure assumed that their goals were the same as the city's, that what was good for them was also good for Charlotte. Providing the city with a reliable morning newspaper that conformed to their views and furthered their vision was looked upon as another of their civic responsibilities. But in the 1870s and 1880s, several movements across the country were causing people to challenge such assumptions.

One was the "new journalism" that publisher Joseph Pulitzer had introduced in St. Louis in the late 1870s. It inspired newsmen to be independent, to look below the surface of news for evidence of social trends and economic forces, to isolate private interests from public interests, and "to serve no party but the people." Pulitzer's St. Louis *Post-Dispatch* and New York *World* were frequently quoted in other newspapers and were a strong influence on other editors. Pulitzer's concern for the downtrodden and for economic justice helped make his newspapers the "conscience" of their communities and helped foster the "Age of the Muckrakers."

Another stimulus to skepticism was the effort by Congress to regulate railroads and break up the trusts that were stifling competition in American business. Public hearings on railroad freight-rate discrimination, which was particularly injurious to the South, and on trust manipulation of consumer prices bred suspicion that what was of benefit to business was not always in the public interest. In February 1888, the *Chronicle* reprinted a story from the *New York Times* concerning one of those investigations. Among the trusts under investigation, according to the story, were those for sugar, castor oil, linseed oil, steel rails, iron ore, steel plows, threshing machines, iron and steel beams, and even one for common nails. The outrage provoked by such investigations resulted in the Interstate Commerce Act and the Sherman Antitrust Act, though both were immediately rendered ineffective by court decisions limiting their enforcement. Even as the Sherman Act was being passed, James B. Duke was incorporating the American Tobacco Company as one of the biggest trusts of all. But the investigations alerted citizens to the self-seeking goals and methods of many businesses.

Two other movements, the organization of labor unions and the establishment of the Farmers' Alliance, also undermined public confidence in business leadership. The union movement dramatized the conflicting interests of labor and management. And the Farmers' Alliance called for a whole new way of thinking about competitive relations between agriculture and business. Frustrated in its efforts to promote reform, the Alliance later became the People's party and provided the ideological thrust for the Populist Revolt.

The influence of the labor movement and the Farmers' Alliance was keenly felt in North Carolina. They stimulated the founding of the North Carolina Bureau of Labor Statistics and the introduction—if not the passage—of the first of many bills to regulate wages and hours in North Carolina factories and to limit the labor of women and children. They also helped bring about the establishment of an agricultural and mechanical college (later North Carolina State University) and a normal school for white school teachers (later the University of North Carolina at Greensboro).

Though business lost some of its collective credibility during this period, individual business leaders still had plenty of verve and continued to energize Charlotte's physical, economic, and cultural growth. In the six years from 1886 to 1892, Charlotte got three more cotton mills, an electric streetcar network, a water-sewer system, its first suburban neighborhood (Dilworth), a new post office building, a new city hall, its first public library, a hospital for blacks, a professional baseball team, a Lutheran seminary for women (Elizabeth College), its first YMCA building, and its first modern superintendent of schools. It also got its first enduring afternoon newspaper, the *Charlotte News*, whose voice contributed to some of the credibility problems of the *Chronicle*.

William S. Hemby was only twenty-five when he came to town to establish the *Chronicle* in opposition to Colonel Jones and the old *Observer*. He was born in 1860 in Union County, the second son of Thomas and Catherine Hemby, who lived at what became known as the Hemby Bridge community near Indian Trail. Thomas Hemby owned 1,600 acres of land and could afford to educate his five children. Some of his descendants recall seeing a picture of William S. in the uniform of Rutherford College, then a military school near Morganton. Hemby edited the school newspaper and at some point apparently went to work for a weekly newspaper, perhaps as an apprentice printer, because by age twenty-three he got a $6,000 advance on his inheritance and was ready to make newspapering a career.

The $6,000 was equal to the investment then needed to equip and operate a newspaper, which is how young Hemby used the money. He went into the mountains west of Asheville and founded the *Waynesville News* in January 1884. He published the *News* for sixteen months, and then sold it to become part owner and city editor—meaning local reporter—of the weekly *Greensboro Patriot*.

In the May 12, 1885, issue welcoming Hemby aboard, the *Patriot* noted that Charlotte had just elected a "liberal" mayor, and alleged that the city had done so "in order to be odd from other municipalities in the state. Anything to advertise Charlotte seems to be that growing city's ambition." The same issue noted that Joseph P. Caldwell, then editor of the *Statesville Landmark*, had been named a trustee of the "Western Insane Asylum" at Morganton. "We'll wager . . . that he was not an applicant for the place. The Statesville post office was offered him on a brand new silver platter, and he modestly declined it. This is a rare case, and Caldwell is a rare fellow," the *Patriot* said.

Hemby remained in Greensboro less than a year. In March 1886, he sold his interest in the *Patriot* and, at the invitation of Democratic party leaders, moved to Charlotte and founded the *Chronicle* as an evening alternative to the morning *Observer*. Hemby was editor and publisher. His city editor was James A. Robinson, who had previously published a weekly in Winston (which had yet to merge with Salem to form Winston-Salem).

The *Chronicle* entered the struggle against the *Observer* as the underdog. Compared with the eight-page morning paper, the *Chronicle* was tiny. It was a single sheet, printed on the front and back and folded to make four pages. Each page had seven columns, about half of them devoted to advertising. But it had no telegraph news, no correspondents in Washington or Raleigh, and no financial or market reports. It relied on the energy and imagination of its editor and reporter and on the items they found to reprint from other newspapers. Its greatest appeal was its political loyalty, which was decidedly pro-Democratic and anti-Jones.

Three weeks before the election—apparently on Monday, October 22, 1886, though the exact date is unknown—the *Chronicle* switched from afternoon to morning publication in order to compete directly against Jones and the *Observer*. With the shift, the *Chronicle* also became a subscriber to telegraph dispatches of the old United Press Association (no relation to the modern United Press International). It also changed its name to the *Charlotte Daily Chronicle*.

The earliest issue of the *Chronicle* preserved on microfilm was published October 26, 1886. It contained a long report of French sculptor Auguste Bartholdi's arrival in New York for ceremonies dedicating his Statue of Liberty. The entire editorial page was devoted to politics and the November elections. Under the editorial masthead was a list of the paper's political endorsements—all Democrats. Like other papers of that era, the *Chronicle* ran the list every day until the election. The lead editorial noted that Col. Oliver H. Dockery, a prominent North Carolina Republican, had said he would vote for Col. Charles R. Jones for Congress, strengthening Democratic charges that the independent Jones was a Republican in disguise. The editorial referred to Jones and the other independents as the "mongrel ticket."

After the election, while continuing to bait Jones, the *Chronicle* began to broaden its appeal. In mid-November, it bragged that improved train service was permitting its early morning delivery in Concord, Lexington, Greensboro, Reidsville, Company Shops (later renamed Burlington), and Graham. It sent reporters into Shelby, Hickory, and Gastonia for stories to interest readers in those communities. It opened news bureaus in Winston and Salisbury, neither of which had a daily paper. It also hurt Jones badly by hiring Wade Harris from the staff of the *Observer*. Harris became city editor, and James A. Robinson went to Durham to edit the *Durham Sun*.

On January 1, 1887, Hemby wrote that his paper had "succeeded beyond our most sanguine expectations and we enter the new year in a healthy and vigorous state, with cheerful hearts, more determined than ever." A few days later, he bought two competing papers, the daily *Evening Times* and the weekly *Citizen's Gazette*. Founded a few months earlier by merchant and real estate man George W. Chalk, both papers were probably on their last legs, but their acquisition cleared the field and enabled the *Chronicle* to focus its energies against the *Observer*.

With the *Chronicle*'s success, Hemby began to act as a spokesman and defender of the Charlotte business community. Though a recession had slowed commerce, he would brook no complaint about Charlotte's economic outlook. On January 5, he bristled editorially at an *Observer* suggestion that the year 1887 was "not as promising as one would wish." Such comments, he said, "are calculated to injure our city, and they will. The fact is that Charlotte has not suffered any more depression in business than is felt throughout the country." Three weeks later, in commenting on local business prospects, he wrote, "We must boom Charlotte by advertising her to the outside world. We must let our advantages be known."

In April 1887, Hemby announced that he was expanding the *Chronicle*'s pages from seven columns to eight to meet an increased demand for advertising space. He also equipped the paper with new typefaces and a cleaner makeup, including a masthead that omitted the word "Daily" from the paper's name, making it simply the *Charlotte Chronicle*. The front page began carrying line scores of major league baseball games and box scores of games played by the Charlotte entry in a professional league that included teams from Columbia, Augusta, Wilmington, Charleston, and Greenville.

To make the paper more appealing to women, Hemby added a "Ladies Column" on page three, in a softer, lighter typeface than that used elsewhere in the paper—a common newspaper practice. In the "Ladies Column" were stories about such things as the origin of throwing old shoes at brides, trends in current fashions, courtship rituals in Singapore, and life among women ranchers.

Curiously, also in the "Ladies Column" was a story that, in view of its significance, should have been on the front page. It was an account of a strange-looking new machine purchased by the *New York Tribune* to set type automatically instead of by hand. The machine, which revolutionized the printing industry, was the Linotype, invented by Ottmar Mergenthaler in 1884 and first used by an American newspaper in 1886. It would be ten years before a newspaper in Charlotte could afford such a machine.

The deference to women in the news columns was not reflected on the editorial pages, where Hemby, like other editors of his day, roundly condemned the campaign for women's suffrage. An editorial of January 12 fussed at New York City for allowing two women to serve on its board of education. While the women might perform as well as men, the editorial said, the true place for a woman was "the domestic circle. . . . Her gentle nature unfits her for noisy political strife." Two weeks later, the *Chronicle* opposed the women's suffrage amendment pending before Congress, saying, "Dear Suffrage Ladies . . . You cannot take the ballot without its attending evils."

Few Charlotte women were brazen enough to challenge those male views. Even Dr. Annie L. Alexander, the first female physician licensed in the Carolinas, carefully restricted her entry into the male domain of medicine. In opening her Charlotte office in 1887, she advertised in the *Chronicle* that her services would be "limited to the diseases of women and children."

The *Chronicle* also adamantly opposed any change in the status of blacks. It defended the county-government system, under which county commissioners were appointed by justices of the peace who were appointed by the legislature. The paper said the system was essential to prevent blacks from holding office in the dozen or so predominantly black counties Down East (though it also rendered county government undemocratic everywhere else). When blacks tried to organize voter leagues to promote their political and economic rights, the *Chronicle* warned that such organizations would only worsen black-white relations and advised "North Carolina darkies to have nothing whatever to do with this wild scheme."

The turning point for the *Chronicle* came in the fall of 1887, following the collapse of the *Observer* in August. Thereafter the *Chronicle* seemed to lose its edge. The paper contained less news and fewer editorials and relied more on matter reprinted from other newspapers. Much of the news from Charlotte was boosterism. That lethargy was more apparent on October 27, 1887, when the paper hit its physical peak in publishing "the largest daily ever issued in this city"—an eight-page edition with eight columns per page. An accompanying editorial called it an example of the "the thrift and push of Charlotte." But the real reason for it was a pair of full-page ads by two dry-goods firms, one of which was going out of business. The *Chronicle* was hard pressed to fill the extra space with fresh material. Several stories were reprinted from previous editions.

Perhaps Hemby and his small staff were simply tired. In the heat of their competition with the *Observer* they had worked long hours, six days a week, for a year and a half. Or maybe they needed the heat of an election campaign to get their adrenaline going. Or Hemby may have been discouraged by the business prospects for his paper. As Colonel Jones often complained, the profits of newspapering were less than commensurate with the effort and risks involved. Despite the *Chronicle*'s claims to the contrary, 1886 and 1887 were recessionary years, and Hemby was having difficulty paying his bills.

Whatever its cause, the lapse could not be attributed to a shortage of news. The winter of 1887–88 saw the unfolding of at least three major local stories. One was the organization of three more cotton mills to fuel Charlotte's growth. Another was the firing of a school superintendent with too many romantic entanglements. The third was the hiring of a new superintendent who turned out to be a man of exceptional ability and character.

The three cotton mills represented a significant breakthrough because they were financed by subscription. Investors pledged to buy shares of stock and pay for them in weekly or monthly installments. Their pledges were used as collateral in dealings with building and loan associations, which advanced the money to build and equip the mills. Such financing methods became important tools in the South's struggle to accumulate the capital for an industrial economy.

The scandal involving the school superintendent was a delicate matter, and the *Chronicle* did not tell the full story until well after the superintendent had been fired. The superintendent was Prof. John T. Corlew, who was so popular in Charlotte that when he tried to resign in 1887 to take a job in another city, the city school board refused to accept his resignation and persuaded him to stay another year. Still a young man, he was apparently single and an inspiration to the women enrolled in his summer teacher-training institutes.

His troubles began after New Year's, 1888, when the mayor of Charlotte, F. B. McDowell, was visiting New Orleans. McDowell met a Louisiana educator who inquired about his old friend Corlew and asked if he had "divorced his Chicago wife yet?" If so, the friend said, a girl in New Orleans was waiting to marry him. The mayor was shocked to learn that Corlew was married.

Back in Charlotte, McDowell confronted Corlew and learned that the professor had been pressured to marry a Chicago woman he dated while teaching there nine years earlier. But Corlew claimed to have never lived with the woman and said he was seeking a divorce. The mayor accused Corlew of "sailing under false colors" and urged the school board to fire him.

The *Chronicle*'s first mention of the story was on January 6, when it reported hearing "lively rumors" about Corlew, but never nailed down the key facts. The school board first rejected Corlew's offer to resign, and then, ten days later, voted to dismiss him—for reasons that were not made clear. Nine days after that, the *Chronicle* reprinted a story from the *Chicago Daily News* in which it was said that Corlew had lived with the Chicago woman, that he apparently had fathered a child, and that if he was ever divorced, another Chicago woman was waiting to marry him.

Three weeks after Corlew's dismissal, the school board appointed Dr. Alexander Graham, superintendent of schools in Fayetteville, as Corlew's successor. The *Chronicle* printed a brief account of Dr. Graham's background, noting that he had a statewide reputation as an educator, that he was a brother of Archibald Graham, a Charlotte banker, and that as an inducement to coming to Charlotte he was provided a home—the Commandant's House of Gen. D. H. Hill's old Carolina Military Institute on East Morehead Street. But the *Chronicle* lacked the enterprise to interview Dr. Graham about his philosophy of education or his plans for enlarging the Charlotte school system.

Over the next twenty-five years, Dr. Graham, a forthright Presbyterian with an old-school charm, steadily built public support for education and attracted a strong faculty. He became "superintendent emeritus" in 1913 and continued to make impromptu visits to classrooms, quizzing students and encouraging teachers, until his death in 1934. Alexander Graham Junior High was named for him. His son, Frank Porter Graham, became president of the University of North Carolina. His Charlotte nephew, Edward Kidder Graham, son of Archibald Graham, also served as president of the university.

Two unexpected events in March 1888 seem to have unsettled the *Chronicle*. One was a leave given city editor Wade Harris to write and edit the first of a long series of illustrated brochures on Charlotte. The brochures were mailed to business leaders up and down the East Coast in hopes of stimulating investment in the city. Their production temporarily deprived the *Chronicle* of its one staff member who knew the city, knew who was who, and therefore knew what was news.

The second event was Colonel Jones's reentry into the newspaper business. When the old *Observer* died in August 1887, its printers bought its equipment and started an afternoon paper known as the *Hornet*. In March 1888, Colonel Jones acquired the *Hornet*, renamed it the *Observer*, published it as an afternoon paper for seven months, and then saw it collapse again. Afterward, another group published it as the *Daily Star*. Though the colonel's challenge was brief and ineffective, it apparently drained off just enough revenue to crimp the *Chronicle*'s slim profit margin.

In early August 1888, William Hemby was forced to mortgage the *Chronicle* to pay an old debt of $430 to his paper supplier, the Virginia Paper Company. Hemby's note, secured by the newspaper's printing equipment, was due on September 3. The effort to pay it apparently forced him out of business because on August 28 he announced he had sold the *Chronicle* to George W. Chalk, the real estate man from whom Hemby had bought two papers to clear the field in the battle with the *Observer*. A few days later it became clear that Chalk had bought the *Chronicle* in behalf of fifty Charlotte business leaders led by Hamilton C. Jones, the lawyer who had written editorials for the 1869 *Observer*.

The fifty investors raised $6,000 to pay off Hemby and formed a $30,000 corporation to operate his newspaper. They included the most prominent businessmen in town, including Col. William Johnston, F. B. McDowell, J. H. Weddington, R. J. Brevard, W. C. Maxwell, Clement Dowd, and F. I. Osborne, each of whom had served or would serve as mayor of Charlotte. They also included J. S. Spencer, E. D. Latta, A. H. Jordan, Samuel Wittkowsky, J. Lenoir Chambers, H. C. Eccles, John Van Landingham, E. K. P. Osborne, E. M. Andrews, George E. Wilson, John Wilkes, and D. A. Tompkins, all leading citizens.

No doubt many of those men were among the Democrats who had invited Hemby to Charlotte. Hamilton Jones was chairman of the Mecklenburg County Democratic Executive Committee. E. K. P. Osborne, who owned the horse-drawn streetcar system and headed one of the three new cotton mills, was chairman of the Democratic Executive Committee for the Sixth Congressional District, which included Charlotte. In raising the $6,000 to buy out Hemby, they were probably fulfilling a promise made in bringing him to Charlotte, that is, that he would not lose the inheritance he was investing here.

Hemby went to Chicago, where he took a job with a publishing house and later enrolled in business school. By the turn of the century, he had gone to Memphis and founded the *Journal of Commerce*, a monthly magazine that he edited until 1907. He is said to have died in Memphis in 1908.

Apparently the effort to buy the *Chronicle* had been under way for some time because by September 3, 1888, when the stock company was formally incorporated, the fifty investors had an editor on hand to succeed Hemby. He was Robert Haydn, previously editor of the *Yeoman's Guard* of Hagerstown, Maryland, managing editor of the Pittsburgh *Dispatch*, and, for eight months before moving to Charlotte, Washington correspondent for the *Chronicle* of Augusta, Georgia.

Haydn turned out to be a poor choice. He was not a good writer or newspaper manager and knew little about the town or the Carolinas. Also, he brought with him some metropolitan newspaper practices ill suited to a city of 10,000 and a surrounding community of small towns. It wasn't long before area newspapers were jeering at the *Chronicle*'s "metropolitan airs."

In taking over the *Chronicle*, Haydn pledged to make it better: "The business people of Charlotte are in earnest in this matter of being properly represented in their legitimate trade territory; and in their plucky endeavor, I know that my hearty and indefatigable cooperation will not be wanting." He increased the size of the *Chronicle*'s one-column headlines. He began running heavy-handed editorial cartoons, most of them on the front page and dealing with issues in the 1888 presidential contest, won by Republican Benjamin Harrison over Democrat Grover Cleveland. In October, he ran stories of the professional baseball championships on page one. Later, when John L. Sullivan defeated Jake Kilrain in a seventy-five-round boxing match, that story went on the front page.

Some of his policies caused immediate resentment. He doubled the *Chronicle*'s advertising rates, then was reduced to begging merchants to advertise. He began charging one dollar for each initial publication of a birth, marriage, death, or funeral notice, and fifty-five cents for each insertion thereafter—a charge certain to offend people who were used to having such notices published free. He abandoned the tradition of suspending publication on Thanksgiving Day and Christmas Day, raising the ire of other newspapers for setting a bad precedent.

Haydn did two other things that must have caused giggles among his readers. He had been editor only a week when he sent reporters out to get man-on-the-street reaction to the "improvements" he had made in the *Chronicle*. Most of the people interviewed were the fifty business leaders who owned the paper. Not surprisingly, their comments—which filled more than two columns!—were congratulatory.

A month later, after weeks of stories about a yellow fever epidemic in Florida and of efforts to raise money for people in stricken areas, Haydn wrote a long editorial suggesting that North Carolina seize this opportunity to replace Florida as a vacation resort. "It has only to advertise—to make its advantages known, to scatter abroad information of its mild climate, its mountain scenery, its mineral springs, its charms for the sportsmen," he said. Even if his idea had been sound—and it wasn't, because North Carolina lacked the hotels, restaurants, and other resort facilities needed to accommodate vacationers—his timing was atrocious.

He followed that two days later with a suggestion that Charlotte itself become a winter resort by advertising the city's "salubrious climate, its bracing air, its crystal water, its exquisite scenery, . . . the welcome it extends strangers and the facilities it possesses for their entertainment." At the time, Charlotte was having trouble raising money for an auditorium to replace the 1,500-seat Opera House, which had been condemned as a firetrap. To finance Charlotte's advertising, Haydn suggested that 200 citizens give ten dollars apiece to create a $2,000 Winter Resort Fund. After the *Chronicle* made the first ten-dollar contribution, nothing further was heard of that suggestion.

City editor Wade Harris could not have been happy in the new regime. His name, which had been a fixture on the masthead of the local page, disappeared the day Haydn took over. For two months, he worked anonymously, then resigned. A one-paragraph item on November 21, 1888, announced that Harris had left the staff, carrying with him "the best wishes of the paper." Seventeen days later, on Saturday, December 8, 1888, Harris published the first issue of the evening *Charlotte News*.

Unlike the town's other new publishing ventures, which usually got a blurb in the *Chronicle* noting their start-up, the *News* was ignored, which suggests there were hard feelings between Harris and

Haydn. But Charlotte readers noticed the new paper, and under Harris's leadership the *News* enjoyed immediate success. It pointedly announced that, unlike the *Chronicle*, it would publish birth, marriage, death, and funeral notices for free.

Wade Harris became a formidable competitor against the *Chronicle*. He was at home among Charlotte's social and business elite and enjoyed their trust. He came from a politically prominent Cabarrus County family—Wade Hampton, the Confederate general and hero of South Carolina's redemption from the radical Republicans, was a third cousin. Harris's wife, Cora, was a member of the socially prominent Springs family from Mecklenburg and South Carolina. Though he had learned printing as a boy, Harris had also gone to college at what is now Virginia Polytechnic Institute, where he edited the student newspaper. He was well read, well traveled, and well versed in history and politics. He had the contacts to get news and advertising even from the *Chronicle*'s financial backers.

Editor Haydn recovered brilliantly by giving Harris's job to an exceptional young woman who was also socially prominent, knew almost everyone in town, and no doubt won many friends for the *Chronicle*. She was Adelaide Williams, a slim, dark-haired, dark-eyed beauty who proved she could out-walk, out-talk, and out-report most male reporters.

Though newswomen were relatively rare in the South, metropolitan dailies in the North and Midwest had employed them for some years. Even as Addie Williams was entering journalism in Charlotte, Nellie Bly was circling the globe for the *New York World*, proving that the trip could be made in a shorter time than Jules Verne's prescribed eighty days. In the South, women who worked outside the home usually did so in cotton mills, hospitals, or school houses.

Before joining the *Chronicle*, "Miss Addie," as Adelaide Williams came to be known, had been a schoolteacher. She was born in July 1862, in a house on West Trade across the street from the United States Mint, then a fashionable neighborhood. Mrs. Stonewall Jackson lived a few doors east. Miss Williams's mother died during her infancy, and she was raised by an aunt who lived in Fourth Ward, another fashionable neighborhood. She grew up playing with the sons and daughters of the city's rich and powerful. She was a bright student and gifted in music—at fourteen she was organist at the Second Presbyterian Church and was later hired away by First Baptist. She attended Charlotte Female Institute (forerunner of Queens College) and Peace College in Raleigh.

In the summer of 1886, she completed one of Prof. John T. Corlew's teacher-training institutes and was teaching at Charlotte's South

Graded School (also known as the D. H. Hill School) when her writings came to the attention of Robert Haydn. He invited her to submit special articles to the *Chronicle*. Before long, she was Wade Harris's successor as city editor and producing three to four columns of news a day. She remained an active newspaperwoman until her death in 1927.

Beyond recruiting Addie Williams, little else seemed to go right for Robert Haydn's *Chronicle*. Though it continued to boast of increased readership and advertising, the paper's appearance and sagging finances were witnesses to the contrary. In January 1889, advertising amounted to about nine columns out of a possible twenty-eight, far below the 50 percent of copy regarded as a break-even point. Yet, on January 11, in announcing a new six-column format, with new typefaces and a cleaner, more modern masthead, Haydn bragged that the improvements were made possible by the "liberality" of the *Chronicle*'s advertisers, who had accepted a 100 percent rate increase.

In the midst of reporting on the Johnstown, Pennsylvania, flood that killed 10,000 to 12,000 people in June 1889, the *Chronicle* moved from its second-floor offices at College and Trade to a two-story building in the third block of West Trade, opposite the First Presbyterian Church. The new home gave the paper a street-floor business office, a press room in the basement, and space for editorial offices and print shops upstairs. But what the paper really needed was a new press. Production failures were causing it to miss trains and disappoint waiting subscribers.

In November, perhaps in response to competition from the *Charlotte News*, it cut subscription rates by two dollars, from seven dollars to five dollars a year, paid in advance. The reduction moved the Lincoln County *Courier* to comment that the *Chronicle* was a newsy paper, priced at bargain rates, though it "sometimes has too much praise for itself." But while the price cut increased circulation, it reduced overall revenues. Within a short time the paper was showing evidence of reduced telegraph news, a lack of typefaces to print effective advertising, and more mechanical breakdowns. Haydn used his editorials to plead for a new press.

Apparently a number of the *Chronicle*'s stockholders agreed to increase their advertising because E. M. Andrews, a staunch supporter of the paper, began running full-page ads for his furniture store, often taking the entire front page on a Sunday morning. But those ads, while supplying income, further highlighted the inadequacy of the paper's printing facilities. The *Chronicle* lacked the large black type essential to printing full-page ads proportional to the space they occupied. The *Chronicle*'s printers tried all kinds of typographical gimmicks—repeating a word many times in small type to approximate the effect of saying it once in big type—but the results were unsatisfactory.

D. A. Tompkins recalled that after two years under the stock company's ownership, the *Chronicle* had lost half of its capital and was $3,000 in debt. The owners were actively looking for someone who could run the paper successfully. Among those they turned to was Joseph P. Caldwell, who remained a great favorite in Charlotte and whose *Statesville Landmark* was one of the most admired weeklies in the state. Not a year went by, he said, that someone from Charlotte didn't approach him about editing a newspaper there. Several times he visited the city to look over possibilities, but did not find the opportunity that interested him. He did accept one offer, only to have the citizens of Statesville change his mind by buying him a new press for the *Landmark*.

The *Chronicle*'s fifty stockholders may have had something similar in mind in February 1890 when they invited Caldwell to be the guest speaker at the annual banquet of the Chamber of Commerce. The dinner, attended by 101 members and guests, marked the opening of the roof-garden restaurant of the newly refurbished Buford Hotel at Tryon and Fourth streets (later the site of Home Federal Savings and Loan). Seated with Caldwell at the head table were Hamilton C. Jones, president of the Chronicle Publishing Company; J. H. Weddington, chamber president and a *Chronicle* stockholder; and D. A. Tompkins, engineer-industrialist and also a *Chronicle* stockholder. Given Joseph Caldwell's interest in Charlotte journalism, it would have been remarkable if the fortunes of the *Chronicle* had not been discussed at that table.

After dinner, when it came Caldwell's turn to speak, he never mentioned the *Chronicle* by name, but his remarks went to the heart of the paper's compromised integrity. He spoke about the need for a fearless, independent, and credible press. A newspaper could depend on its news columns for popularity, "but it is the editorial column which establishes its character," he said. "It exerts a wide and healthful influence if its editor be recognized as a man of information, judgment and integrity; if he be known to be under no outside influence; if he be free of suspicion of any ulterior design." But an editor or a paper with a hidden agenda or secret aspirations "cannot be a faithful, single-hearted or safe guide to others," he said.

Two other visitors to Charlotte that February excited the *Chronicle*'s interest. One was Thomas A. Edison, who arrived with his wife and two children and took a suite of rooms at the Buford (where Alexander Graham Bell had stayed several years earlier). Edison was in town for a few weeks to explore the possibilities of electrically separating gold from ore. On the streets, he talked with townspeople and answered questions about his inventions. He was interviewed by a *Chronicle* reporter—perhaps Addie Williams—who found him at forty-three to be "younger than expected" for a man with 450 patents. "Oh, I'm a young shaver yet," Edison said.

The other exciting visitor was the Reverend Sam P. Jones, an Alabama-born evangelist and a great favorite on the southern tent-meeting and chautauqua circuit. An ex-lawyer and a reformed drunk, Jones was famous for his earthy condemnations of sin and sinners. During his stay in February, he agreed to bring his entertaining evangelistic crusade, which featured a 200-voice choir, to Charlotte for eight days in April. Immediately the city and the *Chronicle* began preparations. The city raised money for a 5,000-seat wooden "tabernacle" at the northwest corner of Tryon and Third streets (later the site of the Northwestern Bank Building), and persuaded the railroads to reduce fares for people from surrounding areas who wanted to attend the services. The *Chronicle* offered free advertising to Charlotteans who would open their homes to visitors, because the city's hotels could not accommodate the crowds. The *Chronicle* also announced it would give Jones's sermons extended coverage and offered reduced rates—two weeks for twenty cents—to anyone who subscribed to the paper for the entire crusade. It was the first use of evangelism to build circulation for a Charlotte newspaper, but it would not be the last. Jones's services drew capacity crowds day and night, and at the final service he raised $10,000 to pay off the debt on the YMCA's then-new stone-turreted building in the second block of South Tryon.

With the opening of a new political season in the spring of 1890, the *Chronicle*'s cozy relations with the Charlotte power structure began to draw complaint. In June, after the *Chronicle*'s vigorous support of a $75,000 bond issue to improve streets and attract a Lutheran seminary for girls (later named Elizabeth College), the paper was accused of a conflict of interest on behalf of its stockholders. Some property owners complained that the street-bond money would be used to improve access to the new plant of the Liddell Company, headed by Mayor F. B. McDowell, a *Chronicle* director and once a partner with Col. Charles Jones in publishing the old *Observer*.

In July, when Hamilton C. Jones, president of the Chronicle Publishing Company, announced that he would run as a Democratic candidate for Congress, political rivals accused the *Chronicle* of another conflict. Jones's Democratic opponent was S. B. Alexander, a respected Mecklenburg farmer, a former state senator, and leader of the North Carolina Farmers' Alliance. When the *Chronicle* took out after Alexander for some of the Populist ideas advocated by the Alliance, other newspapers began to accuse Hamilton Jones of using the *Chronicle* to further his personal ambitions. A sample complaint from the *Monroe Register* said: "*The Charlotte Chronicle* is the personal organ of Col. Ham. C. Jones. Two years ago he bought it, and he is now the President of the Chronicle Publishing Co. and is responsible for the course of that paper. Wonder if he thinks he is improving his chances for Congress by fighting the Alliance as *The Chronicle* is doing?" Within a week, Ham Jones withdrew from the race.

A few days later, the *Chronicle* was involved in controversy with the board of aldermen, which included several *Chronicle* stockholders. In preparing for the street-bond referendum, the city contracted with the *Chronicle* for space in which to publish a required legal notice. Wade Harris of the *Charlotte News* wrote the aldermen, asking that the contract be rescinded until all papers in the city could bid on it. Several aldermen said they resented the implication that they were favoring one paper, but the *Chronicle*'s editorial response made matters worse. Said editor Haydn, "A city is judged by the paper it advertises in."

In January 1891, as stockholders of the Chronicle Publishing Company prepared to hold an annual meeting, Robert Haydn resigned to take a job with the *Journal of Commerce* in Baltimore. Reports were also circulated that a group of investors from Atlanta was bidding to buy the *Chronicle*. At the stockholders' meeting, the Haydn resignation was accepted and the Atlanta offer rejected. F. B. McDowell agreed to take over as manager of the publishing company, making him editor of the morning paper in addition to being mayor of Charlotte, vice-president of the Liddell Company, and a director of E. D. Latta's Charlotte Consolidated Construction Company, which owned the streetcar lines. In the *Chronicle* the next morning, McDowell addressed readers in an editorial that said, "A dignified, newsy, reliable daily newspaper is a necessity to Charlotte. It is by far of more importance than the largest single industry we have."

Despite his multiple roles, McDowell would prove to have very limited powers. Five days after becoming editor, the mayor proposed that Charlotte seek authorization to float $200,000 in bonds and buy the private companies that supplied the city with water and electricity. The *Charlotte News*, which was already hinting of favoritism in plans for the $75,000 street improvements, greeted the new proposal with a jeer that Charlotte should do much more: "While the aldermen are talking about the insignificant matter of $200,000 or $500,000. . . . *The News* wants to suggest something incomparably superior." Sarcastically it proposed that Charlotte "float a million or so" in bonds and buy out the Chicago company recently commissioned to build an airship for the 1893 world's fair. Then, the *News* said, Charlotte would be ahead of all the big cities.

The new editor of the *Chronicle* found he had no way of effectively responding. McDowell was so deeply enmeshed in conflicts of interest that he couldn't argue his own point of view in his own newspaper. Anything he said, especially in an argument with another newspaper, would be seen as self-serving.

Two weeks later, the *Chronicle* announced the appointment of an associate editor to relieve McDowell of the editorial duties. He was David F. St. Clair, formerly editor of the weekly *Central Carolina Express* in Sanford. A twenty-nine-year-old Moore County native, St. Clair had attended Davidson College and taught school in Cleveland County before entering journalism. He was soon joined on the *Chronicle* by another Moore County native, twenty-six-year-old William Carey Dowd, who grew up in Mecklenburg, finished college at Wake Forest in 1889, and taught school for a while in Charlotte. On March 9, 1891, St. Clair was named editor of the *Chronicle* and Dowd was made general manager, allowing Mayor McDowell to bow out. In July, David Vance, son of Sen. Zeb Vance, returned from New Orleans and signed on as news and telegraph editor.

By midsummer, St. Clair and Dowd had bought enough stock to own controlling interest in the paper and were busy making improvements. They opened a news bureau in Concord, bought new type, and ordered a new press, which arrived in late November. It was a two-horsepower, gas-fed Babcock capable of 2,000 impressions an hour (printing one side of a sheet at a time). It arrived just before Thanksgiving Day and inspired a *Chronicle* editorial that said, "Thanksgiving can now be observed devoutly."

The new equipment made a dramatic difference in the newspaper's appearance, but greater investments were needed if the *Chronicle* was to uphold Charlotte's reputation as a forward-looking community. The capital needs worried *Chronicle* stockholders, who were in debt and weary of continued losses. They appealed to D. A. Tompkins, then a director of the company, to take over the paper's management, but he declined. Later they came back to ask under what terms he would consider taking charge. Tompkins said the only way he would assume that obligation would be as owner. If they got together all the stock, he promised to buy it. He wanted a newspaper, he said, that would help him "preach the doctrine of industrial development."

At the time, St. Clair and Dowd had options to buy the remainder of the stock, but they gave them up out of respect for Tompkins's technical skills and his zeal for improving Charlotte and the South. Tompkins had to borrow $3,000 to complete the purchase of the stock.

There are no records of the negotiations leading to the sale, but Tompkins's personal papers provide a lot of clues to what must have been discussed. At some point, other *Chronicle* stockholders probably asked Tompkins, "What are your plans?" Tompkins would have answered, "To provide the machinery to operate efficiently, and a fearless editor whose independence and good judgment will earn respect." When the other stockholders perhaps said, "If you're thinking of getting Joseph Caldwell, forget it—we've been turned down repeatedly," Tompkins may have responded, "Yes, but I think I know how to get him to accept."

Tompkins and Caldwell were well acquainted. Tompkins had done engineering for the town of Statesville when Caldwell was mayor, and the two men had formed a strong friendship. Caldwell had rejected offers to run the *Chronicle* because he didn't want to edit a paper for a stock company, in which he would be subject to the editorial whim of every stockholder, as he was during his ten-month stint with the Raleigh *News* in the 1870s.

Tompkins went to see Caldwell and spent a week discussing the opportunities offered by the *Chronicle*. Assured that he and Caldwell shared the same views about the South and about the role industry could play in pulling the region out of its poverty, he wound up offering Caldwell not a job with a stock company, but a half-interest in the paper.

Even then Caldwell remained reluctant. He talked frankly about the kind of paper he wanted to run, about the extensive investments it would take to make the *Chronicle* into a first-class journal, and about his need for a salary of $2,000 a year. When Tompkins consented to all those conditions, Caldwell accepted. Each man agreed to invest $20,000—200 shares of stock at $100 a share.

Later, in announcing his decision to the people of Statesville, Caldwell said: "My people—those among whom I was born and reared—have been so good to me and to my enterprise that I was quite content to give all the remainder of my days to them. But it was written in the Book of Fate that I am to conduct a daily paper in Charlotte. Twelve years ago I left there after eight years in journalism in that city. The pressure upon me to return has not been exactly continuous since then, but it has been, at least, of annual recurrence. Daily journalism attracts me as Congress does the politician or the bench the learned lawyer. And so I have finally yielded."

The sale was announced in the *Chronicle* on January 16, 1892, with an editorial from Dowd and St. Clair explaining their decision to sell. They were $3,000 in debt, they said, and the paper was not making money. They also pointed out "an important circumstance" that they felt sharply limited the potential for any newspaper in Charlotte. "Were this city with its excellent commercial advantages one hundred miles nearer the center of the state," they said, "*The Chronicle* could happily sustain itself in twice the present size. But Charlotte being so near the [state] line and dealing to such an extent with South Carolina people, *The Chronicle* cannot be made a political paper and a state paper." Caldwell and Tompkins—and a dozen subsequent editors and publishers of the paper—were to demonstrate that that geography, while a partial handicap, could be overcome. The *Chronicle*—or rather, the *Observer*, as it was soon to be called—was not to become a political paper, but a business paper, and Charlotte was not to become a political center, but a commercial capital.

Caldwell and Tompkins assumed control on February 1, with an editorial saying, "We invoke the support of the people of this city, county, state and section, in the end that the *Chronicle* may become not only a potent agency for the promotion of the public welfare, but at the same time an object of pride and affection to its constituency." They also announced they were raising the subscription price from $5 to $6 a year to help finance needed improvements. Both Caldwell and Tompkins were listed on the masthead as publishers and Caldwell was listed as editor. W. Carey Dowd stayed on as the paper's business manager. David St. Clair went to Richmond, where he joined the staff of the *Times-Dispatch* and later became a lawyer. At the time of the sale, the *Chronicle*'s daily circulation had dwindled to 1,100.

Six weeks later, on Sunday, March 13, 1892, the *Chronicle* appeared without warning under the Old English masthead of the *Charlotte Daily Observer*. On page two was an editorial by Joseph Caldwell explaining the change:

The present editor began his newspaper life in Charlotte, now nearly twenty years ago, on the old *Observer*. All his newspaper work here was on it, and the associations which cluster about the name are to him very happy ones. The paper was for a long period of time in great favor with the public of Charlotte and of Western North Carolina, and in going back to the name we fancy we are doing something which, while gratifying a sentiment on the part of the editor, will not in the least be unagreeable to the public. Indeed, suggestions that this be done have not been few. And to the people out of Charlotte the changes will not come awkward, for the people of the western part of the state have persisted in calling the Charlotte morning paper the "Observer," whether its name was *Journal, Chronicle* or what not. So then, it is to be *The Observer* again.

Something of the public's attitude toward the old *Chronicle* was reflected in the next day's editorial in the *Charlotte News*. Editor Wade Harris wrote, "*The News* never speaks ill of the dead, and we stick to the text even in speaking of *The Chronicle*. It's gone. Peace be with it. 'The Observer' sounds much better, and we believe the change will be O.K.'d by all along the line."

If the business and political leaders of Charlotte had paused to look back, they might have seen a moral in the events that had occurred over the previous ten years. They had conspired to put out of business an editor who had produced good newspapers but was outspokenly independent in his politics. In his place they got a succession of editors whose politics pleased them, but whose newspapers failed to win reader respect. Now they were off on a third course with two other men, Caldwell and Tompkins, who were wiping the slate clean. In an effort to put the paper on a new footing, those two reclaimed the vigor and credibility associated with the old name the *Charlotte Observer*. In effect, Caldwell and Tompkins were repairing the past damage to the idea of a free and unfettered press.

CHAPTER 5

BUILDING THE "STATE'S BEST NEWSPAPER"
1892–1904

Under Joseph P. Caldwell and Daniel A. Tompkins, the *Observer* underwent an expansion that propelled it from country newspapering to modern journalism. The two men set out to publish the "very best paper that its patronage would justify," and in the years from 1892 to 1904, they succeeded. They recruited a staff of splendid writers and reporters, installed the latest in news-gathering and printing equipment, enlarged coverage to include books, music, drama, finance, architecture, and medicine, and made the *Observer* a vigorous advocate of education and industrialism. It was a long, expensive, uphill struggle, but by December 1904, when they installed the last piece of essential machinery—a "perfecting" press capable of producing 10,000 sixteen-page papers an hour—they had the satisfaction of hearing the *Observer* acclaimed as "the best newspaper" in North Carolina and often linked with the Atlanta *Constitution* and Louisville *Courier-Journal* as advocates of the New South.

Though Caldwell and Tompkins came from different backgrounds, they shared the same vision of southern progress. Caldwell was a self-taught printer-editor and politician; the patrician Tompkins was a college-educated engineer, financier, and promoter. Both had grown up during the Civil War and had come of age in the poverty of Reconstruction. The experience left neither with much nostalgia for the Old South. They saw in Charlotte an opportunity to build a different, more rewarding way of life, one more like that in the urban, industrial North, full of diversity and aggressive commerce. Together they promoted manufacturing but opposed labor unions; supported education but opposed laws to limit the labor of women and children; urged a diverse agriculture but opposed the agrarian Populists; sought currency reform but opposed the free coinage of silver; befriended blacks but endorsed white-supremacy laws that denied blacks the right to vote and ultimately produced a harsh segregation.

The two men admired each other, complemented each other, depended on each other. Tompkins was restless, blunt, pragmatic, and expansive; Caldwell was calm, reflective, diplomatic, and guided by deeply held principles. Together they rebuilt the *Observer* from the ground up, developing it into a widely read and widely quoted source of news and opinion. In doing so they exerted a profound influence on Charlotte and the Piedmont region of the Carolinas.

Their paper succeeded for at least three reasons. One was the honesty and breadth of its news coverage, including coverage of business and industry. Another was the power and integrity of its editorials, which at one point led to a break with the Democratic party. Even people who disagreed with them admired their cogency. The third was the growth and vitality of the Charlotte region, which assured the paper an expanding economic base.

The period from 1892 to 1904 included one of the most divisive decades in American history. It was marked by the revolt of Populist farmers whose pleas for help had been ignored for twenty years. The revolt included the nomination of William Jennings Bryan for president and the white-hot fight over the coinage of silver. Black involvement in the revolt spurred a white backlash that disfranchised blacks and brought on the evils of segregation. During the period, the panic of 1893 occurred, plunging the nation into a deep depression that lent new urgency to the Populist calls for reform. The modern labor movement emerged in a series of violent industrial and railroad strikes. Seeds for Prohibition were planted, the revelations of muckrackers inspired reforms, President McKinley was shot, and the nation welcomed a dazzling new personality, Theodore Roosevelt, to the White House.

In North Carolina religious leaders provoked an angry clash over the University at Chapel Hill, Southern Railway took over the state-owned railroad through the heart of the state's industrial belt, and the Democratic party took tentative steps toward the establishment of political primaries. In South Carolina the race-baiting "Pitchfork" Ben Tillman came to power as the first of the class-conscious southern demagogues.

The period also had a positive side. The depression induced by the panic of 1893 gave way to prosperity and a rush of expansion. The United States went happily to war against Spain and emerged a world power. A bicycle craze yielded to the age of the automobile and the arrival of Charlotte's first cars. Three years of experiments on the dunes at Kitty Hawk enabled the Wright brothers to make man's first successful flight. The electrification of cities continued, resulting in the harnessing of the Catawba River and the creation of the Southern Power Company (later Duke Power).

Through it all, the *Observer* took vigorous editorial stands that often provoked angry reactions. But Caldwell and Tompkins never found reason to alter their compact, which called for Caldwell to manage the newspaper and Tompkins to continue running his engineering firm and promoting industrialism. Years later, Tompkins recalled, "The partnership was always an easy fitting arrangement. ... There was never a time ... that we had the slightest difference that made a jar of any kind."

That harmony was all the more remarkable in light of the financial obligations the two men assumed. At the outset, Caldwell and Tompkins planned to spend $15,000 modernizing the newspaper's plant and equipment. Before they were through, they had invested more than $75,000, and had to wait nearly five years for the paper to become self-supporting. At times, the costs and delays were enough to shake their confidence, but the two men persisted. They had entered the newspaper business not to get rich, but to build a community institution that would further the economic interests of the entire region.

As the *Observer* was expanding and improving, so were Charlotte and the surrounding cities and towns. From 1892 to 1904, Charlotte broke out of its old boundaries and surged into Dilworth and Elizabeth Heights on the south, Piedmont Park on the east, and various mill villages on the north and west. Communities around Charlotte were also growing as a result of an aggressive industrialization campaign that fostered the establishment of dozens of new cotton mills. In 1896, Mecklenburg and the ten surrounding counties had seventy-three mills; by 1904, they had ninety-nine. Into those mills poured thousands of poor white families, fresh from tenant farms or mountain coves, looking for jobs that would put money in their pockets, perhaps for the first time in their lives. Even so, Mecklenburg remained one of the top cotton-growing counties in the state.

Charlotte shared in the prosperity accompanying that growth. It was in this period that William Henry Belk began to build his department store empire, that Joseph Benjamin Ivey arrived to start his merchandising chain, and that Charlotteans began to share in the mass-produced luxuries enjoyed by other Americans. The advertising and promotion of those and other merchants helped to expand and enliven the *Observer*.

Much of the region's industrial development can be traced to Tompkins's influence. Throughout this period he was busy making speeches, writing books, publishing pamphlets, and providing blueprints for textile mills. When he was not promoting industry, he was fostering the establishment of savings banks and building and loan companies to help the South accumulate the capital to further its industrial ambitions. Having learned thrift as a boy, Tompkins devoted much of his energy as an adult to proclaiming its benefits. In addition to industry, he promoted the development of parks, libraries, hospitals, and YWCAs.

By February 1892, when he and Joseph Caldwell took over the *Chronicle* and turned it into the *Observer*, Tompkins was forty years old. A contemporary described him as "rather stout . . . well-built . . . slow-moving but energetic . . . and quite busy." Growing up on a plantation in Edgefield, South Carolina, he lost an eye in a boyhood accident, but did not let that limit his outlook. Unhappy with a classical education at South Carolina College (later the University of South Carolina), he went north to study engineering at Rensselaer Polytechnic Institute in Troy, New York, and afterward traveled widely in the East, in Europe, and finally in the South. He was a bachelor who spent most of his waking hours working, though his private correspondence indicates that he enjoyed the company of women and was constantly wooing and being wooed by female friends.

Upon acquiring the newspaper, Tompkins applied his mechanic's skills to improving its printing plant. He replaced a two-horsepower gas engine with a four-horsepower engine and rearranged the machinery for greater efficiency. Production immediately went smoother. Tompkins advocated an eight-dollar annual subscription rate (two dollars higher than other papers), which gave the *Observer* extra revenue for hiring talent and acquiring equipment. But Tompkins was too busy traveling, speaking, and supervising industrial projects to participate in day-to-day decisions about the paper's news and feature content.

The man most responsible for the *Observer*'s success was its editor, Joseph P. Caldwell, who became the paper's heart and soul. In an age when most newspapers were dominated by editors, the *Observer* was an extension of his personality. He gave it the standards and editorial force that won public respect. He also had an eye for talent and attracted a brilliant writing staff.

Caldwell was thirty-nine when he took over the *Observer*. Other North Carolina editors, who had admired his work on the weekly *Statesville Landmark*, applauded his move to daily newspapering. In his honor, Charlotte business leaders held a dinner that drew a larger crowd than the big railroad receptions. After dinner, there were cigars and speeches and a response from Caldwell, who said he would not have left Statesville to go anywhere but to Charlotte. He said he intended "to live and to die" in his adopted city, a pledge he did not quite keep.

With Caldwell's arrival, the paper immediately got better. The headlines got smaller and the news and editorial content got larger. The paper was better organized and more tightly edited. Caldwell gave readers plenty to read and discuss. His editorials were clear and strong but judicious. He didn't shout; he reasoned, nudging his readers along with him as he laid out arguments. He often rewarded them with a hint of humor, a bright metaphor, or a pithy conclusion.

H. E. C. ("Red Buck") Bryant, whom Caldwell trained to be a reporter, described Caldwell as "a large blond with clear cut features. . . . His light brown hair was neatly brushed but not carefully parted, and his slightly oval face was clean shaven except for a mustache that matched his hair. He seemed in good health but not robust . . . and it was evident that he . . . spent much time indoors."

According to Bryant, Caldwell was genial and well mannered, but "the boss of the shop, from the press room to the last case in the farthest corner in the composing room. . . . Everybody loved and feared him. He was kind and gentle but most exacting. . . . He could read more papers and see more in them or edit more copy and read more proofs than any two men in the shop. . . . Nothing interesting escaped him. . . . His eye was keen, his hand quick, and his memory true."

At his desk turning out an editorial, Caldwell's "whole soul was in the work," Bryant said. "His coat off, his vest unbuttoned and his strong, Scotch-Irish jaws going on a quid of tobacco." You could tell from the way he chewed whether Caldwell was writing "a roast for some . . . politician or having fun with a local poet," Bryant recalled. Caldwell was fearless in his respect for the truth. He would tell his staff, "Make your reports full and fair, and remember that nothing but the truth endures. Do not write editorials. I will do that."

Caldwell also had a quick wit and a wry humor that seemed to bubble up from deep within him. He found humor in commonplace things and expressed it in editorials, in headlines, and in the nicknames he gave people and dogs. The fretful foreman of his composing room was "the Perturbid Spirit." A good writer on the Asheville paper was "the Sweet Singer of the Swannanoa." Among the many stray dogs he sheltered at the *Observer* was one he called "Lot O'-Trouble"; to another, an ugly, ungainly mutt, he gave the name "Beau." The *Observer*'s editorial exchanges with other newspapers were usually laced with Caldwell's wit.

Though Caldwell loved great poetry and could recite stanza upon stanza of it, he took a perverse delight in running what one writer called "the inept, inadvertently hilarious" verse sent in by readers. When any other editor boasted of having published the worst poetry possible, Caldwell would meet the challenge by publishing another selection from his favorite laureate, Mattie J. Peterson of Bladen County, whose masterpiece was a gaucherie titled "I Kissed Pa Twice After His Death."

For a man who grew up in the rural South, Caldwell displayed a surprising worldliness, testimony to his disciplined reading. When Tchaikovsky died, he wrote a knowledgeable editorial evaluating him as a conductor and composer. He did the same after the deaths of English poet Algernon Charles Swinburne, American poet and novelist Stephen Crane, and Great Britain's Queen Victoria.

Caldwell's major shortcoming was his fondness for alcohol, a failing he shared with many other newspapermen, including Louisville's Henry Watterson. For months he would put in long hours at the office—from 1:00 p.m. to 5:00 a.m., six days a week—and then disappear on a binge. He would return in a few days refreshed and ready to resume his arduous schedule. Discerning readers might have detected his absences in the odd assortment of proverbs, aphorisms, and reprints from other newspapers that occasionally appeared in the *Observer*'s editorial columns.

When Caldwell arrived in Charlotte, his wife and four children remained in Statesville until their new house was ready. Caldwell bought a lot at 603 South Tryon (directly across from the modern *Observer* offices) and had a two-story home built there. During its construction, Caldwell lived at the Central Hotel, where he had roomed as a young reporter. He spent most of his waking hours at the newspaper, staying until nearly dawn to see the last edition off the press.

At the time Caldwell took over the paper, the staff consisted of himself, business manager W. Carey Dowd, and city editor Adelaide Williams. The group was small, but knew the city and had plenty of energy. Miss Addie Williams was said to be known by 90 percent of the town's men, women, children, and dogs, and was popular among rich and poor alike. She met every train, interviewed those who got on and off, attended every public meeting, made the rounds of every bank and government office, and kept her eyes peeled for lively street events. The Atlanta *Constitution* called her "one of the best local reporters in the South," and in the spirit of the New South added, "Miss Williams is a Southerner by birth and rearing but possesses all the energy and progressiveness of her sisters of the North."

Caldwell's first major addition to the staff was Howard A. Banks of Asheville, the scholarly son of a Presbyterian preacher. Banks had finished at Davidson College with honors, worked briefly on the *Chronicle* under editor Robert Haydn, taught school at Ellenboro, and spent two years at the university in Chapel Hill, studying and teaching English. When he arrived at the *Observer* late for his job interview, he told Caldwell a bear on the tracks had delayed his train from Asheville. Caldwell postponed the interview until Banks had written a story about the bear-versus-locomotive encounter, and then hired him as news editor.

Donning a green eyeshade, Banks began editing the daily telegraph report, reading big-city dailies, and marking articles he thought Caldwell ought to see and perhaps reprint. He also learned to imitate Caldwell's writing style and was soon spelling "the Old Man" on the editorial page. Caldwell regarded him as the most polished writer in the state.

Banks and Caldwell grew to be very close. They shared a love for language and poetry, and at dawn, as they left the office, they frequently said their farewells by quoting Shakespeare. Caldwell might look at the graying eastern sky and say, from *Romeo and Juliet*, "Night's candles are burnt out," leaving Banks to complete the line, " . . . and jocund day stands tiptoe on the misty mountain tops." (Many years later, Banks's son Dick would become the *Observer*'s music and drama critic.)

Caldwell's editorial courage came under challenge soon after he took over the paper. After twenty years of frustration within the Democratic party, North Carolina farmers, like farmers across the country, were transforming the Farmers' Alliance into the Populist party. The farmers, who made up about 80 percent of the North Carolina electorate, sought a long list of reforms, including the coinage of silver to increase the currency in circulation, a government-run commodity credit system to replace the ruinous crop-lien financing, the public ownership of railroads and utilities to ensure fairer rates, a parcel post to compete with monopolistic express companies, an income tax to replace the protective tariff, an eight-hour day for wage earners, a limit on immigration, the popular election of United States senators, an Australian ballot for all elections, and direct primaries to replace the clique-run state and local nominating conventions. The demands touched off a rancorous debate that divided Democrats for the remainder of the decade.

Caldwell and the *Observer* responded by stepping up their political coverage and devoting almost as much space to the Populists as they did to the Democrats, though the Populist appeal was strongest in the rural east, where the *Observer* had few readers. But Caldwell understood the gravity of the threat; one leader after another Down East was poised to stampede to the Populists unless the Democrats adopted the farmers' platform.

Caldwell considered himself a "Jeffersonian Democrat" and, like many other Democratic leaders, regarded the Populist proposals as "wild schemes." He argued editorially that free silver and inflation would not cure the farmers' financial problems, which he attributed to the protective tariff, overproduction, and a slavish devotion to cotton. He urged farmers to diversify, to grow grains, to raise dairy cows and beef cattle. He conveniently overlooked the crop-lien system that encouraged overproduction and shackled farmers to cotton because that was the only commodity on which supply merchants would lend money.

Caldwell also resented the farmers' efforts to blackmail Democrats into supporting Populist demands. He urged Democrats to stand by their principles; if the farmers wanted to bolt, let them bolt, even if that meant defeat for the Democrats in the next election. "It would be better on every account for the party to part company with those who want to bring a golden calf into the camp than to fall down and worship it," he said. He held to that position throughout the Populist uprising, even though it did bring about Democratic defeat.

As a reward for his loyalty in that and other party tests, Caldwell was elected chairman of the North Carolina delegation to the 1892 Democratic national convention, which met in Chicago that summer and nominated Grover Cleveland for president. Caldwell admired Cleveland's stand for sound money and the gold standard. When Election Day came, he led his fourteen-man staff to the polls and "voted the Democratic ticket straight to a man," just as Col. Charles R. Jones had done when Caldwell was a reporter. When Cleveland won, the *Observer* celebrated by publishing a drawing of the crowing rooster.

With a Democrat in the White House and party jobs opening in post offices and courthouses across the Carolinas, Caldwell found the money to hire a Washington correspondent. He chose Cicero Harris, an author and Goldsboro native who had been the capital correspondent for Colonel Jones.

By December 1892, ten months after the Caldwell-Tompkins takeover, the *Observer* claimed an average daily circulation of 2,300, double what it was the previous February. It also expanded its pages from six to seven columns to accommodate increased advertising and adopted a 2:30 a.m. press time that enabled it to meet early mail trains and expand its circulation territory. At a time when there were few other dailies, a paper that could get itself widely distributed was likely to attract readers, and, thanks to favorable train schedules, the *Observer* had in fact a broad distribution. On February 1, 1893, in marking the first anniversary of his editorship, Caldwell wrote that the *Observer* "has not become independent enough to throw away its old clothes," but it was prospering and, like St. Paul at the three taverns, had cause "to thank God and take courage."

Caldwell was not a church-going man, but he knew the gospel and its appeal among his Bible Belt readers. In March 1893, when evangelist Dwight L. Moody came to Charlotte for ten days of revivals, he used that appeal to build circulation. He assigned Addie Williams to attend the services and record Moody's sermons. Williams did, and for ten days wrote stories that filled five columns a day. At the last service, Moody recognized her and praised her accuracy. In an editorial, Caldwell called her stories "a piece of longhand reporting . . . unequaled in the history of the state." They increased circulation and created a "demand for back numbers of the paper . . . greater than can be supplied," he said.

Two weeks later, on March 30, 1893, Caldwell and Tompkins put down $2,000 in cash and signed notes for $8,000 more to buy the Bank of Mecklenburg building at 122 South Tryon Street, where the old *Observer*'s initial patrons, James Tate and Thomas Dewey, had conducted business. The building had also been the site of one of the last meetings of the Confederate cabinet, a fact that Caldwell and Tompkins downplayed. They were more interested in the New South than the Old and rarely associated themselves with the "Lost Cause." When they chose to look back, it was usually to the Mecklenburg Declaration of Independence, which united Charlotte and the South with the rest of the country.

Immediately they began to renovate the old building into "the most modern newspaper plant in the state." They electrified it, making it one of the first offices in Charlotte with electric lights. They also equipped it with typewriters and an elevator, added a third floor, and built at the rear a four-story print shop and a power plant. Meanwhile, at its old West Trade Street offices, the *Observer* expanded its Sunday editions from four to six pages, took on B. R. Smith of New York as a correspondent on cotton markets, and began running daily quotations from the New York Stock Exchange. The market summary, which initially listed sixty-three stocks, would double to over 120 stocks by 1904 and would become one of the business-oriented *Observer*'s strongest selling points.

When the *Observer* moved into the new offices in October, Caldwell and Tompkins had to postpone other improvements. A panic had hit the nation's financial markets in June and touched off a depression. By September, the Richmond and Danville Railroad slashed trainmen's salaries 10 percent. By October cotton was selling for four cents a pound, farmers were paying merchants in chickens and eggs, and merchants were paying each other in scrip. The economic miseries of the long-suffering country people were at last felt in the cities.

Two weeks after the June panic, W. Carey Dowd resigned as the *Observer*'s business manager and bought the weekly *Mecklenburg Times*. On July 1, he also bought the *Charlotte News*, paying founder Wade Harris $5,000 for the paper. Dowd found it an inopportune time to enter the publishing business. In the first three days under his ownership, the *News* took in five cents; in the first month, $14.90. Over the next three years, Dowd struggled to keep his paper afloat, accepting hams and chickens in payment of subscriptions, and clothing and coffee in payment for advertising.

The going was less strenuous on the *Observer*, which had a wider circulation and a wealthier clientele. Even so, Caldwell and Tompkins lacked the money to expand their staff. In Dowd's place as business manager, they hired John Van Landingham, Caldwell's brother-in-law. He stayed two years, then left to become one of Charlotte's biggest cotton brokers. His place was taken by George Crater, who had worked for Caldwell in Statesville. Crater later became the *Observer*'s first advertising manager.

For two years, the *Observer*'s reporting and writing staff was stuck at three—Caldwell himself, Addie Williams, and Howard Banks. To fill in, Caldwell occasionally summoned two printers from his composing room, James C. Abernethy of Newton and Gordon H. Cilley of Hickory. Both proved to be exceptional writers.

Caldwell also got part-time help from Charles C. Hook, a draftsman who resigned as the manual arts teacher in the city schools to try his hand at architecture. To get his name before the public, he wrote architectural reviews for the *Observer*. His first was on the pavilions at the Chicago world's fair, some of which were designed by young Frank Lloyd Wright. Later he reviewed the first buildings of Greensboro's new State Normal and Industrial School, which would become the University of North Carolina at Greensboro. With those reviews, Hook launched a distinguished career as an architect and helped make Charlotteans aware of architecture's importance to their emerging city, another instance of the newspaper's enriching the popular culture.

In January 1894, the *Observer* hired a young printer who would also make a name for himself. Having completed his apprenticeship in Shelby, seventeen-year-old Clyde R. Hoey signed on as a journeyman in the *Observer* composing room to set type by hand. His hours were from three in the afternoon until three in the morning. He stayed only a few months and then returned to Shelby to buy the weekly *Shelby Review* on installments. He converted it into the *Cleveland County Star* and finally into the *Shelby Star*, which would later become a daily and would train a number of *Observer* writers and editors. Clyde Hoey went on to be come a lawyer, a congressman (1919–21), a North Carolina governor (1937–41), and a United States senator (1945–54).

When John Van Landingham left the *Observer* business office in June 1895, Caldwell thought he could afford to take on another full-time reporter. So he hired H. E. C. Bryant, a burly redhead fresh from the university at Chapel Hill and the cotton farms of south Mecklenburg. Bryant wound up working three months before Caldwell could pay him a salary. Then it was only twenty dollars a month.

In the fall of 1893, while Joseph Caldwell was working long hours and adjusting to hardships imposed by the panic, he suffered the first of a series of personal losses that might have broken a lesser man. Before he could move her into the new house on South Tryon Street, his wife of sixteen years, the former Maggie Spratt of Charlotte, died after a brief illness. News of her death arrived as carpenters were hanging the front door at the new home. The *Observer* arranged special trains to take Charlotte mourners to the funeral in Statesville.

The depression of 1893–95 gave extra urgency to the Populist cause and put added pressure on Caldwell to soften the *Observer*'s opposition to the Populist agenda, but the editor held firm. He expressed compassion for the farmers, laborers, and miners but did not champion their cause. He stood by President Cleveland and stayed with the gold standard, even after European gold purchases forced the federal government to seek a loan from New York banker J. P. Morgan. Meanwhile, anti-Cleveland sentiment in North Carolina spurred Populists and Republicans to unite and win control of the state legislature in 1894. With that control they restored the popular election of county commissioners and put through other election reforms that encouraged more blacks—who usually voted Republican—to participate in politics.

The depression also spawned a number of bitter strikes that Caldwell opposed. He was sympathetic to the steel, coal, and railroad workers' quest for higher wages, but he disapproved of strikes because they created hardships for innocent people. He dismissed Eugene Debs, leader of the railway workers, as "the latest thing in cranks." In fact, Caldwell frowned on the whole theory of collective bargaining and argued in one editorial that in placing equal value on all workers, unions promoted mediocrity over excellence.

Caldwell's opposition to Populism, free silver, and unions was in line with both his Democratic loyalty and his New South philosophy. In creating the Populist party, the farmers were asking southern Democrats to desert their power base in the industrial East and join with grain growers and silver miners in the West. To Caldwell, an alliance with the West would perpetuate the agrarian economy that the Civil War proved was bankrupt. The East had the industrial spirit the South sought to emulate, and it had the money and markets the South needed. Caldwell courted the East despite the fact that eastern wealth was prolonging the South's colonial status.

Caldwell insisted that the Populist free-silver theories were "impractical" and predicted they would hurt southern farmers more than help them. He acknowledged the need for currency reform, but warned that the United States could not coin silver without international agreements that assured a sound dollar.

In Caldwell's opinion, unions were a threat to the cheap labor that was the South's main attraction to industry. Over and over, he and other New South editors opposed efforts to organize southern unions or regulate the wages and hours of southern workers, including women and children, because such unions and regulations would rob the region of the advantage it had over mills in New England.

Those and other New South attitudes were spelled out in a steady stream of *Observer* editorials. As new mills opened all around, Caldwell and Tompkins stepped up the campaign for industrialism. The *Observer* ran stories about every new mill, every important piece of new machinery, every new bank or building and loan firm established within the Charlotte area. In mid-1893, the paper advertised itself as a clearinghouse for information about industrial development. In addition to news of scientific and technical advances, it ran lists of patents granted to North Carolinians. Almost every edition also included stories reprinted from magazines or other newspapers praising southern industry, many of them mere propaganda pieces.

To these it added editorials and features on Charlotte as a center of manufacturing and commerce and as a supplier of mill machinery and expertise. In mid-1893, it began a weekday column on "Mill Notes and Mill Men" that on Sundays gave way to a longer column on "Mills and Manufacturing." These and other features, including the weekly Dun and Bradstreet report on business conditions, made the *Observer* "must" reading for investors, bankers, managers, merchants, educators, suppliers, salesmen, and professional men— anyone in the region interested in industry. The *Observer* became the paper of the economic elite; the evening *Charlotte News* was more the paper of the working people.

D. A. Tompkins wanted the *Observer* to go even further in catering to the business world. He wanted to leave out stories of crime, personal scandal, train wrecks, and natural disasters to create more space for industrial and financial news. Caldwell and his staff often chuckled over Tompkins's news judgment, but they made sure that industrial news was well displayed elsewhere in the paper, if not always on page one.

The *Observer* and its co-owners took a leading role in organizing the Southern Manufacturers Club, which was chartered and headquartered in the *Observer*'s offices. The club's dining room on the newspaper's third floor became a focal point for talk of industrialization. When an important manufacturer, politician, or journalist visited Charlotte, he was usually entertained at the Manufacturers Club. When Gov. Charles B. Aycock came to town to share his views on industry and education, he spoke at a roof-garden banquet atop the *Observer* building.

Along with industry, Caldwell promoted education, which he saw as essential to an industrial economy, though he had not always done so. As a Statesville editor, he opposed taxes for public schools and regarded any instruction beyond reading as a luxury. But in the summer of 1889, Charles D. McIver (founder of UNC-Greensboro) conducted a teachers' institute in Iredell County and persuaded Caldwell to equate education with economic progress. At the *Observer* he aggressively promoted the public schools at every opportunity. He ran the names of every student who made the honor roll, even when the list consumed more than a column and a half of precious news space. He often ran the names of all the teachers employed in the city schools. He also wrote editorials calling for higher pay and better training for teachers, as well as closer supervision of their work.

In addition to his own editorials, Caldwell ran the Sunday commentaries of a pro-education columnist writing under the pseudonym "Teacher." Years later the writer was identified as Charles L. Coon, who at one time taught in the Charlotte school system and would become superintendent of schools in Salisbury and Wilson. Coon was also the ghost writer for most of D. A. Tompkins's two-volume *History of Mecklenburg County and the City of Charlotte*, published in 1903. When Coon refused to authenticate the Mecklenburg Declaration of Independence, Tompkins fired him and commissioned another writer to complete the project.

Perhaps Caldwell's greatest contribution to education was his support for the University of North Carolina, which he saw as a beacon of progress. In December 1893, as UNC was nearing its 100th anniversary, the state's Baptists, Methodists, and Presbyterians passed resolutions against further state appropriations for it because the public institution was "unfair" competition for church-backed colleges. As the 1894 elections approached, church leaders stumped the state in support of legislators who would cut university appropriations and limit its enrollment to graduate students. Caldwell wrote a thundering, 3,000-word editorial under the heading "The University Must Be Sustained." Remarkable for its cold, sustained anger, the editorial said in part:

> To deny that the State has a right to assist in the higher education of her youth is really to deny that the poor have a right to higher education. The rich can get education under any system. They can go to other States or other lands. But the poor must stay at home. They must struggle and work for education. They must be aided or they cannot go to college. . . . We cannot have an aristocracy of education, based upon wealth or religious affiliations. . . .
>
> The entire sum appropriated to the University of North Carolina during the last 100 years would not sustain our public schools for two months. But the influences that have come from the University . . . have created and sustained the public school system. . . .

Red Buck Bryant, a rising senior at the university that year, wrote that the editorial cut the ground from under the movement opposed to the university. Widely read and reprinted, the editorial endeared Caldwell to university students, alumni, faculty, and friends.

Though Caldwell's *Observer* was forward-looking on industry and education, it was backward-looking on race. Like other New South newspapers, it espoused policies to keep blacks subservient to whites. In some ways, Caldwell befriended blacks and accorded them greater visibility and dignity than had previous *Observer* editors. In addition to covering black churches and institutions, the paper often ran stories about notable black individuals. When a barber named Thad L. Tate went to New York to learn to cut the hair of white women and children, the paper reported it approvingly. At that time there were few white barbers, and a skilled black barber was a community asset. The paper even published regular correspondence about events in the black community—until the black correspondent criticized the racist sermons of a white preacher, and Caldwell publicly fired him.

Elsewhere in the paper, that racial tolerance was contradicted. In the 1890s and the following decade, when lynchings were hitting a peak in the South (155 blacks were lynched in 1892), *Observer* editorials deplored the violence. But the paper subtly contributed to the mob spirit with headlines referring to lynchings as the work of "Judge Lynch," a poisonous euphemism that winked at the truth and cloaked the murders in an aura of legality. Strict segregation was not widespread in the early 1890s, but the *Observer* supported efforts to make it so. Under the headline "A Word of Friendly Warning," a January 1, 1893, editorial cautioned "the colored race" against making further protests about separate railroad waiting rooms and passenger cars. Asserting that waiting rooms and passenger cars for blacks were equal to those for whites, the editorial argued: "The protests against such arrangements subject the colored people to the imputation that they are not seeking equal accommodations . . . but white accommodations—and that is out of the question." Three years later, in *Plessy* v. *Ferguson*, the United States Supreme Court made separate railroad cars the law of the land and cleared the way for a maze of segregated accommodations across the South.

Under Caldwell's management the *Observer* enjoyed steady growth. In the spring of 1894, an eight-page, forty-eight-column Sunday edition became standard, and the Sunday issues began to include book reviews as well as correspondence from New York, Washington, and Raleigh. In the fall of 1894, the paper got a new, cleaner masthead, new headline type, and apparently a head-casting machine that made possible the use of big display type in advertising. Retailers also began to run illustrated ads of hats, coats, shoes, and other goods. The paper ran its first ad for Coca-Cola in May 1895, and, on October 4, 1895, its first ad for Belk stores.

The *Salisbury Herald* was soon calling the *Observer* "the best paper ever printed in North Carolina." In July 1894, Josiah W. Bailey of Raleigh, the future editor of the Baptist *Biblical Recorder* and later a United States senator, called the *Observer* "North Carolina's best" newspaper. But on the horizon, competition was rising. The old *News and Observer* of Raleigh had fallen on hard times and was being sold at auction. Josephus Daniels of Wilson, who previously had edited newspapers in Raleigh, wrote 100 prominent North Carolina Democrats, advising that if they would put up $100 apiece, he would quit his job in the Cleveland administration, buy the *News and Observer*, and turn it into "an aggressive exponent" of the North Carolina Democratic party. The Democrats put up the money; Daniels made the purchase; and soon the *News and Observer* was lashing out at Populists and Republicans. Before the fight for Populism and free silver was over, Josephus Daniels and Joseph Caldwell, once warm friends, would become bitter enemies.

The Populists hit their peak in the 1896 elections. Nationally they joined the Democrats to nominate William Jennings Bryan for president on the free-silver platform. In North Carolina, they teamed with Republicans to split the Democrats and elect Daniel L. Russell as governor, the last Republican to hold that office for seventy-two years. Both outcomes distressed the *Observer*.

The *Observer*'s Howard Banks covered the Democratic convention in Chicago that sweltering summer, but he did not hear the famous speech that vaulted Bryan to the nomination. Like most regional— as opposed to national—reporters, he was busy filing local-angle stories on delegations from back home. He was just returning to the arena when he heard the crowd's roar at Bryan's stirring peroration: "You shall not press down on the brow of labor this crown of thorns, you shall not crucify mankind upon a cross of gold." Dozens of *Observer* reporters who have since covered national conventions—and have missed key moments for the same reasons—can appreciate the disappointment Banks said he felt.

The Bryan nomination put a greater strain on the *Observer*'s editorial commitment to gold, which was already unpopular with many North Carolinians, especially the farmers. North Carolina's preference for free silver showed at the state Democratic convention, where the free-silver platform won, 875 to 31. At the national convention, the North Carolina delegation was among the first to commit to Bryan, even before the "cross of gold" speech.

To endorse Bryan as the Democratic nominee for president, Caldwell would have to swallow all the arguments he had made against free silver and Populism. Some letters to the editor urged him to repudiate Bryan, as New South editors were doing in Richmond, Charleston, Nashville, Louisville, and at least six other major southern cities. But having participated in Democratic conventions at local and state levels, where delegates who picked Bryan were chosen, Caldwell felt a moral obligation to stand by the nominee. Though he continued to oppose free silver, Caldwell and the *Observer* gave Bryan enthusiastic coverage when he spoke in Charlotte and other cities in the Carolinas that fall. Bryan lost the election to William McKinley, but comfortably carried the Carolinas. Democratic leaders were soon inviting Caldwell out of the party.

The election of Republican Gov. Daniel L. Russell upset both Caldwell and the Democrats, for it meant a return of Republicans—and some blacks—to state and county offices and raised the possibility of further election reforms that could open the door to more Republicans and Populists. Caldwell distrusted the secretive Russell and warned North Carolinians to "fortify themselves for the worst and hope for the best" from his administration. But the Populists and Republicans soon fell to fighting among themselves—sometimes with fists—and missed the chance to consolidate their gains.

Fistfights were common in politics and in business, as well as in banking and medicine. It was a scuffle at a Republican nominating convention at Maxton in 1896 that won *Observer* reporter H. E. C. Bryant the nickname "Red Buck." When fighting erupted among contending factions, Bryant fled the rostrum "like a red buck" deer, according to a Raleigh reporter. Joseph Caldwell saw the Raleigh reporter's story, reprinted it in the *Observer* under the headline "Ah, There, Red Buck," and forever afterward referred to Bryant by that name, which helped to make Bryant North Carolina's best-known reporter. So firmly did the name stick that after he was married, friends called his wife "Mrs. Red Buck." His real name was Henry Edward Cowan Bryant.

Given the *Observer*'s editorial stands, several acts of Governor Russell should have drawn Caldwell's praise. He sought increased taxing authority for public schools, greater appropriations for the university, and an annulment of the Southern Railway's ninety-nine-year lease of the North Carolina Railroad running from Charlotte to Greensboro to Raleigh and to Goldsboro. The previous legislature had awarded the lease to the newly organized Southern on terms Caldwell thought were too generous. He warned it would be "repented of in bitterness." But when Russell asked the legislature to revoke it, Caldwell was opposed, saying the lease was granted by duly elected legislators and ratified by North Carolina Railroad stockholders.

Caldwell's opposition to the annulment was further evidence of his loyalty to the Southern Railway, which he regarded as the South's lifeline. While others attacked the railway for corrupting state politics and discriminatory freight rates, Caldwell defended it. The Southern was created in 1894 out of the ruins of the old Richmond and Danville, a victim of the panic of 1893. New York banker J. P. Morgan acquired the line, consolidated it with others, watered its stock by $120 million, and expanded it to dominate the coal and iron fields from Knoxville to Birmingham and the tobacco and textile industries from Virginia to Georgia. Caldwell marveled at the wealth that went into its formation. Though it was owned and controlled by northern investors, he saw the railway as a friend of the New South and overlooked its complicity in perpetuating the region's colonial economy.

Caldwell's respect for the Southern Railway did not extend to other large corporations. He bitterly opposed James B. Duke's American Tobacco Company, and Duke himself. Even after Duke turned his wealth to the generation of electric power, there was a coolness in Caldwell's estimate of him. Caldwell also opposed the manufacture of cigarettes and often wrote editorials condemning them as the worst form of tobacco and a menace to health. He supported bills in Congress to outlaw cigarettes, an idea opposed by most tobacco interests in the state.

Though *Observer* editorials often went unheeded, the paper's reporting had a wide impact, as demonstrated by a series of stories on some remarkable medical advances. The first appeared in January 1896 and described the process used by a German scientist to make X rays. Dr. Henry Louis Smith, a physics professor at Davidson College, read the story and a month later produced an X ray of his own. A story of Dr. Smith's success and a picture of his first X ray, showing a bullet embedded in the hand of a cadaver, were printed on the front page of the *Observer*. Later, when a six-year-old girl in neighboring Cabarrus County swallowed a thimble and efforts to dislodge it from her throat failed, the girl's parents remembered the *Observer*'s story about X rays. They went to see Dr. Smith and persuaded him to x-ray the obstruction so doctors could see how to remove it. Dr. Smith made an X ray, which helped doctors at what would become Presbyterian Hospital open her windpipe and remove the thimble. The thimble was put on public display at the *Observer* office.

A story of that life-saving "miracle" appeared in the *Observer* and immediately inspired another. A Whiteville doctor who was treating a ten-year-old girl for a hatpin stuck in her trachea saw the thimble story and brought the girl to Charlotte. With the help of X rays, he got the pin removed. A story of that success also appeared in the *Observer* and was reprinted around the world.

While reporting those medical "miracles," the *Observer* was taking advantage of some advances in printing. In April 1896 Caldwell and Tompkins signed a contract with the Mergenthaler Corporation of Brooklyn, New York, to lease three Linotype machines for setting type. The machines rented for $1,500 a year. Caldwell and Tompkins put down $650 and signed a note for the remaining $850 plus 6 percent interest. Mergenthaler agreed to deliver and erect the Linotypes and train *Observer* printers to operate them. Caldwell sent two printers, James Abernethy and Gordon Cilley, to the Brooklyn factory for instruction.

The *Observer* put the Linotypes into use on July 17. A little more of the paper was set by machine each day thereafter. A discerning reader knew which stories were set by machine because the type looked light and uniform, while the type set by hand was uneven and worn, and therefore darker. Some sources credit Caldwell and the *Observer* with installing the first Linotypes in North Carolina, but clearly that honor belongs to the *News and Observer*'s Josephus Daniels, who installed the typesetting machines a year earlier.

The *Observer*'s Linotypes came at a high price. For a while, typesetting by machines was slower than by hand, and the *Observer* had to apologize for missing deadlines and mail trains. It also had to defend itself against charges that it was putting loyal hand-set compositors out of work, though all who wanted to could learn to run a Linotype. In all, the Linotypes replaced fifteen printers. Within a year after the Linotypes were installed—and within a week after labor leader Samuel Gompers toured the state—the *Observer*'s printers joined Local 338 of the International Typographical Union.

The union's formation must have wounded Caldwell, who as a former compositor identified with printers and praised their contribution to his newspaper. He often wrote movingly of their exacting work in the stifling heat of a second-floor printshop. He pictured them as standing "half naked, silent and perspiring, under the electric amps, picking up the type, only pausing occasionally to mop their

brows and to mutter a phrase we hope will be forgiven." While printers in Raleigh had been organized for years, a union at the *Observer*
was an embarrassment to Caldwell's labor-management ideals and a
contradiction to the *Observer*'s antiunion editorials. That explains,
perhaps, why there was no story in the paper about the printers'
move to organize. On June 22, 1897, the union label simply appeared on the paper's editorial page.

Once the Linotypes were installed, the *Observer* was in the market
for a new press that could print more pages at greater speed and allow the paper to keep up with its increased advertising and rising
circulation. In July 1897 Caldwell announced that the daily paper
was being standardized at eight pages with six columns to the page,
and more pages on Sundays. He also revealed that the paper was
being printed on a new Cox Duplex press, capable of printing 5,000
copies an hour from rolls of paper (instead of single sheets). The
press would collate, fold, and cut each finished paper. Though it
printed from flatbeds of type, it was a big improvement over the old
Babcock, but still inadequate for the *Observer*'s long-term needs
and would be replaced in seven years. Nevertheless, the new press
arrived just in time to accommodate a period of prosperity and
expansion.

One cause of the expansion was the Spanish-American War. After
much vacillation by McKinley and loud warmongering in Congress,
the United States declared war in April 1898. Joseph Caldwell
watched the rise of war fever with misgivings. "People talk as lightly
of war as of going to a festival," he wrote. "Few realize what it
means. . . . War is the scourge of God and we want none of it." When
North Carolina was asked to send troops, Caldwell wrote that he
hoped they would never be called on to fight. Among the North Carolina volunteers was Gordon Cilley from the *Observer*'s composing
room, who regularly filed stories on his outfit's training and its jour-
ney to Havana. Caldwell's hopes were realized; the North Carolina
regiment did not get to Cuba until the war was over.

The war changed the paper's looks and publication schedule. After
years of one-column headlines a quarter-inch high, the *Observer*
broke out big type for the war news. The upper left corner of page one
became the focal point, with two-column and three-column headlines almost an inch high and three and four lines deep, with sub-
heads below. Compared with the "yellow journals" of William Randolph Hearst, it was tame stuff, but for the staid *Observer* of Joseph
P. Caldwell it was a radical departure. Writing most of those headlines was *Charlotte News* founder Wade Harris, who joined the *Ob-*

server staff as telegraph editor shortly before the war and edited most of the copy from the battlefronts. In addition to the big headlines, the paper added a Monday edition, and became the only paper in North Carolina that published seven days a week, a practice it continued throughout the brief war.

From the day war was declared until it ended, the paper ran a drawing of a furled American flag at the top of its editorial columns. Accompanying it were martial poems by Kipling, Tennyson, and others. At the height of the fighting, Caldwell remarked that patriotism inspired by the war had softened the old North-South bitterness and united the nation. It was in this period that John Philip Sousa's "Stars and Stripes Forever" gained popularity. The patriotism helped persuade the white South to resume its observance of the Fourth of July, which for many years had been celebrated only by blacks. Caldwell wrote an Independence Day editorial applauding the change. At the war's end, the poem accompanying the furled flag was "When Johnny Comes Marching Home Again, Hurrah! Hurrah!"

As the Spanish-American War was ending, a longer, uglier, more tragic war was beginning. But it was a war that Joseph Caldwell and the *Observer* expressed no reluctance about entering. It was the racial war that disfranchised blacks and restored white supremacy to North Carolina government. The goal was not only to eliminate blacks from politics, but also to raise an issue that would divert white farmers from Populism and reunite them behind the Democratic party.

The racist campaign was a backlash from the elections of 1894 and 1896, when the Populists joined blacks and Republicans to oust Democrats from public offices all across the South. The last black to represent North Carolina in Congress was elected during this period. He was Rep. George H. White of Tarboro, who served from 1897 to 1901. During the period a handful of black legislators, county commissioners, and other local officers were elected in predominantly black counties in eastern North Carolina, stirring white resentment.

An *Observer* editorial of August 26, 1898, lamented the ugly tone of the Democratic drive, but blamed it on "arrogant and self-assertive" blacks in Down East counties with majority black populations. The *Observer* dispatched Red Buck Bryant to the eastern part of the state for a series of first-hand reports on black officeholders. His first story, from New Bern, was headlined "Negro Rule: Shall It Last Longer in North Carolina?" The stories were later attacked by Populists as unfair exaggerations and "Democratic lies."

All that fall, the *Observer* carried stories of white vigilantes called "red shirts" terrorizing black voters in Ku Klux Klan style. Many men who would later be leaders in state politics rode in the "red shirt" campaign, including a young, self-educated Richmond County lawyer named Cameron Morrison.

On the day after the November election, when returns showed Democrats winning 134 seats in the legislature to only thirty for the Republicans and six for the Populists, the *Observer*'s triumphant headline said "Whites to Rule." On the editorial page, the paper interpreted the results as a vindication of the state's economic as well as political interests, saying: "The business men of the State are largely responsible for the victory. Not before in years have the bank men, the mill men, and the business men in general—the backbone of the property interest of the State—taken such sincere interest [in state politics]. They worked from start to finish, and furthermore they spent large bits of money in behalf of the cause. . . . Indeed North Carolina is fast changing from an agricultural to a manufacturing state."

In Wilmington, racial feelings boiled over when angry whites stormed and sacked the office of a black newspaper editor. A riot followed and eleven blacks were killed. The whites were led by Col. Alfred M. Waddell, who had edited Charlotte's *Journal-Observer* in the days of Col. Charles R. Jones. Joseph Caldwell deplored the Wilmington violence and regretted that white "wrath" was aimed at blacks instead of the white Populists who incited the blacks.

Democrats spent the next two years drafting, debating, and enacting measures to deny blacks the ballot box without at the same time disfranchising poor and illiterate whites. The proposed "suffrage amendment" to the state Constitution was similar to disfranchisement schemes being enacted throughout the South. It required each voter to prove he had paid a poll tax and could read, write, and interpret the Constitution. Those who could not read and write could still vote if they could prove their grandfathers had been eligible to vote prior to January 1, 1867. After more "red-shirt" nightriding, the plan was approved in an August 1900 referendum in which few blacks voted.

The *Observer* saw the amendment as a means of purifying state politics. It was the product of "a struggle of the white people to rid themselves of the dangers of rule by negroes and the lower class of whites," the paper said. It also meant that power would remain in the hands of the wealthy, the propertied, and the intelligent, a combination that political scientist V. O. Key later termed "a progressive plutocracy." Further, it meant that North Carolina, like other southern states, would become a one-party domain of the Democrats. Without black support, Republicans were a hopeless minority. The white Populists could go nowhere but back to the Democrats, where they became the party's "liberal" wing.

But Populist hopes for free silver were not dead, and the worst of the *Observer*'s political troubles were yet to come. Knowing that the Democrats were likely to nominate Bryan again, Joseph Caldwell stayed away from party conventions leading up to the 1900 election. If the choice was to be Bryan, he wanted the freedom to oppose him. On July 7, two days after Bryan's renomination, Caldwell wrote what must have been one of his most deliberate editorials, a cold dissection of Bryanism and the "evils" it offered the country. It began forthrightly: "*The Observer* cannot support the candidate nominated or the platform promulgated at Kansas City. This is of no consequence to the candidate or the platform, but . . . is of much importance to *The Observer*."

Having seen what happened to Colonel Jones in the 1880s and having suffered party hostility four years earlier, Caldwell knew he was taking "a grave step," one that would alienate many *Observer* readers. He addressed that forthrightly, too, saying: "Four years ago we . . . had no stomach for Bryan or Bryanism. Yet, for the sake of party regularity and old associations, we did the very best we could. . . . We were assailed . . . as 'traitor' and 'assassin' and were frequently invited out of the party. . . . The considerate friends who said those things then now have their wishes gratified. . . . We pray the press and public to attach no responsibility henceforth to the Democratic party for anything this paper says. It does not speak for the Democracy of Charlotte, of Mecklenburg, of North Carolina, but only for itself."

He called Bryan "dangerous . . . self-willed, head-strong, imperious, determined to have his way. . . . He is not a fit man for President; in charge of the craft he would run it upon the rocks." To the thousands of Carolinians who adored Bryan and had given him their votes in 1896, those were bitter words. Caldwell knew it and said he was prepared for "the storm of traduction" that was to come.

The storm came swiftly. Other newspapers jeered, many readers wrote protests, and some warned that the *Observer* would lose advertising and circulation. Even Gordon Cilley, the former printer Caldwell had taught to report and edit, wrote to complain. Quoting Bryan's own speeches on the value of political independence, Caldwell stood his ground.

His editorial was reprinted and praised by newspapers in New York and other eastern cities. But the *News and Observer* of Raleigh alleged that Caldwell was only acting on orders from D. A. Tompkins, and charged that Tompkins, in accepting an appointment to the United States Industrial Commission, had been bought by the Republicans. Caldwell called the *News and Observer* "a liar." Apparently, the truth was just the opposite: it was Caldwell who dictated the stand to Tompkins.

Caldwell told friends that he and Tompkins had often discussed the Bryan issue, and Tompkins had indicated his willingness, for the good of the paper, to accept Bryan again as the nominee. It was Caldwell who was unwilling to compromise. Besides, Caldwell said, the vacancy on the Industrial Commission did not occur until after the anti-Bryan editorial was published. Caldwell had no way of knowing beforehand that it would be offered to his partner. Furthermore, he said, Tompkins was appointed to a Democratic vacancy on the commission.

But the damage had been done. The *News and Observer* charge was widely reprinted and the long-smoldering feud between the two newspapers flashed into open flame. It would be years before old friends Josephus Daniels and Joseph Caldwell again exchanged civil words.

Two other elements in the election of 1900 were defeats for Caldwell and the *Observer*. The Populist push for party primaries and the popular election of United States senators resulted in a trial referendum between industrialist Julian S. Carr of Durham and Democratic party chairman Furnifold M. Simmons of New Bern, both candidates for the United States Senate. The winner would get the state legislature's appointment to the Senate. The *Observer* opposed primaries as expensive, divisive, and encouraging demagoguery, but preferred Carr over Simmons. Simmons won and from the Senate led the North Carolina Democratic machine for the next twenty-eight years.

For the *Observer*, the one redeeming outcome of the 1900 elections was the triumph of Charles B. Aycock of Goldsboro in the contest for governor. The eloquent Aycock partially atoned for his role in the white-supremacy movement by launching a vigorous campaign for public education that benefited both blacks and whites and laid the foundation for a quarter century of progress in the state.

For his stand against Bryan in 1900, Caldwell is often credited with freeing the North Carolina press from domination by political parties. But the freedom cost circulation losses and four years of harassment. In 1908, when Bryan was again the nominee and Caldwell had further cause to bolt over the Democratic nominee for governor, he remained loyal to the party.

Race and politics were not the only cause of controversy and excitement in turn-of-the-century *Observer*s. In November 1900, Osmond L. Barringer and Dr. C. G. McManaway brought the first automobiles to Charlotte and rode them up and down the dusty streets, frightening people and horses. Charlotteans speculated whether they were toys of the arrogant rich or the future of transportation. The *Observer* saw them as heralds of the future.

The continuing growth and development of the city were also a source of excitement. In December 1900, a new census was completed, showing Charlotte had a population of 18,091, enough to pass Raleigh as the second largest city in the state and only 2,885 behind Wilmington. An *Observer* editorial pointed out that if the count had included Dilworth and the mill villages on the urban fringe, Charlotte would have been the largest city in the state with a population of 27,752. With that thought the paper launched a campaign that would extend the city limits in 1907.

Retailing also came in for great attention as competition among Charlotte merchants grew more intense. Store ads included not only pictures of the goods offered for sale, but for the first time also listed prices. The Tapp-Long Company had two stores on the northwest corner of Independence Square, one facing West Trade, the other facing North Tryon, and was aggressively buying full-page ads in the *Observer* to exploit its superior location. In May 1900, Tapp-Long began offering "Red Trading Stamps" with each purchase.

Joining the competition with W. H. Belk and other Charlotte merchants was bespectacled, mild-mannered J. B. Ivey. In February 1900, he opened a store on the street floor of the Leland Hotel at 231 North Tryon Street and rented a room for himself upstairs. The son of a Methodist preacher, Ivey was no stranger to the *Observer*. His letters to the editor objecting to the paper's Sunday publication had preceded him. A staunch Methodist, he refused to advertise on Sundays and throughout his life draped his store's show windows on Sundays. A year later, another merchandising group, the Efird brothers, began doing business in Charlotte, first as the Busy Bee and after 1907 as Efird's Department Store.

As Charlotte emerged as a manufacturing and merchandising center, it created new opportunities in banking and real estate and began attracting ambitious young men from other cities in the Carolinas. Among them was George Stephens from Summerfield, near

Greensboro, an 1896 graduate of the university at Chapel Hill, where he was a star baseball pitcher. Stephens entered the insurance business in Charlotte with Walter Brem and then formed a real estate firm with F. C. Abbott, with whom he developed Piedmont Park, a suburb east of the city. In 1901, he and Abbott summoned Stephens's college friend Word H. Wood from Winston, and the three men organized the Southern States Trust Company, which shortly became the American Trust Company and then, much later, NCNB. In time Stephens and Wood would also own the *Observer*.

The turn-of-the-century prosperity enabled Charlotte's expanding middle class to enjoy many mass-produced goods once available only to the wealthy. Department and specialty stores were advertising such luxuries as diamonds, sterling silver, electric fans, ice-box refrigerators, hand-cranked ice-cream freezers, player pianos, and imported laces and embroidery. Increasingly there were ads for wide-brimmed straw hats for women and girls to wear while bicycling. New consumer services such as steam laundries and home-delivered coal and ice were also publicized. The ads for vacation cottages at Wrightsville Beach and mountain resorts indicate that increasing numbers of people at the turn of the century had leisure time.

Sports pages were not yet a daily feature in the newspaper, but they were on the horizon. Golf and tennis were gaining popularity as weekend recreations requiring newspaper coverage. They got a presidential boost when Theodore Roosevelt moved into the White House. Dilworth's Latta Park was the focus for much sports activity. For the first ten days of April 1901, professional baseball's Brooklyn Nationals (later known as the Dodgers) did their spring training there. And in November 1901 football teams from the University of North Carolina and Clemson College clashed there for the championship of the Carolinas. Clemson won, 22–10, before a crowd of about 1,000.

In this period of prosperity, the *Observer* made significant strides. By becoming a charter member of the reorganized Associated Press in 1900, the paper gained an advantage over its competitors in the area. The *Charlotte News*, for instance, did not get full AP service until 1910 and did not become an AP member until the mid-1930s. Also in 1900 the *Observer* put in a fifty-horsepower Corliss steam engine to power its machinery and generate electricity. And it laid plans for erecting a 300-lamp electric sign atop its Tryon Street building, Charlotte's first lighted sign, said to be visible for miles. On October 15, 1900, the *Observer* permanently resumed the seven-day-a-week publication schedule used during the Spanish-American War, becoming the only true daily in the Carolinas.

The paper was expanded from eight pages to ten on weekdays and from sixteen pages to twenty on Sundays. The Sunday edition included book reviews, music reviews, and essays on religion, travel, and medicine. The paper often ran line drawings of prominent people and events in town. Frequently the paper tried to print photographs, such as a portrait of Mrs. Stonewall Jackson on her birthday. They were always framed in wide white borders in hopes they would get enough ink to reproduce well, but they rarely did. Only a rotary press with stereotype plates and regulated ink fountains would enable the *Observer* to make regular use of photographs.

There were also some important staff changes. Col. Fred Olds, a colorful veteran of capital politics, signed on as Raleigh correspondent and was soon writing Sunday features full of state lore. James C. Abernethy, the "Perturbid Spirit" of the composing room, joined the news staff as a full-time writer on his way toward becoming managing editor. Col. W. S. Pearson, a lawyer and former editor of the *Morganton Herald*, became the Washington correspondent. And in 1901, John Paul Lucas, a seventeen-year-old Charlotte lad fresh out of high school, joined the staff as a reporter. He quickly rose to editing jobs in Charlotte and Winston and later became an officer of Duke Power Company.

The biggest staff change came in December 1899 when Addie Williams resigned to become city editor of the rival *Charlotte News*. At first the move looked like a betrayal of the *Observer*, but in time it made perfect sense. She stayed at the *News* until September 1901, and then took a job in New York. By the year's end she was back in Charlotte—as Mrs. Joseph P. Caldwell. Apparently in working together eight years, she and Caldwell had fallen in love and needed some time outside their editor-reporter relationship to test the strength of their commitment. In late fall, they met in Washington, were married, and returned to live in the editor's house at 603 South Tryon. Having known both over the years, the *News and Observer*'s Josephus Daniels wrote that Addie Williams thought Joseph Caldwell "was the greatest man in the world and almost worshipped him. Praise from him, even before their marriage, was to her the crown of life." But the Caldwells' marriage was apparently a stormy one because the two were soon divorced. They were remarried in 1908 and had one child, a daughter named Adelaide.

Replacing Miss Addie on the *Observer* was Isaac Erwin Avery, one of the most talented of the "bright young men" that Caldwell brought to the *Observer*. A twenty-eight-year-old native of Morganton, Avery had played football at Trinity College (now Duke University), read law under his father, who was a justice on the state supreme court, and afterward wrote editorials for the *Morganton Herald*. He spent four years in Shanghai as secretary to the American consul, returned to North Carolina, and served a stint as a reporter for Col. Fred Olds in Raleigh and Greensboro news bureaus. In joining the *Observer* on January 1, 1900, he was following in the footsteps of his uncle Willoughby F. Avery, who was an associate editor for the *Observer* under Colonel Jones.

Tall, muscular, and "as handsome as Apollo," Avery proved to be a charming personality and gifted writer, with a flair for human-interest stories. After a year as city editor, he began writing the *Observer*'s first personal column, under the heading "A Variety of Idle Comment." It appeared on Monday mornings and usually contained notes on city life, sketches of interesting characters, an occasional tale of joy or sorrow, and, when the occasion arose, a barb for political opportunists. Within a short time, the column enjoyed a wide readership.

The *Observer*'s increasing stature and prestige in this period was reflected in the March 23, 1901, issue of *Charity and Children*, a weekly publication of the Baptist Children's Home at Thomasville. Edited by the highly respected Archibald Johnson (father of *Greensboro News* and *Baltimore Sun* editor Gerald W. Johnson), *Charity and Children* called the *Observer* "the best newspaper that has ever been published in North Carolina. . . . Its news service is superb. . . . Its editorial page is a model." The editorials were not always right and in fact were often wrong, the weekly said, but they were "always interesting, original, pungent, practical . . . clear and candid."

In this time of prosperity, the *Charlotte News* was also flourishing, and in May 1903 the *Observer* moved to compete more directly against its rival by starting an afternoon paper of its own, the *Evening Chronicle*, aimed at workers in the area's textile mills. Howard Banks moved over from the *Observer* to become its editor; John Paul Lucas moved from the *Observer* to become one of its reporters. D. A. Tompkins was said to have discouraged the venture, but across the country evening newspapers were gaining great favor among industrial workers, and Caldwell apparently felt the *Observer* needed an entry in the afternoon field, if only for defensive purposes.

To replace Banks, the *Observer* hired Theo F. Kluttz, Jr., of Salisbury, a nephew of Caldwell and a recent graduate of the University at Chapel Hill and its law school. The son of a Democratic congressman from Salisbury, Kluttz would later become the cause of stormy dissension in the *Observer*'s editorial office. To replace Lucas on the *Ob-*

server, Caldwell hired Charles Phillips Russell of Rockingham, another recent graduate of UNC. Russell stayed two years, then moved on to New York and Europe and a career as an award-winning author. He returned to Chapel Hill in 1931 and taught creative writing in the UNC School of Journalism until his retirement in 1955.

With the arrival of the twentieth century, the *Observer* found itself on the unpopular side of two more vexing political issues. The first was the rising clamor for a limit on the labor of women and children in cotton mills and other industries. The second was Prohibition.

The drive for child-labor laws was part of a broad national movement and gained a champion in North Carolina in the election of Governor Aycock. After years of opposing such measures, Caldwell and Tompkins remained ambivalent on the issue. Tompkins wrote several columns suggesting ways in which the labor of women and children might be limited, but his proposals usually lacked an enforcement mechanism. Caldwell wrote editorials disputing claims in national magazines that children in southern cotton mills often worked in wretched conditions. After long and bitter debate, the state legislature of 1903 enacted a child-labor law that imposed only minimal restrictions, but even that was opposed by the *Observer*.

The Prohibition movement had been building since the 1880s. When the 1903 legislature passed a law allowing local referenda on closing county distilleries and local bars, one of the first cities to hold an election was Charlotte. The *Observer* opposed such moves, saying it believed in the maximum personal freedom that was concurrent with good order. The *Charlotte News*, led by its Baptist owner, W. Carey Dowd, favored them. When the referendum was held in July 1904, the drys won and forced the closing of about twenty Charlotte saloons. But a bid to halt the package sale of alcohol was beaten. The *Observer* accepted the closing of the bars philosophically, saying it hoped the results would benefit the city. But it emphasized that it had not changed its mind on the issue.

A brief front-page story on December 19, 1903, showed that the *Observer* was, nevertheless, a herald of promising events. Headlined "A Flying Machine That Flies," it told of Wilbur and Orville Wright's first successful flight by motor-powered airplane. Though the *Observer* was a day late publishing the news, it had the satisfaction of being one of the few newspapers in the country to sense the significance of the event and publish any notice of it. In an editorial a few days later, the *Observer* said, "Nothing could have better accord . . . with the fitness of things than that this success should have been achieved off the coast of North Carolina, the home of the newspaper which has consistently maintained, amidst universal despair, that we would yet fly." It was further evidence of the paper's unflinching faith in technology.

News of the *Observer's* own technical breakthrough came a year later, when the paper's average daily circulation had grown to 6,800. On December 16, 1904, under the headline "A Beautiful Piece of Machinery," the paper announced that after months of waiting it had installed its long-sought "perfecting" press (one capable of printing on both sides of the paper at once and of assembling, folding, and cutting a finished newspaper). The machine, built by R. Hoe and Company, printed from curved plates attached to rapidly turning cylinders. It would give the *Observer* the speed and flexibility to expand its newspaper without any loss in printing quality. It would also allow the paper to print any number of photos on any page, with little worry about reproduction. In short, it equipped the *Observer* to become a modern, metropolitan newspaper.

Caldwell and Tompkins had every reason to take great pride in their accomplishments. In the twelve years since they had rescued the sinking *Chronicle* and changed its name, they had built the *Observer* into a widely admired, highly influential newspaper. It was read in New York and Washington, as well as in Atlanta and Louisville, and was considered one of the leading newspapers of the South. The paper had a highly talented staff, the most modern offices and printing equipment, an expanding readership, and political independence. But its bright prospects were about to be darkened by a series of cruel misfortunes.

CHAPTER 6

THE DARK SIDE OF A BRIGHT ERA
1904–1911

After twelve years of preparation, the *Observer* concluded the year 1904 poised for a period of accelerated growth. It appeared to have reached a takeoff point in its quest to become, in the words of its owners, "a paper comparable in all respects to the principal dailies in the other Southern states." It had a proven leadership, an experienced staff, a modern physical plant, a flourishing community, and, for the moment at least, a measure of political peace. But the paper never generated the momentum needed to attain its goals. Over the next six years, it was beset by a succession of disasters that sapped its energy and hampered its stride. The calamities included the deaths of three talented young writers, the resignation of several others, a bitter printers' strike, a libelous editorial, a tragic fire, and, finally, a series of strokes that crippled Joseph Caldwell and then took his life, stilling the very heart of the paper.

The *Observer's* reverses were in stark contrast to an otherwise optimistic era that ushered in the Age of Progressivism. People began to realize that industrialism and mass production had significantly changed life and human relationships in America, that frontier individualism had given way to a complex organization of interdependent people. The government was called on to do more to balance competing interests and promote economic equity. In the decade from 1904 to 1914, many of the reforms proposed by the Populists were enacted into law by Democrats or Republicans: an income tax, a parcel post, tighter regulation of railroads, the popular election of United States senators, the Australian ballot, and the direct primary. While the free coinage of silver was never approved, a depression provoked by the panic of 1907 helped bring about long-sought banking and currency reforms resulting in the Federal Reserve System. The age was dominated by the image of an exuberant Theodore Roosevelt, grinning, swaggering, and gesturing as he turned the White House into a bully pulpit for social and economic progress.

The era brought continued growth and prosperity to Charlotte. The city welcomed the first motion pictures and a steady increase in the number of automobiles. The Southern Power Company was organized, bringing dramatic changes in the pace and quality of home and industrial life. An electrified railway network, known as "the interurban," was created to link Charlotte with surrounding counties and towns, making the city a regional hub for financial, retail, medical, and managerial services. Mercy Hospital and the Charlotte Sanatorium took their places alongside Presbyterian and St. Peter's as medical centers.

To serve a growing demand for new entertainment and convention facilities, eight concerned citizens invested private money to build a civic auditorium at Fifth and College streets, and other citizens put up the cash to build a major new hotel, the Selwyn, at West Trade and North Church (later the site of the Marriott City Center). A third group raised money to build the city's first "skyscraper," the steel-framed Independence Building that stood twelve stories above Independence Square, symbolizing Charlotte's ambition to become "a big city." On the western edge of town, along the interurban line to Gastonia, E. D. Latta built Lakewood Park, an amusement center that offered facilities for boating, picnics, concerts, plays, and motion pictures. In the 1910s and 1920s, Lakewood was to Charlotte and the surrounding region what the Carowinds theme park would be in the 1970s and 1980s.

All those additions brought new attention, new people, and new growth to Charlotte. After a long struggle, led in part by the *Observer*, the city won the state legislature's permission to expand its corporate limits 12.8 square miles to include Dilworth, Elizabeth Heights, Piedmont Park, Biddleville, and the villages around the Ada, Alpha, Atherton, Charlotte, and Victor cotton mills. In the 1910 census, that extension enabled Charlotte to surpass Wilmington as the state's most populous city. Immediately afterward, in the spring of 1911, development began on Myers Park, an exclusive residential neighborhood that would become a haven for the area's wealthier residents and a model for future real estate development.

While the *Observer* was suffering setbacks, it was also continuing to grow. Its circulation climbed from 6,500 copies a day to nearly 10,000. It obtained its first automobile advertising, began publishing a sports section, received the first photograph transmitted by telegraph (later known as a wirephoto), installed more Linotype machines, started publishing its first comic strip, opened a news bureau in Columbia, South Carolina, and published a pair of record-setting editions, one containing fifty-six pages and another containing a hundred. During a hotly contested race for mayor, the paper carried political advertising for the first time. Over its weekly calendar of religious services, the *Observer* ran a caption that caught the public's imagination and became a slogan for the entire community. It referred to Charlotte as "the City of Churches," an image Charlotteans would cherish until well into the 1960s.

Even so, the paper's achievements were less than its owners had hoped for, as Joseph Caldwell seemed to suggest in a February 1909 editorial marking the seventeenth anniversary of his and Tompkins's ownership. In his review of events since 1892, there was a hint of regret in Caldwell's tone and a tear "for those who had fallen on the field." He noted that the paper's circulation might have been higher and hoped that it would soon reach 15,000 a day, so he and his staff could show their patrons a newspaper that would "really be worth their time." But the years of hard work and abuse were beginning to tell on him, and within a few months, he too would be among the fallen.

The *Observer*'s misfortunes started in late March 1904, when its popular city editor and human-interest columnist, Isaac Erwin Avery, complained of nervousness, insomnia, and a heart flutter that he attributed to smoking too much. He confided to associates that he felt lightheaded. The complaints were unusual, for Avery seemed to be in robust health and had every reason to be in high spirits. He planned to marry an Alabama socialite, the daughter of former Charlotte lawyer Robert D. Johnston, in late April.

His complaints persisted. On Friday night, April 1, he paused in his work on the next morning's *Observer* to get a prescription filled; he then returned to his desk and was still there at 2:30 a.m., writing letters as the rest of the staff departed. When managing editor James Abernethy left for home at 3:30 a.m., Avery said he felt tired and would soon be going to his room in the Southern Manufacturers Club, one floor above. About an hour later Avery was heard entering his bedroom.

When Avery failed to appear at his desk early the next afternoon, no one worried because Avery often overslept. When he had not appeared by 4:00 p.m., a club servant was sent to awaken him. The servant found Avery unconscious and laboring for breath. Beside his bed was a book he had been reading; scattered about the room were his clothes.

Doctors were summoned, along with managing editor Abernethy, business manager John R. Ross, editor J. P. Caldwell, and the Manufacturers Club steward. Restoratives were applied, and Avery rallied temporarily, but his heartbeat grew faint and in a few moments stopped altogether. To those around him, it seemed incredible that so vital and handsome a young man could possibly be dead. Avery was only thirty-two and widely acclaimed as the best newspaper writer in the state.

Sadly the word was spread, first within the *Observer* building, then throughout the city. J. M. Harry conveyed the remains to his undertaking establishment (later Harry and Bryant Company), and calls were made to Avery's family in Morganton, where the funeral would be held the next day. Arrangements were made to have the body lie in state overnight at the West Trade Street home of his aunt, Mrs. Anna Morrison Jackson, widow of Gen. Stonewall Jackson.

The account of Avery's death was the lead story on the *Observer*'s Sunday morning front page, accompanied by telegrams of condolence from around the Carolinas. On the editorial page was a memorial from the grief-stricken Joseph Caldwell, who said: "This writer, in his most composed moments, when his vision is clearest and his capacity for analysis at its best, would not be fit to write of the man who is dead. He loved him too much. What then, now, when the heart is filled to bursting and tears follow the pencil across the paper?"

For several days expressions of sympathy poured in from notables as well as ordinary readers. The paper published many of them. Banker George Stephens assembled a group of businessmen who put up the money to publish a 272-page book of Avery's best "Idle Comments" columns. The book was praised by some prominent critics, including Walter Hines Page, then editor of Doubleday, Page and Company, who wrote: "The deft and kindly touch with which he drew these little pictures of North Carolina life deepens the regret that he did not live to do a sustained piece of work."

The true story of Erwin Avery's death turned out to be even more sorrowful. Newspaper accounts led readers to conclude that he died of natural causes—the stories said "heart failure." But years later close friends acknowledged that Avery's death was a suicide. While he was making plans to marry the Alabama socialite, he got a telegram from a young Chinese woman with whom he had lived in Shanghai, saying she had arrived in San Francisco and was en route to Charlotte. That explained his insomnia: he faced a dilemma that threatened his personal honor. The prescription he had filled the night before was for a sedative called valerian; apparently, Avery took an overdose of it. His tragedy was a little like the story of Madame Butterfly in reverse. The Puccini opera had its first performance in Milan in February of that same year. It reflects the moral code that existed in 1904.

The redeeming part of the story involves proceeds from *Idle Comments*, the book containing Avery's columns. The publishers originally hoped to endow a scholarship in Avery's name at Trinity College (later Duke University), but royalties were insufficient for that. So they invested the money in a fund for buying books on journalistic topics for the college library. As of 1985, the fund, managed by Perkins Library at Duke University, amounted to $5,115 and was earning about $416 a year for book acquisitions. Over its eighty years, the fund had added hundreds of volumes to the university's collection, each one marked with a bookplate honoring the memory of Isaac Erwin Avery.

Avery's death was the first of two losses that staggered the *Observer* that spring. The other was the resignation of Howard A. Banks, Caldwell's trusted associate who for nearly a year had been editing the *Evening Chronicle*. In April Banks resigned to join a small paper in Asheville. The move was a backward step in his editing career and can be explained only as an effort by Banks to avoid a clash with Caldwell over liquor. In his religious views, Banks was a rigid fundamentalist—Caldwell referred to him as "the Preacher"—and was an ardent prohibitionist. As the temperance campaign to close Charlotte bars heated up that spring, he apparently saw a conflict coming over the editorial stand the *Chronicle* would take on the issue. Knowing that both Caldwell and Tompkins disapproved of sumptuary laws such as prohibition, Banks apparently resigned to prevent an ugly confrontation.

Banks returned to Charlotte in 1907 as city editor of the prohibitionist *Charlotte News*. In 1911 he moved to Hickory to edit a paper called the *Democrat*. During World War I, he went to Washington as private secretary to teetotaler Josephus Daniels, the *News and Observer* publisher who was President Wilson's secretary of the Navy. But he fondly remembered his years on Joseph Caldwell's *Observer* and often told his son Dick that they were among the happiest days of his life.

A month after Banks's resignation, the *Observer* lost a trusted member of its business staff. In May 1905, George Crater, who had accompanied Caldwell from Statesville, resigned as advertising manager to become part owner of the *Raleigh Times*. In announcing the resignation, Caldwell wrote that he could not express his reluctance in parting with Crater, whom he credited with much of the *Observer*'s financial success. While the business staff had a capable replacement for Crater, the fact that he was resigning to buy a newspaper in Raleigh was evidence that the *Observer* was losing a man of exceptional ability and ambition. (He would later own the *Greensboro Daily News*.) Crater's successor was John R. Ross, a Charlotte native who had been the *Observer*'s bookkeeper and would soon gain distinction as one of several private investors who undertook to build Charlotte's Civic Auditorium.

Two weeks after Crater's resignation, the *Observer* suffered a different kind of blow by publishing an angry editorial that tarnished its reputation for fairness and objectivity. It was perhaps the meanest, most intemperate editorial Joseph Caldwell ever wrote and one that by all accounts he later regretted. The target of his tirade was the Reverend A. J. McKelway, a nettlesome Presbyterian preacher and social reformer who had stirred up numerous state and local controversies and opposed the *Observer* on several issues.

McKelway came to Charlotte in 1897 from Fayetteville, bringing with him the offices of the weekly *North Carolina Presbyterian* (later named the *Presbyterian Standard*). He was a vigorous crusader and a forceful writer from a distinguished newspapering family. His uncle St. Clair McKelway was editor of New York's *Brooklyn Eagle* from 1884 to 1915, and one of the nation's most respected journalists. Preacher McKelway's son Benjamin became editor of the *Washington Star*. Another son, St. Clair, edited newspapers in Washington, New York, and the Orient and was for many years a writer and editor for the *New Yorker* magazine. (A grandson, also named A. J. McKelway, is a professor of religion at Davidson College.)

In time, the Reverend McKelway became a hero among social reformers for his brave work in championing child-labor laws and other humane causes across the pre–World War I South. But even his admirers had to admit that he often let his zeal for reform and thirst for combat overcome his religious principles. In those times, he abandoned rational argument in favor of assailing the character of his opponents.

McKelway and Joseph Caldwell had several reasons to distrust each other. McKelway was a militant advocate of prohibition, which Caldwell stoutly opposed. He was a fierce proponent of child-labor laws, which Caldwell resisted. He also had challenged the integrity of the North Carolina delegation in Congress and the ethics of Charlotte's mayor and the recorder's court judge, all of whom Caldwell defended. Moreover, in addition to editing the *Presbyterian Standard*, McKelway was editor of the *Charlotte News*, against which Caldwell and the *Observer* were competing.

During the prohibition campaign, McKelway warned Caldwell several times that unless the *Observer* softened its opposition, he would reveal that Caldwell was a heavy drinker and allege that the paper's support for "the liquor crowd" was based on that fact. Caldwell ignored the threat and nothing came of it until months after the Charlotte referendum was over and the drys had won. Then, in campaigning for a statewide prohibition vote, McKelway repeated the threat and attacked Caldwell in the *Presbyterian Standard*. His comments were reprinted in the Raleigh *News and Observer*, another Caldwell tormentor. That was when Caldwell retaliated.

In a long, signed editorial that appeared on June 20, 1905, Caldwell said:

> For twenty-eight years I have been writing newspaper editorials and it has been my fortune within that time that many curs have barked at my heels. . . . The most malignant and indecent of all these dogs is A. J. McKelway, preacher, reformer, editor of a so-called religious paper and common liar. . . . I have made no war on him nor given him occasion for any grievance. On the other hand, readers of the paper he has edited will bear witness to the steadiness and malignancy of his unprovoked war on me and the *Observer*. Lately he has given a new turn to this—a personal turn in the form of sneaking innuendo, with open threats of exposure to be made unless I shape my editorial policy to square with his opinion.
>
> . . . I shall indulge in no debate with the dog, for he is beyond the pale, but for the sake of this editorial of his last week, I step aside for the moment to bestow the kick for which he has so long begged and so richly earned. Newspaper discussion is frequently interesting and frequently enlightening when conducted by gentlemen who respect the rules of propriety, . . . but there can be no debate with this creature which he does not sooner or later drag down to a personal level, impugning the motives of the antagonist. . . . I engage in controversy with no such cattle, but this fellow has evidently mistaken contempt for timidity and has over-stepped the bounds once too often.

After citing several instances in which he said McKelway had publicly lied, Caldwell reached into his store of literary allusions and dredged up the vilest he could find: John Randolph's description of Edward Livingston as "a man of brilliant attainments, but utterly corrupt. Like rotten mackerel by moonlight, he shines and stinks."

Years later, Gerald W. Johnson, a North Carolina–born editorialist for the *Baltimore Sun*, recalled the shock waves raised by that editorial: "The whole state gasped over its breakfast table the next morning, and men in villages a hundred miles from Charlotte went about with a shocked or awed look on their faces. No modern editor would write so furiously about his most hated enemy." In 1905, when newspapers were the only source of news and editors like Caldwell were trying to give them an aura of authority and respectability, the McKelway editorial was an even greater breach of professional standards. It was a throwback to the old days of personal journalism when a newspaper was considered a weapon with which to club the opposition. Even Red Buck Bryant, Caldwell's pupil and lifelong admirer, conceded that the McKelway editorial was a mistake.

Yet the editorial became a celebrated piece of *Observer* lore, perhaps because it was so widely read and discussed. It fit the old southern ideal of defending one's personal honor, as in answering a challenge to a duel. Requests for extra copies must have come in by the hundreds because *Observer* reprinted it in a little four-page pamphlet. The blast was clearly provoked and devastating in its power. For years afterward it was cited by newspaper people as a fine example of editorial billingsgate.

The Reverend Mr. McKelway did not find it amusing. Sensing the harm it could do, he sued for libel, seeking damages of $50,000 from the *Observer*, $25,000 from Joseph Caldwell, and $25,000 from the *Evening Chronicle*, which had reprinted the editorial. When the case came to trial, a long list of prominent Charlotteans were summoned to testify for Caldwell and the *Observer* about the accuracy of the editorial. But after a jury was selected, attorneys for the two sides got together in the judge's chambers and privately arranged a settlement. The *Observer* pleaded guilty to libel, and McKelway was awarded damages of five cents, which, as someone suggested, was about what the court thought the preacher's reputation was worth. But for McKelway, it was a swaggering victory, for it gave him the upper hand over Caldwell and enabled him to discredit the *Observer* yet another time. During the 1908 campaign for statewide prohibition, the paper had little to say on the subject, except that it was opposed, believing that "a man who prohibits himself [against liquor] was doing very well without undertaking to prohibit his neighbor." The paper characterized the prohibition movement as "organized intimidation."

Among all those untoward events came a few positive developments to sustain the *Observer*'s morale and prestige. One was the hiring of John Charles McNeill as a successor to Erwin Avery. McNeill was a tall, bony, but strikingly handsome country boy who grew up near Laurinburg. He earned a bachelor's and a master's degree at Wake Forest College with honors in English, and taught there one year. He taught another year at Mercer College in Macon, Georgia, then returned to North Carolina, got an attorney's license, and was elected to the 1903 legislature. But the law, politics, and McNeill never harmonized; he was more interested in poetry than polemics. Increasingly his poems began to appear in national magazines.

Red Buck Bryant, who had replaced Avery as the *Observer* city editor, heard about McNeill and visited him at his Laurinburg law office, a second-story cubicle that housed as many wild animals— McNeill befriended squirrels, raccoons, 'possums—as it did law books. Red Buck recalled finding McNeill "with his back to his desk and his long legs propped high on the wall. He was reading. I tapped him on the shoulder and asked, 'How's the law business?' He said, 'The law business is all right, but I've got no clients.'"

Red Buck said he told McNeill that *Observer* editor Joseph Caldwell wanted to see him about a job that might pay him for writing poetry and almost anything else that interested him. To McNeill that sounded better than practicing law, so he called on Caldwell and was signed on as a feature writer without desk or deadline.

Often McNeill was sent to cover a story about one thing, perhaps a local house fire, and came back hours later with a human-interest tale about something entirely different. That upset some of his editors, but not Joseph Caldwell, who loved "the Scotsman" and his poetry about country life along North Carolina's Lumber River. McNeill had a poet's ear as well as a reporter's eye, and his verse caught the sounds of creeks and crickets, horses and hounds, and the soft sibilance of Negro dialect. His poems were published in the *Observer* under the heading "Songs Merry and Sad." That became the title of McNeill's first volume of poetry, published in 1905. A year later he published a second volume, *Lyrics from Cotton Land*. Not all his poems were of peaceful, country scenes. Many were social commentaries with a sharp bite. Among his most famous was a bittersweet portrait of the southern Negro at the dawn of segregation. Titled "Mr. Nigger," it said:

I cannot see, if you were dead,
Mr. Nigger,
How orators could earn their bread,
Mr. Nigger,
For they could never hold the crowd,
Save they abused you long and loud
As being a dark and threatening cloud,
Mr. Nigger.

In addition to McNeill, the *Observer* was hiring others, including James W. Atkins of Asheville, a graduate of Emory and Henry College in Virginia; Julian S. Miller of the Sardis community south of Charlotte, a recent graduate of Erskine College in South Carolina; Victor L. Stephenson of Statesville, a Phi Beta Kappa graduate of UNC–Chapel Hill; and T. W. Chambliss of Wadesboro, a former Baptist minister who took over Red Buck Bryant's job as traveling sales agent and feature writer.

All four men would go on to exceptional careers in journalism. Atkins resigned in 1906 to buy the *Gastonia Gazette* and build it into a successful daily. Julian Miller would become the *Observer*'s first sports editor, editor of the *Evening Chronicle*, editor of the *Charlotte News*, and finally editor of the *Observer*. Victor Stephenson would rise through the *Observer*'s ranks and go on to a newspaper career in New York. T. W. Chambliss would hold several newspaper jobs before becoming press secretary to O. Max Gardner in the 1920 gubernatorial campaign against Charlotte's Cameron Morrison.

The paper hired another poet in those years, though at the time few people recognized him as such. He was James Larkin Pearson, a lean, knobby son of the Wilkes County mountains who worked about a year as a printer in the *Observer* composing room. Pearson later wrote and published five volumes of poetry and in 1953, at age seventy-four, was named poet laureate of North Carolina. He died in 1981 at age 101.

In the 1904–6 period, the *Observer* also had the satisfaction of seeing Charlotte at last invest in public parks, something the newspaper had been urging the city to do for more than ten years. The paper's campaign began in 1893, when the panic deprived developer E. D. Latta of cash to sustain his development of Dilworth. Latta offered to sell the city Latta Park, which then covered a larger area than the modern Latta Park. The *Observer* approved the idea and wrote a series of editorials urging the city to accept Latta's offer—or at least negotiate with him over the price. In addition, the paper published interviews with business leaders, many of whom indicated that they also approved of the park purchase. This was at the height of the "city beautiful" movement in the United States, and cities across the country were becoming conscious of the need to preserve park land and green space as essential elements of the urban landscape. But the mayor and the city aldermen thought Charlotte had more pressing needs and turned Latta down. When business conditions improved, Latta withdrew his proposal.

The *Observer*, editor Caldwell, and copublisher D. A. Tompkins did not let the matter drop. They continued to publish editorials pointing out that "all cities of consequence own their own parks." Urban communities had to have parks to make up for the loss of recreational opportunities their citizens once enjoyed on farms. Parks helped cities maintain a healthy moral and economic climate and attracted new business; the larger the city, the greater the need for parks, the paper argued.

Out of discussions stimulated by those editorials came the formation of the city's Park and Tree Commission (later the Park and Recreation Commission), with D. A. Tompkins as chairman and banker George Stephens and lawyer Heriot Clarkson as key members. Tompkins, Stephens, and Clarkson persuaded the city to convert the marshy ravine east of Sugar Creek into a large park. Much of the land had been given to the city earlier by Col. William R. Myers for use as a municipal water works. Tompkins and Stephens got several property owners, including Stephens's own land development company, to donate adjacent land for park purposes. When city aldermen approved the project in 1904, the *Observer* cheered: "It will unquestionably prove a blessing to the community." Little did anyone realize how big that blessing would become.

Beyond its recreational value, the project brought the city two other benefits. One was John Nolen, a man who left a lasting imprint on the city. At the time, Nolen was a student in the School of Landscape Architecture at Harvard University. When Tompkins, Stephens, and Clarkson solicited ideas for park development from landscape architects, Nolen's responses impressed them the most, and they commissioned him to design what became Independence Park, Charlotte's first public playground.

Nolen's work and manner proved to be so pleasing that a few years later, when Stephens was preparing to develop the cotton farms of his father-in-law, John S. Myers, into a model residential community, he invited Nolen back to design the area known as Myers Park. The graceful landscaping and other amenities that Nolen embodied in that project have enabled Myers Park to retain much of its elegance despite the growth that has since hemmed it in on all sides. Myers Park became a model for other suburban developments and even after seventy-five years remains one of Charlotte's most prestigious neighborhoods.

While working on the Myers Park project, Nolen introduced Charlotteans to the benefits of comprehensive city planning. At the suggestion of Stephens and others, including the *Observer*, he conducted public lectures on landscaping, architecture, and urban design and urged citizens to adopt a comprehensive plan for making Charlotte a more gracious city. His plan, completed about 1916 or 1917, encouraged the landscaping of creek bottoms as park sites and, anticipating the age of the automobile, called for ringing the city with a series of landscaped boulevards. The plan was never acted on: George Stephens got busy with other projects; the *Observer* fell into the hands of different owners; and Nolen went on to found the nation's first professional organization for planners, the American City Planning Institute, established in 1917. In the early 1960s, when Charlotte did get around to drawing a comprehensive plan, it borrowed several elements from Nolen's 1916 blueprint, notably "greenway" parks along creek lands and circumferential highways.

The second benefit offered by Independence Park was its location. Over the years one segment after another of the park's original tract was diverted to other public uses. In 1912, one strip of it became the site for Elizabeth School. In 1929, another section became the site for the Armory Auditorium (later renamed Park Center). In 1935–36, a third part became the site for Memorial Stadium. And in 1947–1950, a fourth section became the roadbed for Independence Boulevard. Even after those intrusions, the park continues to offer Charlotte children and adults a pleasant haven from the brick and asphalt of their urban surroundings.

In the midst of reporting the park's development in 1905, the *Observer* experienced another adversity that diminished much of its joy over the park success. On September 26, the union printers employed by the *Observer*, the Observer Printing House, the *Evening Chronicle*, the *Charlotte News*, and other local printing houses went on strike for an eight-hour day. The strike, part of a national drive coordinated by the American Federation of Labor, grew ugly and bitter. The Charlotte companies employing union printers anticipated the strike, organized ahead of time, and agreed on the settlement they would accept. They elected Joseph Caldwell their spokesman.

When the printers sought contracts for an eight-hour day at the same wages previously paid for nine hours, Caldwell turned them down, and the strike was on.

By pooling their nonunion manpower, the three newspapers continued to publish, though for several days their pages were cluttered with unfamiliar typefaces. Caldwell apologized for his paper's looks and errors and for not answering his mail or keeping regular office hours. Apparently he had gone back to setting type, as had other ex-printers on the three newspaper staffs. In an *Observer* editorial on the morning after the strike began, Caldwell claimed that the wage difference between eight hours and nine hours represented the margin of profit for many printing houses and that owners of those houses could not pay the union wage and remain in business. He also contended that most printers at the *Observer*, the *Evening Chronicle*, and the *Charlotte News* already worked only eight hours though they were being paid for nine.

On the strike's second day, an *Observer* editorial appealed to the striking printers to desert their union and return to work, claiming the printers had no grievance with their employers but were caught in an organizational test of strength. The editorial warned that printers who did not return to work would be replaced as fast as possible by nonunion workers. Obviously, the several employers had decided to use the strike as an opportunity to break the printers' union.

Within a few days, as nonunion printers were hired, the *Observer* resumed its normal appearance and began advertising job openings for young men willing to go to school to learn the operation of Linotype machines. At the same time, there were fights outside the newspaper offices and at least one serious knifing as strikers threatened workers who crossed the picket line. Within three weeks, the newspapers had restaffed their print shops and resumed normal operations. The strike was over, the strikers were out of work, the union was broken. The union label disappeared from the *Observer*'s editorial page masthead.

Charlotte was a test case for the eight-hour campaign, and the stakes were very high. A victory for eight-hour advocates at the *Observer* would have set a precedent for other industries in the region. Members of the National Association of Manufacturers wrote D. A. Tompkins urging him and his fellow employers to "stand pat" against the American Federation's demands. Throughout the strike, the *Observer* ran editorials from other newspapers that cheered the

Charlotte papers for standing firm. Once the showdown ended in Charlotte, similar strikes broke out in other cities. The *Observer* sent experienced printers to help struck newspapers continue publishing.

As the dust from the strike settled, the *Observer* resumed its normal reporting and noted that Charlotteans were flocking to the stage version of Thomas Dixon's novel *The Clansman*, a popular—and blatantly racist—drama that would reappear ten years later as *The Birth of a Nation*, the first of the great movie epics. Within a year, the first nickelodeon—offering scenes of New York filmed from the top of the Flat Iron Building—was showing in town. Charlotteans were also excited by the visit of President Theodore Roosevelt, who spoke before 20,000 people jammed into the block-long Vance Park on West Fourth Street, behind the United States Mint and Post Office. Though the *Observer* had opposed Roosevelt in the 1904 election, it warmly welcomed him to town and praised the literary quality of his public speeches. The *Observer* also proudly reported that its own John Charles McNeill had won the Patterson Cup for producing the state's best literature. During a speaking engagement in Raleigh, President Roosevelt made the presentation to McNeill.

The *Observer* added more Linotypes, hired W. A. Hildebrand as its Washington correspondent, helped promote the opening of the Hotel Selwyn, which drew crowds of visitors to the city, and reported the wreckage left by the San Francisco earthquake in April 1906. For days, the earthquake story filled two and three columns of the paper's front page. The editors also paused in April 1906 to boast that its semiweekly edition, published on Tuesdays and Fridays, was being mailed to more than 5,000 subscribers.

But sorrow continued to stalk the newspaper. This time the victim was James C. Abernethy, the nervous, pacing, determined ex-printer who, following the example of Joseph Caldwell, had risen through the ranks to become the managing editor. In the summer of 1905 he developed a dry cough and the night sweats that signaled the onset of tuberculosis, the dreaded "white plague." He was only thirty-one and had been married but nine months. His doctors ordered him to bed for ten weeks of complete rest. He returned to work in late fall and, taking things easy, appeared to be gathering strength. When the first Linotype machines arrived at the *Charleston Post*, he went down there to oversee their installation and train *Post* printers to operate them. When printer strikes for an eight-hour day hit other newspapers, he went to organize nonunion composing rooms. But in August 1906, he suffered a hemorrhage and was rushed to doctors

in Baltimore. They prescribed more rest, this time at the TB sanatorium in Asheville. But it was too late; the infection had spread to
both lungs, and within a month Jim Abernethy, Joseph Caldwell's
beloved "Perturbid Spirit," was dead.

Perhaps because he saw in Abernethy so much of himself, Caldwell had trouble writing the editorial tribute that appeared on September 2. The piece was heavy with grief and obviously labored over.
It described Abernethy as the paper's pusher, fixer, and organizer,
the man who made the machinery run and the presses start on time.
He had learned the plant routine from mechanical shop to editorial
office, and mastered every job in between, even writing editorials.
Twice in the obituary, as if in torment, Caldwell wrote the same sentence: "We don't know how we shall get along without him."

In truth, the *Observer* under Caldwell never recovered from Abernethy's loss. A week later, R. W. Vincent, a former reporter who had
been moved up to news editor, was named Abernethy's successor as
managing editor, but no other staff member could elicit from Caldwell and Tompkins, or from the rest of the editorial and mechanical
force, the respect and trust Abernethy commanded. In the hard days
ahead, Vincent would see his authority undermined and his orders
countermanded. Abernethy's young widow, the former Margaret
Kelly, would soon join the *Evening Chronicle* as a society reporter
and would become society editor of the *Observer*, a position she held
until 1952.

In the months that the *Observer* was reporting Abernethy's sick-
ness and death, the paper was also introducing three important new
features. One was its first Sunday comic: "Buster Brown and His
Dog Tige," drawn by R. F. Outcault. It was a big, clean strip about a
precocious ten-year-old boy who lived in a well-to-do New York suburb. The strip was highly successful nationally and important socially, for it held up to a generation of young people an example of
what life could be like among the rich and privileged—something
similar to what television was to do in the 1950s. "Buster Brown"
was Outcault's second major success. His first was "The Yellow Kid,"
a mischievous boy who lived at the other end of the economic ladder.
It was "The Yellow Kid" that symbolized the New York journalism
wars between William Randolph Hearst and Joseph Pulitzer and
gave sensational newspapering the nickname "yellow journalism."

The *Observer*'s second new feature was a daily column called
"This Day in History," a compendium of events that occurred in
Charlotte five years, ten years, and twenty-five years earlier. Beyond
eliciting simple nostalgia, such columns were an important service

to newspaper readers, especially in a time of unsettling growth and change. They bridged the past and the present and strengthened the city's identity, stability, and sense of community.

The third new feature was the designation of the first column of page three as the daily sports section, a place readers could turn to for news of baseball, football, golf, tennis, boxing, horseracing, and other organized athletics. Sports sections had been gaining popularity in newspapers since William Randolph Hearst introduced them in the *New York Journal* in 1895. Organized spectator sports were a product of the nation's urbanized, industrial society, and the *Observer*'s introduction of a sports page—one of the first in the South—was another measure of Charlotte's urban growth.

About a week after the introduction of those features, the *Observer* added another: a full page of women's fashion news, complete with illustrations. The page became a regular feature of the Sunday paper and attracted young women to newspapers in the same way that sports pages attracted young men.

As the year 1907 opened, the *Observer* lent its editorial support to a drive to extend Charlotte's city limits. Several bills to accomplish that were introduced in the state legislature. The *Observer* favored those that would bring into the city all the urbanized area on the city's fringe. But city aldermen and Mecklenburg delegates to the state legislature (including Rep. Carey Dowd, publisher of the *Charlotte News*) were under pressure to take a more conservative approach by extending the boundary one mile from Independence Square in all directions. The *Observer* complained that such an arbitrary extension would take in considerable farmland and leave out much industrial property. Debate over the several approaches became very heated.

The final bill was a compromise that took in less than the *Observer* recommended but included most of the urban area—though it left out several politically sensitive mills. Even so, it more than doubled the size of Charlotte to make it the most populous city in the state. Under the ward system, it also increased the board of aldermen to fourteen and later to twenty-two members—the largest government Charlotte ever had. Within a few months, D. A. Tompkins and the *Observer* were spearheading a drive for a smaller, "more efficient" commission form of government then gaining popularity across the South.

Even as these events were occurring, the *Observer* was encountering more tragedy. At 1:30 a.m. on September 9, 1907, as the paper's staff was rushing to complete the first edition of a Monday morning paper, machinist Walter Adams discovered a fire in the third-floor storage room. He ran downstairs to spread the alarm, and work stopped as printers rushed to get a fire hose to the blaze. But water pressure within the building was too low, and flames were soon licking through the electric wires, cutting off power to machines and dousing lights. As the fire alarm was sounded, the printers covered their equipment with tarpaulins and ran for their lives.

By the time firemen arrived from the city fire station (behind City Hall at Fifth and North Tryon), the flames were roaring through most of the third floor print shop and leaping into windows of the Observer Printing House on the fourth floor. Within minutes most of the fourth floor was an inferno and the printing house machinery was in ruins. For a while it looked as if the entire newspaper plant might be lost. The flames could be seen all over town, and spectators soon filled Tryon Street in front of the newspaper office.

With quick work, firemen brought the blaze under control and by 3:00 a.m. had it extinguished. The newspaper's offices and much of its printing plant had been spared, but damage from heat and water prevented their immediate use. Black smoke was still rolling through most of the building.

Publisher Carey Dowd of the *Charlotte News* arrived and offered his printing facilities, which were directly across Tryon Street from the *Observer* office. Caldwell accepted the courtesy, and printers began lugging heavy printing forms and press plates down stairs and across Tryon into the *News*'s print shop. About an hour later, a disheveled-looking edition of the morning *Observer* was printed on presses of the *Charlotte News*.

As *Observer* workmen resumed their tasks, they noticed the absence of George Wilson, the bright, friendly fifteen-year-old deaf and dumb boy who hung around the composing room and occasionally ran errands for printers and reporters. He was not an employee of the paper but often slept on stacks of mats stored on the third floor. Editorial writer Theo Kluttz recalled seeing the boy pop his head into the editorial office at 9:30 p.m., but nobody had seen him since. A search party was sent to comb the third-floor ruins, but the heat and smoke were too intense. About an hour later, the searchers found Wilson's seared body slumped under a blackened window, as if in prayer. Apparently he had been unable to alert anyone that he was there.

The building and equipment were insured and could be replaced, but the boy's death was a heavy blow. Though he had lived with his mother in Mint Hill, the boy had spent most of his time at the newspaper. The newsmen and printers took up a collection to buy a suit in which he could be buried. When firemen speculated that the boy had started the fire by dropping a match or a lighted cigarette as he dozed off, Joseph Caldwell refused to believe it. "If he was the cause of the fire, he did not intend to be, and it seems impossible for him to have caused it," Caldwell wrote. Later, in an editorial praising firemen for saving the newspaper plant and thanking Dowd for making the *News*'s facilities available, Caldwell turned at last to the death of the boy and all but sobbed, "We cannot bring ourselves to dwell upon the lamentable tragedy of the morning. Poor little boy!"

The boy's death was the first of two calamities that befell the paper in 1907. A more damaging loss came six weeks later. In mid-September, John Charles McNeill complained of feeling tired and went to his parents' farmhouse near Laurinburg for a long rest. But he never seemed to get any better. His strength continued to decline, and on October 15 he slipped into a coma. About midafternoon on October 17, he quietly died, apparently of leukemia. He was thirty-three.

Tributes poured in from readers throughout the region. McNeill's poetry had touched something deep within the Carolina soul, and thousands of people grieved with members of the *Observer* family. His colleagues on the newspaper apparently had sensed the end was near, for they had prepared an editorial tribute in advance. It was published the same day as the news story announcing his death. The editorial cited McNeill's naturalness, sincerity, modesty, and simplicity, and called him "the greatest genius our state has yet produced." It mourned that he "died before his time . . . when his genius had budded and was just coming into full flower. There is no guessing what he might have accomplished." That estimate of him was shared by many others, including Josephus Daniels of Raleigh's *News and Observer*.

By now Joseph P. Caldwell and Daniel A. Tompkins had every reason to believe the fates were cruelly arrayed against them. Much of what they had built during the difficult decade of the 1890s was being destroyed by one misfortune after another. Though other enterprises suffered from death and personnel turnover, the *Observer*'s losses had been unusually severe. In three and a half years, they had lost five of their most gifted staff members, had their credibility challenged, and seen their modern plant heavily damaged by fire. Now in their mid-fifties and fatigued from strenuous activities of their own, they faced a long rebuilding process.

Since their purchase of the *Observer*, the nature of the newspaper business had changed—indeed, Caldwell and Tompkins had helped to change it. Newspapers were no longer personal journals, but complex institutions with large staffs and larger community responsibilities. Good newspapers could not be built or rebuilt overnight. They required not only money, talent, and machinery, but also time and a patient blending of personal chemistries. In addition to a collegial relationship, they had to establish a sense of place and an atmosphere of mutual trust, as well as a tacit understanding about what constitutes good judgment, acceptable taste, and the public good. Those things came only with time and experience. With each departure of a key staff member and the introduction of another, a newspaper lost some of the trust and judgment that had been achieved and had to build anew, at least in a small measure. After losing staff members of the quality of Erwin Avery, Howard Banks, George Crater, Jim Abernethy, and John Charles McNeill, rebuilding the *Observer* must have seemed a formidable challenge. As it turned out, there was too little time for such an undertaking. The health of both men would soon break, leaving the paper without strong leadership.

As 1908 approached, though the Bryan tide was rising for one last surge at the presidency, Joseph Caldwell resumed his active participation in Democratic politics. In March 1908 he attended a Raleigh meeting of the state Democratic Executive Committee and was warmly received, his apostasy of 1896 and 1900 about forgiven. In June the Democrats were to hold their state convention in Charlotte, the opening event in the new, privately built Civic Auditorium at Fifth and College streets. Caldwell looked forward to playing host to many of his old friends.

The *Observer* was also writing editorials in support of Asheville lawyer Locke Craig's nomination for governor. His opponent was William W. Kitchin of Roxboro, a Bryanite from the party's liberal wing. Kitchin had been making speeches sharply critical of the state's industrialists. He usually included in his remarks a few choice denunciations of the *Charlotte Observer*, which he said was the state's chief spokesman for the oligarchs who owned the mills.

The Craig-Kitchin showdown in Charlotte that summer proved to be a bitter clash that would leave its mark on North Carolina's Democratic politics for the next forty years. An east-west struggle developed at the convention, pitting the candidate of "the people" (Kitchin) against the favorite of "the machine" (Craig). What was scheduled to be a two-day convention turned into a four-day war. On the sixty-first roll call, Kitchin finally won the nomination, but not before a fistfight disrupted the proceedings. (The fighting stopped when Durham industrialist Julian S. Carr leaped to the stage and began singing the state song, "Carolina, Carolina, Heaven's blessings attend her. . . . ")

The experience taught Democratic leaders two important lessons. One was that if the party hoped to remain united against the Republicans, it would have to find a means of avoiding such divisions. The result was a gentleman's agreement to rotate the governorship between east and west every four years. After the nomination of Kitchin from the east, it was the west's turn, and in 1912 Locke Craig won the nomination without opposition. The rotation continued until 1948, when Kerr Scott of Haw River in the west ran and won in what was supposed to be the east's turn. The second lesson was that to promote peace and avoid "machine" versus "people" divisions, the party would have to stop choosing its nominees in convention and adopt the direct primary used in most other southern states. In the primary, the candidate with the most popular appeal— as opposed to the one with the most party influence—was likely to be the nominee. North Carolina adopted the direct primary in 1915.

The nomination of Kitchin, who had continued to blast the *Observer* right up to the convention, presented editor Caldwell with another dilemma. Would he bolt the party again and support an industrialist candidate for governor (many people were urging Daniel Tompkins to run), or would he swallow his pride, support Kitchin, and stay with the party? Apparently there was never any question in Caldwell's mind. On the morning after Kitchin's victory, the *Observer* carried an editorial saying:

We take off our hats to W. W. Kitchin. It doesn't make any difference whether we were for him or against him before; we are all for him now. . . . We have taken our chances in a council of our peers and whether we are gainers or losers we must abide by the result. . . . To none is this so difficult as it is to *The Observer*. From July of last year up to two weeks ago, from every stump, in every congressional district, . . . he has attacked by innuendo the integrity of this paper, when all the time having perfect confidence in the honor of its editor, whom he has known years upon years. . . . If, therefore, this paper can support Mr. Kitchin, anybody else can.

The state Democratic convention was the first of several major conventions held in the Civic Auditorium that summer, marking Charlotte's emergence as a convention center. After the Democrats came the North Carolina Press Association, the Southern Newspaper Publishers Association, the North Carolina Retail Merchants Association, and the state teacher organization. The Civic Auditorium and the new Selwyn Hotel were achieving results the *Observer* had predicted in promoting their construction. The meetings brought thousands of people to Charlotte for their first look at the city and its new commercial prominence. The steel skeleton of the uncompleted Independence Building at Independence Square promised even greater things in the future.

But the auditorium did not prove to be profitable, and the eight private citizens, including *Observer* business manager John Ross, who put up the money to build it were soon in bankruptcy court. The *Observer* wrote editorials praising the arena, pointing out the good things it had done for Charlotte, and urging the city government to buy it in the name of all the people. Finally, after much vacillation, the aldermen did buy the building, assuring that Charlotte would remain an entertainment center for the region.

Charlotte was proud of its new verve as a convention and business center and invited President William Howard Taft to town in 1909 to help it celebrate. The president's visit coincided with the opening of the Independence Building (originally named the Realty Building) and the May 20 anniversary of the Mecklenburg Declaration of Independence. The *Observer* promoted both events and invited a number of press notables to attend, including Maj. James C. Hemphill, the Charleston *News and Courier* editor who had often dismissed the Mecklenburg Declaration as a "myth." Hemphill and Caldwell admired each other and often humorously crossed editorial swords over the Mecklenburg Declaration and other issues.

On March 1, Caldwell and the *Observer* paused to mark an anniversary of their own. In a long editorial attributed to "the garrulity of old age," Caldwell reflected on the paper's progress in the seventeen years since he and Tompkins bought it in 1892. Back then, he recalled, the paper contained only four pages, six columns to the page; by 1909 it usually contained ten to twelve pages on weekdays and twenty to twenty-six pages on Sundays, with seven columns to the page. He added: "The circulation then was 1,100; the daily average now is 9,813. Its paper bill then was $1,600 per year; it is now $16,200. The mechanical payroll then was $95 per week; it is now

$392. The salary list then called for $75 per week; now, for $573. . . . "

The review acknowledged that the paper's unpopular political stands had limited its influence and impeded its growth. It also noted the heavy toll recently taken by death. But the review ended on an optimistic note, promising growth in size and quality, "if God continues merciful and things go well."

Unfortunately, neither occurred. Six days later, on Sunday afternoon, March 7, as Caldwell returned to his office about 4:00 p.m. and began his editorial writing routine, he felt a "peculiar sensation" in his right hand and arm and down his right side. Instinctively he got up to see if walking around would help any, and fell heavily to the floor. His colleagues rushed to his aid and summoned Dr. E. C. Register, who happened to be nearby. Dr. Register examined him and said Caldwell had suffered a slight stroke involving only the sensory nerves on the right side of the body. It appeared to be a paralysis of the touch, not of the muscles, and was probably temporary. The motor centers did not seem to be damaged, he said.

The editor was taken to Charlotte Sanatorium , a private, for-profit hospital that Tompkins and other stockholders had built at West Seventh and North Church streets. Dr. Register said he thought Caldwell might be up and about in a few days. A brief story to that effect appeared on an inside page of the Monday paper under the terse headline, "Mr. Caldwell Ill."

The paper carried no further stories on his condition, but over the next several weeks there was a steady stream of personal notes from D. A. Tompkins to Caldwell's beloved sister "Miss Jennie" in Statesville, keeping her informed about the editor's progress. At one point Tompkins said Caldwell had regained much of the use of his right arm and leg and was able to stand for a while. He also assured her that doctors were pleased that his speech was not affected, as it usually was in severe strokes. But despite reports of progress, Caldwell remained a patient in the sanatorium. Obviously, he was seriously ill.

Before a week had passed, Red Buck Bryant wrote Tompkins from Washington, where Bryant was the *Observer*'s correspondent, that he feared Caldwell's condition was worse than anyone had admitted. He offered to come home and assume any editing chores that needed doing. Two days later Tompkins replied, "We cannot tell how serious this stroke of paralysis is," and predicted that Caldwell might be out of action at least two or three months. It would be midsummer before doctors would know "whether he can return [to work] and how fully he can return," Tompkins said.

By late March Caldwell was recuperating at home, and by early April he was dropping by the office to answer his mail. He had not regained sufficient use of his right hand to resume writing but had recovered enough to join in the welcome for President Taft. During the May 20 celebration, he posed for a picture with Major Hemphill, standing on the bronze Mecklenburg Declaration marker that was embedded in Independence Square. In June he attended the summer meeting of the North Carolina Press Association in Hendersonville, where his daughter Adelaide played with Jonathan Daniels, son of Raleigh editor Josephus Daniels. But the feuding fathers were still not on speaking terms.

In the meantime, Tompkins, whose own health was precarious— he had suffered several falls and a stroke that left his right arm palsied and was walking with a cane—had begun to assume more of the day-to-day direction of the newspaper. He wrote business manager John Ross, managing editor R. W. Vincent, and associate editor Theo Kluttz several times a week, giving them specific instructions on business and editorial matters. He also got letters from newsmen on other papers, offering to take over Joseph Caldwell's duties. In time, his instructions began to take on a peremptory tone, as if he felt his employees were not responding faithfully. The truth was his employees were arguing among themselves about who had what authority over the newspaper.

Sometime during the summer, perhaps in late July, Caldwell suffered a more severe stroke that left him not only paralyzed but also speechless. That news brought an immediate visit from Red Buck Bryant, who called at the Caldwell home but was turned away by Caldwell's wife, Miss Addie, who said doctors had ordered no visitors. On August 10, Addie wrote Bryant to apologize and revealed Caldwell's true condition. "We just have to wait and see if his physical nature is strong enough to win out," she said. She described his ailment as "aphasia." That is, he was conscious and knew what he wanted to say but couldn't make his mouth and tongue form the words. "He . . . talks in a language all his own," she said. "It just breaks my heart to look at him."

Caldwell never got much better. That fall he was taken to visit the state mental hospital at Morganton, where for many years he had been the unpaid chairman of the board of directors. Later, at his request, it was arranged for him to board at the home of Dr. John McCampbell, the hospital's superintendent, whom Caldwell trusted and admired. Sensing that his career was over, Caldwell sought a quiet retreat. After his newspaper office, the place he loved most was the hospital at Morganton. His wife moved into the Central Hotel and went back to work as society editor for the rival *Charlotte News*.

While Caldwell was at Morganton, he was visited by Josephus Daniels, his old nemesis from Raleigh. Daniels recalled the encounter in his memoirs:

> We had not spoken for years. . . . But, visiting Morganton, I went over to the hospital to call on him. He could speak, but not easily. I did not know how he would receive me, but I recalled our early friendship and deplored the break that had come. I didn't wish him to pass away without knowing that I had for him the same feeling I had had in the early days before political differences brought estrangement. He received me very cordially. We talked about the delightful visits I had made in his home when we were both editors of weekly papers and we parted with friendly greetings. Even before his illness, his last years in Charlotte were sad ones. He had literally burned the candle at both ends and his physical vitality was broken down. . . . His ability had been the great asset of the paper.

In September 1911, Caldwell dictated a letter on state hospital stationery asking "My dear Mr. Tompkins" to advise him "how much money there will be for my son and two daughters each. I am very anxious about the matter." Tompkins replied, "Your children have the stock in The Observer Co. which you gave them [30 percent of the company]. . . . Everything is as you left it as far as stock is concerned."

The last of his old colleagues on the *Observer* to see him alive was Wade Harris, then editor of the *Evening Chronicle* and, like Caldwell, a man who had entered journalism as a boy printer. Harris visited Caldwell in October 1911 and found him waiting for death. Caldwell said he was "marking time, marking time, Wade. Waiting, waiting for the sun to set."

After more than two years of paralysis and despair, Caldwell died on November 22, 1911, at age fifty-eight. His colleagues on the *Observer* published a special edition in his memory. It was filled with tributes from the humble and the great, including President Taft. It credited him with building the *Observer* into a great newspaper. D. A. Tompkins called him "the best newspaper editor in America." But his greatest tributes came from the printers, reporters, and editors who had worked with him. They revered him and spent the rest of their lives telling stories about him—about his honesty, courage, fairness, sense of humor, and gentleness.

Later, in ceremonies in Raleigh dedicating his portrait to the people of the state, Rufus R. Clark, who succeeded Caldwell as editor and publisher of the *Statesville Landmark*, recalled Caldwell's break with the Democratic party in 1900 and credited him with liberating the North Carolina press from political bondage. Until then, newspapers were mere appendages of their political parties, and no editor dared to criticize the candidate or platform of his party, no matter what he privately thought. Caldwell's action in opposing the Democrats, Clark said, "was startling; it was without precedent among us, and the storm of criticism and abuse was violent and incessant. But he quailed not before the storm. . . . Joe Caldwell demonstrated that a newspaper could be independent in North Carolina, and he gave liberty to the press. Today in North Carolina the newspaper editor who speaks his own mind with freedom owes that freedom, whether he knows it or not, to that prince of editors, J. P. Caldwell."

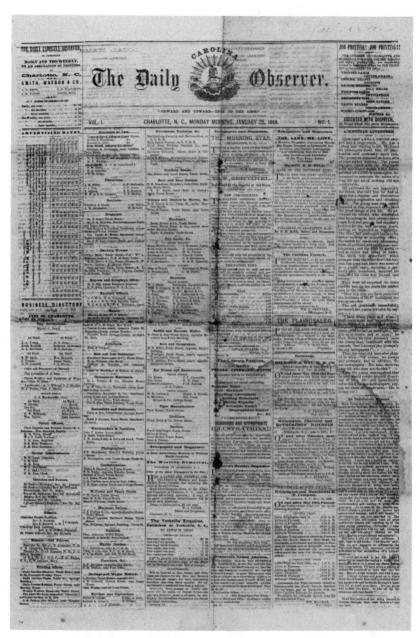

Front page of first Daily Carolina Observer, *January 25, 1869.*

Charles R. Jones.

Artist's sketch of Charlotte in early 1870s, looking south on Tryon Street across Independence Square.

Oates Hall, the two-story building at East Trade and North College streets in which the Charlotte Chronicle *began business in 1886.*

Observer *offices from October 1893, until December 1916. The lighted sign on roof was Charlotte's first.*

Daniel A. Tompkins, Observer *publisher, 1892–1914.*

Joseph Pearson Caldwell, Observer *editor, 1892–1911.*

Adelaide Williams, Joseph Caldwell's city editor and wife.

Business manager George Crater and carriers, about 1900.

Isaac Erwin Avery, first Observer *columnist, 1900–1904.*

Joseph Caldwell (left), and successor James C. Hemphill during Taft's 1909 visit, just after Caldwell's first stroke.

John Charles McNeill, Observer *poet, 1904–1907.*

Tompkins Building and tower housed Observer *from 1916 to 1926.*

Curtis B. Johnson, Observer *publisher, 1916 to 1950.*

Observer *offices at 600 South Tryon as they appeared in 1927. This building was demolished in 1970 to make room for larger plant.*

Mechanical superintendent John P. White (left) and managing editor Ernest B. Hunter.

Observer *composing room as it looked in 1936. The editor at left is* D. G. *Spencer, who drew "Jo Jo."*

Observer *newsroom and staff in August 1936.*

Ralph Nicholson, Observer *editor and publisher, 1951–1953.*

Mrs. Curtis Johnson sells to Knights, December 1954. Knight attorney Blake McDowell, left, and publisher James L. Knight, right.

Observer's top management under Knights: editor Pete McKnight, left, general manager Bill Dowd, center, publisher Jim Knight, right.

Expanded Observer *newsroom in November 1964; in the foreground editor McKnight (in plaid shirt) reads teletype news.*

Knights buy Charlotte News, *January, 1959; left to right, Pete McKnight, John Knight, Brodie Griffith, Lee Hills, Jim Knight.*

Managing editor Tom Fesperman (left) and news editor Carlos Kumpe in Observer *newsroom about 1960; reporters in background.*

Columnist Kays Gary in early 1960s, about the time he accompanied the McRackens to France.

*Cartoonist Gene Payne in mid-1960s, about the time
he won the Pulitzer Prize.*

"DR. KING SAYS, WOULD YOU PLEASE MOVE TO THE BACK OF THE BUS?"

One of the cartoons in Payne's Pulitzer entry.

Block-long Observer *offices occupied in 1972; the previous offices sat on the lawn in the right foreground.*

Editor Jim Batten (center) confers on Nixon resignation; left to right, Luisita Lopez, Jack Claiborne, Pat Carter, Batten, Bob De Piante (seated), Bob Dennis, Bob Conn.

Cartoonist Doug Marlette in 1984.

Marlette cartoon of Christ bearing electric chair; equating the Crucifixion and capital punishment offended some readers.

Exreporter Rolfe Neill became publisher in November 1975.

View of the expanded Observer *newsroom after the folding of the* Charlotte News.

Editor Rich Oppel gets doused in celebrating the 1981 Pulitzer Prize.

Checking the first edition in Observer pressroom, 1986; left to right, John White, Ronnie Mason, Larry Ridge, Jim Page.

Aerial view of downtown Charlotte, May 1984.

CHAPTER 7

TURMOIL, DUPLICITY, AND INTRIGUE
1909–1916

The strokes that felled Joseph Caldwell plunged the *Observer* into prolonged turmoil as various individuals and groups clashed with D. A. Tompkins for control of the newspaper. Tompkins lacked the skills to edit and manage the paper himself but was reluctant to delegate those responsibilities to anyone else. As his own health failed, he grew increasingly irascible and distrusting, issuing a stream of contradictory orders from his mountain retreat. A jealous guarding of his own authority hampered his search for a new editor and new investors in the Observer Company. When he and new partners finally did agree on an editor-manager team, they immediately double-crossed it, touching off a bitter lawsuit and bringing about a startling reversal in the paper's politics in the 1912 presidential election. Even after Tompkins died, the unrest continued until the paper was sold to Curtis B. Johnson of Knoxville, Tennessee.

Though rumors of the power struggle were circulated widely among newspaper people, most of the details remained private. The conflict was played out within the offices of the *Observer* or in secret correspondence between Tompkins and various individuals, including bankers George Stephens and Word H. Wood, who became his partners. But from time to time, the conflict broke the surface and became apparent on the pages of the paper itself, leaving readers to wonder at what was going on behind the scenes. In the course of the struggle, the *Observer* gradually became a different newspaper, in looks, tone, content, and philosophy.

As the *Observer* changed, the nation was changing too. Under the progressivism of Presidents Theodore Roosevelt, William Howard Taft, and Woodrow Wilson, governmental power became more and more centralized in Washington. The Constitution was amended to permit a federal income tax and to require the popular election of United States senators, further eroding powers reserved to the states. Oklahoma, New Mexico, and Arizona were admitted as the forty-sixth, forty-seventh, and forty-eighth states. The Prohibition movement, after years of ferment at local and state levels, became a national cause. Courts broke up trusts to increase competition. (James B. Duke's American Tobacco Company, for instance, became four companies: American, R. J. Reynolds, P. Lorillard, and Liggett and Myers.) In the fall of 1914, war thundered through Europe, raising fears of American involvement, reducing demand for American cotton, and causing a collapse of southern cotton prices.

Charlotte was becoming a different place. More and more it was becoming a service and financial center for cotton mills that dotted its fringe and the twelve-county region beyond. The number of banks more than doubled as Charlotte National (later Wachovia), American Trust Company (later NCNB), Union National (later First Union National), Citizens Savings and Loan Corp. (later Branch Bank and Trust), and Independence Trust (which later went defunct) rose to compete with the older First National, Commercial National, and Merchants and Farmers National banks. Led by Word Wood, efforts were begun to persuade the new Federal Reserve Bank to establish a branch in Charlotte.

Cars and highways were becoming increasingly important. By 1911, there were 190 automobiles domiciled in Charlotte, enough to cause traffic accidents and promote the adoption of laws regulating auto traffic, licensing, and taxation. An auto plant established by Ford Motor Company in the second block of East Sixth Street rolled its first Model T off the assembly line in January 1916. As leaders in the "Good Roads" movement, Charlotte and Mecklenburg County were held up as examples of what could be accomplished through the timely use of local tax money and convict labor to build and maintain highways. In 1915, the "Good Roads" movement, led in part by Charlotteans, promoted the establishment of North Carolina's first State Highway Commission.

In downtown Charlotte, a new mayor, dentist Charles A. Bland, led efforts that felled the stately trees along North Tryon Street and substituted a street-lighting system the mayor liked to call "the Great White Way," after a similar lighting system in New York. It was further evidence of Charlotte's ambition to become a big city.

With the establishment of Myers Park as an exclusive residential community for the wealthy, class distinctions became more evident. Until then, the rich and poor had lived in the same neighborhoods and attended the same churches. After the rise of Myers Park, that changed, and people began to speak of "rich" and "poor" areas of the city. The change was reflected in the personal-news column of the *Observer*. For years the column appeared under the heading "Personal and Social." After the rise of Myers Park, the column was renamed "Society," which implied something different. It was said that Charlotteans believed in "the fatherhood of God, the brotherhood of Man and the neighborhood of Myers Park."

Through all the change, the *Observer* slowly relinquished its role as a leader of public opinion and became a follower instead, abandoning the independence that Col. Charles Jones and Joseph P. Caldwell stubbornly fought to achieve for it. The shift was directly attributable to D. A. Tompkins's brand of journalism. Unlike Caldwell, who thought editorials were the heart of a good newspaper and insisted on printing the truth as he saw it, Tompkins had little respect for editorials. His letters of instruction to *Observer* editors suggest that he expected his paper to produce propaganda, not reporting. He didn't want the *Observer* to reveal the true extent of Joseph Caldwell's illness or to report that he had suffered a relapse.

Tompkins was introducing the *Observer* to the age of the publisher, a developmental stage when newspapers were looked upon more as businesses than as forums for an editor's personal views or as auditors of community affairs. It was a stage when the need to show a profit made the newspaper vulnerable to the thought and feeling of the communities in which they were published. Tompkins, for instance, expected his editorial writers to express views that reflected popular opinion. "Popularity counts for everything in the newspaper business," he said. He suggested that "the last function of a good editor is criticism." A critic has to point out what is wrong, and Tompkins wanted none of that. He wanted a paper that was "a constructive force," not one that stirred up trouble.

Once in full control of the paper, he ordered his editors to leave out news of crime, scandal, and other unpleasantness and put greater emphasis on industrial and financial developments, a practice his editors were reluctant to follow. He wrote managing editor R. W. Vincent in January 1910 that the paper was looking better but "the principle of eschewing criminal news is far from being carried out. . . . You never do emphasize industrial or economic news. In fact, the organization seems to have an idea that nothing but criminal news is worth headlining." Tompkins only agreed to abandon that policy after his editors pointed out that it was causing reader complaint and a decline in circulation.

By 1909, Tompkins was fifty-eight years old, and his own health was failing. Three years earlier he had suffered the first of several bad falls that left his left arm and leg slightly palsied. Once he was thrown from a runaway buggy and knocked unconscious. The accident laid him up several weeks and left him with a hard lump in his chest. Later he stumbled on some steps and broke a bone in his left leg. Still later he slipped in a bathtub and broke two ribs. After that he fell in a Washington hotel, landing heavily on his left arm and rendering it stiff and trembly.

Those accidents, plus the strenuous pace of his business life, left their mark on Tompkins's nerves. In September 1909, as he left on a two-week trip to New York, his private secretary, Anna Twelvetrees, wrote Dr. W. Gil Wylie, a South Carolinian practicing in Manhattan, asking for his help. (Wylie was more than a physician; he was a pioneer in hydroelectric power generation and a cofounder of Duke Power Company. Lake Wylie, into which the Catawba River feeds, is named for him.) Knowing that Tompkins was likely to see Wylie on business while in New York, she urged the doctor to look him over and "do something . . . to get his nervous system in normal condition. Perhaps I should not write this, but I feel his nerves should have treatment before much longer or they will get the best of him." That plea came just after a second stroke had rendered Joseph Caldwell speechless and Tompkins had assumed responsibility for the day-to-day management of the *Observer*.

Whatever treatment Dr. Wylie prescribed did not help because Tompkins got little better and spent the next four years going from doctor to doctor in search of relief from various aches and pains. When doctors in Charlotte and New York diagnosed his illness as Parkinson's disease, Tompkins refused to accept that and began a vain search for other opinions. He wrote resorts in Hot Springs, Arkansas, asking whether their baths would offer him any relief. During this search Tompkins bought a mountain retreat at Blowing Rock and, later, another at Montreat.

Though his health was precarious, Tompkins continued to travel, make speeches, and set a brisk business pace. He was often in New York, Boston, and Washington, attending meetings of boards and commissions on which he served. He also carried on a large correspondence and went to great lengths to assist people who wrote requesting his help: students who wanted advice (and sometimes financial aid) in going to college; out-of-state businessmen who wanted the name of a reliable Charlotte lawyer; even a New York banker who wanted to know whether a North Carolina manufacturer named James W. Cannon (founder of Cannon Mills) was a good credit risk. One of the letters was from banker George Stephens, who complained that the *Observer* was not doing enough to promote James B. Duke's electrified "interurban" railroad, linking the Piedmont's major industrial centers. The letter offered an insight into the kind of publisher Stephens would later become.

Some months before the arrival of President Taft in May 1909, Tompkins got a letter from Dr. Henry McCrorey, president of Biddle Institute (later Johnson C. Smith University), asking for Tompkins's help in getting Taft to speak to Biddle students during the president's visit to Charlotte. Tompkins was a militant racist in his public speeches, but he wrote Dr. McCrorey that he would do what he could, even though he was not on the committee planning President Taft's itinerary. His efforts were successful; Taft added a 6:00 p.m. speech at Biddle to his Charlotte schedule. One of Johnson C. Smith's prized possessions is a huge chair purchased especially for the 300-pound Taft.

Like other elitist whites, Tompkins believed blacks to be inferior, but he was kind to them as long as they stayed in their place and did not challenge the status quo. Later that year, Tompkins wrote U.S. Sen. Lee Overman of North Carolina, recommending Dr. J. T. Williams, a black physician from Charlotte, as a candidate for an ambassadorship. When Williams was considered for an appointment to Liberia, Tompkins wrote letters in his behalf. Williams was later appointed ambassador to Sierra Leone.

In June 1909, Tompkins consented to have his own name put forward as a nominee for United States ambassador to China. While he was being considered, the White House received a flurry of supporting mail from his friends in Congress, the newspaper business, and the cotton, textile, and steel industries. Even the *Charlotte News* endorsed his candidacy. He lost the bid when Republicans in the United States Senate objected to seeing Taft appoint a Democrat. So Taft nominated a safe Republican who quit the post after a few months. Tompkins's candidacy was revived, but the second effort met the same fate as the first.

In trying to fill the void left by Joseph Caldwell, Tompkins frequently submitted editorials to Theo Kluttz, Caldwell's nephew who took charge of the *Observer*'s editorial page after the editor's first stroke in March 1909. Unlike Caldwell's editorials, which were usually well reasoned and conversational in tone, those written by Tompkins were more like formal essays. All dealt with predictably safe subjects. One reviewed the ruinous impact of slavery on the development of industry in the pre–Civil War South, a favorite Tompkins theme. Another called for an expansion of foreign markets for American-made textiles. A third championed the Australian ballot, an idea the *Observer* opposed in the 1890s, when it was part of the Populist agenda.

In addition to writing his own editorials, Tompkins was constantly peppering Theo Kluttz with suggestions for others (including one about the dubious moral value of vaudeville shows). He warned Kluttz against being too strident or aggressive in editorials. When Kluttz wrote that capital cities like Raleigh often expected to be subsidized by the rest of the state, Tompkins hit the ceiling. "*The Observer* should never enter Charlotte as a competitor of any city in the state or South Carolina," he said. When Kluttz wrote an editorial mildly disapproving the proposed federal income tax, Tompkins sent him a stronger version from the New Haven *Journal-Courier*, which the publisher said more nearly expressed his views. Later, Tompkins wrote Kluttz that he did not want the paper expressing opinions contrary to his without good reason. He warned Kluttz that such conflicts were "liable to make disagreement between us." Tompkins did not trust Kluttz and often said so in letters to his secretary and *Observer* editors.

In August 1909, he appointed John Ross, the *Observer*'s corpulent business manager, to head a four-member executive committee to run the paper in Caldwell's absence. The other members were managing editor R. W. Vincent, city editor Winston Adams, and associate editor Kluttz. "When you get to a point where you cannot settle things by yourself, I will be glad to join you in a conference," he said. He established a similar committee for the *Evening Chronicle*, also chaired by Ross, whose salary was raised $150—to $1,800 a year—as compensation for the extra responsibilities.

As a check on the efficiency of those committees, Tompkins commissioned Joel Hunter, an Atlanta accountant, to look over the books of the *Observer* and the *Chronicle*. Specifically, he was unhappy about the rate of collections from subscribers and the level of profits. Tompkins wrote Ross several times claiming both should be higher. When Hunter's studies showed the *Observer* and *Chronicle* had higher collection rates than most newspapers, Tompkins groused. He asked for an appointment with Hunter when they could discuss matters that went beyond bookkeeping. Tompkins was beginning to doubt Ross's loyalty.

Throughout most of 1909 and 1910, Tompkins got letters from newsmen interested in filling the Caldwell vacancy. One of the earliest came from Red Buck Bryant, who offered to leave Washington and assume the editorial chores. Another came from Alfred B. Williams, editor of the *News-Leader*, an afternoon newspaper in Richmond, Virginia. Williams was a Greenville, South Carolina, native who wanted to buy into a profitable newspaper in the Carolinas. His credentials as a New South disciple apparently appealed to Tompkins, and, later, to George Stephens and Word Wood, because Williams remained a contender for Caldwell's job until 1912. Apparently he was not chosen because Tompkins did not want a rival in setting *Observer* editorial policy. In one letter he said, "While I have a high regard of Mr. Williams's talents, . . . he is the kind of man who would run the whole machine." Other applicants included T. W. Clawson of Wilmington, formerly of the *Washington Star*; A. R. Parkhurst, Jr., of the *New York Times*, R. N. Dersholme of the *Savannah Press*, and A. D. Weightman of the *Washington Post*. Weightman was willing to give up an $8,000 salary and come to the *Observer* for $3,000 a year. Tompkins feared he "would not long be satisfied."

Tompkins encouraged many of the applications by writing friends all over the country in search of an editor who met his qualifications—able, loyal, obedient, and a consistent advocate of New South industrialism. His letter to R. H. Edmonds, founder of the *Manufacturers Record* of Baltimore, a New South paper Tompkins greatly admired, all but invited Edmonds to become Tompkins's partner in publishing the *Observer*. Written in January 1910, the letter said in part:

> After Mr. Caldwell's serious illness, I purchased all of his interest in the *Observer*. I own about 70 per cent of the stock. He had previously given to his children 10 per cent each, making about $30,000 which stands to their credit on the books.
>
> If I could find a man of somewhat Mr. Caldwell's type with the addition of some of your qualifications, I would like to discuss with him the feasibility of coming here and buying all or some of Mr. Caldwell's stock and becoming practically my partner. I would want a man who would know something of industrial development and that could give the paper a more industrial feature than it has had.

The letter indicates that Tompkins was not fully committed to publishing a general-interest newspaper, but was more interested in an industrial organ or journal of commerce like the *Manufacturers Record*.

Yet the *Observer* was a general-interest newspaper, and by this stage of its development a highly profitable one with a broad influence in the Carolinas. With costs of starting a new publication now beyond the reach of most people, a newspaper as established as the *Observer* was worth fighting for. Many people were vying for control of its business and editorial policies.

Jealousy, suspicion, and in-fighting within the *Observer* itself kept the paper in an uproar throughout 1909, 1910, and 1911 and spurred Tompkins's search for a successor to Caldwell. A letter Tompkins got from Red Buck Bryant in November 1909 provides an insight into the power struggle. Bryant said:

> The following I throw out to you as a suggestion in the event you think any changes necessary upstairs: Kluttz is constantly making trouble, for the reason that he will not take a friendly suggestion. Why not, if this keeps up, put Mr. [Wade] Harris [editor of the *Evening Chronicle*] in charge of the editorial department of *The Observer*, and let Kluttz write at his suggestion, as he did for Mr. Caldwell, and put [Edmund P.] Wideman [city editor of the *Chronicle*] in Mr. Harris's place. [John Paul] Lucas, who now handles telegraph matter for *The Chronicle* could take Wideman's place as city editor, and Mr. [Sam T.] Ashe could succeed him. This would give the following lineup: Harris, editor-in-chief of *The Observer*; Kluttz, his assistant; Wideman, editor of *The Chronicle*; Lucas, city editor, and Mr. Ashe, telegraph editor. Vincent and all others hold their present positions. Mr. Harris is the best man for the place. You could not get a better in the state. He and John would not be at war.
>
> . . . Having known the shop for fourteen years, I feel certain this arrangement would work. Kluttz would not like this but it does not seem reasonable that a young fellow [Kluttz was thirty-one] should fill so responsible place as editor of *The Observer*. Mr. Harris [who was fifty-two] has much better judgment and would not be courting trouble all the time. Wideman, with your occasional suggestions, would make *The Chronicle* go. He is a bright, snappy writer and knows news. . . . Somebody should be in charge.

Tompkins did not act on Bryant's suggestion—at least, not immediately. Tompkins did not trust Bryant, and the two quarreled often about whether Bryant should return to Washington and report political news or travel the Carolinas writing stories and selling *Observer* subscriptions. Believing that newspapers ran too much political news, Tompkins put little value on Bryant's Washington correspondence. After such a quarrel in 1910, Bryant quit the *Observer* and took a fling at journalism in Missoula, Montana. When Bryant returned ten months later and asked for his job back, Tompkins refused to hire him. Instead, Bryant went to Washington as a correspondent for Joseph Pulitzer's New York *World*, which suggests that Tompkins did not recognize Bryant's stature as a Washington journalist.

As 1910 dawned, Tompkins's troubles with the *Observer* came not only from within the staff but also from the outside. After years of effort, the *Charlotte News* finally secured lease-wire services of the Associated Press and could at last compete with the *Observer* on nearly equal terms. In announcing the acquisition, *News* publisher Carey Dowd issued a challenge to the *Observer*. The *News*, he said, would soon begin publishing a Sunday morning edition—the first of which appeared on February 6, 1910—and was also considering the publication of a morning paper during the week (in addition to its regular afternoon edition). Dowd obviously wanted to get even with the *Observer* for publishing the afternoon *Chronicle* in competition with the *News*. Nothing came of the threat, but rumors about a second morning paper added to the anxiety at the *Observer*.

As soon as the *News* got AP service, a circulation war broke out between the two papers. At the time, the *News* probably had as many Charlotte subscribers as the *Observer*, whose 11,600 circulation included a large number of state readers. The *News* claimed a circulation of 6,000; the *Chronicle* claimed 7,500. Such figures were often inflated, and there was no way to verify them until the independent Audit Bureau of Circulation was established in 1914, with the *Observer* as a charter member.

In response to the *News* challenge, the *Observer* and the *Chronicle* cut their street-sale prices. The *Chronicle* went from five cents a copy to a penny, and the *Observer* went from five cents to two cents. The *News* answered with a front-page box saying, "*The News* has not reduced its price. It hasn't found it necessary to do so." The first day of lower prices brought the *Chronicle* 880 street sales and fifty new subscriptions—but at a sizable loss in total income. In time the price war ended, and the *Chronicle* and *News* resumed their previous level of coexistence. The *News* recognized that its real competitor was the *Observer*, whose profits subsidized the *Chronicle*.

Sensing the *Observer*'s managerial vacuum, Dowd offered to buy the *Observer* and *Chronicle* and combine all Charlotte newspapers under one owner, but was turned down. Likewise, *Observer* business manager John Ross, acting for himself and not for The Observer Company, looked into possibilities of buying the *Charlotte News*, but found Dowd's $75,000 price tag beyond his means—and beyond the *News*'s real worth. Ross also offered to buy the *Observer*, a move that angered Tompkins and gave him further cause to doubt Ross's loyalty.

Throughout 1910 and much of 1911 rumors of instability at the *Observer* floated through the newspaper industry. A group of wealthy investors was said to be planning a new morning paper. Tompkins believed Ross was conspiring with that group and wrote his secretary, Anna Twelvetrees, in January 1911, "I would hate dreadfully to think John was a traitor and working for an opposition while he is drawing a salary from The Observer Company." Ross protested, but could not regain Tompkins's confidence.

Other rumors said Frank Caldwell, son of Joseph Caldwell's first marriage, was involved with the wealthy investors. After his father's stroke, young Caldwell came home from Panama, took a reporter's job on the *Chronicle* and later moved over to the *Observer*. Tompkins distrusted him, too, and with good reason. In August 1911, Caldwell wrote Tompkins that the investors were ready to start a new morning daily or buy the *Charlotte News* and convert it into a morning paper. He and his sister were ready to sell them their 30 percent interest in the *Observer* rather than see the paper get into a fight that would diminish its value. He urged Tompkins to sell too, so the investors could have a controlling interest, a suggestion that inflamed Tompkins.

All the time the rumors were flying, Tompkins's letters from Blowing Rock to his editors and managers in Charlotte grew more acrimonious. He accused them of disobeying his commands, of writing editorials contrary to his views, and of refusing to publish stories he requested. He also complained about their news judgment, headlines, photo captions, length of stories, typography, and conduct of business affairs. From the opposite direction, Tompkins got letters from employees suggesting that his instructions were contradictory, that he was telling one editor one thing and another something else. Ross, Kluttz, Vincent, and Charles H. Slack (a newcomer Tompkins hired from Nashville, Tennessee) wrote such complaints. Slack soon resigned, saying Tompkins had reneged on promises made during his hiring.

For several years before Joseph Caldwell's stroke, Tompkins had been encouraging George Stephens, his friend from the Tree and Park Commission, to buy stock in the *Observer*. Early in the summer of 1911, at the height of rumors about a new morning paper, Tompkins began earnest negotiations with Stephens and his banking partner, Word Wood, about investing in the *Observer*. The three men were already partners in a real estate venture, and Tompkins saw in Stephens and Wood qualities he wanted in future *Observer* leaders. They were sound businessmen, cautious but progressive, and showed a deep interest in the economic growth of Charlotte and the South. They also shared Tompkins's zeal for industrial development, and both were Democrats.

Born in 1878 in Guilford County, Stephens was a graduate of Oak Ridge Institute and the University of North Carolina. At UNC he had been a star baseball pitcher and might have made it to the major leagues had he chosen to pursue a professional career. (New York Giants manager John McGraw once called the left-handed Stephens, "one of the best college pitchers I've ever seen.") Nine years after graduation, Stephens became a UNC trustee and maintained his interest in its athletic program by chairing the athletic council, which drew up rules governing athletic scholarships and academic eligibility. He was drawn to Charlotte by his friendship with insurance man Walter Brem, his UNC roommate, and his interest in the Mecklenburg "Good Roads" program. Stephens wrote his senior thesis at Chapel Hill on roads and road building. In Charlotte he developed Piedmont Park (a residential subdivision along Central Avenue from Seventh to Tenth streets), helped to found the American Trust Company in 1901, and was a partner in the construction of the Trust Building at 212 South Tryon Street, the early home of Duke Power and the Academy of Music. (The Trust Building burned in the mid-1920s and was replaced by the Johnston Building, later renamed the United Carolina Bank Building.) In 1902 Stephens married Sophie Myers, daughter of John S. Myers, and at the time of his negotiations with Tompkins was developing the Myers farms south of town into Myers Park. He became a strong advocate of city planning and later, after moving to Asheville, was chairman of that city's planning board. He also was publisher of the *Asheville Citizen*.

Word Wood was also thirty-eight. Born near Elkin in Surry County, he attended public schools in Winston and went on to the University of North Carolina, where he became friends with Stephens. He dropped out of UNC, studied for a year at a business college in Baltimore, where he apparently learned accounting, and returned to Winston to become a runner for Wachovia Bank and Trust Company. He had worked his way up to a teller's job in July 1901 when Stephens and F. C. Abbott invited him to join them in creating the

Southern States Trust Company, which became American Trust. He became the bank's president in 1918 and led its growth into one of the nation's 100 largest banks. His seven-year effort to bring a branch of the Federal Reserve Bank to Charlotte won him an honored place among Carolinas bankers and assured the city's eventual stature as the banking capital of the two states.

Tompkins's choice of such men helped set the *Observer*'s course for the next forty years. Had he chosen men of broader backgrounds, of larger experience in public affairs or a different political bent, the *Observer* might have become a more moderate newspaper, like the literate *Daily News* in Greensboro or the lusty *News and Observer* in Raleigh. But Tompkins gave every indication of having made his choice deliberately, because he wanted the *Observer* to remain a conservative spokesman for Carolinas business and industry. So he chose two gilt-edged bankers. In turn, when Stephens and Wood decided to sell the paper, they made the same decision, turning the *Observer* over to Curtis B. Johnson, a publisher whose interests were those of a business conservative.

Tompkins's negotiations with Stephens and Wood dragged on for months. One reason was the distance between them—they were dealing by letter and telegram. Tompkins complained at one point that the visits of Stephens and Wood to his Blowing Rock retreat were too brief to permit conclusive discussions. Another reason was that the three men could not agree on a method of payment. Stephens and Wood wanted to put up securities as collateral. An impatient Tompkins was driven to write his secretary that perhaps he should go find buyers who "could afford to pay cash." But the major reason for the delay was Tompkins's reluctance to surrender his control over the newspaper. Throughout the negotiations, the issue of "control" remained a sticking point.

In August 1911, the three men agreed that Stephens and Wood would buy some of Tompkins's stock and become officers of the company. But they did not agree on every detail, so a contract to that effect was left unsigned. A few days later, Tompkins showed the agreement to his friend Ambrose E. Gonzales, publisher of the *State*, the morning paper in Columbia, South Carolina. Gonzales warned that the agreement would give Stephens and Wood controlling interest in the *Observer*. With that, Tompkins abandoned the proposal and began negotiations anew.

The introduction of Gonzales compounded the negotiating difficulties. Tompkins included the Columbia publisher to ensure there was someone besides himself who understood the business end of newspapers. He told Stephens and Wood, "I think it would be a mighty good thing if he [Gonzales] could be made the fourth man. There is no better newspaper man in the South. . . . I am putting myself in Mr. Gonzales's hands." At the same time, Tompkins sent Gonzales to Charlotte to look over the *Observer* office and determine what needed to be done. He wrote John Ross instructing him to show Gonzales anything the Columbian wanted to see. The visit was probably the first inkling anyone in Charlotte had that the publisher of the *State* might acquire an interest in the *Observer*.

At first, Stephens and Wood were dubious about expanding the partnership puzzle. But after meeting Gonzales and discovering him to be frank, Stephens wrote Tompkins that "Mr. Gonzales would bring to the Company a knowledge and experience that would be invaluable and would relieve you of a great deal of detail that Wood and I would probably have to impose on you if you had only us with you." It was understood that Gonzales would serve as business manager of the *Observer* while retaining ownership of the *State*.

At that point, the goal of everyone seemed to be that of relieving Tompkins of his publishing burdens so he could concentrate on regaining his health—everyone, that is, except Tompkins. The industrialist may have wanted to relax his grip on the newspaper but could never bring himself to do so. His secretary observed a few months later, "He seems to think there is nothing else he wants to do, or can do as well as this." Over the next six months, that obsession contributed to the most bizarre intrigue in the *Observer*'s long history.

After several rounds of correspondence, Tompkins, Stephens, Wood, and Gonzales formed a partnership to share Tompkins's 70 percent interest in the *Observer* and try to buy the 30 percent owned by Caldwell's heirs. They also agreed that Gonzales would become publisher and general manager and would try to persuade Maj. James C. Hemphill, previously editor of the Charleston, South Carolina, *News and Courier*, to come to Charlotte as editor. The conservative Hemphill, a tall, stately man with a bushy, handlebar mustache, was one of the South's best-known newspaper writers. He had friends in high places, including President Taft.

Though he had moved to the *Times-Dispatch* in Richmond, Virginia, only a year earlier, Hemphill was willing to go to Charlotte if he could have a free editorial hand and a chance to buy into the paper. Gonzales warned that relations with Tompkins might be difficult. Tompkins honored the Mecklenburg Declaration of Independence that Hemphill dismissed as "a myth." Gonzales said, "You will have to achieve a straddle in comparison with which the Colossus of Rhodes will seem to be wearing a sheath gown." Hemphill said he would make that sacrifice for a chance to buy a fifth interest in the newspaper.

Tompkins, Gonzales, Stephens, and Wood met at Blowing Rock on September 23, 1911, to formalize their partnership. Gonzales offered to bring a lawyer, but Tompkins said that was unnecessary, that a simple memorandum would do, since the whole arrangement was to be built on mutual trust. Gonzales accepted that—much to his later regret. The agreement called for all four men (and Hemphill when he arrived) to share ownership of Tompkins's stock—and the Caldwell stock when it was available. Tompkins valued the entire company at $100,000 and his holdings at $70,000; each of the other partners gave him notes for $14,000 at 6 percent interest, renewable after six months.

The company's reorganization plans were announced in an *Observer* editorial on October 6 and were greeted with sighs of relief by some staff members. Sports editor Julian S. Miller approvingly wrote Hemphill, "The paper has finally emerged from a chaotic condition of management into the oversight of such capable and experienced craftsmen." Like Miller, Hemphill was a graduate of Erskine College and the son of a Presbyterian minister. For the next several weeks, the *Observer* ran congratulations from other newspapers, most of whom applauded the Hemphill appointment. Said the *New York Times*: "Richmond, Va., is to be condoled with, and Charlotte, N.C., to be congratulated on the transfer of the valuable services of Maj. James Calvin Hemphill. . . . No other journalist of the South excels Major Hemphill in clearness of vision, sagacity and fairness of mind, while his command of humor and the perspective of large experience, which shows in all he writes, lend unusual charm and force to his work. He leaves Richmond to take editorial control of a long-established and influential newspaper in an important center of the South."

It soon became clear that the paper had four publishers: Tompkins, Gonzales, Stephens, and Wood. Tompkins was angered when general manager Gonzales did not fire John Ross and Frank Caldwell. Later he was even angrier when he felt Gonzales was moving too rapidly to reorganize the company. He feared outsiders might think the Columbia *State* was taking over the *Charlotte Observer*. He summed up his feelings in a letter to Gonzales: "To Blowing Rock you came as a Samaritan. To Charlotte you came as a conquering general."

The two bankers did not like the choice of Hemphill as editor and preferred Alfred B. Williams, editor of Richmond's afternoon *News-Leader*. Also, they assumed *they* were to oversee the paper's business affairs.

Even before Hemphill arrived, Tompkins, Stephens, and Wood discovered that the September 23 partnership memorandum was illegal under North Carolina law. They notified Gonzales, but made no move to draw up another pact. Later the three men informed Gonzales that as publisher and general manager he had no authority except to give "advice" and "counsel" about office problems. Tompkins told him he was not to take possession of the *Observer* or try to run it from Columbia.

A week after Hemphill's arrival, Stephens, Wood, and Tompkins struck harder. They held a directors' meeting without Gonzales and passed resolutions formalizing the Columbian's "advisory" role. They also hired E. W. Thompson to manage the Observer Company in Gonzales's place. Thompson, a member of the Charlotte Board of Aldermen from Dilworth, and chairman of the aldermen's finance committee, had been Charlotte district manager for the Southern Cotton Oil Company and a close friend of Tompkins. An announcement in the *Observer* said he was succeeding John Ross, "who resigned his place . . . Nov. 1." No mention was made of Gonzales. The hiring of Thompson, who was inexperienced in newspaper management, was contrary to earlier plans to bring in someone with newspaper expertise.

Hemphill was alarmed at those developments and urged Gonzales to come to Charlotte and straighten them out. Gonzales claimed the Tompkins-Stephens-Wood cabal had no legal or moral justification, but said there was little he could do. He later filed suit on behalf of himself and Hemphill, charging a breach of the September 23 contract, but the case took two years to review and was ultimately settled in favor of Tompkins, Stephens, and Wood, on the basis that the September 23 agreement was illegal.

In the meantime, Gonzales urged Hemphill to purchase the stock he had been promised. Hemphill wrote Tompkins, asserting, "My understanding when I came here was that I was to have $14,000 worth of stock in The Observer Company, which you were to carry for me on six months notes at 6 per cent interest annually on payment of $1,000." Hemphill enclosed a check for $1,000 but was refused the stock on grounds that he lacked the collateral to fulfill the contract. After Joseph Caldwell's death on November 21, Tompkins, Stephens, and Wood quietly acquired the stock owned by his heirs (at $125 a share), but did not inform Gonzales or Hemphill.

In a letter to Red Buck Bryant, dated December 11, 1911, ex–business manager John Ross described the chaos within the *Observer* as "a hell of a mess: Everybody [is] quarreling as to who is really in authority. The thing can't go on indefinitely. . . . You can look for further developments in a comparatively short time."

Though Hemphill's status at the *Observer* was cloudy, his editorials were not. On November 2 he introduced himself to the paper's readers as the grandson of a Scotch-Irish Presbyterian minister who came to Chester, South Carolina, a century earlier, a pedigree that he knew would win friends among Mecklenburg Presbyterians. He expressed his intent to "help in the building up of this splendid city." He said he could not fill the place of his friend Joseph Caldwell, but hoped "to follow in his footsteps, to emulate his virtues, to cherish his friends and win their approval." He pledged to build the *Observer* into one of the nation's great newspapers, "to print all the news that is fit to print, to be conservative in the treatment of all honest business enterprises." It was a strong, clear, forceful beginning.

Hemphill held to those promises. His daily editorial output was prodigious. He drew on deep wells of experience and a broad knowledge of public men and affairs. He wrote clearly, persuasively, and seemingly without effort. On Sundays, he delved into his Presbyterian upbringing and wrote editorials with a theological thrust. He brought with him a pet editorial project: to promote the adoption of a businesslike commission form of city government to replace the "corrosion of politics" within the board of aldermen. His first editorial on the subject was headlined "How to Make Charlotte Grow," a play on the civic boosters' motto "Watch Charlotte Grow." It was a subject dear to the heart of the elitist Tompkins, who abhorred aldermanic politics. Commission governments of three to five members were part of a local-government reform that began in Galveston, Texas. Hemphill and Tompkins thought that Charlotte, as an up-and-coming southern city, ought to have one. Hemphill also urged Charlotte to develop a downtown farmers' market similar to the one in Columbia, South Carolina, and he encouraged the establishment of a charity hospital. He opposed the direct primary, the initiative, the recall, and the referendum as invitations to demagoguery.

Tompkins approved those ideas and found Hemphill to be "very charming" and popular among *Observer* readers. The paper's circulation had risen with the news of Hemphill's appointment, and Tompkins's brother Arthur detected a "higher moral tone and social uplift" on Hemphill's editorial pages.

But Hemphill had some surprises in store for his fellow Presbyterians. In a November 9, 1911, analysis of national politics he lit into the methods and ambitions of Woodrow Wilson, the former Princeton University president who was governor of New Jersey. Hemphill had been a Wilson admirer until the New Jersey governor proved to be a progressive reformer rather than a states' rights conservative. In December, when Wilson applied for a Carnegie Foundation grant he was entitled to as a retired professor, Hemphill accused him of a "pension grab" at the expense of indigent teachers and began to accuse Wilson of greed, selfishness, duplicity, and other character flaws. Though North Carolina was witnessing a vigorous primary for the United States Senate among incumbent Sen. Furnifold Simmons, State Supreme Court Justice Walter Clark, and Gov. W. W. Kitchin, editor Hemphill hardly noticed. He focused instead on the upcoming presidential campaign, praising the Republican Taft, touting Democratic Congressman Oscar W. Underwood of Alabama, and blistering Wilson. The *Observer* was one of a few newspapers in North Carolina opposing Wilson. The *News and Observer* of Raleigh led a large group of papers, including the *Charlotte News*, in promoting Wilson; other, more conservative journals were divided among House Speaker Champ Clark of Missouri, the candidate of Tammany Hall, and Congressman Oscar W. Underwood, chairman of the House Ways and Means Committee and the choice of eastern financiers and southern "Bourbons."

In early January, Hemphill joined two other former Wilson backers in a conspiracy to derail the Princetonian's presidential campaign. The co-conspirators were George Harvey, editor of *Harper's Weekly*, and Henry Watterson, editor of the Louisville *Courier-Journal*. Hemphill was to be the point man in exposing Wilson as an "ingrate" and a hypocrite for asking that Harvey withdraw *Harper's Weekly*'s endorsement of Wilson because it implied the support of eastern financial interests who were offensive to Democrats in the West. Hemphill not only wrote editorials to that effect but created a national sensation on January 5, 1912, by placing an anonymous story on the *Observer*'s front page alleging that Wilson had insulted Harvey, the man who brought him to national prominence. The story was widely reprinted across the country, citing the *Observer* as the source. It brought vehement denials from Wilson. At this point, the conspiracy called for Watterson and Harvey to corroborate the story, but for reasons of their own, they remained silent.

That didn't stop Hemphill. He continued to hammer at Wilson as unfit for the presidency and as a traitor to southern traditions. At the same time, he pointed to Underwood as the ablest Democrat and the South's best hope. So persistent were Hemphill's attacks that *Observer* readers began to complain and cancel their subscriptions. "Your tiresome knocking of Woodrow Wilson is, to be mild, nauseating," wrote one offended reader. D. A. Tompkins did not care for Wilson, but the complaints from readers worried him. Former *Observer* hand Howard A. Banks, the fundamentalist Presbyterian who was then editing his own paper in Hickory, wrote Tompkins that "the bitter and unjust attacks" on Wilson were alienating "the strong clientele of *The Observer*" in the Hickory area. Tompkins's brother Arthur wrote from Edgefield, South Carolina, that people in his state were upset by the *Observer*'s "fight against Wilson."

On February 4, 1912, Tompkins wrote Hemphill that the *Observer*'s past policy called for "fairness and due regard" for the opinion of subscribers and that the *Observer*'s anti-Wilson editorials amounted to "persecution." He cited Wilson's "high attainments, excellent character and good standing before the masses of the people" and suggested that Hemphill "desist." Hemphill replied that he was only writing the truth, but promised to adopt a "dignified reticence" toward Wilson. Quietly Hemphill began looking for another editing opportunity. In the meantime, though silent on Wilson, he continued to pour on the coals for Underwood and redoubled his praise for President Taft, who was rapidly losing ground to an aroused and aggressive Theodore Roosevelt.

Hemphill used praise for Underwood to indict Wilson. He pointed out that Underwood had "broken no promises . . . violated no friendships . . . given way to none of the fads and follies of the time." He portrayed Underwood as a Democratic guardian against Bryanism in the past and progressivism in the future. He lumped Wilson and Roosevelt together as "high speed progressives." Such views raised the ire of *Observer* directors and on February 29 brought a remonstrance from Tompkins, who ordered Hemphill to show a "decent respect" for "any man seeking the presidential nomination."

By early spring, Hemphill had given up hopes of buying *Observer* stock and was making plans to leave. He resumed his assault on Wilson and Roosevelt and his campaign for Underwood and Taft. In April, an angry Word Wood suggested that further references to Wilson be banned from *Observer* editorials. In May, Tompkins wrote Hemphill, "I appreciate that Mr. Taft is a good friend of yours, but it is not necessary to so violently emphasize this in a Democratic paper."

In early May, having failed to buy into another newspaper, Hemphill accepted an offer from publisher Adolph Ochs to become a roving editorial writer for the *New York Times*, and on May 13 he gave the *Observer* a month's notice of his intention to resign. The directors of the company did not want him around that long. They stripped him of his duties and forced him to quit fifteen days ahead of schedule. His last editorial appeared on May 30, 1912, under the heading "Good Luck to Everybody." It announced, "My connection with *The Observer* ceased yesterday." He reiterated his respect for the memory of Joseph Caldwell and his admiration for Charlotte. "I shall hereafter be attached to *The New York Times*, one of the greatest newspapers of the world." In a larger place, "where the vision is broad," he said, "it will be a pleasant entertainment to 'Watch Charlotte Grow.' " It was the paper's only notice of his departure.

A week later, on the eve of the North Carolina Democratic Convention, the *Observer* endorsed Woodrow Wilson for president and urged delegates to the state convention to do the same. Wilson backers hastily reprinted the *Observer* editorial and placed a copy in the chair of every delegate at the Raleigh meeting. The endorsement stands as one of the fastest political turnabouts in *Observer* editorial history, rivaled only by the sudden endorsement of Republican Richard Nixon over Democrat John F. Kennedy in 1960.

Six days after the Wilson endorsement, the *Observer* carried an unheaded, one-sentence announcement that "Mr. Wade H. Harris has been appointed editor of this paper." The announcement said nothing about his successor as editor of the *Evening Chronicle*; nor did it make any reference to Harris's deep roots in Charlotte journalism. A native of Concord, Harris had come to Charlotte via Wilmington in the 1870s to work for the *Observer* under Col. Charles R. Jones. He left the embattled Jones to join the old morning *Chronicle* in 1886. He quit the *Chronicle* in 1888 and founded the *Charlotte News*. He sold the *News* in 1893 and rejoined the *Observer* under Joseph Caldwell. When Howard Banks quit in 1904, Harris left the *Observer* to become editor of the *Evening Chronicle*. No other newsman knew Charlotte, its leaders, and its history as well as Harris. The announcement indicated that Tompkins finally had taken the advice that Red Buck Bryant gave him two years earlier.

A staunch Democrat whose personal views ran toward progressivism, Harris was probably the one who persuaded Tompkins, Stephens, and Wood to endorse Wilson. Harris was well acquainted with state political leaders and perhaps knew of Wilson's strength among delegates to the state convention. He could have argued that Underwood was out of the running, that an endorsement of Tammany's Champ Clark would be meaningless in North Carolina, and that an endorsement of Wilson (an 1873 freshman at Davidson College and later a resident of Wilmington) was likely to put the Princetonian over the top in the state. If that was Harris's contention, he was correct, for after an all-night session punctuated by parliamentary ploys and exhausting roll calls, North Carolina Democrats endorsed Wilson, 503 to 393.

When Wilson won the national nomination a month later, the *Observer* headlined its approving editorial "Our Next President," asserting that Wilson's sane progressivism would attract Democrats, Republicans, and independents to his campaign. Even so, only a yawning split between Republicans backing Taft and those supporting Roosevelt enabled Wilson to win in November. Huge crowds stood in Tryon Street on election night, watching *Observer* bulletin boards and cheering at returns showing a nationwide Democratic triumph. The next day, the *Observer* ran a drawing of the crowing rooster breaking through the front page of the paper. It celebrated the victories of Wilson, Gov. Locke Craig, and Sen. Furnifold Simmons, each of whom the paper had endorsed. A leader in the hard-fought Simmons campaign was Cameron Morrison, the former Rockingham mayor and accomplished stump speaker who had moved to Charlotte and become an active member in the conservative wing of the Democratic party.

After Joseph Caldwell's stroke, the *Observer*'s appearance changed dramatically. As time passed, the paper departed more and more from his severe, space-conserving makeup. The rigid style that had lined small, one-column headlines across the top of page one like a row of tombstones gradually gave way to alternate headlines in bigger, bolder type. When the *Titanic* sank on April 15, 1912, the paper told the story with big type and multicolumn headlines, unseen since the Spanish-American War.

When the Democratic National Convention opened in Baltimore to nominate Wilson, the *Observer* ran its first streamer headline extending across the full seven-column width of the page. It ran its first two-line full-page streamer on May 8, 1915, after German submarines had sunk the *Lusitania* with 1,198 passengers aboard (including 128 Americans), an event that brought the war in Europe chillingly close to the United States.

Meanwhile, the *Observer* was looking more like a profitable business. Under Tompkins's prodding, it had installed its own engraving facilities and was running pictures, maps, and drawings on almost every page. By October 1912, local theater owners began buying daily ads to inform readers what was currently playing at the silent movies. To automobile advertisements had been added big, illustrated ads for tires and auto accessories. The classified ad section, previously called "The People's Column" and tucked modestly into a half-column on the editorial page, had grown to more than a column in length and had been moved to the back of the paper, along with reports from stock and commodity markets. By April 1915, the classifieds had been renamed "Want Ads" and were filling a full page.

The paper's most distinctive ad was one inaugurated January 22, 1912, by Ivey's department store. Unwilling to profane the Sabbath by advertising on Sundays, Ivey's advertised on Mondays instead—in a highly visible way. At the suggestion of its general manager, Canadian-born David Ovens (for whom Ovens Auditorium is named), Ivey's bought the top third of a page every Monday and inserted what looked like the front page of its own newspaper, "Ivey's Weekly Store News." In the "Store News" were announcements of sales, changes in store hours or policies, observations on buying trends, tips on fashions, the introduction of new Ivey's personnel, and tart comments by David Ovens, who had a wicked sense of humor. The ad was a regular feature of the Monday *Observer* for twenty years and attracted a wide following.

Other changes in the paper included the introduction on March 1, 1913, of "Mutt and Jeff" as the first daily comic strip (drawn originally as a code for gamblers on the West Coast). Its slapstick violence and racist humor were apparently too coarse for Carolinas readers, for the strip was replaced in October 1915 by "Bringing Up Father," featuring the trials of a carousing, nouveau-riche husband named Jiggs and his suspicious, rolling-pin-wielding wife, Maggie. On January 5, 1916, the paper introduced the first women's page under the headline "Of Interest to Women." About the same time, it expanded its books and arts page to include a column on classical music. It also began using various promotional slogans, such as "All the News That's Fit to Print" (later a trademark of the *New York Times*), and "The Foremost Newspaper of the Carolinas," an *Observer* standby for the next sixty years.

The editorial page masthead was changed to list J. P. Caldwell and D. A. Tompkins as "founders" instead of "publishers." Though that was incorrect, nobody seemed to care, even when the paper compounded the error in January 1913 by adding the line "Founded 1869" to its front-page nameplate. The "1869" claim remained a front-page fixture until the 1960s.

Other changes were taking place on the staff. In the reorganization attempted by Gonzales, old Caldwell hands were replaced, among them managing editor R. W. Vincent, who was followed by a succession of newsroom executives. In 1912, Red Buck Bryant was rehired as the Washington correspondent and began writing a political column called "Under the Dome" (not to be confused with the "Under the Dome" column begun thirty-two years later in the Raleigh *News and Observer*). In the fall of 1915, Red Buck left again and was replaced by Nixon S. Plummer. About the same time, Raleigh correspondent Col. Fred Olds was replaced by A. L. Fletcher of Ashe County (later elected state commissioner of labor). Julian S. Miller left the sports pages to become executive director of the Greater Charlotte Club, a forerunner of the modern Chamber of Commerce. He was replaced as sports editor by Bailey T. Groome, who later became executive director of the Statesville Chamber of Commerce. Theo Kluttz left to take a Washington job as editor of congressional publications. After about a year general manager E. W. Thompson was replaced by J. V. Simms, formerly of the *Raleigh Times*, a man experienced in the business side of newspapering.

One of the most notable personnel changes was the hiring of Oscar J. ("Skipper") Coffin, later to become dean of the UNC School of Journalism and one of the university's most storied faculty members. During the brief Gonzales reign, Coffin was hired as the *Observer*'s news editor. Before that he had been a high school principal. Over the next four years he developed two editorial-page columns, one called "The Side Table," a daily essay on interesting elements in the flow of news. For example, when trench combat in World War I led to the slaughter of thousands of cavalry and draft horses, the embattled armies sought replacements from America. "The Side Table" discussed the brisk business done by American horse traders, how the animals were sold and shipped to Europe, and what their life expectancy was after they arrived. Later, under the heading "Playful Plinkings" (afterward changed to "Graveyard Talk") Coffin produced a saucy column of limericks, verse, and other banter often aimed at Charlotte or North Carolina personalities.

In October 1915, Coffin got a letter from William Henry Jones of Yanceyville, a recent graduate of UNC, asking for help in getting a newspaper job, preferably on the *Observer*. Coffin's reply offers insight into newspaper wages and working conditions at the time. He wrote Jones:

> The best chance I know of in this state to get work at a living wage as a reporter is with James H. Caine of the *Asheville Citizen*. He works his men like the devil and he never pays big wages, but he seems to start them at enough to pay board and laundry. If you really want to start newspapering, don't be surprised if you have to wear the same suit of clothes for two years.

Frankly, no man without training is worth more than ten dollars a week as a reporter for a good while. Some pick up the trade more quickly than others; but it's easy enough to a man with common sense, who realizes he's learning a trade, not practicing a profession.

... There may be a lot of money in a newspaper if you own it. . . . But there aren't six jobs in the news departments of North Carolina papers that pay $1,500 a year. Still, you'll be mighty welcome [in the business]. Come on in—there's nothing the matter with the water except all the sewers empty into it.

Jones later got a newspaper job but did not stay in journalism long. He went into education and later founded Asheville-Biltmore College (which became UNC-Asheville).

Under Wade Harris, the *Observer*'s conservative editorial policy gradually became what Harris liked to call "cautiously progressive." It no longer hooted at the idea of women's rights; it endorsed the concept of "equal pay for equal work" and, within a short time, was advocating the vote for women. Unlike Major Hemphill, who hammered home his editorial points, Harris had a softer style, often writing editorials that were little more than news summaries and containing little opinion. He rarely approached subjects head on, but usually came at them obliquely, striking only a glancing blow, then waiting for the reaction. If the public's response was favorable, he pushed on; if it was unfavorable, he altered his approach or dropped the idea.

That is not to say that Harris was not forceful, because at times he was, especially in behalf of education and teacher pay. And he could be eloquent, as he often was in championing the conservation of North Carolina's mountains. But on many issues he seemed to be testing the waters and, encountering a chill, falling back. When the Anti-Saloon League was promoting Prohibition in 1915, he straddled the issue. When direct primaries were being debated, he was opposed to them. After they were adopted, he said something like "Well, maybe they won't be so bad." When opposition arose to his calls for a city farmers' market, he agreed that Charlotte had enough "clean, sanitary" retail outlets. In the harshest days of segregation, he would write solicitously of the aspirations of black people and the courageous rise they had made. Then, he would undo any good he had done by referring in print to an individual black as a "nigger," just as editors of the first *Observer* had done in the bad old days of Reconstruction.

Just before Harris's appointment as editor, another event occurred that should have reminded readers of the *Observer*'s Reconstruction origins. It was the death of Peter S. McLauchlin, the last of the four printers who founded the old *Observer* in 1869. Like Wade Harris, McLauchlin had served the old *Observer*, the old *Chronicle*, and the new *Observer*. Several times over the years, he had written reminiscences of those early days on the paper, so regular readers of the *Observer* knew who he was. He died on April 23, 1912, at age sixty-nine, having retired only two years earlier from the *Observer*'s print shop.

A third event in those years might have touched old-time readers of the paper, but it went unreported. It was the death, on January 24, 1911, of Anthony Rivers, the big, taciturn ex-slave who had been the old *Observer*'s first pressman. Though Rivers left the paper years earlier, it was unlikely that he was forgotten. The sad truth is that in the segregation of 1911, the *Observer* didn't run death notices for black people. Neither did most other white-owned southern newspapers.

Other societal changes were reflected in the newspaper. In reaction to scandals dug up by muckrakers—including revelations that the putative Lydia E. Pinkham, whose newspaper articles invited women to write for her advice, had been dead more than twenty-five years—Congress passed the Newspaper Publicity Law of 1912. Still in effect today, that law required papers to label paid matter as advertising and to file with local postmasters periodic reports on their ownership, indebtedness, and circulation. Citing freedom of the press, newspapers protested but had to comply or stop using the mails. A few years later, when the post office ended Sunday mail deliveries, and the Southern and other railroads began reducing passenger train service, newspapers like the *Observer* began developing alternative delivery systems. The day of delivering newspapers by auto and truck was fast approaching.

The *Observer* of 1909–16 also felt the pressure of increased competition. In 1909, the *Greensboro Daily News* was founded as a Republican successor to that city's old *Industrial News*. In 1911, the *Daily News* was bought by ex-*Observer* hands George Crater and W. A. Hildebrand and became a Democratic paper. Thereafter it grew rapidly, paralleling the rise of Greensboro as a railroad and industrial center. Further competition arose in Winston, which voted to merge with Salem in 1913 and, in doing so, eclipsed Charlotte as the state's largest city. That boost in population helped the *Winston-Salem Journal* become a major competitor of the *Observer*.

But the greatest change in the tone and direction of the *Observer* came with the death of Daniel Tompkins in October 1914. After the Gonzales-Hemphill disaster of 1912, Tompkins's health worsened.

He moved into a mountain home at Montreat, where he required the constant care of nurses. He continued his correspondence, though his signature became all but illegible. Perhaps for the first time in his adult life, he took up a hobby: cooking. He had five different types of ranges installed in his mountain home, to determine which was the most efficient. He experimented with different cooking styles and said that if he had his life to live over, he might become a chef and run a chain of great hotels. Had he developed that recreational outlet earlier, he might have avoided the nervous disorders that plagued his last years. Gradually the paralysis that affected his legs and arms moved up to claim the rest of his body and stilled his active brain at noon on October 18, 1914. His death inspired numerous tributes in the *Observer* and other newspapers in the Carolinas. In his will, he left most of his estate to churches, hospitals, libraries, and YWCAs.

The record he wrote on the pages of the *Observer* and in voluminous personal papers now at UNC and Duke University libraries reveals that Tompkins was not the "tight-fisted despot" described by some historians or the saintly genius portrayed by Dr. George Winston, his official biographer. Tompkins was a little of both, but more than anything else, he was a product of his times. The experience of growing up on a plantation in Edgefield, South Carolina, during the Civil War and undergoing the poverty of the South during Reconstruction profoundly shaped his character. He never shed the paternalism of the planter class, and he remained a strong advocate of social Darwinism, but he also demonstrated a boundless energy, an insatiable curiosity, and a generous spirit, especially in helping young people. He left his imprint on the newspaper he helped Joseph Caldwell build, and also on the industrial region the paper served. The schools of textiles at Clemson University and North Carolina State are among his legacies. He was a product as well as a prophet of the New South creed.

As Tompkins became an invalid, George Stephens and Word H. Wood took over the *Observer*, and after his death gradually acquired his stock. Like Tompkins they sought to use the paper to promote causes they were interested in. The *Observer* wrote glowingly of Myers Park's development and of efforts to attract the Federal Reserve Bank to Charlotte. An August 1914 letter from Word Wood to Red Buck Bryant revealed the two bankers' approach to newspaper politics. The letter encouraged Bryant to promote Cameron Morrison as the Democratic candidate for governor in 1916. Saying that "*The Observer* crowd" was strong for Morrison, the letter instructed Bryant to "do whatever you can from that end [Washington] to help him out from now on." The letter continued:

> The old question of "East and West" is not applicable to Morrison. There has never been a Governor from this section of the State. We really could not be called an "Eastern County" or a "Western County," strictly speaking. This section of the State is entitled to a Governor sometime in the history of the country. Morrison was an Eastern man up to six or eight years ago when he moved here. We do not want to bring up in *The Observer* any difficulties or impediments in the way of Morrison's prospective candidacy. . . . Let's be careful not to bring out in public other candidates for nomination until they have been so talked about that good news service necessitates it.

Wood overlooked Nathaniel Alexander and Zeb Vance, who were previous governors from Mecklenburg, but that mattered little because talk of Cameron Morrison's candidacy soon began to appear in *Observer* political reports. Once Morrison's interest in the race was known, he found the east-west rotation of the governorship did indeed apply to Charlotte, which is above the fall line and therefore decidedly in the west. It wasn't long before Morrison took himself out of contention, for in 1916 it was the east's turn to supply the gubernatorial candidates. Morrison would have to await the west's turn in 1920.

That misstep and others soon convinced Stephens and Wood that they lacked the time and inclination to master the myriad details that go into day-to-day supervision of a successful newspaper. Many of their decisions backfired on them. When they discovered that the *Evening Chronicle* was a burden on *Observer* resources, they sold it to the *Charlotte News*—then watched a bigger, better *News* compete more aggressively against the *Observer*.

Throughout 1914 and 1915, the *Observer* ran campaigns to rebuild its sagging circulation. When war broke out in 1914, closing off European markets for American exports, southern cotton prices plummeted. The *Observer* offered to accept a bale of cotton as payment for a year's subscription. When the Chapman-Alexander evangelistic team launched a month-long crusade in a temporary tabernacle on East Trade, the *Observer* again used evangelism as a circulation builder. The paper ran subscription contests to determine the best teacher in city and county schools and the prettiest girl in Mecklenburg County.

None of the gains seemed to last, and at the end of 1915 the *Observer*'s circulation remained at 10,394 daily and 13,611 on Sundays, about where it was when Joseph Caldwell was stricken six years earlier—though the city-county population had increased more than six thousand.

Stephens and Wood decided to sell the paper and asked newspaper brokers in New York to find them a buyer. During the 1915 convention of the American Newspaper Publishers Association in New York, the brokers contacted Curtis B. Johnson, a forty-year-old bachelor from Knoxville, Tennessee, owner of Knoxville's afternoon *Sentinel* and widely admired as a conservative southern publisher.

At first, Johnson showed no interest in the brokers' offer. He had just sold a one-third interest in the *Chattanooga Times* to devote full time to running the *Sentinel*, and had no desire to leave Knoxville, which was only a few miles north of his birthplace in Lenoir City, Tennessee. But when a broker confided that the paper being offered was the *Charlotte Observer*, Johnson was intrigued. He knew the *Observer* from the Caldwell and Tompkins days and thought of Charlotte as an emerging commercial and industrial center with a bright future. He agreed to consider the purchase if the brokers would not offer the paper to anyone else in the meantime. The brokers agreed. He knew he would need an able manager who would move to Charlotte and run the paper for him. Someone told him about thirty-one-year-old Walter B. Sullivan, a handsome and urbane advertising promoter who was doing great things for the afternoon *Record* in Columbia, South Carolina. Johnson knew Sullivan only by reputation, but wired him that if he was interested in the presidency of an old, established, well-financed morning paper in the South, he should meet Johnson's train at Asheville. Sullivan met the train, and the two men reached an agreement.

Johnson then went to Charlotte to negotiate the *Observer*'s purchase. He took rooms at the newly opened Mecklenburg Hotel, near the Southern Railway's West Trade Street railroad terminal. He strolled around town and looked over the *Observer* offices at 132–34 South Tryon Street. Then he called Wood and Stephens and invited them to meet him at the Mecklenburg. The bankers looked up Johnson in Dun and Bradstreet and found him to be a publisher of substantial wealth. Johnson made it clear that he wasn't interested in the *Observer*'s real estate, commercial printing house, or engraving company. All he wanted was the newspaper, with its good will and subscription lists. What would the bankers sell that for? Johnson left the room while they conferred. When he returned, he took an option to buy the paper at a price of $125,000. That was in February 1916. The sale was completed in Asheville in mid-March and announced on April 2. At the time, the *Observer*'s circulation was 12,986 daily and 16,414 on Sundays. Over the next thirty-four years, Johnson would see those figures increase nearly 1,000 percent.

CHAPTER 8

GROWING INTO A BIG BUSINESS
1916-1936

Under the keen eye and crisp command of Curtis Johnson, the *Observer* grew into a big business. Unlike Caldwell and Tompkins, who regarded the paper as a pulpit for expounding social and economic ideas, Johnson bought it as an investment that would pay increasing dividends. In the twenty years from 1916 to 1936, he made it highly profitable by tightening its management, modernizing its printing plant, and building a cargo line that greatly expanded its market. Under his prodding, the paper doubled, tripled, and quadrupled its circulation to become the Carolinas' preeminent daily and a powerful promoter of Charlotte as the commercial and industrial "metropolis of the Carolinas." Even in the Great Depression, when other newspapers cut costs and reduced coverage, the *Observer* was expanding. It widened its news and feature content and further extended its circulation territory. Step by step, it built a staff of writers and editors who would dominate its pages for the next twenty-five years.

Johnson was a shrewd businessman who also had good fortune on his side. His management of the *Observer* benefited from three favorable circumstances that promoted newspaper growth and earnings. One was a lack of competition. Few of the cities and towns in the *Observer*'s circulation territory had daily papers. By making the *Observer* available in those communities, Johnson was all but assured of increased sales. A second was the growth in national wire services and syndicated features, such as sports columns and political comment. It cost less to buy syndicated material than to hire people to write and edit, an economic reality that Johnson and the *Observer* exploited again and again. A third was the growth of mass advertising that relied heavily on newspapers to reach the American consumer, increasing newspaper revenues and allowing newspapers to expand.

Across the country, newspapers were becoming big business as the focus of American journalism shifted from the era of the editor to the era of the publisher. Wealthy newspaper owners were buying up competing publications, consolidating operations, and increasing profits. Following the example of Hearst and Scripps-Howard, newspaper chains became common in this era. While newspapers declined in number, those that survived grew in size and circulation: from 2,580 dailies with 28.7 million copies sold in 1914 to 2,037 dailies with 40 million copies sold in 1930.

That increase in sales was enhanced by a steady movement of Americans into cities and an increase in adult literacy. Nationally, the number of cities with 8,000 or more people rose from 768 in 1910 to 1,208 in 1930. In North Carolina, the urban population more than doubled, from 318,000 to 810,000. Most of the gains were in the industrial Piedmont where the *Observer* was circulated. Thanks to the public schools that Gov. Charles Aycock began building in 1901, an increasing number of adult North Carolinians were literate by 1916. Their readership sent state newspaper circulation soaring from 75,000 copies a day in 1908 to more than 324,000 copies a day by 1928.

The age itself was a stimulus to newspaper readership. Full of excitement and change—from war to prosperity to depression—it was a time when the course of world and national affairs was profoundly altered. By March 1917, in addition to the war in Europe, there were revolutions in Mexico, Ireland, and Russia. After the wars came upheavals in lifestyles, marked by Prohibition and gangsterism, the rise of radio, jazz music, and talking movies. A more militant and aggressive labor movement raised new tensions between workers and management. The continued mechanization of agriculture brought overproduction, falling prices, and an accelerated migration to the cities, marked by the movement of southern blacks into industrial centers in the Midwest. A roaring stock market hit new peaks, then fell, provoking the nation's worst depression. Altogether, life got more complicated, and newspaper reading became almost a necessity.

In an effort to maintain old values, Americans embraced a religious fundamentalism that opposed evolution and other scientific theories. But they maintained their faith in technology and material progress, welcoming the advent of aviation as well as an increase in motor cars. Cities and states rushed to build airports along with highways. An emphasis on advertising and promotion led to greater boosterism, augmented by the rise of civic clubs and slicker, more resourceful chambers of commerce. The modern Charlotte Chamber of Commerce was organized in 1915, and from 1921 to 1948 was led by Clarence O. ("Booster") Kuester, a dynamo at civic promotion.

Charlotte and the surrounding region experienced a heady growth. Once the cotton economy recovered from war-induced disruptions in 1914 and 1917, mills in the Carolinas began to whir with activity, and throughout the 1920s, more mills moved to the South from New England in what became the "Second Cotton Mill Campaign." Unlike the first campaign in the 1880s and 1890s, which was fueled largely by local capital, the second was funded by northern financiers whose investments deepened the South's colonial dependency. But the South welcomed the expansion nonetheless. Gaston County adopted the slogan "Organize a Mill a Month."

The growth reinforced Charlotte's role as a textile banking and service center. The city extended its boundaries to take in mill villages on its perimeter. It also reached south to annex previously incorporated Myers Park, which decided it did not like being a separate city. As its population doubled—from about 40,000 in 1916 to about 91,000 in 1936—Charlotte regained its rank as the state's largest city, surpassing Winston-Salem by 7,300 in the 1930 Census.

With the increase in population and commercial prominence came a rising skyline. In 1923 the twelve-story Hotel Charlotte joined the twelve-story Independence Trust Building and the twelve-story Commercial National Bank tower as "skyscrapers." In 1924, they were overtaken by the fifteen-story Johnston Building, featuring a roof-top restaurant (which disappeared when the building was expanded to seventeen floors). In 1927 came the loftiest of them all, the twenty-one-story First National Bank Building (later renamed the Liberty Life Building, the Baugh Building, and, more recently, One Tryon Center). It eclipsed the eighteen-story R. J. Reynolds Building in Winston-Salem as the state's tallest office tower.

But the apparent prosperity was misleading. Buoyant claims of New South vigor overlooked the grinding poverty in the countryside. While Piedmont mills were booming, the farmers who supplied their food and fiber were suffering from low prices caused by overproduction, market manipulation, absentee ownership, and other economic evils. In time, the overproduction curse also fell upon the cotton manufacturers, who resorted to cutting prices and stretching out work schedules, economies that soon provoked labor unrest and attracted union organizers. The era was marked by a wave of textile strikes, the most famous at Gastonia's Loray Mill in 1929, the memories of which still haunt that community.

Curtis Johnson and Walter Sullivan bought the *Observer* on credit, issuing $125,000 in bonds that were to be paid off in ten years, beginning in 1919. The bonds were secured by Johnson's credit and the plant and equipment of the *Observer*. Johnson took 500 shares of stock; Sullivan took 497. *Observer* editor Wade Harris, business manager Knox Henry, and managing editor Edward Cowles each bought one share. Sullivan became president and moved to Charlotte to run the newspaper. Johnson became vice-president and remained in Knoxville. Johnson agreed that Sullivan could buy his stock out of earnings of the company. When Sullivan died five years later, Johnson stuck by that agreement. He offered to buy Sullivan's paid-up stock from his widow or let her continue paying for the remaining shares out of future earnings. Mrs. Sullivan chose the latter course and remained an *Observer* stockholder until the mid-1950s.

In assuming control of the paper in 1916, Johnson and Sullivan paid their respects to the New South legacy of Caldwell and Tompkins and pledged to continue the campaign for industrial and commercial growth. They said the paper would remain Democratic but would not hesitate to criticize "wrongdoing within the party." They pledged to promote the city as a good place to do business.

They also had praise for the *Charlotte News* and assured their competitor that the city was large enough for two newspapers. But within a short time, competition between the papers intensified and altered the management styles of both companies. Their battles for new circulation were more than a matter of pride; advertising revenues were riding on the outcome. Because the *Observer* led in total circulation, its ad rates were higher, though much of its readership was outside the city. The *News* was first among local readers, who were the customers Charlotte merchants most wanted to reach. As the *Observer*'s total circulation rose, *News* ad salesmen hammered away at the local differential in ad rates, turning what had been a polite contest into a dogfight.

While the two papers were competing, they were drawing from the same pool of talent. Over time, many writers and editors worked for both papers. J. A. Daly was an *Observer* reporter and later a *News* city editor and business writer. Bailey T. Groome was sports editor of the *Observer* and city editor for both papers. *Observer* sportswriters Eddie Brietz and Jake Wade had previously apprenticed on the *News*, as had reporters LeGette Blythe and Mason Hood. Even W. J. Cash, the *Charlotte News* editorial writer famed for his book *The Mind of the South*, spent a summer as an *Observer* reporter in 1923.

Curtis Johnson had been a newspaper man nineteen years when he bought the *Observer*. He had grown up near Knoxville, gone to business school in Chattanooga, and taught penmanship in Nashville. He quit teaching to take a job as a bookkeeper in a Knoxville department store. When a fire destroyed the store in 1897, Johnson, then twenty-one, persuaded the publisher of the *Knoxville Sentinel* to take him on as the paper's first advertising salesman. He not only sold advertising but wrote the copy, read proof, and kept an eye on collections. Johnson rapidly increased the *Sentinel's* advertising linage and invested his commissions in shares of the newspaper. By 1911, at age thirty-six, he was owner and publisher.

His background in advertising deeply influenced his conduct as a publisher. His newspapers catered to advertising and business interests. When Charlotte merchants staged "Dollar Day" sales, the *Observer* gave the events front-page display, often with a headline over the newspaper's masthead. When haberdashers celebrated "Straw Hat Week," the paper ran front-page stories about the event. When auto dealers came to town to map sales strategy, the paper ran their pictures and a story.

Johnson was a short, rotund man who usually hid his baldness under a hat (a bowler in winter, a boater in summer) that he wore even while seated at his desk. He had piercing, deep-set eyes, a stolid countenance, and a reserved manner that terrified most of his employees. He was fond of dark blue, three-piece suits and double-breasted overcoats that only added to his severe appearance. Eudora Garrison, his secretary for nineteen years at the *Observer*, recalled that he was a relatively shy man who was all business and did not mingle easily with associates or employees. "He was a very private person, but he was as honest, as ethical, as principled as he could be," she said. "If he said he was going to do something, you could count on it. His word was his bond."

She said Johnson was "the smartest man I ever met in my life. Working for him was a liberal education." He was quick at sizing up people and a good judge of personal character. He usually hired good people and expected them to work hard. "He was firm, but he was fair," she said, and he let his people know that he expected a full day's work for a full day's pay.

He prized loyalty and he rewarded loyalty. "If the truth were known," Mrs. Garrison suggested, "he sometimes admired loyalty more than he did ability." He had a reputation for being cold and tight-fisted, but he was privately caring and often went to considerable lengths to aid a troubled employee. During the Depression, he signed notes securing loans for more than a dozen employees.

Many people who met Johnson were struck by his unusual smoking habits. He loosely rolled his own cigarettes from a pouch of Bull Durham tobacco. As the cigarettes burned, they dropped bits of hot tobacco onto his vests and silk shirts, leaving them pock-marked with small holes and littered with ash.

Though he was careless about smoking, he was precise about business. He took an aggressive role in managing the newspaper and could look at the daily cash report and know what was happening in every department. He was also fastidious about his paper's appearance and accuracy. Any errors he found were ripped out and sent to editors upstairs with a demand for an explanation.

His integrity and respect for loyalty were important elements in his relations with Walter Sullivan, his early partner. Like Johnson, Sullivan entered the newspaper business by way of the advertising department. A native of Savannah, Georgia, he started out to be a dentist but chose newspapering instead. A big, handsome man with easy grace and a winning smile, he became a promoter of special advertising sections and traveled the South working for various newspapers. He married Ella Sayre of Montgomery, Alabama, a beautiful socialite who was a cousin of Zelda Sayre, wife of the novelist F. Scott Fitzgerald. In 1912 he acquired an interest in the Columbia, South Carolina, *Record* and in three years doubled its circulation. When he came to the *Observer* as a thirty-six-year-old president and publisher, he took a vigorous role in community affairs.

Weekly and semiweekly editions of the paper were discontinued and "Daily" was dropped from its name, making the masthead simply *The Charlotte Observer*. Just under the nameplate was a line describing Charlotte as "The Metropolis of the Carolinas." In the first month there were editorials touting Charlotte as "The Factory City," as a center for medical services, and as a supplier of automobiles and auto parts. From time to time, the paper ran a boldfaced box on the editorial page touting Charlotte's assets: a center of hydroelectric power, a junction for four railroads and sixty-two daily passenger trains, the heart of the largest telephone exchange between Washington and Atlanta, a supplier of more than 400 surrounding cotton mills, the home of eight banks and four building and loan associations, and a retailing center with the lowest per capita taxes of any city in the state. Under Walter Sullivan and Curtis Johnson, the *Observer* was a civic booster as well as a promoter of business.

It took Sullivan and Johnson more than a year to find the right chemistry for producing a lively paper. In the first fifteen months, they went through four managing editors, and the paper veered erratically in journalistic style. From day to day, the appearance of the front page varied from conservative to spectacular. On some mornings, the page might contain ten to twelve relatively long, modestly displayed stories, usually under one-column heads. On other days, it might have twenty-two to twenty-five stories, most of them short pieces of one to three paragraphs, some with multicolumn headlines that consumed more space than the stories themselves.

In the summer of 1917, Sullivan brought in thirty-nine-year-old James A. Parham from the *Wilmington Star* as managing editor. Under Parham, the paper achieved order and consistency in a combination of conservative makeup and a variety of stories, some long and serious, others short and light. A native of Lumberton, Parham had entered newspaper work on his hometown weekly, the *Robesonian*. Later he worked on the *Fayetteville Index* and the Raleigh *News and Observer*. He had been in Wilmington four years before coming to the *Observer*. A thin man with thick glasses, a professorial manner, and a prodigious memory, he brought to the newsroom a regional outreach. Soon afterward, circulation began to rise.

While some of the paper's success can be attributed to promotional ventures—six weeks after Walter Sullivan's arrival it offered seven automobiles and forty-two other prizes to readers who sold new subscriptions—much of the growth was a result of its broader news coverage. Though it maintained a relatively small newsroom staff (about fourteen to sixteen full-time people), the paper recruited correspondents in every town and hamlet across the Carolinas and ran every scrap of news gleaned by those stringers: every new business, train wreck, murder, or fatal accident; every major trial or courthouse proceeding; and every marriage, birth, and death (at least among white people). Most of the stories were little more than notices of the basic facts, without depth or perspective. In addition, the paper also ran acres of Sunday features from a stable of contributors, including writers employed by colleges, religious denominations, and other institutions, whose services to the paper were usually free. It bought a wide variety of syndicated columns, cartoons, games, and other features, including crossword puzzles, a 1920s craze.

It also doubled the space for sports news from one page to two. The additional space was filled with syndicated matter, such as a series of illustrated stories on "How My Dad Taught Me to Play Baseball," supposedly written by the son of Joe Tinker of professional baseball's famous double-play combination, Tinker to Evers to Chance. The sports pages also subscribed to Grantland Rice's *New York Tribune* column, "The Sport Light." Sports proved to be a strong circulation builder, and got continued emphasis throughout the 1920s, when interest in athletics exploded and nearly every textile mill or major business fielded a baseball team.

But Walter Sullivan knew that in many households women determined which newspaper the family read, so he added more stories of interest to women. One was "The Heart of a Vampire," supposedly written by movie star Theda Bara, known as "the Vamp." Many stories had lurid headlines such as "Girls Are Saved from Immorality as the Standard of Their Homelife Is Raised" or "Gang of Thieves Teach Girl to Steal and She Becomes Steeped in Crime." Such sensationalism was soon abandoned, and the *Observer* returned to its old formula, which called for a daily dose of social news by Margaret Kelly Abernethy and on Sundays a heavy run of fashion and glamour, plus stories on the wealthy at play.

In 1917, the *Observer*'s editors added a Sunday feature called "The Home Circle," which included tips on cooking, sewing, and housekeeping. In 1919, when the Piggly Wiggly chain opened the first supermarkets in Charlotte and began to advertise aggressively, the *Observer* inaugurated a weekly "Market Basket" page that mixed grocery advertising with features on foods, cooking, and recipes.

One of the paper's most notable concessions to women was its editorial endorsement of women's suffrage, the result of a gradual change in editorial opinion that began when D. A. Tompkins appointed Wade Harris editor in 1912. The stature of many vigorous Charlotte women—Jane Wilkes, the mother of local hospitals; Dr. Annie Alexander, one of the first women to practice medicine in the South; Anna Morrison Jackson, widow of Stonewall Jackson; her sister, Harriet Morrison Irwin, who designed her own octagonal house; Julia Alexander, one of the city's first female lawyers; and reporter Adelaide Caldwell, Joseph Caldwell's widow—may have encouraged that enlightened view. Buttressing its editorial stand, the paper acquired in December 1916 a syndicated column by Rep. Jeannette Rankin, the first woman elected to Congress. (Women could vote in Montana, where Rankin lived, before they could in many other states.)

Under Curtis Johnson and Walter Sullivan, as under D. A. Tompkins, the editor's jurisdiction was limited to the editorial page, where he was expected to express opinions closely attuned to those of the general public. Having inherited editor Wade Harris from the Stephens-Wood regime, Johnson and Sullivan allowed him wide latitude in political matters, perhaps out of deference to his high standing among local and state Democratic leaders. Harris was a delegate to the 1916 Democratic National Convention that renominated Wilson. Afterward he wrote editorials soliciting contributions to the campaign for Wilson's reelection. Harris was one of the Charlotteans who visited the White House and persuaded Wilson to visit Charlotte in May 1916. But when it came to economic issues, Harris was an orthodox conservative whose views reflected those of Curtis Johnson.

One feature introduced by Sullivan and Johnson in 1916 became a fixture on *Observer* front pages for the next thirty-five years. It was Jo Jo, a chimpanzee who forecast the weather. Modeled after a similar chimp in the *Knoxville Sentinel*, Jo Jo became the *Observer's* most popular feature. Crudely drawn at first, the chimp gradually acquired polish and style. From 1924 to 1934, he was sketched by Col. DeLeon G. Spencer, a wispy copy editor with a head full of Shakespeare and a devilish grin. Spencer had entered journalism as a boy printer's apprentice in Orangeburg, South Carolina, in 1892. He went to Wofford College with hopes of becoming a preacher, but his love for newspapering interfered. When he came to the *Observer* in 1924 from the *Spartanburg Herald*, he took over the drawing of Jo Jo. Many people thought the chimp resembled Spencer himself. Later, Spencer embellished Jo Jo's daily forecasts with a piece of doggerel, usually about the perversities of man or the weather.

In 1934, reporter–movie critic Dick Pitts took over the art work, giving Jo Jo clothes and a more sophisticated look—though people still said he looked like Colonel Spencer. As Jo Jo's appearance improved, so did Spencer's verse. A sample: "Got a jug of buttermilk / Cooling in the well / Go and fetch an onion / And ring the dinner bell."

Other enduring features introduced by Sullivan and Johnson in the early months included colored comics on Sunday, a doctor's advice column, and the anchoring of letters to the editor on the editorial page, under the heading "The Open Forum." Until then letters had floated through the paper, often appearing in news columns as separate stories. On the editorial page, the *Observer* gave reader opinion a prominence rivaling that of its own editors.

Shortly after taking over the paper, Johnson and Sullivan announced plans to relocate the paper in the Tompkins Building, which fronted South Church Street and backed up to the paper's Tryon Street site. Erected in 1902 to house D. A. Tompkins's foundry, the brick building had the look of an old textile mill. The move was requested by George Stephens and Word Wood to accommodate an Asheville developer who wanted to turn a portion of the newspaper's Tryon Street site into a movie house, later known as the Imperial Theater. Johnson and Sullivan agreed to the shift because it gave them an opportunity to expand the paper's printing facilities. The move also meant that the *Observer* and the *News* would again oppose each other from across-the-street offices, the *News* having previously moved off South Tryon to the northwest corner of Fourth and Church.

Plans for the move were accelerated in December 1916, when a fire destroyed much of the *Observer*'s Tryon Street plant, melting type and warping machinery. For two weeks, the *Observer* was printed on the presses of the *Charlotte News*. On January 1, 1917, it began publishing on a new Goss Duplex press in the Church Street building that would remain its home for the next ten years. A lighted sign spelling out "The Charlotte Observer" in big green letters was erected atop an eight-story tower on the south side of the building. It could be seen for miles until taller structures obscured it in the 1920s. The big sign was lighted in March 1917, three days before President Wilson mobilized United States troops for World War I.

Efforts to make Charlotte a military training base involved the *Observer* in a new kind of boosterism and showed off the promotional skills of Walter Sullivan. Learning that training sites would be chosen by Gen. Leonard Wood who was traveling through the South, Sullivan got on the telephone, tracked down the general in Alabama (no small feat in 1916), and wrung from him a commitment to delay his decision until his Charlotte visit. When General Wood arrived, he was entertained like a prince, shown several properties, and, at the conclusion of his tour, presented a leather-bound volume of his photos and proclamations, compiled and printed by the *Observer*. Later, Wood chose a huge farm southwest of town as a training site, and the Army turned it into Camp Greene, a base for 60,000 soldiers— about one and a half times more than the population of Charlotte. Suddenly the city was flooded with people and had the feel of a boomtown.

Other successful *Observer* promotions in those early years included a big thermometer marking daily progress in a drive for $100,000 to move Presbyterian Hospital from downtown to the vacant Elizabeth College campus at Elizabeth Avenue and Hawthorne Lane; ballots asking readers to indicate their support for $350,000 in bonds to relieve overcrowding in city schools—a straw poll that persuaded aldermen to call a referendum in which the bonds were approved; a series of editorials and features that aroused public support for replacing the twenty-two-member board of aldermen with a three-member city commission that Tompkins and J. C. Hemphill had earlier championed. With World War I under way, the paper also put its prestige behind a campaign that raised $4,000 to organize a Charlotte chapter of the Red Cross.

Three years before, when the fighting had begun in Europe, *Observer* headlines had portrayed warfare as a romantic adventure. They referred to clashing swords, dashing horsemen, and thrilling contests, as if the conflict were like something from Tennyson's "Charge of the Light Brigade." But as a fierce stalemate developed between entrenched forces, the tone of the reporting changed. By 1917, when America entered the struggle, the coverage had begun to convey the pain and misery of the exhausted armies. It left mothers with sons in uniform and soldiers training at Camp Greene no illusions about what life was like on the battlefields of France. Dispatches from combat zones made it clear that war had changed for the worse.

Other stories in the 1917 *Observer* made it clear that in many ways life in America was also changing for the worse. With the war's outbreak, immigration from Europe slowed to a trickle, and the great factories of the North and Midwest were forced to look elsewhere for willing labor. For the first time, southern whites and southern blacks began moving north in significant numbers to take jobs in expanding industries. The reception given many blacks was cruel notice that racism was not restricted to the South. White residents of Cincinnati, St. Louis, Pittsburgh, Chicago, and other manufacturing centers rioted over the increased presence of blacks among them.

The incidents moved *Observer* editors to write several editorials more sympathetic to blacks than any in the paper's previous history. The editors conceded that southerners had not always accorded blacks the dignity and kindness that was their due and that blacks were entitled to decent places to live, raise and educate their children, and pursue a livelihood—startling concessions in light of the prevailing racism. But the concessions were not entirely altruistic; the black exodus threatened to deplete the South of its cotton hands. Even so, the commentaries represented a significant change in the newspaper's tone and outlook toward blacks, who were being portrayed for the first time as valued citizens with hopes, feelings, and human rights. Even while expressing such sympathy, however, *Observer* editors could, in the next edition, support a campaign to erect a statue to early organizers of the Ku Klux Klan.

In the fall of 1918, when it was clear that American involvement had turned the tide of the war, Walter Sullivan told pressman Charles M. Wills that he wanted the *Observer* to be the first paper in town to report the war's end. He said he would give Wills fifty dollars if he got out an extra announcing the armistice ahead of the *Charlotte News*. Wills, an *Observer* pressman since Joseph Caldwell days, wanted that bonus. So he took an ordinary day's paper, had a special front-page plate made with the word "Peace" in large letters across the top, and ran off fifty copies to keep on hand. As soon as news came that the war was over, he planned to put those on the street and claim the fifty dollars.

As it turned out, news of the war's end arrived at 3:00 a.m., just as the *Observer* was completing its regular press run, so his ersatz extras were not needed. The *Observer* published a legitimate extra and sent to Camp Greene for an Army bugler who, from the top of the paper's eight-story tower, played "Church Call" in the chill, gray dawn. His solemn song awoke the town to news that the hostilities had ended and that the soldiers would soon be coming home. A long, loud celebration erupted, climaxed by a bonfire in a field off East Morehead Street.

Four months later, as the first troops from the Carolinas were returning to the United States, the promotion-minded *Observer* dispatched reporter J. A. Daly to Newport News, Virginia, and rented a launch in which he could meet their transport as it entered the harbor. Informed by radio of his identity, soldiers lining the decks cheered as he approached. Once on board, he sent telegrams to more than 300 cities and towns across the Carolinas, informing next-of-kin that their husbands and sons had safely returned. The cost of those telegrams was more than offset by the excitement and good will they purchased.

The war in Europe was soon replaced by war on American streets as labor unions throughout the country fought for better wages and working conditions. In Charlotte, motormen who ran streetcars for the Southern Public Utility Company (a Duke Power subsidiary) went on strike in the fall of 1919. When the strike threatened to disrupt the city, the *Observer* offered its services as an arbitrator but was spurned by the union leader, who said the newspaper was controlled by "the same capitalists" who owned the power company. The strike turned mean; police were called to restore order; and shooting erupted in front of the streetcar barn at Bland Street and South Boulevard. Five strikers were killed and twenty-five wounded. Strikers blamed city officials and began circulating petitions to recall the mayor and commissioners who had summoned the police. Though the *Observer* was sympathetic to the streetcar workers, it vigorously opposed the recall petition.

As it did so, the *Observer* itself became the target of union agents. On October 8, 1919, the logo of the International Typographical Union suddenly reappeared on the paper's editorial page masthead, signaling that during the turmoil over the streetcar strike, the paper's composing room had again been organized. That typographers' union would remain part of the *Observer* organization until the paper's complete conversion to electronic typesetting in 1982.

In November 1919, Walter Sullivan, who had given the *Observer* much of its verve, learned he had diabetes and had to retire for "an indefinite period of rest." It was a setback for both Sullivan and the *Observer* because the paper had made rapid progress under his leadership. Advertising, circulation, and profits had grown in each of his three years at the helm. The paper paid dividends of 19.5 percent in 1916, 21 percent in 1917, 28 percent in 1918, 10 percent in 1919, and 34 percent in 1920. It also retired the bonds that had financed the Johnson-Sullivan purchase far ahead of schedule. By 1920 only $30,000 of the original $125,000 were outstanding.

Sullivan went to a health resort in Denver, Colorado, and adopted a strict regimen. After two years he was much improved and went with his wife to New York to attend the 1921 World Series. There he suffered a relapse and died of diabetic shock, at age forty-one. Six months later, two Canadian doctors developed an insulin therapy that would have saved his life.

After Sullivan's death, his stock in the paper was held in trust for his wife and daughter. As executor of the trust, the American Trust Company became a voting member of the Observer Company for thirty-two years.

Sullivan's retirement and death forced a reorganization in the *Observer*'s management. Curtis Johnson assumed the presidency and Col. Albert W. Burch, the paper's courtly, white-bearded advertising director, moved up to general manager. Burch was succeeded in the advertising department by the ebullient Tom Pierson, who never met a stranger. Pierson led the *Observer* to new advertising records year after year in the 1920s, especially in publishing special sections that helped promote Charlotte and the Piedmont region.

In 1920, the *Observer* hit a promotional peak. It crowed over a shift from a seven-column to an eight-column format that created more room for news and advertising. (The eight-column page was to remain its standard for the next fifty-five years.) It vigorously promoted citizen investment in a new hotel, opened in 1923 as the Hotel Charlotte. (The site at West Trade and South Poplar streets offended real estate developer Edward D. Latta, who wanted the hotel built on

South Tryon where he owned property. When he refused to honor his $50,000 pledge to the citizens' corporation, he was taken to court and forced to pay. In anger, Latta sold his Charlotte holdings and moved to Asheville.) Also in 1920 the *Observer* sponsored a huge auto show, began devoting an entire Sunday section, with a separate front page, to sports news, promoted women's suffrage (Julia Alexander wrote a series of articles advising women what to expect in the voting booth), and helped elect Cameron Morrison governor of North Carolina.

Then forty-nine years old, Morrison announced his candidacy in 1918 and immediately received an *Observer* fanfare. In 1919, he was endorsed by U.S. Sen. Furnifold M. Simmons, leader of the Democrats' conservative "machine." Morrison's chief opponent was progressive O. Max Gardner of Shelby, who in 1916 had been the youngest man, at age thirty-four, ever elected lieutenant governor. Gardner also announced his candidacy in 1918 and as presiding officer of the North Carolina Senate was building support among fellow legislators. Gardner was considered the front-runner even after another progressive, ex-congressman Robert N. Page, brother of author-editor Walter Hines Page, entered the primary.

When Morrison's wife died in November 1919, he went into seclusion, missing important party events and doing little to put together a campaign organization. His friends began to worry, and by the winter of 1920 they were threatening to abandon him in favor of Gardner. In a speech on March 4 in Charlotte, he came out fighting. He charged that Gardner was leading a "Shelby ring" in manipulating state and federal offices, a claim that weakened Gardner's use of the "machine" issue against Morrison. He ridiculed Page as a member of the effete "House of Page." With Charlotte lawyer Heriot Clarkson as an effective campaign manager, Morrison ran flat-out until the June 5 primary.

The crucial issue became women's suffrage, which Gardner supported and Morrison opposed. If women were given the right to vote, Morrison argued, what would keep Negro women from voting and reviving "Negro domination"? His question was highly effective Down East. Though the *Observer* supported women's suffrage, it ignored Morrison's opposition and between March 4 and June 5 published twenty-two editorials in Morrison's favor, many portraying him as a "progressive." It ran seven others opposing Gardner.

It turned out that Morrison needed every one of those editorials, because when all the ballots were finally counted—eleven suspenseful days after the primary—the Charlotte lawyer led by only eighty-seven votes and faced a runoff against Gardner. In the next four weeks, as Morrison and Gardner grasped for the 30,000 votes that had gone to Page, the *Observer* resumed its editorial drumroll, publishing ten editorials favoring Morrison and nine opposing Gardner. The paper's fairness was publicly challenged by the *Shelby Star* and by Gardner spokesman T. W. Chambliss, a former *Observer* reporter. On July 2, the eve of the runoff, the *Observer* carried a long editorial, urging Mecklenburg Democrats to vote for "the home man." The next day, Morrison won the nomination by 9,259 votes.

In the fall, Morrison forgot his opposition to female suffrage and sought the support of women (then eligible to vote for the first time) in defeating Monroe lawyer John J. Parker, who polled more votes than any previous Republican gubernatorial candidate. In the campaign, Parker tried to shed the stigma of black support by calling for "the political ostracism of the Negro" and a "lily white" Republican party. Those tactics came back to haunt him nine years later when, as a Charlottean, he was nominated for a seat on the United States Supreme Court but was denied confirmation by the Senate.

As governor, Cameron Morrison proved to be as progressive as *Observer* editorials promised. He pushed through a bill to replace the state property tax with an income tax. He strengthened public schools, expanded state ports, and increased appropriations to the university, enabling it to attain national stature. His greatest accomplishment was a $50 million bond issue for building and maintaining roads to every county seat and state institution, a measure that when fully implemented gave Charlotte the best highway access of any city in the state—and paved the way for future *Observer* growth.

The Morrison campaign deeply influenced the career of the *Observer* reporter who covered it. He was Brock Barkley, a Charlotte native who apprenticed on the weekly *Charlotte Review* before joining the *Observer* staff in 1920. When the Morrison-Gardner campaign heated up, Barkley, then twenty-three, traveled with Morrison and covered his speeches. After Morrison won, Barkley was sent to Raleigh to cover the governor's office for the *Observer* and the *Asheville Citizen*. While there he found time to take courses at Wake Forest College (then in Wake County) and read law under a local judge. He passed the state bar exam in 1927 and a year later left journalism to practice law. During the Depression, he worked part time on the *Observer* copy desk, where he was one of the staff's fastest headline writers. Barkley's departure from Raleigh left the *Observer* without a full-time representative in the state capital until the 1950s, which accounts in part for the paper's declining influence in state affairs in the 1930s and 1940s.

In the excitement over Morrison's election, women's suffrage, and the onset of Prohibition, the *Observer* neglected to report two significant "firsts" that occurred in Charlotte in 1920—events that the promotion-minded paper might normally have trumpeted. One was the July 15 opening of the first cafeteria in the Carolinas, the S&W, owned by Frank Sherrill and Fred Weber, a pair of ex–army mess sergeants who previously had run the lunchroom at Ivey's department store. Their establishment, in the first block of West Trade (later the site of Marriott City Center), immediately became one of the city's most popular eating places and the anchor of an S&W chain that extended from Washington, D.C., to Atlanta.

The other "first" unreported in the *Observer* was the inaugural broadcast of the South's premier radio station, 4XD, which went on the air in December 1920 from the basement of Fred M. Laxton's home at Belvedere and Mecklenburg avenues, near the Charlotte Country Club. Two years later, when the Federal Communications Commission issued a license to Southern Radio Company, the station was renamed WBT, with studios in the Independence Building. One of the *Observer*'s first notices of its existence came in April 1922 in a small story saying that the "wireless telephone" operated by Southern Radio would soon begin broadcasting daily weather reports. Within a year the paper was running nationally syndicated stories about how radios worked and carrying ads for radio receivers. Within six years, it was publishing daily guides to WBT programming, similar to those later published for television. In 1928, the *Observer* joined WBT in sponsoring a radio-appliances exhibit that drew 20,000 people a day. In 1930, the *Observer* referred to WBT as a "blessed" asset, an opinion the paper would later retract.

In the fall of 1923, the *Observer* was part of a promotional effort that built a temporary "tabernacle" on the southeast corner of South Church and West Third streets and brought evangelist Billy Sunday to town for six weeks of fiery sermons. The *Observer* ran the text of Sunday's daily condemnations, with the result that subscriptions climbed 3,000 to 27,000 on weekdays and 30,000 on Sundays.

About the same time, evangelist Mordecai Ham was conducting a crusade in Raleigh. Both Sunday and Ham opposed the evolution theory of Charles Darwin. Their sermons fueled an uproar over state-approved biology texts for public schools. As ex officio chairman of the state school board, Governor Morrison banned two of the books, claiming, "One . . . teaches that man is descended from a monkey and the other that he is a cousin to the monkey. I don't believe either." Mordecai Ham called Morrison's purge, "the greatest act" of any governor of any state. The *Observer* praised Morrison for keeping the state's public schools "pure and undefiled." It was the only major daily in the state to do so.

The biology battle was the opening shot in a war over Darwinism. The 1925 legislature was asked to pass a bill to ban any reference to evolution in public schools. The proposal brought the presidents of the University of North Carolina and Wake Forest College to Raleigh to defend intellectual freedom and scientific inquiry. In an editorial headlined "Monkey or Bible," the *Observer* again sided with the antievolutionists and was the only major daily in the state to do so. According to one scholar, the paper blamed the whole conflict on "high brow professors" who would rather "stick by the monkey" than "live by the Bible." Ultimately, good sense prevailed, and the antievolution bill was beaten.

After the excitement over the Billy Sunday crusade, Charlotte and the *Observer* resumed business as usual. The paper dropped "The Metropolis of the Carolinas" from its front-page masthead and replaced it with a slogan describing itself as "A Clean, Constructive Newspaper" and a pledge that "When You See It in the Observer, It's So." That fall it added a Sunday supplement called the *Observer Junior*, a miniature newspaper published for and about schoolchildren. Edited by a woman named Willie Irvine Shelby, the supplement remained part of the *Observer*'s Sunday package until World War II, when it was a casualty of a newsprint shortage. Also that fall, the *Observer* welcomed auto racing to a big dirt racetrack off South Boulevard, near Pineville. In December, it helped to found the Charlotte Engraving Company, incorporated by publisher Curtis Johnson, mechanical superintendent Harry Fentress, and Charlotte artist Kenneth Whitsett. With its own engraving plant, the paper could run more and larger photographs.

In the fall of 1924, sixty-three-year-old Col. A. W. Burch, the second advertising man Johnson recruited to run the paper, died after a six-month illness. By then, Johnson had sold the *Knoxville Sentinel* and moved to New York to play the stock market. He came to Charlotte and rented rooms in the new Hotel Charlotte with the intention of putting the *Observer* in shape to sell. The longer he stayed, the more he was impressed by the local business climate. Soon his goal was to stay and help make Charlotte the largest city in the Carolinas and the *Observer* the largest newspaper. When he arrived, the paper was selling 29,937 copies a day and 33,832 on Sundays, double what it was at the time of his purchase in 1916. Over the next twelve years, circulation would double again under his management.

Johnson assumed direct control of the paper just as its circulation manager, Henry J. Strickland, was completing work toward a night school law degree. A year later, Strickland passed the bar exam and left the newspaper to practice law. With the *Observer* locked in a circulation war with the *Charlotte News*, Johnson looked for a circulation man who could give his paper a competitive edge. He found one in M. H. ("Mooch") Brandon, a thirty-four-year-old promoter who was circulation manager for the *Knickerbocker Press* in Albany, New York.

Soon after he arrived, Brandon began to modernize the *Observer*'s delivery system. With the aid of Fred W. Hunter, the city circulation manager, he divided Charlotte into four circulation districts, each with its own manager, and launched door-to-door subscription campaigns. He took the carriers off the payroll and made them independent merchants who bought their papers at a discount and sold them at a profit. He organized a carriers' club that held monthly meetings and taught boys how to sell, how to keep books, and how to save money. To promote salesmanship, he ran contests among carriers, offering as prizes trips to New York, San Francisco, Mexico, Canada, even South America. He also ran contests among readers, offering prizes for the most subscriptions sold. One year, when the *Charlotte News* offered readers a Packard car as first prize in a subscription drive, Brandon and the *Observer* countered by offering seven cars and a new bungalow. Steadily the *Observer* closed the gap in local circulation.

Brandon's most ingenious move was the formation of what is now the Observer Transportation Company, an overnight delivery service that was begun almost by accident. For more than ten years, the Post Office and the railroads, previously the *Observer*'s chief means of circulating its newspapers outside Mecklenburg County, had been curtailing service, mostly because of increased travel by automobile. As an alternative the paper contracted with owners of small trucks to distribute its papers. As those trucks pulled up to the paper's loading dock behind the South Church Street building each night, the manager of a movie house on West Trade was closing his theater, the rear of which backed up to the *Observer*. Often the theater manager asked an *Observer* truck driver to deliver his film to the next exhibitor in a nearby town. That kept the movie film in circulation without the usual transit delays. Brandon immediately saw the business potential of that practice: Charlotte was the film exchange for the Carolinas, and with the development of talkies, traffic in film was doubling and tripling.

He and Curtis Johnson took steps to put the *Observer* in the film delivery business. They bought trucks, formed a subsidiary called the Inter-Carolina Delivery Company, and got a federal license to haul freight across state lines. Taking advantage of Cam Morrison's "Good Roads" program, the delivery company was soon distributing film to 450 theaters. Gradually it added other commodities from Charlotte warehouses: dry ice, farm implements, auto parts, drugs—even bread from the A&P bakery. By offering overnight delivery, the company enhanced Charlotte's wholesaling and distributing business.

By the 1930s, *Observer* trucks were making deliveries in seventy counties—and getting the *Observer* in the hands of readers who could get no other morning paper. As the freight business increased and the paper added more trucks and loading equipment, publisher Johnson complained, "You boys are going to break me." But in his bookkeeper's heart he knew better. The trucking company not only delivered his papers free but did so at a profit. When the Depression hit and other newspapers were forced to retrench, Johnson, Brandon, and the *Observer* could continue expanding their business ventures, thanks to cheap newsprint and the trucks of Inter-Carolina Delivery Company (later renamed the Observer Transportation Company).

Arriving about the same time as Brandon were two young men who became his pupils. One was tall, angular Granbery ("Granny") Ward, who came to the paper from the *Asheville Citizen*. The son of eastern North Carolina tobacco fields, he had a slow drawl but a quick mind and learned everything Mooch Brandon was willing to teach. He would succeed Brandon as the *Observer* circulation manager and director of the Observer Transportation Company. The other pupil was a short, stocky redhead named Bruce Rogers, son of a police detective who moved to Charlotte in the early 1920s. Young Rogers began at the *Observer* as a school boy, taking morning circulation complaints before going to school and later working in the mailroom as an inserter. When Brandon arrived, he went into the field as a district manager. In time, Rogers succeeded Ward as *Observer* circulation manager.

In addition to bringing in Brandon, Johnson reached back to Knoxville and summoned the *Sentinel*'s crusty John P. White to become the *Observer*'s mechanical superintendent. Under the previous superintendent, the paper was often late going to press and missed mail trains. John White was a stern clock-watcher. When he arrived he found typesetters working from nine copy spikes, one for each of the different types of copy to be set: sports, markets, women's news, editorial, etc. The spike for the easiest copy was always clear; the spike for the most difficult copy was always full. The second night White was there, he hammered down the last eight spikes and announced to all typesetters, "From now on, boys, we work from the same hook, and set it as it comes." Quick, blunt, often caustic, White was the driving force of *Observer* composing rooms for the next twenty-five years. He was hard, but the men loved him for his honesty and fairness.

With reliable production and a strong circulation and sales force, only one other factor limited the *Observer*'s prospects: its plant. The Tompkins Building was hardly suited for a modern newspaper. The place was drafty in winter, sweltering in summer, and always filthy. Its yard offered little room for loading and servicing trucks, and there was no space for storing ink and newsprint. Tons of paper had to be trucked in daily. Often the presses were stopped while trucks raced to a railroad siding where reserve newsprint was stored in boxcars. The cost-conscious Johnson winced over the extra expense of storing, handling, and trucking.

After studying sites, he chose to build a new plant on the southwest corner of Stonewall and Tryon streets, on the edge of an aging residential district. The site's main asset was a rail line along its southern boundary. It would let the *Observer* receive newsprint directly from freight cars at a savings of $1,500 a month—about half the newsroom payroll.

Ground was broken for the new building on February 22, 1926, but workmen dug only a few feet before hitting solid rock. Excavation for a fifteen-foot basement pressroom required two months of constant blasting. Curtis Johnson visited the construction site daily, stared at the granite being gouged from the earth, and uttered to the foreman his standard complaint, "You boys are going to break me." The three-story building was completed in ten months—a little behind schedule—at a cost of $425,000. Of that sum, $275,000 came from the newspaper's cash reserves. Johnson borrowed only $150,000, which by 1930 he had repaid at 5¼ percent interest.

The trim new building was opened to the public on Sunday, January 1, 1927, and occupied by the newspaper early the next morning, after the final press run at the Church Street plant. The new building had business offices on the first floor, advertising offices on the mezzanine, a newsroom on the second floor (including an alcove occupied by the Associated Press), and an auditorium on the third floor, where the paper invited the public to come watch the tallying of election returns. Its eight new press units and fourteen Linotype machines were expected to meet the newspaper's needs for the next fifty years. But that expectation did not take into account the *Observer*'s accelerating growth.

Before and after the move into the new plant, the *Observer* hired two reporters who would make a significant impact on the paper and on the town. One was Hazel Mizelle (later Hazel Trotter) of Robersonville, a 1922 graduate of the Woman's College at Greensboro (later UNC-Greensboro). She came to the *Observer* in July 1926 after teaching English and working for newspapers in Asheville and Hendersonville. She began as a reporter for the *Observer*'s "Made in Carolinas" Sunday supplement promoting local industry. Two years later she joined the city desk staff and was assigned to banking, commerce, real estate, and labor relations, traditionally a male domain. Her honesty and accuracy quickly won the trust of business leaders and gave the *Observer* an edge over the *News* in business coverage. She kept the job for twenty-seven years.

The *Observer*'s assignment of a woman to such an important news beat reinforced a feminist movement that was under way in Charlotte. In 1925, lawyer Julia Alexander became the first woman from Mecklenburg (and the second in the state) to be elected to the North Carolina legislature. Two years later, Carrie L. McLean became the county's second female legislator. Women were also taking leadership roles in Democratic politics, among them Gladys Tillett.

A year after Hazel Mizelle joined the news staff, Stanford R. Brookshire, an Iredell County native who finished at Duke University in June 1927, came to the *Observer* to produce a special section on colleges and universities in the Carolinas. He was made a reporter and covered the opening of the First National Bank Building as North Carolina's tallest structure (with the Charlotte branch of the Federal Reserve Bank on the top floors). But six months of trudging streets and hopping trolley cars in quest of news dimmed his enthusiasm for journalism. One night his city editor, J. M. ("Buddy") Roberts, suggested that he would be happier in business. Brookshire quit, took a job with his father, a Charlotte building contractor, and later formed a partnership with his brother in distributing industrial equipment. In the late 1950s, with *Observer* support, he was elected mayor of Charlotte and led the city peacefully through the civil rights revolution.

In the 1928 presidential election, the *Observer* deserted the Democratic party for the first time since Joseph Caldwell opposed Bryan in 1900. All spring, Wade Harris, like other southern editors, watched in dread as New York Gov. Al Smith sewed up the Democratic presidential nomination. They knew that many southerners would never accept Smith, a Catholic and an outspoken "wet." Even Sen. Furnifold Simmons, leader of the state's Democratic loyalists, openly opposed Smith. Letters from readers hostile to Smith overflowed the "Open Forum." Soon the *Observer* was running editorials attacking Smith. Unlike Caldwell's 1900 stand against Bryan, the paper's opposition to Smith was highly popular. Herbert Hoover easily carried North Carolina.

As the election campaign ended, the *Observer* heaved an editorial sigh and welcomed the chance to listen to the radio without having to hear political speeches—but complained about the raucous jazz music that was becoming increasingly popular. It suggested that jazz was less than dignified.

The paper resumed its subscription war against the *Charlotte News* by offering eight new cars as prizes to readers who sold the most subscriptions. By January 1929, the paper was giving subscribers more for their money. Walter Lippmann's column, "Today and Tomorrow," appeared daily on the front page, along with the humor of Will Rogers. The back page featured columnists Arthur Brisbane, Kathleen Norris, Elsie Robinson, O. O. McIntyre, and poet Edgar A. Guest. By March 1929, the weekday paper was big enough to divide into two sections, with the front page of the second section—called "the second front"—devoted to local news.

As part of the drive for local subscriptions, the *Observer* expanded its reporting staff. Among those taken on was LeGette Blythe, the smooth-writing "Squire of Huntersville." After nearly ten years in daily and weekly journalism, Blythe knew most of the leading citizens in town and would remain the *Observer*'s star reporter and literary critic until 1950. One of his reporting coups occurred in the early 1930s. Nosing around the courthouse, he picked up a hint that Robert Rice Reynolds, an Asheville lawyer and Al Smith loyalist, was thinking about running against Mecklenburg's wealthy Cam Morrison for the United States Senate. Morrison was appointed to the Senate after the death of Lee S. Overman and had to run for election in 1932. Blythe went back to the *Observer*'s offices, got the managing editor's permission to make a long-distance telephone call, and put the question to Reynolds: "Bob, they tell me you're going to run against Cam Morrison for the Senate." To the shock of many people, Reynolds said that, yes, he was. Thus began one of the most bizarre—and most shameful—Senate campaigns in North Carolina history. Posing as a poor boy, Reynolds drove a steaming Model T from town to town, with a great flourish unrolled a red carpet in front of the town square, and, aping Cam Morrison's mincing walk, ambled across it to a speaker's stand. He accused the wealthy Morrison of eating "caviaaar" for breakfast, and defined caviar as "feesh aigs, red Rooshian feesh aigs." In the depths of the Depression, he laughed the popular ex-governor out of the United States Senate.

Joining Blythe on the reporting staff was portly, moon-faced Porter Munn, a genial, drawling South Carolinian who covered county government for the next thirty years. He was slow walking and slow talking, but had a firm command of English, was an excellent speller, and could be dogged in the pursuit of news.

But the most colorful addition was John Thomas ("Jake") Houston, who in 1929 became the first staff photographer on any newspaper in the Carolinas. Houston was a flamboyant character whose sartorial splendor and unintended malaprops (he once described a woman in an auto wreck as "lying prostitute across the pavement") made him one of the *Observer*'s most storied employees. In hiring him, Curtis Johnson indicated that he wanted more and better pictures in the *Observer*. Houston gained immediate notice by flying to football games with pilot Johnny Crowell and sports editor Harry Griffin, prowling the sidelines for action shots, and flying home in time to get his photos prominently displayed in the Sunday morning paper. Houston's photographic feats were remarkable in light of the rude facilities in which he worked. His lab was an abandoned women's restroom, with plumbing stubs protruding from the floor. His developing tanks were a couple of hollowed-out automobile batteries. His thermometer was his index finger.

To interest women, *Observer* editors added two new features. One was "Shopping with Miss Charlotte," a chatty advertising gimmick that kept readers abreast with what was popular in Charlotte stores. The column was begun in 1928 by Cora Harris, daughter of editor Wade Harris, but she lacked the tact and writing touch to sustain an audience. In November 1932, the column was taken over by Queens graduate Mabel Biggers, whose polite charm made it an *Observer* institution for the next thirty-two years. Mrs. Biggers wrote one column from the maternity ward of St. Peter's Hospital, where she had given birth to a son. Later, when she was crippled by illness, she continued the column from a wheelchair.

The second feature was "Caroline Chatfield," a column of advice to the lovelorn written by Irving Harding McGeachy, daughter of Dr. R. A. ("Dicky") Harding, a popular Davidson College professor, and widow of Dr. A. A. McGeachy (pronounced Mac-GAY-he), pastor of Charlotte's Second Presbyterian Church (later Covenant Presbyterian). The "Ann Landers" of its day, the column was launched in October 1930, and was syndicated nationally.

Throughout the late 1920s, much of the paper's energy and resources were devoted to covering strikes in the textile industry, including the communist-inspired walkout by workers at Gastonia's huge Loray Mill, a manufacturer of cord for tires. In two years the number of workers at the Gastonia plant had been reduced from 3,200 to 2,200 and wages twice cut by 10 percent, reducing operating costs by $500,000 a year. During the strike, Gastonia Police Chief O. F. Aderholt was shot and killed, and a female striker, Ella Mae Wiggins, a mother of five children, was murdered.

Observer editorials blamed communists for the Gastonia strike and suggested that the union organizers were not entitled to constitutional rights. Strike leader Fred Beal and fifteen others were tried in Charlotte for the murder of Chief Aderholt. The trial attracted national press coverage, and the *Observer* and the Postal Telegraph Company rented rooms in the Court Arcade and equipped them with typewriters and telephones for use by visiting reporters. Beal was convicted along with most of his fellow defendants, but fled to Russia before he could be imprisoned. He later returned, disillusioned with communism.

In the meantime, events in the United States were giving many Americans cause to be disillusioned with capitalism. On August 27, 1929, the *Observer* leased a special telegraph wire and installed equipment to receive and set into type the "long line" summary of each security listed on the New York Stock Exchange. Included in the quotation were the high and low prices for the year, the previous dividend, each day's sales in hundreds, the high and low for the day, and the net change. In the days before teletype machines, that data had to be transmitted by ticker tape, pasted onto copy sheets, edited, set into type, and read by proofreaders, line by line. It took nearly eight hours to get it into type. Rupert Gillett, a scholarly, soft-spoken Texan who had fought in World War I, studied at the Sorbonne, and worked on newspapers in Fort Worth, Nashville, Cleveland, and Miami, was hired to oversee the stock wire's installation and to expand the financial pages into the most complete in the South. Two months later, those stock quotations became the most sensational news in the paper as the bull market collapsed and the nation plummeted into an ever-deepening depression.

For several days, *Observer* headlines minimized the market's fall. On October 29, a headline on page one said, "Stock Crash Doesn't Alarm Business," but a streamer on the financial pages was more forthright. It said, "Stocks Collapse—Most Active Decline Ever Experienced." For ten days, as news of the market's plunge was bannered in newspapers across the country, the *Observer* gave the story the same understated play and minimized its impact. One front-page headline said, "Market Crash Laid to Prosperity Talk." Another said, "Business Men Predict Market Crash to Aid Charlotte." Even in 1930, when Charlotte's First National Bank closed the gleaming brass doors to its twenty-one-story building, a victim of the crash, the *Observer* put a positive slant on the story by emphasizing the soundness of other Charlotte banks. When two other Charlotte banks failed after the March 1933 "bank holiday," the *Observer* downplayed that news.

Observer publisher Curtis Johnson had sensed danger and before the crash sold off much of his stock at a handsome profit. With that wealth, plus the *Observer*'s rock-solid financial condition, he entered the Depression with the means to take full advantage of cheap newsprint by expanding operations.

The man who led the editorial side of that expansion was Ernest B. Hunter, a tall, tireless, and martial news editor brought in by Curtis Johnson in November 1929 to give the *Observer* a combative edge against the *News*. Johnson had previously employed Hunter on the *Knoxville Sentinel* and knew him to be a driver. Since 1925 the *News*, led by the aggressive Brodie S. Griffith, had been giving the *Observer* fits. Rapidly, Hunter became the *Observer*'s heart and soul.

Hunter knew Charlotte well. He grew up between Pine and Poplar streets in Fourth Ward, attended the D. H. Hill School on East Morehead, sold the weekly *Grit* on Tryon Street, and hung around the *Observer*'s offices to catch a glimpse of Joseph Caldwell and other heroes. He learned the telegrapher's code from Charles Wister, an Associated Press operator who, in the days before teletype machines, decoded dispatches sent by ticker over the *Observer*'s leased wire. That skill landed Hunter a job with the Associated Press and later with the *Greensboro Daily News*.

During World War I he earned a captain's bars in France and afterward returned to the newspaper business in Greensboro, where for a time he was a colleague of Brodie Griffith. He married in the early

1920s and accepted a daytime job on Johnson's *Knoxville Sentinel.* But Greensboro called him back. He was executive editor of the morning *Daily News* before joining the *Observer.*

Quick, incisive, and restless, Hunter could edit copy faster than anyone on the *Observer* staff. He not only edited copy, he carried it to the composing room, reading and correcting as he went. He remained chief of the newsroom—and its highest priced copy boy— for thirty years. He had high ethical standards and the will to enforce them. Though he carried out Curtis Johnson's cost-cutting economies, he kept the confidence of most staff members, who admired his soft heart. He might bawl them out one minute and crunch them in a viselike embrace the next. He liked to sit around after work, telling stories and discussing current events. He also offered advice on how to live, how to save money, how to stay away from strong drink. To protect those who could not handle liquor, Hunter often turned over their pay to their wives.

It was under Hunter that the *Observer* developed the distinctive, old-style appearance that made it instantly identifiable across the Carolinas and earned it the nickname "the *New York Times* of the South." Hunter liked old-fashioned vertical makeup, with a careful mixture of typefaces that set each story off from its neighbor. He also liked a balance of pictures, cartoons, and other graphics that gave readers an impression that excitement was waiting on the page. Though *Observer* pages were jammed with stories, Hunter used column rules, stars, dashes, and cut-off rules to guide the hurried reader's eye.

Sad to say, Hunter, like most other *Observer* employees, stood in awe of Curtis Johnson and yielded to the publisher's wishes in backing away from controversy or stories that raised sensitive issues. With a soldier's instinct for authority, he executed his commander's orders, even though he might disagree with them. He allowed the paper to prominently display "puff" stories about advertisers or to soft-pedal news that was embarrassing to commercial interests. The paper's pale coverage of the Depression was just one example. Even under Ernest Hunter, the *Observer* was dominated by advertisers and the business community.

While the *Observer* avoided local controversy, it gave generous space to national and international news not available to other papers in the area. When advertising declined during the Depression, Johnson and Hunter filled the space with more news and features. They purchased syndicated features at bargain rates, expanded

Sunday comics to twelve pages, and added more photographs and cartoons. On many days, the paper contained less than 20 percent advertising (as opposed to a normal 50 to 60 percent).

The *Observer*'s business interest showed in its reaction to Franklin Roosevelt. When the New York governor won the Democratic nomination for president in 1932, *Observer* editorials welcomed him as a man capable of balancing the budget and restoring national confidence. When Roosevelt defeated Hoover, an *Observer* editorial called his triumph "a revolution by ballot," and cheered prospects for the end of Prohibition and "beer by Christmas." *Observer* editors approved of most of the emergency measures in Roosevelt's first 100 days and the general thrust of the New Deal. But as the economy revived, they expressed increasing doubt about the long-term implications of the New Deal and its labor relations policies. To Johnson and *Observer* editors, they looked like socialism.

The paper reflected the same business conservatism at the state level, where Gov. O. Max Gardner was trying to cut costs, relieve indebted cities and counties, and find money to compensate school teachers and public employees who were being paid in scrip. The *Observer* urged a reduction in taxes and spending, but Gardner and his successor, J. C. B. Ehringhaus, sought a 3 percent sales tax. Torn between a love for education and a commitment to commerce, the *Observer* vacillated, but then joined merchants in opposing the sales tax—in front-page editorials.

To increase reader appeal, Curtis Johnson and Ernest Hunter hired two more staff writers early in the Depression. They brought back as sports editor the gifted Julius Jennings ("Jake") Wade, whose sports columns had been a big favorite in the mid-1920s. A native of Dunn and a graduate of UNC, Wade was a shy, reserved, but well-read man with ambitions to write serious fiction. As a sports, news, and Associated Press writer, he had worked in several cities during the 1920s, but returned to the *Observer* in December 1930, about the time Duke University was hiring coach Wallace Wade from Alabama and giving new emphasis to college football. Jake Wade's first assignment for the *Observer* was an interview with coach Wade. His column, "Jake Wade's Sports Parade," would highlight *Observer* sports pages until after World War II.

A second major addition to the staff was Julian S. Miller, whose association with the *Observer* dated from Joseph Caldwell's days. Miller spent the years from 1915 to 1931 on the *Charlotte News*. As the Depression bit deeper in September 1931, he left to aid the work of a state relief commission. Six months later, he accepted the *Ob-*

server's offer to become associate editor, assisting Wade Harris, who was beginning to look old and to sound tired after more than fifty years in Charlotte journalism. In addition to editorials, Miller wrote a second-front column on people and politics in the Carolinas. When the seventy-seven-year-old Harris died in September 1935, the forty-nine-year-old Miller was appointed to succeed him.

Throughout the Depression, Johnson maintained his expansionist strategy and continued to show a profit. He never cut back the size of the paper or reduced its staff. Nobody was laid off, though when circulation dipped (from 46,657 in 1929 to 45,143 in 1932) wages were cut 10 percent one year and 5 percent the next. Beginning in 1933, at the bottom of the Depression, the total effect of the *Observer*'s superior resources—an expanded staff, broader news coverage, more and better features, a distinctive appearance, an efficient delivery system, and an aggressive selling force—began to wear down the *News* and show up in circulation figures. As the *Observer*'s sales climbed from 47,867 a day in 1933 to 66,211 in 1936, its local circulation rose from 12,393 to 15,994, exceeding the *News* by 481 papers daily and 1,533 on Sundays. After that, the *Observer* was never again headed. With the lead in circulation came a supremacy in advertising as well. Yet Charlotte's newspaper wars were far from over.

CHAPTER 9

WAR, CONSERVATISM, AND RECORD GROWTH
1936-1950

With the key elements in place, the *Observer* hit a stride in the mid-1930s that produced the greatest growth in the paper's history. From 1936 to 1950, it twice expanded its plant and staff and again doubled its circulation, pushing sales to 135,473 copies a day—1,431 more than the number of men, women, and children within the corporate limits of Charlotte. The *Observer* became one of the few newspapers in the country with a circulation exceeding the population of its hometown. While growing, it altered its attitude toward radio, lent crucial support to community projects, began developing a local columnist, and further softened its attitude toward blacks. Its growth continued despite manpower and paper shortages during World War II, the death of an editor, and the departure of a popular sports columnist. But storm signals arose in the fall of 1950, when Curtis Johnson died and left the paper under clouded ownership.

Again it was an age, just before the rise of television, when world and national events encouraged an eager reading of newspapers. In every corner of the globe, the winds of war were blowing. Hitler was rising in Germany, Franco in Spain, and Mussolini in Italy. Stalin was tightening his grip on Russia, and the Japanese were seizing an empire in the Pacific. When the fighting erupted, human beings found new and more terrible ways of killing each other. By the end of the decade, the mushroom cloud of the atom bomb towered over the horizon, leaving man no refuge from his own destructive tendencies.

In the United States, where a second depression began in 1937, the Roosevelt administration embarked on a second phase of the New Deal that was even more reformist than the first. During this period, the South was singled out as "the Nation's No. 1 economic problem" and targeted for more assistance in the form of public welfare, improved health facilities, and more public works projects, many of them under the Works Progress Administration (WPA), a program of huge benefit to Charlotte and the Carolinas. Douglas Airport, the Mint Museum of Art, Revolution Park, and even the indexing of titles and trusts in the Mecklenburg County Office of the Register of Deeds were wholly or in part products of that program. Under the New Deal, the federal government became much more of a partner in state and local government.

The Depression and the world war that followed produced a different kind of America, one that traveled on rubber tires and concrete rather than on steel wheels and rails. Cities gave up streetcars in favor of buses, and railways quickened their curtailment of passenger service. Airports built and expanded for wartime use were turned over to civilian aviation. The Depression and war brought dramatic changes in wages, hours, working conditions, and housing. The first rush of residents from the inner cities to the suburbs showed up in the 1940 census, and the exodus from urban centers became a stampede in the years after World War II.

The Depression and the war also gave rise to a continuing crusade for education and a dramatic expansion of educational resources, from the public school to the graduate school. And they stirred a new awareness of human rights and expectations, inspiring efforts to open wider opportunities for blacks and women. It was in this period that Charlotte blacks began voting in significant numbers, that Joe Louis came to prominence as an American hero, that the armed services were desegregated, that Jackie Robinson broke the color barrier in professional baseball, and that universities in the white South were forced to admit blacks to selected graduate schools. That increase in black awareness, plus the increase in black purchasing power, made many newspapers, including the *Observer*, more attentive to black interests and more responsive to black readership.

During the period, radio emerged as a competitor for news and advertising. Throughout the Depression, newspapers were losing advertising and radio was gaining. The American Newspaper Publishers Association urged publishers to stop promoting radio. For two years, the *Observer*, which had befriended WBT, joined other papers in halting publication of daily radio schedules. Some papers, including the *Observer*, tried to ban the word "radio" from their pages. They also retouched photographs to eliminate microphones in front of speakers.

The publishers' most serious effort to restrict radio was a move to prevent the Associated Press, and by extension the United Press, from supplying news to radio stations. The move brought a lawsuit against the AP for restraint of trade. Slowly the case worked its way to the United States Supreme Court, which ruled in June 1945 in favor of the broadcasters, forcing the AP to revise its membership rules and extend service to all media. Like many newspapers, the *Observer* condemned the judgment as a limit on the First Amendment. But in time, the decision had the opposite effect: it increased the flow of news and information and ultimately benefited publishers as much as broadcasters, especially after 1950, when television entered the picture as an additional gatherer of news.

After first promoting radio and then opposing it, Curtis Johnson and the *Observer* tried in 1936 to enter broadcasting themselves. Johnson spurned a chance to buy WBT in the late 1920s because he thought it was a passing—and unprofitable—fad. Instead the station was sold to the Columbia Broadcasting System. That failure to see a business opportunity was unlike Johnson, who was usually ahead of fellow publishers in exploiting an opening. But in this case, publishers in Greensboro, Winston-Salem, Asheville, Durham, High Point, Wilmington, and cities across the country were buying radio stations while Johnson was dismissing them as beneath the dignity of a good newspaper. Later, after radio had demonstrated its worth, Johnson and the *Observer* joined W. Carey Dowd, Jr., and the *Charlotte News* in forming a $50,000 corporation to seek a radio license. The corporation was chartered in October 1936. A year later, when the license it sought was awarded to another city, the firm was dissolved.

The joint effort to enter broadcasting did not lessen competition between the *Observer* and the *News*. They continued to fight for every story, every ad contract, and every new subscriber. With both papers publishing Sunday editions, Saturday was the best news day of the week. That was when news makers in business and government usually chose to divulge their plans. They knew both papers were likely to give their stories good display the next morning. The rest of the week, a story that appeared in one paper was usually buried in the other.

If anything, the two papers were competing more vigorously as a result of bolder leadership at the *News*. When W. Carey Dowd, Sr., died in 1927, his second son, J. Edward ("Bill") Dowd, came home from Richmond, Virginia, and joined his brother, W. Carey Dowd, Jr., in running the business side of the newspaper. In 1931, when Julian Miller went to Raleigh and thence to the *Observer*, Bill Dowd moved into the editor's office and began breathing fire and humor into *News* opinions. Bill Dowd wrote short, incisive, often funny editorials that gave the *News* a waspish style. He had a knack for descriptions that stuck in the imagination. When Charlotte's city council split seven-to-four on a series of hotly contested issues, Dowd characterized the council as "the Seven Iron Dukes and the Four Blocks of Granite," names that soon turned up even in the *Observer*.

Under Bill Dowd, the *News* adopted an enterprising style of reporting. Not satisfied with telling what happened, Bill Dowd and Brodie Griffith sent reporters to find out why things happened. Out of those inquiries came a crusading zeal that sparked reform. Reporter Cameron Shipp's 1937 series on Charlotte's slum housing led to the construction of Piedmont Courts and Fairview Homes as the city's first public housing. The *News*'s most celebrated crusade was a sixteen-part series written by reporter Tom Jimison who pretended to be a patient at the state mental hospital at Morganton. It inspired mental-hospital reforms.

Reporters on the *Observer* were infected by that crusading spirit and tried to emulate it. City hall reporter Tom Watkins wrote a long and, for the *Observer*, bold series on the public-health threat posed by syphilis. His series avoided any reference to sexual relations but relied on such euphemisms as "pleasure" and "sin." Hazel Trotter wrote stories about the need for charity medical care for indigent patients. But reform was not the mission of *Observer* publisher Curtis Johnson and managing editor Ernest Hunter, and under their leadership the paper steered clear of sensitive issues. When a reporter visited the Catawba Indian Reservation near Rock Hill, South Carolina, and wrote of Indian claims to much of the land in York County, South Carolina, Johnson sent a note upstairs banning further stories on that subject. The *Observer* usually stuck to who-what-where-when reporting and left the why to others. It concentrated on covering organizations, their meetings, memberships, officers, speakers, and goals, and sought to be the newspaper of record for the city and the region. Day in and day out it produced a big, fat, newsy paper crammed full of stories and features. What it lacked in quality it made up in quantity, though its overall tone was a trifle stodgy.

On the editorial page, the stodginess was more pronounced. Shortly after becoming editor of the *Observer*, Julian Miller received an honorary degree from Erskine College, his alma mater, and thereafter was known as "Doctor Miller." He was a popular public speaker and was often called on to address education groups. He was also a fast writer whose typewriter sounded like a machine gun. But his editorials were usually long and windy, and often inconclusive. He obviously did not agree with Curtis Johnson on many issues and wound up writing editorials that straddled differences between them. In one area, however, his editorials were strong, lucid, and right on target. That was when the alarmed Miller turned his eye toward Europe where dictators were rising in Germany, Italy, and Spain. As war clouds gathered, he warned of the price the world would pay for having bungled the peace talks after World War I.

On controversial issues closer to home, the *Observer* rarely took strong stands. The one exception was education and teacher pay, which Miller consistently supported, often in vigorous language—though he remained imprecise about how the public should be taxed to pay for education improvements. On economic issues, the *Observer* reflected a safe, sober, big-business point of view, boosting industry, boasting of growth, and opposing all efforts to regulate wages, hours, and working conditions. It bitterly opposed labor unions. It campaigned for an end to North Carolina's corporate income tax as a means of attracting more industry to the state. That was the pro-business formula that had brought the *Observer* its prosperity and an ever-expanding readership, and the publisher and his editors were not about to abandon it.

In 1936 and 1937, in fact, the paper geared up for another round of expansion. The press it had installed ten years earlier was no longer adequate for printing 60,000 daily and 68,000 Sunday papers. To get papers printed in time for delivery to distant points in the Carolinas, the *Observer* had to complete its printing cycle between 11:00 p.m. and 4:00 a.m. A paper printed earlier would not contain late-breaking news and sports scores that readers expected. One printed later could not be delivered before breakfast. On many nights, the old press could not meet that schedule. In late 1936, a new press was installed, one capable of printing more pages per paper and more papers per hour.

At the same time, the paper was expanding its business and editorial staffs. To the business side it added Pryor Hamlin ("P. H.") Batte, a portly, bald, smooth-talking Virginian who came to the *Observer* from Anderson, South Carolina, in September 1936 to head the advertising department. Affable, confident, and good humored, Batte might have been a professional entertainer. He could sing, play a piano, pick a guitar, and tell an endless stream of funny stories in Amos-and-Andy style. His favorite expression was "yowsa, yowsa," which he used to put people at ease or soothe ruffled feelings. He quickly won friends among Charlotte merchants.

Like others at the *Observer*, Batte wore a hat even while seated at his desk. He removed it only when summoned by Curtis Johnson. Then, setting the hat aside, he would pass his palms over the sweaty fringe of hair on his bald head and, with a jaunty stride, trip across the mezzanine to Johnson's office. Batte was one of the few people in the company who knew how to talk to Johnson and get the publisher's approval. He was an able man and was soon promoted to business manager and then to general manager. His genial style and access to Johnson made him a power within the Observer Company and a leader in the Charlotte business community.

Among other business office changes in 1936 was the departure of M. H. Brandon, the resourceful promoter who had modernized the circulation department and created the Observer Transportation Company. He also made a lasting contribution by helping to organize the Carolinas Golden Gloves, an amateur boxing tournament that the *Observer* sponsored each year. In addition to his work for the *Observer*, Brandon was engaged in several sideline businesses. He had invented a special hand truck for use in newspaper mailrooms and was marketing it among other newspapers. He had also built a number of bowling alleys and was promoting their use. When Curtis Johnson decided Brandon's private interests were compromising his loyalty to the newspaper, he asked him to leave. Brandon moved to Memphis, where he organized a trucking company similar to the *Observer*'s, only this time Brandon got to keep the profits. Brandon was succeeded by J. Granbery Ward.

On the second floor, additions were also being made to the news and feature staffs. Dick Banks, son of Howard Banks, Joseph Caldwell's Shakespeare-quoting associate in the 1890s, finished Davidson College and followed his father's footsteps to the *Observer*. Like most people who enrolled in the Ernest B. Hunter school of journalism, Banks began as a proofreader. After demonstrating a grasp of grammar, punctuation, and spelling, he was promoted in 1936 to the news desk, where he learned to edit copy and write headlines. He would remain an *Observer* writer and editor until his retirement in the mid-1970s.

About the same time, twenty-three-year-old Carlos Kumpe, son of the head proofreader, J. E. Kumpe, was transferred from the proof room to the newsroom clerk's desk. There he kept his eyes open, his mouth shut, and absorbed the welter of details that go into putting together a morning newspaper. His sure knowledge of Carolinas people and places and keen eye for news made him a key figure in *Observer* newsrooms for the next forty-one years.

Three other additions to the newsroom in 1936 proved to be significant. One was Sam Justice, an Asheville native and University of Missouri graduate who left the proof room to become a reporter and later developed a local column. The second was Robert C. ("Bob") Page, a Charlotte native and UNC graduate who joined the *Observer* as a headline writer and after World War II became city editor. The third was pipe-smoking Wilton Garrison, an Easley, South Carolina, native and Washington and Lee graduate whose coverage of Spartanburg's 1936 American Legion Junior Baseball champions caught Jake Wade's eye. He joined the sports department as Wade's assistant. A gentle, soft-spoken man, he later succeeded Wade and remained sports editor until retiring in 1966.

Garrison came to the sports department to replace Hayward M. ("Hayti") Thompson, who was transferred to the state news desk. Old-timers credit Thompson, a slim, dark, good-humored left-hander who was lightning on a typewriter, with extending the *Observer*'s state news coverage further than anyone. In an amiable, Georgia boy's drawl, he recruited correspondents in distant towns, taught them what he wanted reported, and edited their copy with a thick black pencil and blinding speed. It was that coverage of events out in the state that enabled the *Observer* to sell more papers than Charlotte had population. Thompson stayed five years on the state desk, was drafted in 1943, and after World War II came back to develop a flair for typography and page design as editor of the Sunday features section. He was a mainstay on the editing staff and a favorite among *Observer* employees until his retirement in 1966.

Like Hayti Thompson on the state desk, sports editor Jake Wade was also recruiting far-flung correspondents. Among Wade's recruits was a slight, ruddy-faced, sandy-haired student at Presbyterian Junior College, then located at Maxton. The young man was James B. McMillan, who would later make a name for himself as a Golden Gloves boxer, a champion debater, a trial lawyer, a court reformer, and a United States district court judge. It was Judge McMillan who presided over the Charlotte-Mecklenburg school-busing case in the early 1970s.

Another of Wade's correspondents was a lanky, dark-haired Baptist who was a student at Wake Forest College, then located in Wake County, a few miles northeast of Raleigh. The son of the Monroe police chief, he signed his stories "By Jesse Helms Jr." He later became a Raleigh newsman and radio-TV commentator and now represents North Carolina in the United States Senate.

The *Observer* was also attracting distinguished carriers during those years. One of them was William Clyde Friday, a high school student in the town of Dallas in Gaston County. Fifty years later Friday said he could still remember the cold feet and chapped hands he endured while delivering papers in the dark, icy dawns during the Depression. In 1986 he retired after having served thirty years as president of the University of North Carolina.

From 1936 to 1942 the *Observer* tried to develop a personal column to anchor the front page of the local news section, known as the "second front." Such columns help to break the formality of a newspaper and blend warmth and personality with the flow of news. They also give readers someone on the paper to identify with, to contact about stories, and to hear their pleas for various causes. But local columnists require a rare combination of talents, and the *Observer* had not had a successful practitioner of the craft since Isaac Erwin Avery wrote "Idle Comments" at the turn of the century.

In the early 1930s, T. D. Kemp, Jr., a slight Alabamian who had traveled widely on his father's railroad pass and studied in Europe, persuaded Curtis Johnson to let him write a local column. Kemp had an easy writing style and shared Johnson's conservative views. From 1932 to 1934, his columns ran five days a week on the second front but were editorial in tone and did not invite reader participation. Later, he wrote profiles for the editorial page on people in the news. They were good enough to be syndicated. Kemp expanded his profile on Hitler into a thin paperback that sold nationwide in the late 1930s, when it was one of the few available biographies of the Führer.

But Kemp's heart was in show business—his brother Hal Kemp led a nationally known dance band—and he gave up the daily column in the mid-1930s to develop a show-business booking agency. He reduced his column output to three a week, then two, and finally one, which appeared on Sunday mornings until 1952. The booking agency was a success—it was Kemp who brought Elvis Presley to the Carolina Theater in 1956 for the rock-'n'-roll singer's first appearance in Charlotte.

Kemp's second-front columns were replaced by "Event and Comment," a daily commentary by Julian Miller after his return to the *Observer* as associate editor. But Miller's columns, like Kemp's, were editorial in style and not about everyday people. When Miller was appointed editor, his column moved to the editorial page with him. Ernest Hunter then offered the second-front space to members of the reporting staff for columns about interesting people or situations on their news beats. Dick Pitts often filled it with notes about theater people. Hazel Trotter filled it once with a column on the increasing prominence of women in local business and civic affairs. Even photographer Jake Houston used it; he took candid photos of people and wrote funny captions. But for most reporters, the column was a chore on top of their other duties.

From 1936 to 1940, the reporter who most often filled that space was tall, thin, mustachioed Sam Justice, who converted the column into a collection of around-town vignettes and notes on local people. In January 1940, the column was made his alone under the name "Justice for All." Accompanying the column was a photo of Justice brandishing a judge's gavel. Justice often used the space to engage readers in the paper. In 1940, he offered $100 in prizes for the three best names suggested for the big new hotel going up on North Tryon Street. The entries poured in, many with a historic theme. But the developers ruined his contest by naming the hotel for their father, William R. Barringer.

During World War II, Justice accepted a navy commission and signed off the column, vowing to come back when the nation was at peace. He did, but by then yearned for bright lights and big cities and took a public relations job in New York. Someone else would have to establish the second-front column.

While the *Observer* was undergoing its 1936–37 expansions, the widow of Walter Sullivan complained that she was not getting a fair share of the company's profits. Under a trust established by Sullivan, his wife and daughter shared income from his *Observer* stock, which by 1937 amounted to 42.5 percent of the company. The widow charged that the American Trust Company, executor of her husband's estate, was conspiring with Curtis Johnson to undermine her interests. The bank protested the widow's charge, disagreed with her assessment of Johnson's management, and asked to be relieved of its trust obligation.

Behind Mrs. Sullivan's complaint was some personal history. For some years, Curtis Johnson had spent Sunday afternoons as a guest at Mrs. Sullivan's home in Myers Park. When Mrs. Sullivan and her daughter, Clayton, toured Europe, she asked her friend and *Observer* columnist Mrs. Irving Harding McGeachy to look after her "favorite boyfriend." When Mrs. Sullivan returned from the Continent, she found Johnson was spending his Sunday afternoons with Mrs. McGeachy. Shortly afterward Mrs. Sullivan filed her complaint against the bank and Johnson.

Mrs. Sullivan's charge deeply offended Johnson, who felt his integrity was publicly impugned. He told friends that out of loyalty to his late partner, he tried to be generous to the Sullivan estate. He certainly made the *Observer* a profitable investment for Sullivan heirs. A month later, Mrs. Sullivan withdrew the allegations, and the bank remained trustee for the estate. But for Johnson the incident ended his friendship with Mrs. Sullivan.

By 1936 Ernest Hunter had toned down the *Observer*'s brassy self-promotion, but the paper was still tooting horns for special causes, especially those that enhanced its image. Over the next few years the paper lent its voice and news columns to the support of sports, the arts, music, and other causes benefiting the community.

The paper's Golden Gloves boxing tournaments gave boys, many of whom were idle and unskilled, a goal to work toward that would improve their bodies and raise their self-esteem. A second promotion aimed at improving the health and outlook of boys was the Observer Fresh Air Camp. It grew out of Curtis Johnson's concern for Frank Vita, a pale, thin, twelve-year-old who regularly came through the *Observer* office selling candy, gum, and crackers. Johnson took an interest in the boy and coached him on the meaning and spelling of big words. Several times he gave his secretary, Eudora Parker (later Mrs. Wilton Garrison), money to buy the boy a decent lunch. Once he gave her money to buy him a suit of clothes. Despite Johnson's attentions, the boy remained pale and spindly. One summer Johnson sent him to a boys' camp. Two weeks later, young Vita came home tanned and glowing. That success persuaded Johnson to create a camp for other less-privileged boys, much like the one sponsored by the *Herald-Tribune* in New York.

In the spring of 1937 he bought 115 acres of wooded land on the banks of Lake Wylie, just inside South Carolina, and put up money for a camp consisting of four main buildings and seventeen cabins. The camp could accommodate 150 boys at a time for vacations that included instruction in swimming, boating, hiking, baseball, and other games. It would also teach safety, hygiene, nutrition, and crafts. Proceeds from each year's Golden Gloves boxing tournament went to the Fresh Air Fund. The public was encouraged to give: seven dollars to send a boy to camp for one week, fourteen dollars to send him for two weeks. When J. B. Ivey's autobiography, *My Memoirs*, entered a second printing, the merchant donated his royalties to the Fresh Air Fund. From July 1937 through the summer of 1945, the camp welcomed more than 500 boys each season, at least 100 of them from South Carolina communities served by the *Observer*. In

1946, Johnson gave the $150,000 complex, including twenty-five buildings and $98,000 in cash, to the YMCA, which renamed it Camp Thunderbird. The Fresh Air Fund became Observer Charities, Inc.

Also in the 1930s, the *Observer* joined efforts that preserved the United States Mint as an art museum. The mint was dismantled at its West Trade Street site to make room for an expansion of the United States Courthouse and Post Office, a Depression project to create jobs. The newspaper wrote editorials favoring the mint's preservation and opened its columns to citizens like lawyer Julia Alexander who wrote about the mint's history and architecture. But it was not a popular project. Raising money to move a century-old building to a new location was all but impossible. Like most southern cities, Charlotte lacked the money and sophistication to support an art museum. The project was finally completed with the help of a federal grant. When the museum was dedicated in October 1936, the *Observer* noted that "community esteem for this new venture may appear . . . at low ebb," but the paper was convinced that "it is a development . . . which will come to hold a higher and higher place in the lofty regards of our people."

About the time the Mint Museum was dedicated, the community was celebrating the completion of another federally assisted facility that the *Observer* helped to promote. It was the 15,600-seat American Legion Memorial Stadium, built with a WPA grant, as the third largest arena in North Carolina. President Roosevelt spoke there in September 1936, at a rally for more than 30,000 people. Despite a drenching shower, the ceremonies got off to a propitious start. Just as Roosevelt reached the podium, the clouds parted, the sun broke through, and the president said, "My friends, I notice there is a rainbow in the sky."

In 1939–40, the *Observer* gave editorial support to strenuous efforts to revive the public library, another victim of southern poverty and lagging sophistication. It was discovered that annual city and county grants to operate the library were illegal because under North Carolina law libraries were not a "necessary expense" of local government. A referendum was scheduled to give taxpayers a chance to authorize the grants. Most people assumed the voters would approve a modest library tax, but in the June 1939 election, held during a hubbub over waste in local government, the tax was defeated and the library forced to close. Fearing that Charlotte would look like a bastion of philistinism, *Observer* editor Julian Miller leaped to the city's defense with soothing editorials attributing the defeat to general unrest instead of opposition to the library. He urged city officials to schedule another vote as soon as possible. After many more *Observer* editorials, a four-cent tax was approved in May 1940. The relieved *Observer* said, "a black mark [on Charlotte's reputation] has been erased."

The *Observer* was an important participant in three other campaigns during 1940. In cooperation with the Charlotte Symphony, founded eight years earlier, the paper launched a drive to stimulate interest in classical music. It brought to town a panel of experts for a forum attended by more than 500 guests, and it published a series of articles by Guillermo de Roxlo, the orchestra's first conductor, introducing ten famous symphonic works. In conjunction with the series, the paper sold recordings of the ten works being performed.

A second 1940 campaign raised money and public support to build Charlotte Memorial Hospital as the community's first venture into public medicine. Despite expansions at St. Peter's, Presbyterian, and Mercy hospitals, Charlotte's growth as a medical center put new pressure on existing facilities. Studies in 1938 led to plans for the creation of Memorial as a successor to St. Peter's. The new hospital was to be financed by $500,000 in federal grants, $350,000 in bonds approved by Charlotte voters, and $135,000 donated by private citizens. *Observer* stories and editorials helped create a favorable climate for the bonds and a week-long drive for $135,000 in private donations.

The third 1940 promotion was an all-out effort during the federal census to make Charlotte the first city in the Carolinas with a 100,000 population, a distinction that was expected to attract new business. As census takers completed their first count in April, the Chamber of Commerce moaned that Charlotte was falling short of its goal. The *Charlotte News* persuaded federal officials to check their census lists against names of uncounted residents the paper would supply. The *News* began publishing a coupon that uncounted residents could send to the Census Bureau. The *Observer* joined the campaign by publishing a similar coupon, and throughout the month of May both papers bombarded readers with the question "Have You Been Counted?" On Sunday, June 9, a day when both papers could publish the results simultaneously, the Census Bureau announced that Charlotte's population stood at 100,337 (later revised upward to 100,899). There was great celebration.

Among the Charlotteans that both papers were careful to count were the 31,403 blacks, who were becoming increasingly important to the social and economic life of the community as entrepreneurs as well as servants. Previously, the papers, like most white-owned newspapers in the South, barely mentioned blacks or black institutions except in crime stories. In the late 1930s, as the black middle class expanded and blacks gained purchasing power, that began to change.

Under President Roosevelt, blacks for the first time were holding important positions in the government, not as department heads but as highly visible assistants. The president's New Deal opened job opportunities for blacks and raised the level of black wages. In the South Brevard Street area of Charlotte, then the main street of the black community, young men like A. E. Spears, Fred Alexander, and Bishop Dale were organizing to improve black opportunities and to register black voters. As blacks shifted their political allegiance from the Republican to the Democratic party, they found it easier to register in Charlotte precincts.

In October 1936, a local lawyer, acting on a Supreme Court decision in the Scottsboro case, threatened to seek the dismissal of charges against his client unless blacks were included in the Mecklenburg jury pool. Unlike other southern newspapers, which urged the repudiation of that ruling, the *Observer* conceded that under the Constitution blacks were entitled to serve on juries and should be accorded that privilege.

In May 1937, when Johnson C. Smith University launched a campaign to raise $120,000 for a new dormitory, the *Observer* gave the story a streamer headline on an inside page. In that story, the paper did something even more significant. It referred to the wife of the president of Johnson C. Smith as "Mrs. H. L. McCrorey," perhaps the first time the paper extended a courtesy title to a Negro woman. According to newsroom lore, as the wife of Dr. McCrorey was giving details for the fund-raising story to Haywood Trotter, an *Observer* editor, she asked if he would do her a favor. When Trotter said he would try, she asked, "Could you please refer to me in the story as 'Mrs. McCrorey' instead of by my first name?" Trotter said he would, and thereafter courtesy titles for black women became almost routine in the paper.

In the third week of March 1940, the *Observer* accorded blacks another level of dignity. Almost overnight the paper began capitalizing the *n* in the word *Negro* wherever it appeared in the paper. Twenty years earlier, in an exchange with a New York newspaper, *Observer* editors had defended their consistent practice of lowercasing "negro" on grounds that the paper did not capitalize the *w* in "white." Of course, the paper did not often use "white" to identify Caucasians in its news columns in the same way that it used "negro" to identify blacks. The use of "negro" without a capital letter was seen by many people as an effort to demean the black race.

Why the *Observer* adopted the capitalization is unclear. People who worked for the paper at the time do not remember. The fact that the change was uniform throughout the paper suggests that it was probably a policy decision, made perhaps after a delegation of blacks called upon the editors and requested it. The *Charlotte News* began capitalizing *negro* in January 1938, during national debate over an antilynching law. By March 1940, the Raleigh *News and Observer* was also using the capitalized form of the word, but the *Greensboro Daily News* was not.

A delegation of influential blacks may have called on *Observer* editors in 1941 and prevailed on them to editorialize in behalf of hiring blacks on the city police force, for in February of that year the paper carried an editorial questioning the city's reasons for not employing blacks as policemen. (At about the same time, blacks in Atlanta were lobbying to have blacks on their city's police force.)

During World War II, when blacks were in the armed services and working in defense plants, many more references to Negroes and to Negro organizations began appearing in the paper. The rigidity and repressiveness of the New South creed was beginning to break down and give way to reforms.

The approach of World War II brought other changes. Warning that sooner or later Hitler had to be confronted, editor Julian Miller saw the war coming. On September 2, 1939, after German troops invaded Poland, bringing France and England to Poland's aid, Miller's editorial said, "Ruthless, conscienceless, man-hating, God-sneering Hitler has unleashed his legions against Poland. . . . It is unutterable folly."

Once the war was under way, Miller was impatient for the United States to join it, a view that was not popular among his readers. He complained that American neutrality was a sham and that Hitler's lightning conquest of France left England to suffer in America's stead. Putting aside its old alarm about federal debts and public spending, the *Observer* supported Roosevelt's decision to send the British surplus American destroyers. It also supported the president's mobilization of the National Guard and his call for a revival of the draft. In the international emergency, the paper's doubts about a third term for Roosevelt also vanished, as was true among the American people in general.

As in World War I, war news from Europe benefited the *Charlotte News* more than it did the *Observer*. The five-hour time difference between England and the United States gave the *News* first crack at most battle stories. The *News*, for instance, was on the street with an extra about Germany's invasion of Poland before most *Observer* editors were out of bed. Despite that advantage, the *News* moved in February 1941 to abandon its Sunday morning edition.

The decision was announced at a meeting of merchant-advertisers. Publisher W. Carey Dowd, Jr., and his brother Bill said discontinuing the Sunday edition would improve the evening paper the rest of the week. As it was, reporters and editors saved their best stories until Sunday, often starving the Thursday, Friday, and Saturday editions. Producing a Saturday afternoon paper followed by a Sunday morning edition worked a hardship on *News* personnel. The paper's last Sunday edition was published on February 23.

The Dowds made no mention of three other factors that influenced their decision. One was a newsprint shortage. As military cargoes filled railroad cars, there was less room for rolls of newsprint. Newspapers were assigned a monthly allotment, based on previous consumption. The *News* had been using up its allotment in an effort to increase circulation around military bases, such as Fort Bragg. Eliminating the Sunday paper eased that crunch. A second factor was the lack of Sunday Associated Press service. In deference to the *Observer*, an AP founder, the agency refused to serve the *News* on Sunday mornings. That made putting out a newsy Sunday paper very difficult. A third factor was the *Observer*'s superiority in circulation and advertising. By February 1941, *Observer* Sunday editions contained between seventy-two and seventy-six pages, compared with thirty and thirty-two pages in the *News*. *Observer* circulation inside Charlotte averaged 20,331 copies a Sunday; *News* circulation inside the city averaged 16,503 on Sundays.

Even so, the *News* was still a lively, aggressive paper and had added Charlotte natives Tom Fesperman and Reed Sarratt to its reporting staff, Harriet Doar to its women's staff, and Burke Davis to its sports staff. Clever and lightfooted, they usually ran rings around the ponderous *Observer* in local coverage. The *News* had also taken on a tall, thin, nervous young intellectual named C. A. ("Pete") McKnight. A Shelby native who finished Davidson College with high honors and served a brief apprenticeship on the *Shelby Star*, McKnight wrote bright, clean stories that crackled with energy and hard facts. In ten years he climbed from reporter to city editor, news editor, and managing editor to become, in 1949, a prize-winning editor at age thirty-three.

War, Conservatism, and Record Growth

About the only place the *News* was not routinely beating the *Observer* was in covering business, where Hazel Trotter was untouchable, and at city hall, where Hal Tribble, an *Observer* newcomer from Anderson, South Carolina, was beginning to sew up stories. Tribble brought to the *Observer* a brassy writing style that was apparent in his first story, an interview with orchestra leader Paul Whiteman, which was memorable for its rhythms and trumpet flourishes.

The *Observer* did not comment on the demise of its Sunday competitor. At the time it was nervous about what newsprint rationing might do to its own Sunday edition. As the shortage worsened, Curtis Johnson asked Ernest Hunter to have his staff look over the Sunday paper and suggest what might be eliminated. He got back a thick Sunday edition with suggested cuts marked in pencil. He turned through those carefully as a worried Hunter looked on. When he was finished, Johnson stood, closed the paper, folded it, and put both hands on top of it. "I will not be party to the destruction of my newspaper," he said. So nothing was dropped, though for a time the size of the paper was frozen, as was its circulation. On occasion, Johnson even ordered advertising left out to conserve newsprint.

The absence of a Sunday morning edition did not prevent the *Charlotte News* from exploiting an advantage it had on Sunday, December 7, 1941, when the Japanese bombed Pearl Harbor. Word of the attack reached Charlotte by radio around noon, and by early afternoon *News* executives had summoned a makeshift staff and produced an extra that newsboys sold as fast as they could make change. Pete McKnight recalled editing a wire story in which a Pearl Harbor resident was quoted as saying, "I'll bet the papers on the Mainland will exaggerate this." But the disaster proved to be one of those events that could hardly be exaggerated. News of the bombing all but broke up a professional football game at Memorial Stadium. Fans leaving the stadium encountered *News* vendors selling papers with big, ugly headlines that everybody knew meant war, even if few people had ever heard of Pearl Harbor or knew of its strategic importance in the Pacific.

Members of the *Observer* staff rushed to their newsroom that Sunday, but their hands were tied for the afternoon. Under a prior agreement between Ernest Hunter and the *News*'s Brodie Griffith, the *Observer* would not produce an extra before 6:00 p.m. and the *News* would not produce one before 6:00 a.m. By the time the *Observer* got an extra on the street, the edge was off the Pearl Harbor story, so *Observer* headlines focused on the Japanese raid on Guam and the fact that war had been declared. With the stories, it ran maps showing where Japan was in relation to Guam, the Philippines, and other Pacific islands. The maps gave readers a chilling view of the war's immense theater.

Earlier that year the *Observer* lost its first staff member to military service. Impatient for combat, copy editor Charles Lesesne joined the Royal Canadian Air Force in February 1941. After Pearl Harbor there was a steady drain of employees from all departments of the paper. Dick Banks and photographer Jimmy Dumbell, a Charlotte native who had joined the staff in 1940, went into the army in January 1942. In all, the paper sent 110 people into military service during the war. Eighteen of those came from the twenty-five-member newsroom, meaning that the *Observer* had to replace almost an entire news staff.

Ernest Hunter anticipated the manpower shortage, and in 1940 began hiring older men unlikely to be called into service. They included John and Granbery Dickson, brothers with whom he had worked in Greensboro. Granbery Dickson brought with him an old-timer's habit of clipping and filing significant stories; in the process he accumulated on his desk top the beginnings of the *Observer* library. His brother John, a reformed alcoholic, was an inspiration to other *Observer* drinkers. To test his resolve, he kept a full bottle on his living room mantel, and at work sang temperance songs under his breath. John Dickson also maintained Hayti Thompson's pace on the state desk and ran a journalism school that turned out several skilled deskmen.

Later, as the armed services claimed more of the staff, Hunter began hiring women. The first was Marjorie Dumbell, Jimmy Dumbell's sister, hired in October 1942 out of Queens College. After her came Adelaide Butler, Joseph Caldwell's daughter whose husband had gone into service; Mary Gillett, wife of news editor Rupert Gillett; Valerie Varnon; and Mary Pressley. Hunter also called Henry Daugherty out of retirement. In addition to women and the elderly, Hunter hired the young before they could be drafted. When Eddie Allen and Earl Heffner finished Central High in 1942, they joined the *Observer* sports department. Hunter also hired Bryan Caldwell, Joseph Caldwell's grandson, who was later drafted. Early in the war, many key staff members began working a six-day week.

In the composing room, which then employed twice as many people as the newsroom, the war hit even harder. Superintendent John P. White was constantly seeking replacements and ultimately hired several female printers.

Throughout the war, the *Observer*, like other firms in the city, patriotically displayed the names of its employees in service. The *Observer*'s "Honor Roll" appeared every Sunday on the editorial page. At Christmas, Curtis Johnson remembered the people on the list with a gift of twenty-five dollars. The gifts were a precedent for the Christmas bonuses that Johnson began awarding after the war—twenty-five dollars for each employee, plus five dollars for each year with the company. During the war, Johnson also began providing group life insurance with $2,500 benefits for each employee. The company paid the premium.

On May 2, 1942, the bachelor Johnson took a wife. A brief, two-column item on the *Observer*'s front page the next day announced that Johnson and Mrs. Irving Harding McGeachy had been married in private ceremonies at New York's Waldorf-Astoria Hotel. The union was the result of several years of Sunday afternoon courting. Johnson was sixty-seven; Mrs. McGeachy was fifty-two. The story did not mention that the bride was "Caroline Chatfield," author of the paper's advice-to-the-lovelorn column, a feature she continued to write until August 1943.

During the war, the *Observer* often appeared with three streamer headlines eight columns wide across the front page. One might be on the war in Europe, another on the war in the Pacific, and a third on some political development in Washington or Raleigh. To help readers orient themselves to the fighting, the paper ran illustrated maps locating battle sites: where Stalingrad was, or Iwo Jima, or Bastogne. Rarely did the paper make the war look glamorous. Photos were usually of blackened ruins, twisted wreckage, or the faces of battle-weary soldiers. To help people at home cope with the war, the paper promoted every bond drive and campaign for scrap metal, wastepaper, and animal fat. When rationing began in 1942, the paper ran a daily "Ration Guide" on the local front page, informing readers which coupons merchants were accepting for the purchase of sugar, gasoline, shoes, meat, butter, and other scarce commodities.

As young men and women in the *Observer*'s circulation territory left civilian jobs to enter the armed forces, the paper ran stories and pictures marking their progress: when they completed training, when they were promoted, when they were decorated. The paper also ran one-column pictures of all who were killed, wounded, or missing in action. In 1944 and 1945, as the tide of the war turned and Americans could see victory on the horizon, the number of casualties increased because Americans were engaged in more of the front-line fighting. In those years each day's *Observer* might contain eight, nine, maybe even ten or twelve such photos, brought in by the next-of-kin from Charlotte and surrounding towns. Marjorie Dumbell recalled consoling tear-streaked mothers, widows, or sisters as she got from them biographical data to be published with photos of the dead or missing. Often, she recounted, the women brought with them the telegram from the War Department saying, "We regret to inform you that . . . " Such encounters were deeply moving, she said, even for the normally hard-bitten news staff.

In February 1944, one of those killed in action was S. Sgt. Julian S. Miller, Jr., son of the *Observer* editor. Young Miller, a waist gunner on a B-24 Liberator, was lost in the battle for New Guinea. In January 1945, one of the missing in action was Ernest B. Hunter, Jr., son of the *Observer*'s managing editor. Young Hunter turned up later as a prisoner of war in Germany. In April 1945, Charles Lesesne, the ex–*Observer* copy editor who had joined the Canadian Air Force, was missing after a bombing raid over Germany. He was later declared dead, the war's only casualty from the newsroom. One other *Observer* employee, Lowden Blue Suggs, was killed in action. Another, John F. Jenkins, died in service. Several were prisoners of war.

The most shocking casualty of all came on April 13, 1945, when *Observer* headlines announced that President Roosevelt was dead. It was staggering, unbelievable news that brought many people to tears. For three days, the *Observer* carried long, solemn editorials reviewing the late president's accomplishments and forgetting past quarrels with him over the New Deal. Like the rest of America, the paper was in mourning.

One of the most moving stories about the president's death was reporter LeGette Blythe's account of the huge crowd that watched the Roosevelt funeral train pass through Charlotte on April 14. It began:

> Franklin Roosevelt, honorably discharged from all his wars, rode slowly through Charlotte's sorrowing thousands last night toward the high banks of the Hudson and his long home. Stretching the length of the railroad station and packing the streets that opened out upon the tracks, the people who had come out to see the late President's funeral train . . . paid him the greatest tribute they knew how to pay—the homage of utter silence.
>
> It was one of the greatest throngs ever to assemble at the Southern station. And it was the most orderly. As the crowd awaited the arrival of the train, it stood quietly and talked in low

tones. And as the train came slowly and solemnly through, the only noise was that of the soldiers as they brought their rifles smartly to the salute.

Even as headlines about Roosevelt's death were capturing public attention, the *Observer* was supporting a drive to raise funds for a park memorializing the city's World War II heroes and heroines. Daily the paper ran a headline over the second-front masthead, urging Charlotteans to "Do Your Part!" The drive was a success, and the memorial became Freedom Park.

In August 1945, in reporting the single most important event of the war—America's use of nuclear power—the *Observer's* headlines were ambiguous. News of the bombing of Hiroshima was carried in a six-column rather than eight-column streamer. It said, "Atomic Bomb May Flatten Japan," as if the bomb had yet to be dropped. Only a close reading of the story made it clear that the first bomb had already fallen. The paper's best perspective on the bomb came the next day in a long editorial headlined, "Friend of Man or Frankenstein?" The editorial made it clear that in dropping the bomb America had thrust the world into a new era, filled with both promise and peril.

With the war's end, the nation entered a period of prosperity and expansion, frustrated by a shortage of manpower and materials and by a volatile political climate. Fears of communism were rampant; the race issue was beginning to boil; the public was disagreeing over how and where growth should take place. Over the next five years, uncertainty, discord, deaths, and departures would slow *Observer* efforts to build and equip a new plant. In that period, the *Observer's* political outlook became even more conservative.

The war years had been good to Charlotte and the *Observer*. The city had grown, but the newspaper had grown faster. From 1940 to 1945, its daily circulation had risen from 80,653 to 108,143—a 34 percent increase that was again taxing the paper's physical facilities. In November 1945, two months after the Japanese surrender, Curtis Johnson announced plans for expanding the *Observer* plant. He had been accumulating cash reserves and had acquired the entire block along South Tryon from Stonewall Street to the Southern Railway line (which then crossed Tryon), and from Tryon back to Church Street. On the block he proposed to duplicate the 1926 building twice over, tripling the paper's office and production space. The new buildings would be air-conditioned and have elevators, a cafeteria, and conference rooms. Work would be started as soon as construction plans could be drawn and materials were available, Johnson said.

Several things upset Johnson's timetable. Col. J. N. Pease, who was Johnson's architect, recalled that the publisher was uncertain about what size expansion to make. At one point, the colonel said, Johnson was dickering to buy the *Charlotte News*. By the war's end, W. Carey Dowd, Jr.'s health was declining, and members of the Dowd family were anxious to sell the paper. It is quite likely that Johnson (known among the Dowds as "C. Buzzard Johnson") talked with the family about purchasing the *News*, but the negotiations did not succeed. In January 1947, the *News* was sold for an undisclosed sum to Thomas L. Robinson of Boston and a syndicate of blue-chip businessmen from the Carolinas. Whatever the price, it was too high, because throughout his tenure as *News* publisher, Robinson was strapped to pay the paper's debts and had little reserves with which to improve its plant. Under Robinson, Bill Dowd stayed on as general manager.

Johnson's bid for the *News* was his second unsuccessful postwar effort to broaden his communications base. A year earlier, when the Federal Communications Commission ordered the Columbia Broadcasting System to dispose of Charlotte radio station WBT, Johnson put in a bid for that property. According to Charles Crutchfield, WBT's general manager at the time, Johnson offered $1.5 million, but Jefferson Standard Life Insurance Company offered $1,505,000. In July 1949, Jefferson Standard put WBTV on the air as one of the South's first television stations. It is interesting to speculate how Charlotte's communications industry might have developed had Johnson succeeded in buying both the *News* and WBT.

The greatest obstacle to Johnson's 1945 plan for expanding the *Observer* was a scarcity of materials and equipment. Other businesses had similar plans, and the nation's conversion to peacetime production could not meet the demand. The *Observer* was put on a waiting list for a new press, and by the time it arrived in the fall of 1949, construction costs had led Johnson to limit the expansion to a new wing, with a basement and first floor for the new press, a mailroom overhead, and a composing room addition on the third floor. The wing was added to the south side of the building, forming an "L" with the existing structure. The new ten-unit press could print 50,000 copies of an eighty-page paper per hour and complete the *Observer*'s Sunday morning press run in about four hours. But within a decade the decision not to go on with a larger expansion would prove costly.

While people at the *Observer* were studying blueprints, the city of Charlotte was also making plans. In February 1944, the city council adopted a sixteen-item agenda for postwar development. It included covering Sugar Creek and building a crosstown boulevard over it, creating a new auditorium and civic center, enlarging the water-sewer system, improving streets, building a new library, and expanding the airport. Three weeks later, the *Observer* drew up its own eighteen-point program that included many items on the city's list but added these others: citywide zoning, then a highly controversial issue among many property owners; vigorous efforts to develop industrial parks around the city; a new concept in land-use planning; and efforts to exploit Charlotte's location as a Carolinas distribution center. In the Joseph Caldwell–Daniel Tompkins tradition, the business-minded *Observer* was still promoting the New South creed.

Before work was begun on any of those projects, the *Observer* got a new and different editorial voice. After two years of declining health, Julian S. Miller died of a heart attack on July 28, 1946, at Lumberton, on his way home from a vacation at Wrightsville Beach. Though his career at the *Observer* had begun forty years earlier, he was only fifty-nine. At the time of his death, he was chairman of the state Board of Education, on which he had served for three years. In those days, editors of major newspapers often headed state boards and agencies, including the politically powerful Highway Commission. The idea that such service might compromise their journalistic objectivity had yet to dawn on them.

Curtis Johnson did not appoint anyone to replace Miller as editor. He waited a few weeks before moving news editor Rupert Gillett to the editorial page as an associate editor along with James A. Parham. The closest he came to naming an editor was his appointment of managing editor Ernest Hunter to the editorial board, giving Hunter a voice in the making of both news and editorial policy. The result was a harder edge on the *Observer*'s conservative editorials, most of them by Gillett.

Rupert Gillett was stiff, formal, scholarly, and soft-spoken. Many people thought he had the best mind on the paper. He was more of an ideologue than Julian Miller, and his editorials were more tightly reasoned and better focused. Gillett did not like President Truman, the people around him, or his "shoot-from-the-hip" style. He feared Truman was leading the country toward socialism. In 1948, in protest to a civil rights plank in the Democratic party platform, he wrote an editorial severing the paper's ties to the Democrats. But he did not go to the extreme of other southern editors and support South Carolina Gov. Strom Thurmond, then a Democrat who became the "Dixiecrat" candidate for president. The *Observer* did not endorse a candidate in the 1948 elections, but left little doubt that it favored Thomas E. Dewey over Truman.

In international affairs, Gillett was a "cold warrior" and never missed an opportunity to scorn the Soviets. When Truman ordered American troops to Korea to contain the communists, Gillett approved. At home, Gillett feared the communist menace and often cited FBI Director J. Edgar Hoover's warnings about the presence of communists within the United States government. Initially, Gillett approved of Sen. Joseph McCarthy's communist witch-hunts.

Gillett was barely interested in state and local matters and, like Julian Miller, usually avoided controversial issues. Before the 1947 referendum that gave Mecklenburg County state-owned liquor stores, the *Observer* was silent. The paper continued to support public education and higher teacher pay, but without the fervor Miller usually brought to the subject.

On the most divisive issue to confront the community in the postwar years, the *Observer*'s position was set not on the editorial page but in the print shop. John P. White, the paper's mechanical superintendent, was a member of the Charlotte City Council from 1945 to 1949, during the long wrangle over the route for a crosstown boulevard. A state survey of drivers entering and leaving the city revealed that most motorists wanted to make at least one stop in the inner city. Engineers recommended a route skirting the edge of downtown. Many people argued for a circumferential route that would bypass the city altogether. Placing his faith in the engineers' survey, the crusty, plainspoken White put together four votes on the seven-man council and held firm for the crosstown route through months of sulfurous debate. The crosstown route became Independence Boulevard and a savior of downtown Charlotte. Had the city taken the bypass option, the flight of business and offices from the inner city would have begun sooner and been more severe. As it was, Charlotte's downtown remained strong while that of many other cities declined.

The *Observer* also expressed no preference in the Democrats' 1948 primary for governor, a hot race that changed the course of North Carolina politics. W. Kerr Scott, an Alamance County dairy farmer, upset tradition and party discipline by running from the west when it was the east's turn to nominate the governor. Scott's victory was a defeat for the state's economic oligarchy, which had been hand-picking governors since the turn of the century. The east-west rotation helped the oligarchs control the selection of candidates, avoid regional conflicts, and maintain party unity. After the triumph of Scott, the first nonlawyer to be governor in the twentieth century, the rotation died. East-west rivalry was resumed, sapping party loyalty and draining Democratic strength.

Given *Observer* loyalty to business interests, it is remarkable that the paper did not back Scott's opponent, state treasurer Charles M. Johnson, a conservative who had the support of industrialists, bankers, and financiers. Scott was a Democratic reformer who, fifty years earlier, might have been a Populist. *Observer* editorials reflected none of that. In one of its few comments on the election, the *Observer* straddled the rotation issue by contending that Alamance County was in neither the east nor the west but in neutral territory. In fact, Alamance is west of the fall line that divides the western Piedmont from the eastern Coastal Plain.

Neutrality also initially characterized the paper's stand in the infamous 1950 Democratic primary for the United States Senate. The candidates were Sen. Frank Graham, a Charlottean and former president of the University of North Carolina who had served on President Truman's Civil Rights Commission, and Willis Smith, a Raleigh lawyer, former president of the American Bar Association, and former chairman of the trustees of Duke University. In the first primary, the *Observer* expressed no preference. Graham came within 5,000 votes of winning the nomination outright, though he lost Mecklenburg County by 4,718 votes.

While Smith was deciding whether to call a runoff, the United States Supreme Court handed down two decisions ordering the desegregation of graduate schools in Texas and Oklahoma. The thrust of the decisions clearly indicated that the court was close to condemning "separate but equal" public schools in the South. In the anxiety provoked by those decisions, Smith called for a second primary and zeroed in on Graham's record as a liberal and an advocate of civil rights for blacks. Race became the key issue.

Within a week, the *Observer* abandoned its neutrality and endorsed Smith. It attacked Graham as a friend of the Truman administration and as a senator who would continue "the national drift toward a socialistic state." The *Observer* also rebuked Graham for his conditional approval of Truman's proposed Fair Employment Practices Act, a civil rights measure that the paper feared would promote government interference in hiring decisions.

The campaign degenerated into one of the dirtiest in North Carolina's history. Dr. Graham, who had consolidated the University of North Carolina and led it to greatness for nearly twenty years, was made to look like a dim-witted dupe of blacks and communists. He was falsely accused of appointing a black to West Point. The black votes he received in Piedmont cities in the first primary were heavily emphasized by his opponent. Among the leaders of the Smith campaign was the *Observer*'s former sports stringer, Jesse Helms, Jr., then a radio commentator in Raleigh. In a stunning reversal, Smith won the second primary by more than 20,000 votes, carrying Mecklenburg County by 5,362.

Rupert Gillett's appointment to the editorial page left a big hole in the newsroom. Succeeding him as news editor was city editor Haywood Trotter, and succeeding Trotter on the city desk was Bob Page. Hired as a special writer was Randolph Norton, forty, a gentle Virginian with a graduate degree from Duke University. Norton had been editing a daily newspaper in Beckley, West Virginia, but moved to Mecklenburg County to be near his wife's family. His age, his editing background, and his hiring by Curtis Johnson himself stirred newsroom suspicions that he was being groomed for a bigger job, perhaps Julian Miller's successor as editor. That suspicion dogged Norton, an earnest and conscientious man, the rest of his career.

As those shifts were made, the *Observer* was resolving its uncertainty over a columnist for the second-front page. It gave the honor to a slim, zany man with the improbable name of Augustus Zollicoffer Travis. Gus Travis was no stranger to Charlotte readers. He had come to the *Charlotte News* in the 1920s as a sportswriter who wrote stories in verse. During the Florida land boom, he and UNC classmate Bill Dowd went south in search of riches in real estate. When that went bust, Travis returned to Charlotte as an ad salesman for the *Observer*, often writing ads in verse. Throughout the 1930s, Travis wrote humorous vignettes that appeared on the second front, under the heading "Gus Travis's Flash" and later as "Travisties." During the wartime personnel shortage, Travis left the ad department and moved upstairs to edit copy and write headlines. During slack hours, he regaled his deskmates with tall tales about this or that luminary in town. Those tall tales landed him the columnist's job in April 1946.

Travis could take an ordinary event—somebody putting a penny in a gumball machine and not getting any gum—and turn it into a riotous incident. He made up funny stories about his neighbors, his wife Laura Ann, his maid Edna, his dog Tar Baby, and his fellow staff members at the *Observer*. He also wrote about the mayor, the president of the Chamber of Commerce, the chairman of the board of the bank, even the governor. All notables were fair game for the lively

Travis imagination. Readers loved him, especially those out in the state, who appreciated the fun he made of Charlotte's stuffed shirts. Travis was in constant demand as a banquet speaker and might show up with a snake up his sleeve or a frog in his pocket. His columns were comic strips in prose.

As Gus Travis was establishing his local-front column, the sports pages were losing their anchor. In 1946 Jake Wade resigned as sports editor and later accepted a job as sports publicity director for the University of North Carolina at Chapel Hill, just in time to help promote the Charlie Justice era in Tar Heel football. In sixteen years as the *Observer*'s sports columnist, Wade built a huge following, but he had grown tired of the late hours and the burden of producing six columns a week. He was succeeded by Wilton Garrison, who had often run the department in Wade's absence. Garrison had a wide knowledge of sports and a following of his own, but lacked Wade's touch as a writer.

With the war over and newsprint plentiful, the paper was growing rapidly, and the staff was again expanding. Among the newly hired members was Harry Golden, Jr., a bright, cocky, fast-talking New Yorker who, at the urging of his father, had come south to enroll at Belmont Abbey College. Golden's father, Harry Golden, Sr., a former *Observer* ad salesman, had yet to achieve national fame as editor of the *Carolina Israelite* and author of best-selling books. Young Golden was only eighteen and about to be drafted, but he talked Ernest Hunter into giving him a temporary job on the state desk. Hunter did and discovered a talent. In those days, the *Observer* state desk took stories of all kinds by mail, telephone, and telegraph: weddings, obituaries, elections, accidents, auctions, trials, etc. Golden quickly learned to trim the excess from the essential and make the copy brighter.

He was also a clever writer who often won the five-dollar prize Ernest Hunter offered for the week's best headline. One of his winners was on the story of a tobacco farmer who, after selling his crop, celebrated with more drinks than he could remember and awoke to find he had been robbed. In informing the police, the farmer suggested that God was punishing him for his overindulgence. Golden's headline said, "Farmer's Roll Is Called Up Yonder."

Others hired in the 1946–49 expansion included copy editors Bill Lamkin, Gerry Leland, and Clyde Osborne, reporter Ralph Mulford, society writer Katharine Halyburton, and sportswriters Dick Pierce and Herman Helms, each of whom would add to the paper's overall strength. One of the most significant additions was a part-time reporter. He was Bill Johnson, a postal worker who became the paper's first black writer. A 1938 graduate of Second Ward High School, Johnson studied journalism in the army and afterward sought jobs on black newspapers. When he applied to the *Observer* in 1946, Wilton Garrison told him the paper was looking for someone to cover black sports on a part-time basis. After working his mail route, Johnson would visit black high schools and Johnson C. Smith, then go to the *Observer* at night to type out his reports. At first, he said, the sports desk doubted there was an audience for black sports news, but over time more and more of his copy turned up in print. Johnson remained a sports correspondent until the 1970s and later became editor and publisher of the weekly *Charlotte Post*.

The racial tolerance that greeted Bill Johnson was reflected in the sports department's handling of the Jackie Robinson story. When the Brooklyn Dodgers signed Robinson as the first black in major league baseball, the *Observer* played the story under a streamer headline on the second sports page, neither sensationalizing the racial angle nor ignoring it. It was handled routinely, as were subsequent stories about Robinson's trials as baseball's first black rookie.

In January 1950, as work was completed on an addition to the pressroom and composing room, the *Observer* published a promotion ad saying that 1949 had been the paper's best year in history. During the year it had published 20.2 million lines of advertising and enjoyed a circulation of 134,000 daily and 140,000 on Sundays. The ad did not say so, but profits during the year amounted to more than $800,000 on operating revenues of $3.4 million.

To celebrate, the paper was gearing up to publish a special edition, marking its eightieth anniversary—based on the assumption that the paper had been founded in 1869, as the date on its masthead claimed. Plans for such a celebration drew protests from J. E. Dowd and the *Charlotte News*, who wrote Curtis Johnson, pointing out that the *Observer* of 1869 died in 1887 and that the modern *Observer* should be dated either from the start of the *Chronicle* in March 1886 or from the date of the *Chronicle*'s conversion to the *Observer* in March 1892. Those dates would make the *Observer* either sixty-three or fifty-seven years old—and closer in age to the *Charlotte News*, which was sixty-one. If the *Observer* published an eightieth anniversary edition, the *News* threatened to charge publicly that the claim was false.

Curtis Johnson and P. H. Batte yielded to the *News* complaint and recast the special edition. Instead of the eightieth anniversary, it would celebrate the progress of Charlotte and the Carolinas. The final product, published on February 28, 1950, contained 212 pages and weighed more than three pounds.

Just before the special edition was published, its driving force, general manager P. H. Batte, suffered a stroke and died. He was stricken at the newspaper on a Saturday night and died at home four hours later. He was only fifty-four. His unexpected death was one of three losses the newspaper suffered that year.

The second came in July, when LeGette Blythe, the paper's ablest reporter and most polished writer, resigned in a dispute over a leave of absence in which to finish writing *A Tear for Judas*, a Book-of-the-Month Club novel. To accommodate newsroom needs, Blythe took his vacation early that year, with an understanding that he could take unpaid leave later to finish the book. When he requested the leave, Hunter refused to grant it, apparently on instructions from Johnson, who felt Blythe's fiction writing interfered with his reporting and editing. Blythe left, taking with him a prodigious memory of Mecklenburg people and events. Hunter and others predicted he would be back, seeking his old job, but Blythe found he could earn a comfortable living as a full-time author and went on to write more than thirty novels, biographies, and dramas, twice winning the Mayflower Award for the best nonfiction by a North Carolinian.

The third loss came on October 6, 1950, when Curtis Johnson died at Presbyterian Hospital. His death was not unexpected—Johnson was seventy-four, was suffering from emphysema, and had nearly died a few weeks earlier after emergency surgery for a strangulated hernia. But at his death, Johnson left no clear instructions for the disposition of his newspaper. During his hospital stay, he was drafting and redrafting his will, unable to decide what to do with the *Observer*. According to one account, he asked his nurse as she made evening rounds whether he would live through the night. He said he had important papers he wanted to get signed. The nurse assured him he would survive. During the night he slipped into a coma and died at five o'clock the next afternoon. Under his pillow was an unsigned will leaving the *Observer* to its employees.

For three weeks, his widow and lawyers assumed he had died without a valid will and were preparing for legal snarls that were certain to occur. Then, in the pocket of an old Gladstone bag that the publisher used in traveling to New York, they found a second will, dated April 19, 1947. It was written in pencil in Johnson's firm hand and on stationery of the Waldorf-Astoria Hotel. It was signed by Johnson and witnessed by two Waldorf employees. It was perfectly legal, but before being executed, it would cause the *Observer* all manner of trouble.

CHAPTER 10

STRUGGLES FOR MONEY AND POWER
1950-1954

The terms of Curtis Johnson's handwritten will embroiled the *Observer* in an extended crisis. Competing banks fought over the privilege of administering Johnson's $4.5 million estate, and competing individuals clashed for control of his $6 million newspaper. The fighting continued for four years and involved a dozen lawyers, several publishers, three managing editors, various newspaper department heads, and a bitter union election. When the storms were over, the *Observer* emerged as a different newspaper, with a different look, different owners, and plans to pursue a different brand of journalism.

The conflict sapped the paper's energy and momentum. After thirty-four years of steady gains, circulation hit a standstill. Daily sales stood at 135,473 in October 1950 and at 135,448 in January 1955. Even with an expanded staff, higher wages, new machinery, improved employee benefits, and better working conditions, the editorial and mechanical staffs were divided and demoralized.

During those same years, however, the paper could take pride in some significant accomplishments. It discovered three splendid reporters, reestablished news bureaus in Raleigh and Columbia, South Carolina, changed its typographical dress, and won a national award for its new and youthful appearance. Furthermore, it took a courageous stand in favor of ending segregation in the public schools. People in the Carolinas and newsmen elsewhere in the country were beginning to look upon the once-stodgy *Observer* with new respect.

While the *Observer*'s growth was entering a pause, that of Charlotte and the surrounding region was not. Modern Charlotte as the heart of a network of sprawling suburbs began to emerge in this period. At the end of Independence Boulevard on the eastern edge of town, the city was building a 2,500-seat auditorium and a 12,000-seat coliseum that enlarged its role as an entertainment center for the region. On the other side of town, across the runway from the old airport, the city was building a modern airport terminal that strengthened its position as an aviation and transportation hub. Thanks to the coaxial cable, WBTV was beaming live television into homes across the Carolinas, introducing live college football in the fall of 1951, live coverage of national political conventions in 1952, and live coverage of news from the Charlotte area. The effect enhanced Charlotte's image as a communications center. In the fall of 1954, on a forty-acre slope off Park Road, Paul Younts and others were grading land for the city's first suburban shopping center, touching off a marketing trend that would first expand and later shrink Charlotte's potential as the retailing center of the Carolinas.

Nationally, the focus of interest was the Korean War and the toll it was taking in American lives, dollars, and prestige. Americans wondered how their country could defeat enemies like Germany and Japan and yet be bogged down in a nasty little war against Korea. When Gen. Douglas MacArthur publicly proposed to end the war by widening it in an attack on China, President Truman fired him, creating a national uproar and arousing new suspicions that a communist conspiracy was undermining American leadership. Gen. Dwight Eisenhower was elected president to bring the war to an honorable end, but fears of communist subversion continued to rise, thanks to Sen. Joseph R. McCarthy of Wisconsin, who saw security risks lurking at every level of government. Ultimately, his exaggerated charges exceeded the bounds of political tolerance, and he was formally censured by the Senate, but not before his allegations had created a climate of fear in the country.

Even as McCarthyism was dying, national concerns were shifting from communism to race. The 1950 court decisions that had forced Texas and Oklahoma to admit blacks to graduate schools were applied to North Carolina in 1951. The UNC Law School was ordered to admit three black students. Attentive southerners could foresee trouble brewing at high school and elementary school levels. The NAACP's Legal Defense Fund was challenging "separate but equal" education in the public schools of Clarendon County, South Carolina. South Carolina Gov. Jimmy Byrnes launched an ambitious effort to make his state's schools for blacks equal to those for whites, but it was too late. In May 1954, after reviewing the Clarendon County case and four others, the Supreme Court ruled that "separate was inherently unequal" in public education. A year later, in May 1955, the court ordered that public schools be desegregated "with all deliberate speed."

Rising enrollments were beginning to put great stress on public schools. Children born of returning World War II veterans were reaching school age, and schools had neither the classrooms nor the teachers to accommodate them. Cities, counties, and states rushed to pass bond issues for more school buildings and to raise taxes for teacher salaries.

The South was changing in other ways. Its cotton economy was moving west into Texas, Arizona, and the Imperial Valley of California. Western cattle-raising was moving east into abandoned cotton fields. Southern blacks were moving north for higher paying jobs in industry, and northern industry was moving south to take advantage of southern markets and cheap labor. Politically, the region's old Democratic loyalties were being tested. Strom Thurmond's 1948 campaign and Dwight Eisenhower's success in 1952 had opened fissures in the once-solid South and encouraged two-party politics.

It was in that changing, volatile climate that Curtis Johnson's will was contested and the fight for control of the *Observer* took place.

One of the important figures in both aspects of the *Observer* struggle was banker Carl G. McCraw, a handsome, aggressive, but unfailingly polite Kings Mountain native who came to Charlotte in 1924 as a runner for Union National Bank (later First Union National) and by 1950 was poised to become the bank's next president (a position he assumed in 1952). His personal success and business acumen had long impressed Mrs. Curtis Johnson, who, despite her husband's loyalty to the American Trust Company, did her banking at Union National.

Shortly after Johnson's death, when no valid will was found and it appeared that Mrs. Johnson might have to administer his estate without one, she went to McCraw for advice. He accompanied her to the county clerk of court's office and had Union National Bank named as coadministrator of the Johnson estate. The appointment galled the American Trust Company, where Johnson had been the sixth largest stockholder. American Trust was trustee for the Sullivan estate, which owned 42.5 percent of the *Observer*. American Trust executives had been voting members of the *Observer*'s board of directors since the early 1920s.

A few days later, when Johnson's 1947 will was discovered, the clerk's designation of Union National as coexecutor of the estate was open to challenge. In one ambiguous sentence in his will, Johnson named his wife as executor and American Trust as "trustee" of his estate. American Trust sued to replace Union National as coexecutor. Union National objected on grounds that it was the choice of the executrix. In December 1950 the trial judge ruled for the American Trust Company, and in May 1951 so did the state supreme court.

In the meantime, at Mrs. Johnson's suggestion, the *Observer* was being run by an executive committee composed of circulation manager Granny Ward, mechanical superintendent John White, advertising director O. A. ("Bo") Robinson, treasurer Harry Allen, and managing editor Ernest B. Hunter. The makeup of the committee increased the commercial influence on the newsroom; Ernest Hunter was outnumbered by spokesmen for business and advertising.

During litigation over the executor issue, a second set of complications arose. In his will Curtis Johnson gave $750 a month to a sister in California for the rest of her life, one-time grants of $25,000 each to three nephews in Michigan and California, and gifts to the following long-term employees of the *Observer*: $5,000 each to Harry A. Allen, Granbery Ward, Ernest B. Hunter, J. A. Parham, John P. White, and P. H. Batte (since deceased); $2,500 each to secretaries Eudora Garrison and Carrie J. Cook; $1,000 each to all employees who had worked for the paper more than twenty years, and $500 each to all employees who had worked for the paper ten to twenty years. The rest of his estate was to go to his widow. After her death, the remainder, including his 57.5 percent interest in the *Observer*, was to be equally divided among the three nephews or, in the event of their deaths, among children of the nephews.

Mrs. Johnson, then sixty-one, did not like the thought of those three nephews' waiting for her to die. Both her father and mother lived long lives, and she worried that her longevity might postpone the nephews' inheritance for many years. (Her fears were well-founded; she lived to be ninety-six.) On the advice of Carl McCraw, she chose to dissent from the will, a move that under North Carolina law entitled her to half the estate and gave the nephews immediate access to the other half. But in dissenting, she gave up her role as coexecutor, leaving American Trust as administrator until the estate was settled. That meant that as of May 1951 the trust department of American Trust was managing the *Charlotte Observer*, a newspaper that had no publisher, no editor, and no business manager.

The trust officer at American Trust was vice-president Bascomb W. ("Barney") Barnard, an Asheville native, then fifty-seven years old, with a bachelor's degree from Trinity College (later Duke University), a master's from Princeton, and a privately earned license to practice law. An amiable and proper man with the manner of a prep school dean, he was on the telephone daily to members of the *Observer*'s executive committee and often invited them, one at a time, to stop by his office at the bank for person-to-person talks. As a result, business leaders and advertisers had even greater leverage over the paper's news and editorial content.

After several weeks, Barnard was convinced the *Observer* needed the supervision of an experienced newspaper manager. He was helped to that conviction by Henry Lineberger, a wealthy Belmont textile manufacturer who had married Walter Sullivan's daughter Clayton and was voting her one-third interest in the Sullivan estate. At Lineberger's urging, Barnard made inquiries among southern publishers, several of whom recommended Ralph Nicholson, recently of New Orleans, a man with a reputation for making money-losing newspapers into money-makers. Nicholson had sold a half interest in the *Tampa Times* but had just bought the *Independent* in St. Petersburg and might not be available. When Barnard tried to reach him, Nicholson was said to be traveling in Mexico.

Later, it was Nicholson who reached Barnard. Hearing of the Charlotte banker's search, one of Nicholson's friends asked him to call Barnard and put in a good word for him. Nicholson did and learned of Barnard's effort to contact *him*. At Barnard's invitation, Nicholson arrived in Charlotte on July 21, 1951, ostensibly to visit his daughter, a Wellesley student in summer school at Chapel Hill. That night, while dining at the Charlotte Country Club, he ran into Thomas L. Robinson, publisher of the *Charlotte News*. Robinson suspected Nicholson was looking over the *Observer* and so informed his editors at the *News*.

Nicholson spent six days in Charlotte, conferring with Barnard and dining first with Mrs. Johnson and then with Mrs. Sullivan, two old friends who were then barely speaking to each other. He also spent considerable time with the Henry Linebergers. He told all parties that having just made more than a million dollars in selling the *New Orleans Item* and the *Tampa Times*, he did not need a job but would come to Charlotte as president and publisher of the *Observer* if he could buy a block of stock in the paper when the Johnson estate was settled. All parties wanted him to come but were reluctant to sell him stock. Nicholson flew to his plantation near Tallahassee, leaving them to think about his offer.

He also left behind a reputation for clipped speech and brassy personal relations. At one point during negotiations, he thought he might need a lawyer and, after asking around, phoned F. Grainger

Pierce, who had been well recommended. "Mr. Pierce, I understand you are a good lawyer," Nicholson said. When Pierce replied that he was "pretty good," Nicholson responded, "You'd better be damned good, Mr. Pierce, because I'm pretty good myself."

Three days later, Barnard called Nicholson with news that all his conditions had been accepted. He invited Nicholson back to Charlotte on Wednesday, August 1, for a joint meeting of *Observer* stockholders. They elected Mrs. Curtis Johnson chairman of the board, Ralph Nicholson president, Henry Lineberger vice-president, and Harry A. Allen secretary-treasurer. They offered Nicholson a contract, but he declined to sign it, saying the situation was "turbulent" and he preferred the freedom to leave anytime. So he was hired on a handshake at a salary of $30,000 (which Nicholson led reporters to believe was $50,000), with the expectation that he would soon buy into the company.

On the front page of the August 2, 1951, *Observer* was a four-column story and photo spread, announcing that fifty-two-year-old Ralph Nicholson, native of Greens Fork, Indiana, had been named president, editor, and publisher of the *Observer*. The photo showed a dapper Nicholson wearing glasses and smoking a pipe. The story briefly reviewed his background: he began in newspapering as a carrier boy, became a high school sportswriter, and after graduating from the Quaker-run Earlham College in Richmond, Indiana, traveled in Europe as a foreign correspondent for the *Philadelphia Ledger*. He earned a master's degree from Harvard University, held executive posts on newspapers in New York, Pittsburgh, and Japan, and served a year as public affairs director for the high commissioner in the American sector of occupied Germany. The story also cited his ownership of newspapers in New Orleans and Florida.

Ten days later *Time* magazine reported his appointment under the headline "Hoosier Bargain." The story said: "Charlotte's *Observer*, the biggest (circ. 138,183) daily in the Carolinas, is a newspapering nugget of gold that seldom glitters. Its news pages are a typographical mishmash, its editorial voice a whisper. Yet, because in its leisurely stride it picks up every crumb of news in its territory, the 82-year-old *Observer* is one of the biggest profitmakers of its size in the United States."

Time went on to detail Nicholson's hiring, his reputation for buying newspaper bargains, and his intention to buy into the *Observer*. With the story was a photo of Nicholson smoking a pipe. The photo caption said, "New Brass for a Gold Mine."

Shortly after Nicholson's appointment, the American Trust Company honored him at a luncheon for business moguls whom he assured that he was their kind of publisher. Afterward, he went to Roaring Gap with the Linebergers to hobnob with more of the financial elite. In the offices of the *Charlotte News*, one editor observed, "The *Charlotte Observer* has not had a social conscience for twenty years, why should it have one now?"

Nicholson's hiring gave American Trust and the Johnson family time to pursue other questions about the effect of Mrs. Johnson's dissent from her husband's will. What did the dissent do to the disposition of *Observer* stock? Would Mrs. Johnson own 28.75 percent and each of the nephews 9.58 percent? Would that give the Sullivan estate controlling interest? To make sure it was proceeding properly, American Trust filed a "friendly suit" in Mecklenburg Superior Court, asking those and other questions. The issues took two years to resolve.

In the meantime, Nicholson moved into Curtis Johnson's office and began to transform the *Observer*. Stung by *Time* magazine's dismissal of the paper as "a typographical mishmash," he set out to modernize its appearance. He hired Gilbert P. Farrar of New York, a consultant who had redesigned more than thirty American newspapers, including the *Los Angeles Times*, *Houston Post*, and *Atlanta Journal*. Farrar spent a month in Charlotte, trying out various formats, then chose to replace the dozen or more typefaces used for *Observer* headlines with only one—Bodoni—and to abandon the paper's vertical makeup in favor of a modular style that divided each page into blocks. Gone were the daily eight-column streamers; in their place would be headlines two, three, and four columns wide and one, two, or three lines deep. Farrar made up a stylebook for the *Observer* staff and conducted classes on how to use it. Farrar's fee, plus the cost of new type and machinery, totaled $75,000.

On September 17, 1951, the paper's new dress was introduced to the public, all at once. On the previous Sunday the *Observer* appeared as it had every day for twenty years. On Monday it came out looking like a different newspaper. Not only were the typeface and layout different, but so was the placement of the paper's regular features. The editorial page, for instance, was moved from Section A to Section B. Many long-standing features were dropped, and the larger Corona type used for the text of stories reduced the volume of material that could be published. A three-column display at the bottom of page one explained the change under the headline "Observer's New Style Makes Reading Easier." The story included predictions from Nicholson and other *Observer* executives that readers were going to love the paper's new look.

They reckoned without considering the basic conservatism of people in Charlotte and the Carolinas. Many readers complained that the new *Observer* was "a stranger" at their breakfast table. Circulation manager Granny Ward, who joined Ernest Hunter in urging Nicholson to implement the new style gradually, said the paper lost from 8,000 to 10,000 subscribers overnight.

Learning that Gilbert Farrar was in town, *Charlotte News* managing editor Brodie Griffith guessed what he was up to and tried to anticipate changes the consultant might make in the *Observer*. He studied copies of other newspapers Farrar had designed. One Farrar trademark was Bodoni type, which the *News* already used. Another was stacking ads from the bottom of the page at the inside fold diagonally across to the top of the page at the outside edge. Griffith got the *News* to adopt that ad layout. As a result, when the *Observer* appeared in its new look, the *News and Observer* in Raleigh took one glimpse and suggested, "*The Charlotte Observer* just spent $75,000 to make itself look like *The Charlotte News*."

Circulation losses due to the *Observer*'s new dress were short-lived. People who canceled subscriptions soon reordered the paper. The March 1952 circulation audit showed average daily sales of 139,149, up 470 from a year earlier. The *Observer* entered its new design in the N. W. Ayer & Son typographical exhibition of 1953 and won third place, behind the *Washington Star* and the *New York Times* and ahead of the *Washington Post*. Not bad company for a southern newspaper that eighteen months earlier looked like something from a journalism museum.

In the fall of 1951, Nicholson made other improvements in the paper. He hired Ralph Howland, Carolinas news director for the Associated Press, to establish an *Observer* office in Raleigh, the paper's first full-time news bureau in the state capital since the 1920s. He also hired William D. Workman, Jr., then South Carolina's most respected political reporter, to correspond for the *Observer* from Columbia, South Carolina. In October, Nicholson ordered two more press units from the Hoe Company, giving the paper twelve units in all and sufficient printing capacity to publish the entire Sunday paper without having to print some sections early. In January 1952, he added the syndicated magazine *This Week* to the Sunday edition.

Nicholson cut costs by installing modern typesetting procedures. He replaced worn-out Linotype machines with new, high-speed Comets and equipped them to set type by "reading" a perforated tape in the same way that player pianos read perforated scrolls of music. With experience, a good tape puncher could set type faster than a

Linotype operator working the keyboard by hand. The tape also could be fed to the typesetting machine straight from an Associated Press wire. The tape marked the beginning of automation in the composing room.

Nicholson had the *Observer* building air-conditioned, ending the necessity of opening windows on summer nights and letting in swarms of gnats and moths. He also had an elevator installed as well as new lockers and showers for printers and pressmen. He raised salaries throughout the building, expanded the news staff, and put in a pension plan that forced the retirement of eight employees who were more than seventy years old. Among the retirees was society editor Margaret Kelly Abernethy, widow of Jim Abernethy, Joseph Caldwell's managing editor who died in 1906. Mrs. Abernethy had been with the *Observer* since 1924. She was replaced by Katharine Halyburton, whose title was "women's editor" instead of society editor, reflecting a changing emphasis in women's news. Others retiring were associate editor James A. Parham, who joined the *Observer* as managing editor in 1917; mechanical superintendent John P. White, who came from Knoxville in 1926; and DeLeon G. Spencer, the copy desk chief who came to the *Observer* in 1924.

The retirement of Spencer spelled the doom of Jo Jo, the chimp who for thirty-five years had forecast the weather on the *Observer*'s front page. From 1924 to 1934, Spencer had drawn Jo Jo and since 1934 had written the daily verse that accompanied Jo Jo's weather report. When Dick Pitts resigned in 1950 to work as a Hollywood press agent, and Spencer retired in 1951, no one was left to carry on the Jo Jo tradition. Having already banned photos of children and animals from the newspaper's front page, Nicholson ordered Jo Jo dropped. The *Observer* did not announce that the feature was ending. After December 3, 1951, Jo Jo was simply not there.

The retirement of J. A. Parham also brought an end to the weekly "Letters from General Mecklenburg," a front-page feature of the Sunday *Observer* since 1926. The open letters, usually addressed to local officials in cities and counties surrounding Charlotte, were brief editorials reflecting Parham's conservatism and conscientious civic outlook. They were part of the *Observer*'s effort to promote the region. Again, there was no announcement about discontinuing them. Like Jo Jo, General Mecklenburg simply vanished.

Parham's personal leave-taking was more painful. He wrote a brief note to *Observer* officers, thanking them for the "substantial and liberal income" provided him, but he added that his "separation from . . . the paper . . . has been a rather sad experience." Reporter

Randolph Norton, who drove Parham home after his last day at the office, remembers the old man gathering up his few belongings, including an old upright typewriter with extra-large keys to aid his fading eyesight, and going home to a lonely apartment on East Morehead Street. His job at the *Observer* had been his joy in life.

The day after Parham's retirement, Nicholson announced the appointment of city hall reporter Hal Tribble as Parham's successor on the editorial page. The *Observer* gained hugely in the exchange, for Tribble was one of the paper's brightest writers whose wit and brevity were welcome additions to the long-faced editorial columns. Tribble's interests were also local and state, and complemented Rupert Gillett's preoccupation with world and national events. At last the *Observer* was expressing opinions on matters close to home.

Having killed two long-standing *Observer* features, Nicholson took aim at a third—the riotous Gus Travis column, which he felt was beneath the dignity of a serious newspaper. He ordered the column discontinued. Again, there was no announcement or farewell; the column just stopped. Somehow, Travis made sure his fans noticed. At hundreds of speeches and public appearances, he had made many friends in and out of town, and they began to protest. As the mail arrived in sacks, Travis, wearing a loud sport coat and puffing the stub of a cigar, watched with amused satisfaction. Soon, Nicholson ordered the column reinstated.

For reasons that were never quite clear, Nicholson also ordered the paper to print a summary of each day's police blotter. Again Ernest Hunter objected, pointing out that the blotter routinely listed many people who were innocent. But Nicholson was adamant, and Hunter gave the order: Run the police blotter. Many people complained, and one night the practice provoked a crisis. When the son of a prominent merchant was charged with drunken driving, his name turned up on the county police blotter and was duly recorded in the daily *Observer* summary. Before it could appear in print, Barney Barnard, trust officer for American Trust, arrived in the newsroom and asked Hunter not to publish it. Hunter said he was under orders from the publisher. Barnard asked to speak to the publisher. "He's in Spain," Hunter said. "Where in Spain?" Barnard asked, and got Nicholson on the telephone. Nicholson asked to speak to Hunter and instructed him to omit the name of the merchant's son. Gritting his teeth, Hunter said, "Yes, sir," and with a heavy heart relayed the order to his editing staff.

When Nicholson arrived the *Observer* had no library—the popular term then was "morgue"—containing photos and background matter on important people and institutions. The lack of such a resource indicated the degree to which the *Observer* was an event-oriented paper, with little concern for the context of stories. In that, the paper was far behind other dailies its size. Many metropolitan newspapers began accumulating morgues in the 1920s. Newspapers in the South had been creating them since the late 1930s, when the trend toward in-depth reporting began. Under Nicholson, the *Observer* started building a morgue in 1952. When Elizabeth Page, mother of city editor Bob Page, retired from Western Union, she began assembling an *Observer* library in a small storage bin between the newsroom and the composing room. She started with clippings from the top of reporter Granbery Dickson's desk. It was haphazard but better than nothing.

The changes Nicholson made in the *Observer* were being noticed at the *Charlotte News*, where money for improvements was scarce. When Kays Gary of the *Shelby Star* was in Charlotte one Sunday afternoon, he learned from a former *Star* staffer, Dick Young, Jr., who had recently joined the *News*, that he might find an opening at the *Observer*. "They seem to be spending a lot of money down there," Young said.

Gary, a short, intense, hurrying young man with a thick shock of black hair, grew up in Fallston on the outskirts of Shelby, went to college at Mars Hill and UNC, and, after World War II, took a job at the *Shelby Star* in his first week out of the army. By the fall of 1951, he had developed a love-hate relationship with the newspaper. He loved it because it was home and familiar and gave him the opportunity to write about anything that interested him. He covered the courts, politics, and the police, and he got to write about sports, his first love. He not only covered sports, but made money on the side as official scorer, public address announcer, and radio play-by-play commentator. He also learned to hate the paper because it was home and familiar, and because the pay was low and the hours were long, and he usually wound up working every weekend. His wife, by then the mother of two children, had begun to complain. Besides, Buck Hardin, foreman of the *Star*'s composing room and a man who had seen *Star* talent come and go over the years, had advised Gary that it was time he moved on. If he didn't go soon, Hardin warned, he might never leave.

So Gary took Dick Young's suggestion and stopped at the *Observer* on his way back to Shelby that Sunday. He found managing editor Ernest Hunter at his desk in the middle of the newsroom. Hunter knew about Gary's talent from stories he had read in the *Shelby Star* and from feature stories Gary had sold to the *Observer*. He also knew that Gary had earlier turned down a job on the staff of the *Charlotte News*, where he had a chance to succeed Furman Bisher as sports editor and columnist, and that he also had hemmed and hawed over Miss Beatrice Cobb's offer to let him manage her Morganton *News-Herald*.

The lean, impatient Hunter had a way of leveling his gaze at job applicants as if to plumb their insides, and he fixed Gary with one of those stares. "I just want to know one thing," he said. "Are you ready to come to work here? I don't want to count on you and have you not show up." For an instant, Gary's knees wobbled, but he managed a firm response: "Yes, sir." Hunter seemed impressed. "Okay," he said, "be here in two weeks." As an afterthought, he asked if eighty dollars a week would be satisfactory. Gary, who made less than that at the *Star* but more when side money was added, said eighty dollars a week would be just fine.

That agreement almost came apart. When Gary notified his managing editor, an avuncular veteran named Holt McPherson, that he would be leaving to join the *Charlotte Observer*, McPherson let the matter stew a day or so. Then, not wanting to lose his best reporter, he called his friend Ernest Hunter and confided that this kid Gary was in dreadful agony over the prospect of leaving Shelby and Fallston and the people he had grown up with. He asked if Hunter could let Gary out of their bargain. In a flash, Hunter was on the phone to Gary, demanding to know what was going on. Gary laughed at McPherson's ploy. "Oh, you know what a mother hen Holt is," he said. He assured Hunter that he was not agonizing, that his mind was made up and his commitment firm. He would be there on the appointed date. Hunter said, "Well, all right," and hung up. The incident apparently impressed Hunter, because in Gary's first paycheck at the *Observer* his salary was pegged at ninety dollars a week instead of eighty.

When the day came for Gary to leave Shelby, his colleagues in the *Star* newsroom and Buck Hardin's mechanical department pitched in seventy-five dollars to rent a truck to move the Garys to Charlotte. It was a sweet-sad farewell. Gary and his wife and two infant children arrived on a Saturday afternoon at Charlotte's Sedgefield Apartments with the seventy-five-dollar-a-month rent paid in advance but no lights and running water. Gary called Hunter at the *Observer*, but he wasn't in. He tried Dick Young and couldn't reach him. Knowing no one else, he called Ralph Nicholson, the editor and publisher, and explained his predicament: with a wife and two babies, he couldn't get through the weekend without lights and water.

Several times Nicholson asked Gary for his name. "And you're a new reporter on our staff?" he asked. Gary explained again, but Nicholson obviously knew nothing about Gary's hiring. Finally the publisher asked for Gary's phone number and promised to call back. In a few minutes he was on the line, instructing Gary to be at the Church Street office of Duke Power Company in thirty minutes. Somebody would meet him there. A few minutes later, Duke vice-president J. Paul Lucas, whose father had once been an *Observer* reporter, arrived to get the lights and water turned on at the Gary apartment. The next Monday, when Gary showed up for work at the *Observer*, he was a celebrity. Among staff members who knew Nicholson only as a powerful but remote force in their lives, Gary was introduced as "the man who got the publisher to turn on his lights and water." The staff soon learned to respect Gary for other qualities.

Back in Shelby, Gary was used to writing maybe a dozen stories a day on everything from winning teams to lost cats. At the *Observer*, all he got from city editor Bob Page was a few *Charlotte News* clippings to rewrite each afternoon. After polishing off those, Gary paced the floor. One day news editor Haywood Trotter told him about a Dilworth man who had just returned from a year in Alaska. Gary rushed to the man's home on Kingston Avenue, took copious notes in an interview, and returned to write a story that might have filled two whole columns. When the copy was pasted end to end, Trotter stood on a chair and held it up for all to see, asking in acid tones at what lengths Gary might report the Second Coming.

The ice-breaker for Gary came a few days later on a story Hunter suggested about an otherwise healthy little girl with a baffling illness. Gary paid the girl a visit, sat with her in a backyard swing, and listened as she talked about the hopes and dreams of a six-year-old. News editor Trotter gave his story, full of the girl's innocence and charm, prominent play on the front page. The shocker came in its last line, when Gary revealed the girl's illness: leukemia.

Ralph Nicholson called upstairs to protest and ordered that there be no more "sob-sister" stories on the front page of his newspaper. But to people in the *Observer* newsroom, the story signaled that Gary was no ordinary reporter or writer. The guy had a gift for getting inside the hearts and minds of both his subjects and his readers. Within a year or so, Gary was writing a column on the front page of the local section. It was called "Politics and People," but slowly its subject matter became more people than politics.

Gary was one of eight people hired in the newsroom that year as Hunter and Nicholson filled vacancies and expanded the staff. Others included Virgil Patterson, the paper's third photographer; Randy Hancock, a farm editor; Helen Boone, a society writer; Jim Henderson, Jack Meder, and Dick Hagood, copy editors; and Wriston H. ("Wink") Locklair, a movie, drama, and music critic. A Charlotte native who had attended Belmont Abbey and UNC, the tall, thin, dark-eyed Locklair was a polished writer and perhaps the most knowledgeable music critic the paper ever had. He was engaging, well read, and well traveled, and was as much at home talking sports and politics as he was discussing music and drama. He rapidly became a favorite among staff members.

A second extraordinary reporter hired during Nicholson's tenure was Harry Golden, Jr., the ex–state desk whiz who in the fall of 1952 completed a two-year army hitch and returned to the *Observer* seeking a more exciting assignment. Golden's image of a reporter was patterned after Hildy Johnson in *The Front Page*. He could hear himself phoning the switchboard and saying, "Hello, sweetheart, give me rewrite." Ernest Hunter put him on general assignment and promised more later. Every time a beat opened, Golden dashed to the boss's desk to claim it, but Hunter kept putting him off. In the spring of 1953, Hal Tribble's old city hall beat again came open, and Hunter summoned Golden into the privacy of the photo lab and said, "Okay, hotshot, here's your chance."

For Golden, it was heaven. The *Charlotte News* had been thumping the *Observer* at city hall, and Golden vowed to stop that. On day-to-day stories, he did okay, establishing contacts and bird-dogging them daily. Lillian Hoffman, the city clerk, took a special liking to him and tipped him off occasionally. So did Herman Hoose, the traffic engineer. Golden began to break a story or two every week. It was the city council's weekly meetings that stymied him. They began at 10:00 a.m. on Mondays and ended in time for the *News* to get a complete report in the afternoon edition, leaving Golden to do rewrites. Golden began working to change that. It took two years, but he succeeded. In 1955, Martha Evans became the first woman elected to the council, largely on the strength of frequent stories Golden wrote about her campaign. Golden had also kept warm the close relations Hal Tribble had established with ex-mayor Herb Baxter, still a member of the council. In time, he learned that Councilman Ebb Wilkinson disliked Monday morning meetings because they took him out of his transfer-and-storage office at an hour when the snags of weekend moves were being resolved.

All Golden needed was one more vote. He targeted Steve Dellinger, the happy-go-lucky auto parts dealer from Iron Station in Lincoln County. Golden argued that Dellinger would get more exposure before Iron Station readers in the *Observer* than he was getting in the *News*. "Oh, yeah?" Dellinger asked. The councilman hesitated, then said okay. So in the spring of 1955, just after Mrs. Evans's election, the city council voted to reschedule its weekly meetings to 3:00 p.m. on Mondays. The vote was five to two. When Councilman Herman Brown, a Dilworth tire dealer, sensed the outcome, he voted with the winners. Charlotte councils have met on Monday afternoons ever since.

Once the council was meeting in the afternoons, it added a new element to its weekly schedule. It gathered informally in the mayor's office an hour early for a preliminary conference that gave members a chance to glance at the agenda, compare notes on what might spark controversy, and do a little vote trading. Golden attended those conferences and began writing informal stories under the heading "Council Day at City Hall." His stories took the public behind the scenes and portrayed council members as real people. He quoted their gibes about each others' ties, shoes, cigars, and voting habits. His reports added spice to old city hall gruel.

Though Ralph Nicholson was rarely in the newsroom, he was visible in the community and region, making speeches about world and national affairs to civic clubs, business groups, and college students. He was vice-chairman of an executive committee that studied fund-raising among Charlotte's charitable agencies and recommended a United Fund (now United Way) campaign. As the 1952 elections approached, his speeches got more political. He showed a decided distaste for the "socialistic" Truman and a heavy preference for Ohio Sen. Robert Taft, a fellow midwestern Republican. Nicholson favored Taft over General Eisenhower, who was popular among Carolinians. He had editorials written jeering at Eisenhower's not knowing which party he belonged to. He reminded readers that when Eisenhower was president of Columbia University he claimed he was no educator and when he became a presidential candidate he claimed he was no politician.

In July, he sent Raleigh correspondent Ralph Howland to Chicago to cover the North Carolina delegation to the Republican National Convention and left instructions that Howland's stories were to go on the front page. On the convention's opening day Howland filed a blatant editorial that alleged Eisenhower's eastern backers were playing into Truman's hands by splitting the party with claims that Taft couldn't win. The concluding paragraph said, "It seems a bit cowardly for delegates to say, 'We believe Taft is the better man but we're for Ike because we believe he's the only man who can win.' If that isn't cowardly, it is at least dishonest. No party can flourish under such hypocrisy."

Ernest Hunter and his news editors stood fretfully over the teletype as that dispatch arrived, shaking their heads over its tone and content. All agreed it was an out-and-out editorial and wondered how they could disguise it as front-page news. Hunter had already gone to the mat in opposition to other Nicholson edicts and was reluctant to beard the publisher again, lest he risk being fired. So he put the story on page one, under a small headline, hoping that most readers might miss it.

Anyone who read the story had to be impressed with its similarity to *Observer* editorials accusing Eisenhower supporters of trying to "smear" Taft with "Big Lie" tactics. Under Nicholson, the once-Democratic *Observer* was promoting not only a Republican but the least popular Republican. The paper was probably the only daily in the Carolinas, perhaps in the South, supporting Taft. Charles R. Jonas of Lincolnton, the Republican candidate for Congress from the Charlotte district, was supporting Eisenhower because the general had the greatest appeal among Carolinians and would improve Jonas's chances of being elected.

When Taft lost the nomination, *Observer* editorials cheered his good sportsmanship and urged Eisenhower forces to show the same spirit. As the general election approached, the paper endorsed Eisenhower and Nixon, saying "a vote for Stevenson would be an endorsement of Truman." It was the first time the *Observer* had openly supported a Republican for president, though it came close in 1928 and 1948. The *Observer* was not alone in switching parties; a broad shift to the Republicans was under way in newly urbanized areas of the South. Nicholson had the *Observer* publish a story about the "unprecedented" volume of letters from Charlotte-area readers who were supporting Eisenhower. The paper made no reference to angry letters it got from disappointed Democrats. Eisenhower and the Republicans swept middle-class Charlotte and Mecklenburg County, winning 57 percent of the vote. But North Carolina went for the Democrats by 54 percent.

A month after the 1952 elections, Nicholson's prospects at the *Observer* began to fade. The North Carolina Supreme Court ruled that as a result of Mrs. Johnson's dissent from her husband's will she was entitled to half the estate and the three nephews were immediately entitled to the other half, including 958.3 shares apiece of *Observer* stock. By April 1953, it was clear that the three nephews had agreed to sell Mrs. Johnson their stock as soon as it was distributed and that she was not going to sell Nicholson the stock he sought.

Indeed, Mrs. Johnson let Nicholson know that she was displeased with his stewardship of the newspaper and that, as soon as possible, she intended to elect herself president and publisher. She disliked his high-handed manner, his use of big pictures on the front page ("The *New York Times* doesn't do it," she sniffed), his decision to accept beer advertising, the shed he had built at the rear of the building to protect his company-owned Cadillac, and his having the car washed weekly in the company garage. Most of all, she did not like his overnight redesign of the newspaper. She and her husband had taken great pride in the old *Observer*'s distinction as "the *New York Times* of the South."

Nicholson was so certain of being dismissed that he began looking for other newspapers to buy. He expressed an interest in the *Raleigh Times*. Later, he visited Asheville, agreed on a price for the morning *Citizen* and afternoon *Times*, and put a $50,000 binder in escrow at the American Trust Company. But one of the two families that owned the Asheville papers chose to sell out to the other instead.

It was early August before Mrs. Johnson could act. She had to wait until attorneys computed inheritance taxes on the Johnson estate, based on the distribution approved by the courts. Finally, a stockholders' meeting was held August 12. Mrs. Johnson was elected president, publisher, and chairman of the board. Henry Lineberger was made vice-president, and bankers Carl McCraw and B. W. Barnard were named directors. They passed a carefully worded resolution thanking Nicholson for his services and sending him on his way.

Though his two years at the *Observer* were ridiculed by some *Observer* veterans, Ralph Nicholson did much to improve the paper and position it for a later rise to national prominence. It was not what he did that offended people, but the way he did it. The retirement plan he established was long overdue, and the air-conditioning alone should have won him everlasting gratitude. But in their comfort *Observer* staffers soon forgot how steamy that newsroom could get and what a nuisance it got to have electric fans blowing their papers away and gnats and moths buzzing inside their collars. In later years, as efforts to expand the paper's production capacity brought few results, the two units he added to the printing press proved to be of critical importance. What most *Observer* hands found hardest to forgive was his overnight redesign of an old-style newspaper that they and Carolina readers had loved. The same changes might have been accomplished over time, with less loss in identity and loyalty. But as one old-timer recalled, "Mr. Nicholson was not one to seek advice nor accept it."

After leaving Charlotte, Nicholson retired to a plantation near Tallahassee, Florida, and in June 1956 bought the afternoon *Eagle* in Dothan, Alabama, just north of the Florida line. In 1961, when the *Observer* published Ernest Hunter's seventy-five-year history of the newspaper, correcting early errors about the date of its founding, Nicholson wrote to complain that Hunter's references to his tenure at the paper had been "mighty chinche" and that Hunter's assessment of Nicholson improvements was "something short of fulsome." A few years later in an autobiography, *A Long Way From Greens Fork*, Nicholson was more generous in evaluating his accomplishments at the *Observer*. He died in July 1972 at age seventy-three.

Mrs. Johnson gained control of the *Observer* three months before her sixty-fifth birthday. She was a heavy-set woman but not obese. She had a large frame, big bones, a high forehead, and a firm jaw. When she smiled, she resembled Ethel Barrymore. She liked big hats that showed off her strong face, she smoked cigarettes from a long, black holder, and she spoke in a melodious contralto voice. The key to her personality was her brown eyes. They were bright, lively, and active, recording all that they saw around her. She was obviously an intelligent woman and confident of her own intellectual powers. It was she who in the early 1920s conducted James B. Duke on the tour of Davidson College that persuaded him to make Davidson one of the four educational institutions included in the trust fund he was establishing (later the $650 million Duke Endowment).

In later years, the story was told—indeed, Mrs. Johnson told it herself—that on an airplane flight to New York she sat next to a Manhattan businessman who, on learning she was from Charlotte, said, "I knew two brilliant men from Charlotte. One was a Presbyterian preacher and the other a newspaper publisher." Mrs. Johnson replied, "Yes, and I married them both."

Though Mrs. Johnson resented Nicholson, she maintained many of the improvements he made and added others. She subscribed to the Washington correspondence of Frank Van der Linden, who represented several papers in the capital. She joined AP's regional wirephoto network, which supplied the paper with live photos it would otherwise have received a day later by mail. She put in a group insurance program that combined life insurance with a hospitalization policy, the first medical insurance offered to *Observer* employees. The company paid part of the premiums and the employees paid part. In October, she accepted congratulations as the *Observer* won national honors for a "Home Week" special section containing 104,000 lines of classified advertising, an indication that Charlotte was in a thriving region.

Also that fall, Mrs. Johnson saw the *Observer* hire another exceptional reporter. He was Roy B. Covington, a tall, shy, soft-spoken native of Ripley, Mississippi, who had finished Davidson College in 1950 and spent six months reading proof at the *Observer* until being called to active duty in the army as an ROTC officer. After two years in Korea, he returned in September 1953 to become a reporter covering federal agencies in Charlotte. Covington's lean but lucid prose would later win him national distinction as a writer of religion and business.

Mrs. Johnson also presided over a transition in the paper's reporting of women's news. Since 1912, when the *Observer* renamed its personals column "Society," the paper's coverage of women's affairs had run primarily to social events, weddings, engagements, parties, and the comings and goings of the well-to-do. For years, it devoted the front page of the society section each Sunday to big photos of young women who were being married that weekend or were engaged to be married. The pictures on that page and the relative prominence of the families represented were a matter of the highest concern at the *Observer*. Even the placement of photos on the page was a sensitive issue occasionally resolved in the publisher's office. It simply wouldn't do to offend the wrong merchant, banker, or other moneyed citizen by mishandling his daughter's wedding picture or engagement announcement.

As Charlotte grew and the number of moneyed people increased, such decisions became more difficult. The number of weddings and bridal announcements was crowding out other matters of interest to women. Finally, Mrs. Johnson put an end to it. In February 1954, she approved "a more metropolitan" handling of bridal pictures and announcements. Brides were removed from the section front and replaced with stories about food, furniture, fashions, schools, child rearing, and other cultural activities, all of them written to appeal to female readers. There was an immediate uproar. Women whose daughters were about to be married were furious. So were matrons who considered themselves arbiters of who was "Society" and who wasn't. But Mrs. Johnson stood her ground, and bridal news was relegated to inside pages. In June, Jane Rogers, a recent graduate of Winthrop College in Rock Hill, South Carolina, was hired as women's editor and authorized to make the *Observer*'s society section into "women's pages."

The move was part of a national trend, encouraged no doubt by advertisers who wanted to reach a broader audience than people who were mainly interested in brides. In the post–World War II baby boom and the rush to the suburbs, women were broadening their concerns, and matters related to the home and the family as well as the activities of women's organizations were becoming subjects of greater interest. The war and its aftermath had produced a generation of young women who, while not asking for these changes, were certainly receptive to them. The *Observer*'s shift to a more "metropolitan" presentation of women's news was duplicated by other major dailies in the state.

In managing the paper Mrs. Johnson revived the executive committee that had set policy for nearly a year before Nicholson's arrival. Composed of circulation manager Granny Ward, business manager Harry Allen, advertising manager Bo Robinson, mechanical superintendent Clarence Capps, and managing editor Ernest Hunter, the committee met over tea in her office each afternoon to discuss plans for the next day's paper. In those sessions, the tall, drawling Ward, to whom other department heads looked for leadership, was clearly a powerful influence. Again, Ernest Hunter was outgunned and felt the pressure of business and advertising interests. Often he wound up having to run photos and stories of such non-news events as the unveiling of a new model washing machine or the unwrapping of a new brand of automobile tire. In guarding the newspaper's editorial integrity, Hunter offended other department heads, who regarded him as brusque and autocratic. A few months later, when Hunter fell deathly ill and was not expected to live (one doctor mistakenly diagnosed his ailment as lung cancer), Mrs. Johnson invited Randolph Norton to take his place at the executive teas.

In April 1954, while Hunter was ill and presumed to be dying, Mrs. Johnson promoted him to executive editor and distributed memos asking other editors to spare him many of the burdens he had been carrying. At the same time, she appointed Randolph Norton as Hunter's assistant and news editor Haywood Trotter as managing editor. The move gave Hunter a title but uncertain authority. Trotter urged Mrs. Johnson to delay the appointments until Hunter could be consulted about them. But Mrs. Johnson refused. As a result, a move intended to resolve conflict in the newsroom only caused more. After three weeks, Trotter resigned, saying he could not work under Norton, and his wife Hazel, the paper's highly respected business reporter, resigned with him. Their departure sent shock waves through the newsroom, causing deep division among members of the staff and breeding suspicion that a circulation-business-advertising "palace guard" was taking over the newspaper. Actually, Mrs. Johnson made the moves in an effort to buy time in which to sell the newspaper, but at that point she could not divulge her intentions.

She later acknowledged that she had been publisher only a few weeks when she recognized that she "wasn't up" to running a newspaper as complex as the *Observer*. She and her banker-adviser Carl McCraw agreed that the paper needed an experienced publisher to attend to daily details and plan for the needed expansion. Secretly she asked McCraw to look for the best buyer.

McCraw spent several months reading newspapers, Dun and Bradstreet ratings, and annual reports. By early spring of 1954, his discreet inquiries led him to recommend that Mrs. Johnson sell the *Observer* to the Knight brothers, John S. and James L., publishers of the *Akron Beacon-Journal*, the *Miami Herald*, the *Detroit Free Press*, and the *Chicago Daily News*. His findings indicated that they ran honest, highly professional newspapers that showed great concern for their communities. The group they had acquired was not subject to a single point of view coming down from headquarters; it was more like a federation, with a local company, board of directors, and editor for each paper.

Mrs. Johnson was pleased. She knew and respected the Knights. When her husband was alive, she and Curtis Johnson had visited the Knights in Florida and entertained them in North Carolina. At the April 1954 meeting of the American Newspaper Publishers Association in New York—at about the time that Ernest Hunter was being appointed executive editor—Mrs. Johnson sat with forty-four-year-old Jim Knight and his attorney Blake McDowell and asked whether they would be interested in buying her newspaper.

Jim Knight knew a great deal about the *Charlotte Observer*. Like other Miamians, he used to vacation at Highlands in the mountains of western North Carolina and read the *Observer* while he was there. During World War II, when getting to Highlands was difficult, he bought a place at Roaring Gap, northwest of Winston-Salem. His retreat there was next door to one owned by Henry and Clayton Sullivan Lineberger, *Observer* stockholders. Knight knew Charlotte to be the fast-growing financial capital of the Carolinas and the center of an industrial region with a strong growth potential. Yes, he said, he was interested in buying Mrs. Johnson's paper.

Jim Knight's older brother John, then fifty-seven, was less enthusiastic. He and Jim looked at newspapering differently. Jim Knight was oriented to the business and production side; John Knight to the news, editorial, and political side. When John Knight thought of expanding the family's publishing activity, he usually looked toward the older, larger, more industrial cities of the North, where business and politics were separate and distinct. John Knight was a little suspicious of southern cities, where politics and business were usually entwined and where regional and family loyalties strongly influenced community attitudes. If Jim Knight wanted to buy a newspaper in Charlotte, North Carolina, he could do so, but John wanted it known that it would be Jim's baby.

When Mrs. Johnson got back to Charlotte, she had other worries. The Trotter resignation occurred in early May, creating new tensions within the staff. She got work started on an expansion of the newsroom to make room for more reporting desks. A waist-high partition topped by a glass panel about shoulder height was built in the northeast corner, directly overlooking Stonewall and Tryon. After years of working at an open desk in the newsroom, "Boss" Hunter was about to get a sanctum. Staff members speculated whether Hunter's first act upon returning would be to order it demolished as an unnecessary barrier to communication. But when Hunter returned, looking thin and pale and old, the partition was allowed to stay, though he rarely used it.

On May 17, 1954, the paper faced a crisis. A bulletin over the AP teletype brought news that a unanimous United States Supreme Court had ruled that segregated public schools were "inherently unequal" and therefore unconstitutional. The bulletin was ripped off the printer and taken to Mrs. Johnson, who called in her senior editors for advice. Rupert Gillett, Hal Tribble, Randolph Norton, and Ernest Hunter gathered in her office. The court's decision was not a surprise; Mrs. Johnson and the four editors had talked earlier about the likelihood of such a ruling. Now what was the *Observer* going to say about it? Randolph Norton remembered the discussion as calm and brief. "I don't think we ever sat down," he said.

They talked about what the decision meant and what southern reaction might be. Mrs. Johnson had the last word. She said she knew the decision would be unpopular, but it was the law, and she thought the paper should uphold the law. The next day an ambiguous two-line heading over the lead editorial said, "The Segregation Ruling Demands More Than Loud-Mouthed Resistance," but the editorial itself stated the case more clearly. It pointed out that the South had overcome many obstacles and with time could overcome this one. The court had indicated it would allow the South time to adjust. Indeed, the court itself asked for time in which to write a second order implementing its decision. The editorial continued:

> Whatever the emotional forces involved, the order, when it comes, must be complied with. To resist it with violence would be to beg inevitable grief.
>
> The ruling will bring changes; it must not bring revolution. It calls for clear thinking; it demands a reappraisal of educational policies at the public school level; it requires the emergence of educators trained in social techniques; it needs a people resolved to realism and conditioned to restraint.
>
> The South has a new problem. It may turn out to be the greatest problem of the region's history. But it calls for analysis and solution in calm, orderly fashion. That is the South's responsibility—to itself and its children.

The *Observer* was one of a handful of southern newspapers to respond positively to the landmark decision. Others, including newspapers in Richmond, Charleston, and cities in the Deep South, challenged the authority of the Supreme Court to make such a ruling, though it was the high court that legitimized the separate-but-equal concept fifty-eight years earlier in *Plessy* v. *Ferguson*. Those papers called for defiance and resistance. The *Observer*'s more moderate stance cost it several thousand subscribers, especially in South Carolina, where subscription agents from Charleston compared the Charlotte paper's stand with that of the defiant *News and Courier*.

When asked later about her "bold and courageous" stand, Mrs. Johnson said, "There was nothing bold or courageous about it. It came straight out of my conscience." She said she had long recognized the inequity of "the Negroes' position"; she knew it was wrong and knew that "one day that would have to change." The Supreme Court provided an opportunity to bring about that change. She realized the paper's positive statement might cause some circulation losses, but she thought in the long run the court order would be accepted. "These old Scotch-Irish people around here, they're by and large fair-minded," she said.

The *Observer*'s call for compliance was another step in its long, slow departure from the New South oppression of blacks. It put the paper on stronger moral footing and changed its image in the eyes of its staff, its readers, and other newspapers around the country. It helped to strengthen the climate for moderation in Charlotte, where civic leaders felt resistance might lead to violence that would be bad for business. A year after the court order, the Mecklenburg Medical Society voted to admit black doctors and, in doing so, forced the desegregation of the state medical society.

Throughout the summer and fall of 1954, Jim Knight, attorney Blake McDowell, and their editorial expert, the precise Lee Hills, then executive editor of both the *Detroit Free Press* and the *Miami Herald*, explored the possibilities of buying the *Observer*. Jim Knight visited the city, looked over the paper, and continued to indicate an interest. But serious discussions between Mrs. Johnson and the Knights were postponed until after *Observer* newsroom employees held an election on whether to make the American Newspaper Guild their bargaining agent. The Knights did not want rumors of their interest to influence that election.

Agitation for a guild had been under way at the *Observer* several years, since a successful guild vote at the *Charlotte News* had sharply raised salaries there. Employees of the Associated Press were in the guild, and their presence in both newsrooms was a constant source of guild talk. Members of the AP often bragged to *Observer* employees about guild wage scales. Rancor over the Norton-Trotter conflict increased interest in the union, and so did rumors that the *Observer* was about to be sold. Up and down Tryon Street reporters were hearing that Carl McCraw was acting as broker for this or that publishing interest and that a sale was imminent. As the election approached, the possibility of a sale became the major issue, ahead of wages and working conditions. Guild sentiment seemed to be growing; the outcome was expected to be close.

Just before the vote Mrs. Johnson invited the newsroom staff into her office and spoke openly against the union, saying the paper needed no outside agent bargaining for its reporters and editors. She said that under her husband's ownership the *Observer* had treated its employees like members of a family, and she intended to maintain that tradition. She cited the case of reporter Granbery Dickson who had been sick for months but continued to draw his salary. She said people who were worried about their jobs should put their minds at rest because the paper was not being sold, which at that moment was only technically correct.

That session apparently changed several minds because when the election was held a few days later, the result was not close. The union was defeated by a wide margin, much to the shock of some of its advocates. But the election left deep scars. Some staff members who had expressed support for the union refused to speak to those who had spoken for the company.

With the union election out of the way, talks between Knight interests and Mrs. Johnson grew more serious. Audits of *Observer* books for the previous six years were studied. At meetings in Mrs. Johnson's home on Pembroke Avenue in Myers Park, banker Carl McCraw was much in evidence, asking questions and advising Mrs. Johnson. Jim Knight and Lee Hills were there often, as was Akron attorney Blake McDowell, who had negotiated the Knights' other newspaper purchases. On Monday night, December 6, over dinner and some of Curtis Johnson's stash of rare pinch-bottle Scotch, the parties held long talks and reached a firm agreement. It called for Mrs. Johnson to sell 5,750 shares of *Observer* stock to the *Miami Herald* for $4,250,000 (about $739.13 a share). When the Knight contingent called for a taxi to take them back to their hotel, it was after midnight and they noticed for the first time that it had been snowing.

With controlling interest in hand, the Knights approached the Sullivan-Lineberger families for the rest of the stock. Mrs. Sullivan and the Linebergers were reluctant to sell until Blake McDowell suggested that the Knights would be investing so much in expanding the newspaper that dividends on *Observer* stock were unlikely for many years. Mrs. Sullivan and the Linebergers agreed to accept $2,975,000 for their 4,250 shares (about $700 a share).

That made the paper's total cost $7,225,000 when the parties met to close the transaction on December 29. As the papers were being signed, Jim Knight discovered that he needed a cashier's check for $1 million to complete the purchase. He looked at Barney Barnard, the American Trust vice-president, who said he could arrange that in a day or so. Carl McCraw, president of Union National, said he would credit the Knight account with that sum. A few minutes later, the transfer was complete and the *Charlotte Observer* was the property of Knight Newspapers, Inc. The next day, Jim Knight ordered the *Observer*'s bank account moved from American Trust to Union National. Union National also became administrator of trusts established by Mrs. Johnson and two of the three nephews.

Before the settlement Mrs. Johnson alerted a few of her executive committee of her intention to sell. One evening she invited Granny

Ward to her home and told him a sale was imminent. The next day, as Randolph Norton passed the door of Ward's tiny first-floor office at the *Observer*, Ward pulled him aside and said, "You know the ol' lady has sold the paper?" When Norton said no, Ward whispered the news. An evening or two later, at a gathering of the executive staff in her home, Mrs. Johnson revealed her plans. Ernest Hunter looked stricken, as if it were his first inkling that a sale was imminent.

On the afternoon of the final settlement, Mrs. Johnson called the entire company to the business office on the main floor. People stood, sat on counters, lined the stairs to the mezzanine, and gathered at the railing around the mezzanine. Mrs. Johnson announced the sale, praised the Knights as newspaper publishers, and said they would operate the *Observer* with local people and local directors. Then she introduced Jim Knight, who promised good things for the paper and the community. He spoke of the paper's long and distinguished history and of his intentions to build on that. He promised to give the staff the tools and financial support to put out a complete, well-edited, vigorous newspaper. He pledged that it would be independent politically as well as independent from business and advertiser influence. He spoke of the need to guard the news columns against advertising "puff." The paper could not give away the space it was in business to sell, he said.

The staff listened in silence and considerable apprehension. In a little more than four years it had suffered through the deaths of P. H. Batte and Curtis Johnson, the uncertainty over the Johnson will, the upheaval wrought by Ralph Nicholson, the momentary relief brought by Mrs. Johnson's control, the illness of Ernest Hunter, the Trotter-Norton division, the anger of a union election, and now the sale of the paper. Most of them had never heard of the Knights. They had no idea whether the sale was good or bad for the paper. Many feared for their jobs.

The *Observer*'s sale reflected a national trend that was affecting newspapers. With rising costs of publishing, the increased complexity of newspaper management, a lack of heirs interested in newspaper publishing, and the impact of state and federal inheritance taxes, many family-owned newspapers were sold to national chains or newspaper groups. In 1900, eight publishing groups owned 27 dailies; by 1935, 63 groups owned 328 papers, and by 1960, 109 groups owned 560 papers. When the Knights bought the *Observer*, most of North Carolina's major dailies were owned by families or local corporations, but a decade later most were owned by large, corporate publishing groups. Having passed successively through the age of the printer, of the editor, and of the publisher, the *Observer* was entering the era of the corporate conglomerate, a stage when the resources of an outside ownership freed newspapers large and small from domination by narrow local interests and allowed them to deal objectively with sensitive issues, even if those issues did involve a powerful business or industry. Nationally, the trade-off was that newspapers became more alike in appearance and opinion. They reflected more of the views of mainstream America and were less receptive to individualism and eccentricity.

CHAPTER 11

THE KNIGHT-McKNIGHT REVOLUTION
1955–1965

Under the Knights the *Observer* was rebuilt from top to bottom. What had been a stodgy, lumbering giant became a vigorous, assertive advocate of social and economic progress. The new owners gave the paper greater financial and managerial resources and the benefits of local autonomy. They hired a perceptive editor in C. A. ("Pete") McKnight and helped him recruit one of the South's brightest newspaper staffs. Freed from the dominance of business and advertising interests, the paper exerted a broader influence in local, state, and regional affairs. It resumed its growth and achieved a national stature exceeding that of the *Observer* published a half-century earlier by Joseph Caldwell and Daniel Tompkins.

But the ten years in which that growth occurred were among the most contentious in American history, and in that time the *Observer* all but exhausted its store of reader good will. In standing again and again for what it thought was wise and just, even when that proved unpopular, the paper got ahead of its audience and nearly crossed the line between community conscience and arrogant scold. As a result, the paper itself was often an object of controversy.

The *Observer* was not alone in its unease. Those years were hard on most newspapers, which were having to report news many Americans did not want to read. From 1955 to 1965, the nation confronted one upheaval after another, including the civil rights movement for blacks, the equal rights movement for women, and the movements to protect the environment, the elderly, the consumer, and to correct the rural bias of Congress and state legislatures by reapportioning on the basis of one person, one vote.

While absorbing those quakes, Americans were further upset by rising discord over the war in Vietnam and unrest on college campuses, by the decay of cities and violent urban riots, by an explosive growth in crime and traffic in illicit drugs, by a startling increase in public obscenity, sexuality, and pornography, and by the sounds and gyrations of a rebellious rock music.

Those and other events raised tensions in Charlotte and the Carolinas, where traditions died hard and change was often grudgingly accepted. Many people resented the new and aggressive *Observer* and wanted back the predictably safe paper they had grown up reading. Some accused it of being "meddlesome"; others, of expressing the "Yankee" views of its "Northern" owners. Still others alleged it was "communist" or "nigger-loving."

In the racial unrest of the 1950s and 1960s, the single gauge for measuring a newspaper in the South was its stance on civil rights. Newspapers that supported the black cause were "liberal" no matter what other views they held. In the minds of thousands of Carolina readers, the once-conservative *Observer* became a "liberal" newspaper.

Pete McKnight tells of one long-time *Observer* reader who called to ask which Northern states his "carpetbag" editorial writers were from. McKnight told the caller that he was an import from Shelby and a graduate of Davidson College, that the rascal Hal Tribble was a transplant from Anderson, South Carolina, and a graduate of the University of South Carolina, and that the scoundrel Simmons Fentress was a refugee from coastal Pamlico County who went north to college at Wake Forest. The caller paused to take that in, then drawled, "If there's anything worse than a no-'count carpetbagger, it's a low-down scalawag."

The caller's suspicions may have been strengthened by a larger phenomenon distressing residents of Charlotte and the Carolinas at about that time. Throughout the 1950s and 1960s many home-grown companies, such as the *Observer*, were being bought and merged into national corporations and staffed with a succession of executives from other parts of the country. The rapid turnover among such corporate nomads was disconcerting to Charlotteans, who felt their city was losing stability and becoming just another stop on the corporate ladder. For many years, the *Observer* itself, as the smallest member of the Knight organization, was a "boot camp" for ambitious young people who were seeking bigger jobs in journalism. They came and went at three- and four-year intervals.

Though the Knights learned newspapering in Akron, Ohio, their roots were southern. Their grandfather, William Knight, was living in Milledgeville, Georgia, in 1864 when Sherman's army torched the town and poured molasses into the church organ. Their father, Charles Landon Knight, known as "C. L.," was born in Milledgeville in 1867, went west to work on cattle ranches, was educated at Vanderbilt University, got a law degree from Columbia University, and started a law practice in Bluefield, West Virginia. His eldest son, John S. Knight, known as "Jack," was born in Bluefield in October 1894.

Three years later, C. L. Knight moved to Winston, North Carolina, where in April 1897 he founded the evening *Winston Journal*, forerunner of the morning *Winston-Salem Journal*. He sold the Winston paper to Bowman Gray, moved to Springfield, Ohio, to edit the *Woman's Home Companion*, and in 1903 began his thirty-year career on the *Akron Beacon-Journal*. By 1909, the year his second son, James L., was born, he was editor and publisher. In addition to editing the *Beacon-Journal*, C. L. Knight served a term in Congress (1921–23) and ran for governor (1922). When he died in September 1933, at the bottom of the Depression, he left an estate of $515,000 and debts and inheritance taxes of $800,000.

The tall, intense Jack Knight took command and in four years put the paper on its feet. He did it in much the same way Curtis B. Johnson had expanded the *Observer*. When other papers in Ohio were retrenching, Jack Knight opened up the *Beacon-Journal*, poured in more news and features, gained circulation and advertising, and paid off the paper's debts. In October 1937, he and his brother bought the *Miami Herald*. In May 1940, they added the *Detroit Free Press*, and in October 1944 acquired the *Chicago Daily News*.

Jack Knight grew up on his father's newspaper, working as a printer's devil, then as a copy boy, and later as a reporter. He entered Cornell University and was about to graduate when World War I broke out. He enlisted in the army and was sent to France, where he earned a lieutenant's commission in the infantry. He was training to be an airborne artillery observer when the war ended. He roamed Europe a few months, spending $5,000 he had won shooting craps, and weighing whether to go to law school or return to newspapering. At his father's invitation, he went back to the *Beacon-Journal* and by 1925 was managing editor, the post he held at his father's death.

The stocky, thick-chested Jim Knight had a different background. Coming of age in his father's later years, when C. L. Knight no longer sought political office and family life was calmer, he developed a warmer, more relaxed personality than his assertive brother. He attended Brown University until the Depression, then left school to work in the business end of newspapering. He learned newspaper production by looking beyond the accounting ledgers at the condition of machinery, the maintenance of buildings, and the morale of employees.

His interests in the nuts and bolts of the business were apparent in the Knights' purchase of the *Observer*. He told *Observer* employees it was his job to provide the best plant and equipment and their job to produce the best newspaper. One of his first moves was to summon potbellied William B. Sandlin, a grizzled, squint-eyed, cigar-chomping ex-printer with a top-sergeant's bearing. "Uncle Bill" Sandlin had retired as production manager of the *Miami Herald* and knew all the tricks of the printing trades. Until his arrival, the composing room had jurisdiction over *Observer* deadlines, ad layout, page makeup, and press starts. Under Sandlin that changed; the composing room became a servant of the editorial and advertising departments. For the first time in many years *Observer* editors could control the size and content of each day's paper.

The most dramatic change came in advertiser access to the news columns. Previously, ad manager Bo Robinson could send a note upstairs and get an *Observer* reporter and photographer assigned to an advertiser's ribbon-cutting ceremony. Under the Knights, that practice ended. They made it clear that the *Observer* was in business to sell newspaper space, not give it away, that news was news and advertising was advertising, and the two were rarely the same. The new policy brought howls from merchants who had assumed a proprietary interest in the newspaper.

In those first months, Jim Knight and his editorial director, Lee Hills, were in and out of Charlotte frequently, conferring with executive editor Ernest Hunter and managing editor Ran Norton, meeting local business leaders, and speaking at state press gatherings. They tinkered with the typography to give the paper a cleaner look. They pulled the column rules from editorial, women's, and feature pages, and removed the ads from page two, opening up space for more news and an improved weather summary. They evaluated personnel, eliminated the six-day work week, expanded the staff, raised salaries, enlivened the women's pages, and began preparing the sixty-six-year-old Hunter for a transition to younger management. The visits of Lee Hills were especially important, for he was the Knights' most trusted lieutenant and would make crucial decisions in shaping the paper's future.

A slim, quick, efficient man who was exact in speech and dress, Hills grew up with an appetite for work. Born in North Dakota and reared in Utah, he entered journalism at fourteen as a copy boy, cub reporter, and general handyman on his hometown weekly. By eighteen, he was editing the weekly and winning prizes in state press contests. He went to college at Brigham Young and the University of Missouri, and in 1929 joined the *Oklahoma City Times*. Three years later he moved over to Scripps-Howard's *Oklahoma City News*, and spent the next ten years with the Scripps-Howard chain, acquiring expertise in both the editorial and business sides of newspapering. He worked in Cleveland, Indianapolis, and Memphis, as well as Oklahoma City. He was in Cleveland in 1942, awaiting other assignments, when he learned that Akron's Jack Knight was looking for an editor and went to talk with him.

Jack Knight said later he had "never talked with a newspaperman who had better credentials." He offered the thirty-six-year-old Hills a job as city editor of the *Miami Herald*. Hills accepted and was barely on the job in September 1942 when he was charged with rebuilding a staff decimated by the draft and military enlistments. He made the *Herald* a servant of readers, as well as a source of news, and in 1950 led it to a Pulitzer Prize for investigating gangsterism in Miami. The following year, he became executive editor of both the *Herald* and the *Detroit Free Press*. In 1955, he won a Pulitzer in Detroit for reporting secret negotiations between auto makers and auto workers over a guaranteed annual wage.

Hills was also the Knights' chief talent hunter, a man who took joy in spotting people with potential and guiding their development. On flights between Miami and Detroit, he often stopped in Charlotte. In the back of his mind he had begun to seek an editor who could turn the *Observer* into a Knight newspaper. Quietly, one candidate had already explored with him the paper's possibilities. That was Pete McKnight.

After the Supreme Court outlawed segregated public schools in May 1954, the Ford Foundation put up money to create an agency that would monitor southern progress in obeying that order. The goal was to provide facts and dispel rumors in the impending social revolution. In July 1954, Pete McKnight took leave as editor of the *Charlotte News* to head that agency, known as the Southern Education Reporting Service (SERS), with offices in Nashville.

In early February 1955, six weeks after the Knights bought the *Observer*, McKnight was traveling through the East and Midwest to inform editors about the SERS mission and to suggest that segregation was not exclusively a southern problem. On the trip McKnight stopped in Detroit to talk with Lee Hills, ostensibly about desegregation but also about the *Charlotte Observer*. At one point, Hills asked McKnight to go to a typewriter in the next office and write out what he thought should be done with the *Observer*. What McKnight wrote closely matched what Hills and Jim Knight had discussed doing, which was to raise the paper's standard of journalism.

Between interviews with other candidates, Hills called around the South to check McKnight's credentials and found him to be highly respected as an editor and an intellectual. He had the reputation and personality to attract talent, and the brains to develop it. He was a North Carolinian, knew Charlotte inside out, and had been away long enough to get a new perspective on the city and its region, to see them against the whole southern backdrop.

McKnight visited Miami for talks with Jack and Jim Knight and at their suggestion went to New York to be interviewed by Cle Althaus, an expert in personnel testing. The encounter was significant, for Althaus soon became the *Observer*'s personnel director and pioneered the paper's personnel testing. Until then, editors had done their hiring on the basis of first impressions and seat-of-the-pants hunches. After helping the *Observer* identify a long list of highly talented men and women, the tests were adopted throughout the Knight organization.

By late February, the Knights and their lieutenants had agreed that McKnight would be the next editor of the *Observer*, but the decision remained secret. McKnight had commitments to keep in Nashville, and the Knights had groundwork to lay in Charlotte. The secrecy proved painful that spring when McKnight spoke to North Carolina newspaper editors in Chapel Hill. There he ran into Charles Kuralt, a UNC senior from Charlotte who was editing the *Daily Tar Heel* and showing great promise as a journalist. McKnight had been encouraging Kuralt to consider a career in newspapers instead of television. With a big grin, Kuralt announced he had decided to join the *Charlotte News*. McKnight later recalled he had to bite his tongue and could only congratulate the young man, knowing that he and Kuralt would soon be on opposing papers. After several years on the *News*, Kuralt joined CBS.

On Sunday night, July 3, Lee Hills invited *Observer* managing editor Ran Norton to dinner at Charlotte's Barringer Hotel (later named Hall House). When Norton arrived, McKnight was introduced to him as "the new editor of the *Observer*." Norton remembers being stunned, but pleased because he admired McKnight's talent. Two days later, McKnight was introduced to the *Observer* staff at a meeting in the newspaper's third-floor auditorium. He played it low-key, talking about how he had read the paper as a boy in Shelby, and asking for help and patience as he learned the *Observer* way of doing things. He made no allusions to lofty goals or to changes that might be forthcoming, but as the staff, still sore over the union election and the paper's sale, trooped back to the newsroom, its members buzzed with excitement. Knowing McKnight's reputation, they sensed that the good gray *Observer* was in for brighter days.

The next morning's *Observer* contained a three-column story headlined, "Knight Moves to Strengthen *Observer*'s Local Autonomy." It announced that Ernest B. Hunter had been named assistant to the publisher and would be Jim Knight's personal spokesman in the community, and that thirty-nine-year-old C. A. McKnight, former editor of the *Charlotte News*, had been appointed editor of the *Observer*, "with full responsibility over the news and editorial functions of the newspaper." His authority did not equal that of Joseph Caldwell, but it was greater than any *Observer* editor had enjoyed since 1909.

In announcing the appointments, Jim Knight repeated his pledge to maintain the *Observer* as a "locally edited and operated" newspaper. McKnight promised to tell "the story of Charlotte and its surrounding region better than it has been told before." He saw "a tremendous opportunity for the *Observer* to speak for the Carolinas, and to report and interpret their key role in the growth and development of the New South. . . . The dynamic economic and industrial expansion of the New South has barely begun, and it holds out great promise."

Like Joseph Caldwell and Daniel Tompkins, McKnight had a singular vision of the emerging South. He saw it advancing in education, industrialism, and racial understanding. Unlike Caldwell and Tompkins, whose portrayal of the region often lapsed into propaganda, McKnight sought to depict the South flaws and all. Like other southerners who grew up reading the social research of UNC's Howard Odum and Rupert Vance, he believed the region stood little chance of ending its poverty until it ended its ignorance and segregation. When the South learned the real costs of backwardness and prejudice, its own self-interest would bring about change. That idea, an expression of the southern liberal's faith in education, would later be misinterpreted by many *Observer* readers who accused McKnight and the *Observer* of "tearing down" instead of "building up" the South.

McKnight was one of three talented sons of wholesale grocer John S. McKnight of Shelby. He was christened Colbert Augustus, but early on was dubbed "Pete" by a neighbor who said he was "too puny" to hold up so formal a name. His mother, Norva Proctor McKnight, taught him to read at age four. At age twelve, he built a radio and became a ham operator. At thirteen, he lost his left eye when a rusty .22 rifle backfired and a piece of shell casing ripped through his eyeball. Like D. A. Tompkins, he did not let that narrow his vision. He made straight A's in school, and played the piano and four brass instruments. In the valedictory address at his high school commencement in 1933, he said, "Our schools can do more than any other influence to break down the walls of prejudice. If the schools have a world-wide mission, it is to clear up the idea that some are born superior to others in human rights."

That summer he visited Cuba, where his older brother John was an Associated Press correspondent. While there, he witnessed a hurricane and helped cover a revolution. Returning to North Carolina too late to enter college, he got a job on the *Shelby Star*, partly because he could type fast. In those days, the *Star*'s only AP service was the "pony wire" via telephone from Charlotte. The faster someone at a "pony" subscriber could take dictation, the more news the paper got.

The next year he entered Davidson College on a half scholarship and earned the rest waiting tables, selling men's clothes, delivering the *Observer*, clerking in the library, and grading papers for Spanish and English professors. He still had time to compile an academic average of 97. He had intended to be a Spanish professor like his other brother Bill, but the summer in Cuba and the year at the *Star* turned him toward newspapers.

He joined the *Charlotte News* as a reporter in 1939 and rose to city editor, news editor, managing editor, and, in 1949, at age thirty-three, to editor. He was a routine winner of North Carolina Press Association editorial writing contests, winning first prize in 1950, 1951, and 1953. In 1951 he also won second place and honorable mention out of four possible prizes.

McKnight's reputation for editorial brilliance was a burden to him at the *Observer*. John S. Knight, whose heart was on the editorial side of newspapering, grumbled repeatedly that once McKnight became the *Observer* editor, he quit writing editorials. In complaining about "dull" *Observer* editorial pages, he urged McKnight to return to the typewriter. But at the *Observer* McKnight's responsibilities were broader than they were at the *News*. On the *News* he supervised only the editorial page; Brodie Griffith ran the news department. When McKnight arrived at the *Observer*, there was no Brodie Griffith. For several years, McKnight was busy revitalizing the newsroom, recruiting talent, representing the paper in the community, planning for the future, and serving as a director of Knight Newspapers, Inc.

In breathing life into the news department, McKnight made the *Observer* a morning version of what the *Charlotte News* had been— bright, lively, and enterprising. Overnight, the *Observer*, which had previously asked few questions, was poking around in government and business affairs, stirring up stories and covering local news with a new aggressiveness. At the *News*, publisher Thomas L. Robinson, editor Brodie Griffith, and managing editor Tom Fesperman felt the heat of stronger competition. Strapped for money and equipment, they were now up against not only superior financial resources, but also a big-city organization.

The Knights soon gave the *News* cause for greater apprehension. They followed up the hiring of former *News* editor Pete McKnight by hiring *News* general manager Bill Dowd to run the business side of the *Observer*. Jim Knight and Bill Dowd had admired each other since they were thrown together several years earlier at an unscheduled airline stop. After they had swapped stories for a couple of hours, Bill Dowd said he would like to work for Knight someday. Jim Knight remembered the incident and in October 1955 took Dowd up on the offer.

After years of competing against the morning giant, Dowd had trouble making the shift. The old loyalties were hard to cast off. On his first trip to the *Observer*, he got a block from home and could not go on. He stopped at the home of a neighboring physician for tea and fortification, then went home and called in sick. The next day, he stopped again at the neighbor's, and then went on to the office— late.

In appointing Dowd, the Knights separated the news and business departments of the *Observer*. Dowd was to represent the paper in business and civic affairs, and have authority over all *Observer* departments except news and editorial, which were McKnight's preserve. "What happens if I want Pete to do something?" Dowd asked. The answer: "You can't reach him; he is supreme in his field." That division enabled the *Observer* to throw off the business-advertiser influence that had compromised its news coverage.

Merchant-advertisers continued to test that division, largely at the urging of ad manager Bo Robinson, who did not support it. He blamed the new policy on "those bastards" in the *Observer* newsroom. It was not long before Dowd and Jim Knight relieved Robinson—who had been with the paper thirty-one years—and reached a third time into the executive ranks of the *Charlotte News*. Just after Christmas 1955, they hired Robert J. ("Bob") Alander, a popular, laugh-a-minute ad salesman who came to Charlotte from the *Miami News*, where he was advertising director. Though born in Oak Park, Illinois, Alander was at home among southerners and had become deeply involved in Charlotte's civic and cultural affairs.

The hiring of Alander provoked *News* publisher Thomas L. Robinson to quip, only half in jest, that though he had heard of afternoon papers being bought up by their morning competitors, this was the first time he had heard of one "being dismembered." But the *Observer* still had another raid to make on *News* personnel. In what was perhaps the most damaging swipe of all, Pete McKnight reached into the opposition's newsroom and hired its spark plug, managing editor Tom Fesperman, a Charlotte native who grew up reading proof on the *News*, honed his reporting and writing skills there, and developed a warm and chatty local column. He was father confessor to a generation of bright young writers, among them Charles Kuralt, Julian Scheer, and Sandy Grady.

The wise and winsome Fesperman had known McKnight for many years. They had spent hours together, drinking beer, listening to opera, and trading newspaper talk. They liked each other and complemented each other. McKnight was brainy, analytical, and abstract; Fesperman, intuitive, personable, specific.

McKnight began recruiting Fesperman in late 1955, when he sensed that the chemistry between himself and managing editor Randolph Norton was not generating energy. They met at McKnight's home to remember the past and discuss the future. Fesperman was reluctant to cut his ties to the *News* and the rough-hewn but lovable Brodie Griffith. Like Bill Dowd, his loyalties went deep. But lacking capital, the *Charlotte News* had poor long-run prospects, and Fesperman had a family to educate. Knight Newspapers, Inc. could offer more career options.

Having passed the Cle Althaus tests, Fesperman met Lee Hills at the Barringer Hotel. They discussed Fesperman's coming to the *Observer* as "night managing editor" until he learned the morning-paper routine and got to know the staff. Later, with Norton's approval, he would move up to managing editor. Fesperman checked and found Norton willing to take another job, as director of public service. In the spring of 1956, Fesperman accepted the *Observer* offer and, with a heavy heart, went to inform Brodie Griffith. "Mr. G." had seen lots of *News* talent come and go; he would understand. Griffith did little to make Fesperman's leave-taking anything but excruciating. Griffith was persuasive, Fesperman was sweating. But Fesperman stuck by his decision and finally "Mr. G" wished him well. When the move was announced, people at the *News* cried.

The infusion of *News* executives did not bring joy to the *Observer*, especially among veteran employees who saw their careers being short-circuited. Advertising and circulation workers who had competed against the *News* cringed at the idea of working for Bill Dowd. A number of people left, among them business manager Harry Allen, who had been with the *Observer* for thirty-four years, and city circulation manager Dave Cauble, who had been with the paper thirty-two years. Circulation manager Granny Ward saw his job cut in half as Bruce Rogers took over circulation; Ward was left to run the Observer Transportation Company.

There was also resentment in the newsroom. Though personal relations between Pete McKnight and associate editor Hal Tribble remained cordial, old-timers groused that Tribble should have been named editor. Five years later, Tribble resigned. Some desk men looked upon Tom Fesperman as an intruder and an obstacle to their advancement. When the *Miami Herald*'s Walter B. ("Whitey") Kelley was appointed executive sports editor in August 1955, it was seen as a slight to sports editor Wilton Garrison. Younger sportswriters regarded Kelley as a barrier to their ambitions.

Two newsroom firings also upset people. One, before McKnight arrived, was the dismissal of Wriston H. ("Wink") Locklair, the paper's popular music, drama, and book critic, whose arrest in a roundup of homosexuals shocked the press and cultural communities. He was fired even before standing trial. Sentenced to five years in prison, he was later paroled when Harry Golden gave him a job selling ads for the *Carolina Israelite*. He earned enough to pay his debts and go to New York, where he got jobs with the American Newspaper Publishers Association, American Express, and, finally, the Juilliard School of Music. He was assistant to the president of Juilliard when he died in March 1984.

The second firing was of Scott Summers, a journeyman reporter with a history of alcohol problems. Summers won praise for his coverage of the "Jack-in-the-Box" murder trial (so called because a man hid in the trunk of his wife's car and then jumped out and killed her lover at a drive-in rendezvous). Later, while driving to an assignment, Summers was wrecked by another car and received an injury requiring a neck brace. He was reassigned to the editing desk, where the constant bending over aggravated his injury. One day he came to work drunk, backed his car into a bus in front of the *Observer* office, and was fired on the spot. Some staffers said that the firing was unjust, that other drinkers on the staff had kept their jobs after worse incidents.

The firing was the result of a new policy laid down by Pete McKnight. The first to test the policy was reporter Porter Munn, who in twenty-six years under Ernest Hunter had been fired several times for drunkenness, then rehired after much pleading. The first time he showed up soused under McKnight, he was summoned by the editor and told in no uncertain terms that the next time he came to work with liquor on his breath would be the last. He would be fired and never rehired. "Is that clear?" McKnight asked. Munn said yes—and never touched liquor again. He retired seventeen years later, hearing praise for his coverage of state and local highway planning. After seeing the results of the Munn-McKnight encounter, Ernest Hunter said, "And all those years I thought I was doing Porter a favor."

During the time it took for that and other policies to prove their worth, the divided *Observer* newsroom was an unhappy place in which to build loyalty and pride. McKnight and Fesperman had their work cut out for them. Their success was partly a tribute to their skills and partly a result of the quality of young people who were entering the newspaper business.

During the 1950s, the image of newspapering as an occupation began to improve. One reason was that newspapers were changing their style and content to meet the expectations of better-educated readers, whose numbers had grown with the huge increase in college graduates since the end of the war. Another was the greater sophistication of journalism schools, which were turning out better-qualified graduates. A third was the spread of newspaper chains, which had the resources to recruit and train better talent and could afford to employ newspaper specialists. And of special significance in the South was the realization among idealistic young people that the racial story unfolding in the mid-1950s was likely to be a drama of historic significance, and they wanted to be on hand to witness and interpret it.

With the resources of Knight Newspapers and an abundance of available talent, McKnight and Fesperman set about rebuilding the *Observer*'s news and editorial staff and raising its journalistic standards. The process had begun even before McKnight's arrival. In the spring of 1955, Atlanta native Don Oberdorfer was looking for a reporting job on a southern newspaper. He had graduated from Princeton in 1952, done an army tour in Korea, and was recovering from an attack of polio. He called on William Howland, chief of *Time* magazine's Atlanta bureau, who had just written a story on the Knights' plans for stepping up the voltage at their newly acquired *Charlotte Observer*. Howland told Oberdorfer the place to go was Charlotte.

With Oberdorfer sitting there, Howland called Detroit and told Lee Hills about Oberdorfer's interest. Hills urged Oberdorfer to see Ran Norton, then the *Observer*'s managing editor. A few weeks later, Oberdorfer was hired and told to report Tuesday, July 5. As he was settling into a Charlotte apartment over the July 4th weekend, Oberdorfer got a call from Norton suggesting that he report for work an hour early the next day to attend a staff meeting. That was when McKnight was introduced as the new *Observer* editor.

McKnight quickly recognized Oberdorfer's talent and began grooming him for major assignments. With hurricane season approaching (Hurricane Hazel had struck the Carolina coast the previous fall), he sent Oberdorfer to the weather bureau and the library to learn about cyclones and their habits. When three more storms struck the seaboard that fall, Oberdorfer's expertise proved invaluable. Wearing wide-striped shirts, garish ties, and orange-and-black Princeton suspenders, he performed a number of reporting chores before becoming the paper's first full-time Washington correspondent since Red Buck Bryant. During the Vietnam War, he covered the Tet offensive that was the beginning of the end of American involvement. Later he became chief diplomatic correspondent for the *Washington Post*.

Seeing one of its alumni move up in the newspaper business was a relatively new experience for the *Observer*. The *Charlotte News* had employed a number of people who had gone on to jobs on bigger newspapers, but most *Observer* staffers tended to stay put. Soon after the Knights took over, Harry Golden, Jr., moved to the *Detroit Free Press* and later to the *Chicago Sun-Times*, where he became the senior city hall reporter.

In the decade following the Knights' purchase, the Oberdorfer-Golden pattern was repeated over and over as the *Observer* recruited and trained a succession of bright young men and women and sent them on to bigger jobs in journalism. Every spring and fall, McKnight and Fesperman made recruiting trips to major journalism schools. McKnight developed a knack for spotting people of exceptional promise. His test was, "If I was a news source, would I like being interviewed by this person?" When he felt the hair rise on the back of his neck during an interview, he knew he was facing an extraordinary applicant.

Fesperman was also a shrewd judge of talent and a sensitive tutor. He knew how to coax from young people the best that was in them, often without their knowing it. Fesperman got to the office early each morning, read the paper closely, and wrote clever little notes to reporters and editors about their previous night's work. The notes, usually droll, were mostly praising and taught by positive reinforcement. On occasion they were also gently critical—Fesperman could chasten and praise in the same sentence. Young people who were terrified of McKnight found Fesperman to be sunny and approachable.

As improvements by McKnight and Fesperman began to show up, word spread that the reviving *Charlotte Observer* was "a reporter's newspaper" where ideas bubbled up from the bottom instead of coming down from the top. McKnight and Fesperman not only gave their protégés wide latitude, but also invited their suggestions for improving the paper.

That atmosphere, training, and encouragement helped prepare at least a dozen of McKnight and Fesperman's early recruits for careers as editors, publishers, or major executives in the Knight organization. Going on to become editors were W. Davis ("Buzz") Merritt, a Morehead Scholar at UNC, who became editor of the *Wichita Eagle-Beacon*; Larry Tarleton, from Wadesboro and UNC, who rose through the sports department to become managing editor of the *Dallas Times Herald*; Charles M. ("Chuck") Hauser of Fayetteville, a UNC graduate, who became executive editor of the *Journal-Bulletin* in Providence, Rhode Island; and Dale Allen of Arkansas, a University of Missouri graduate, who became editor of the *Akron Beacon-Journal*.

Becoming publishers were Rolfe Neill, a Mt. Airy native and UNC graduate, who became publisher of the *Observer*; Sam S. McKeel of Greene County, a UNC and Columbia School of Journalism graduate, who joined the *Observer* as a reporter and went on to become president of the *Philadelphia Inquirer* and the *Philadelphia Daily News*; Joseph C. Doster, Jr., of Rutherford County, a Phi Beta Kappa graduate of UNC, who joined the *Observer* as a reporter and went on to become publisher of the *Winston-Salem Journal*; John Ginn, a Texan who trained at the University of Missouri, who came to the *Observer* as a copy editor, and went on to become publisher of the *Anderson* (S.C.) *Independent*; John C. Gardner, a graduate of Northwestern University and the Columbia School of Journalism, who held a number of reporting and editing jobs at the *Observer* and went on to be publisher of the *Quad-City Times* in Davenport, Iowa; and Fred Sheheen, a Camden, South Carolina, native and Angier Duke scholar at Duke University, who represented the *Observer* in Rock Hill and Columbia, South Carolina, and went on to publish a variety of community newspapers in South Carolina.

Two former *Observer* reporters and editors became major executives in the Knight-Ridder corporation, parent of Knight Publishing Company, the local firm that owns the *Observer*. They were Larry Jinks, Knight-Ridder's senior vice-president for news and operations, and James K. Batten, the president of the corporation. The Batten story is a good example of the *Observer*'s impact in those heady years.

A native of Tidewater, Virginia, Batten went to Davidson College intending to study chemistry and become a plant pathologist and experimental farmer like his father. As a senior he edited the *Davidsonian*, and after graduation, with eight months to kill until his Army ROTC commission, he took a reporting job at the *Observer*, hoping to rid himself of a nagging interest in journalism. The excitement of the reporting stint changed his mind. After serving in the army, he was accepted in the graduate plant-pathology program at North Carolina State University, but he enrolled in Princeton's Woodrow Wilson School instead, returned to the *Observer* as a reporter, and wrote stories about politics, poverty, hunger, and racial unrest. In the mid-sixties he joined the paper's Washington bureau, moved to the *Detroit Free Press*, returned to the *Observer* as executive editor, and in 1975 joined the executive organization of Knight-Ridder.

In the first decade of the Knight-McKnight years, the *Observer* employed many others who became exceptional writers and reporters. Medical writer Don Seaver won state and national prizes before joining the medical news staff at Duke University. His stories forced the desegregation of Charlotte Memorial Hospital and the public takeover of Good Samaritan. Courthouse reporter Loye Miller went on to *Time* magazine, as did business writer John DeMott. Georgian John Eslinger became editorial page editor of the *Fayetteville Observer*. Texan William S. Delaney went on to the *Washington Star*. Robert Rosenblatt became a Washington correspondent for the *Los Angeles Times*. Victor McElheny became a science writer for the *New York Times* and later director of a graduate program for science and technical writers at Massachusetts Institute of Technology. Hickory's dogged Dwayne Walls won prizes for stories done in partnership with either Joe Doster or Jim Batten about absentee-ballot fraud in the mountains, Ku Klux Klan terror in the Piedmont, and hunger among rural families. He left the *Observer* to become a journalism teacher and writing coach.

In his tenure at the *Observer* Walls was involved in the last and one of the best of the Gus Travis stories. Walls had been out all day covering Vice-President Lyndon Johnson's leapfrogging, arm-waving campaign swing through the Piedmont. The exhausted Walls had written his story and gone home. At Douglas Airport, the vice-president saw an early edition of the *Observer* and, admiring the Walls account of his visit, phoned the newsroom to thank him. Gus Travis answered the phone. Johnson said, "This is Lyndon Baines Johnson, vice-president of the United States, and I'd like to speak to Mr. Dwayne Walls." Travis replied testily, "Well this is Augustus Zollicoffer Travis, copy editor and headline writer, and Mr. Walls is not here." Johnson sputtered and asked for Walls's home phone number. The snickering Travis put down the phone and asked if anyone knew how to reach Dwayne Walls. News editor Carlos Kumpe was sitting nearby and asked what was going on. "Oh, just some nut claiming to be Lyndon Johnson," Travis said. Kumpe picked up the phone, recognized the LBJ drawl, and gave him Walls's home number. When Travis learned the caller really was Lyndon Johnson, he cackled. He had deflated another stuffed shirt.

McKnight did not always hire the exceptional applicants he interviewed. He recalled two that he deliberately let get away. One was Tom Wicker, a Hamlet native then working for the *Winston-Salem Journal*. McKnight interviewed him for an editorial writing job and decided he was too liberal for the *Observer*. He suggested that Wicker go to Nashville instead. Wicker did and from there went to the *New York Times*, where he became an associate editor. A second exception was Patrick J. Buchanan, whom McKnight interviewed at Columbia University. Buchanan showed up with Sen. Barry Goldwater's book, *The Conscience of a Conservative*, under his arm. McKnight said he decided Buchanan was too conservative and advised him to look elsewhere. Buchanan went to the *Globe-Democrat* in St. Louis and later to the White House during the Nixon and Reagan administrations, serving as director of communications.

McKnight and Fesperman strengthened the *Observer*'s outreach by recruiting veteran reporters for its Raleigh and Columbia bureaus and by plugging into the Knight bureau in Washington. For the Raleigh bureau, a critical post on a paper that had been outside the mainstream of state politics, McKnight hired an old friend, James L. ("Jay") Jenkins, Jr., in the fall of 1955. It was a splendid choice, for Jenkins wrote quickly and cleanly, knew the state well, and was familiar with its political traditions and leaders. Like McKnight, he had grown up in Cleveland County, then the home of ex-governor O. Max Gardner's "Shelby Ring" and a hotbed of North Carolina politics. Jenkins's father was pastor of Boiling Springs Baptist Church and president of Boiling Springs Junior College (later a four-year school named Gardner-Webb). Jenkins attended Boiling Springs and worked his way through Wake Forest College by writing sports news. After graduation he got a job on the *Shelby Star*, served in the air corps during World War II, and afterward was a reporter for the *Wilmington Star* until joining the Raleigh *News and Observer* in 1948. When Pete McKnight formed the Southern Education Reporting Service, he signed up Jenkins as a North Carolina stringer.

Jenkins had not been the *Observer*'s Raleigh correspondent long before he was giving the paper exclusive stories of statewide interest and raising the ire of his former editors at the *News and Observer*. Legislators who felt the sting of the *Observer*'s reporting (largely by Jenkins) began taking the floor on "a point of personal privilege" to condemn "the acrid smoke of Akron that now swirls around Charlotte"—a sure sign that the *Observer* was again doing its job and being taken seriously in the state capital.

During legislative sessions, the *Observer* sent other reporters to Raleigh to assist Jenkins. Beginning in 1961, one of those was Joe Doster, an emerging political specialist. In addition to hard-news stories and analyses, Jenkins and Doster often wrote anecdotes about the foibles of legislators. When Doster wrote that Sen. William D. James, a Hamlet physician, named the children he delivered for unwed mothers after his political enemies, Dr. James was not amused. At his next meeting with Doster and Jenkins, he said, "Guess who I'm naming those illegitimate kids for now?"

The Columbia bureau was more difficult to staff. Though the *Observer* had a significant South Carolina circulation (then about 25,000 a day), it was often regarded as a "foreign" newspaper. McKnight's first choice for the job was Hoke Smith May, grandson of Hoke Smith, a former *Atlanta Journal* editor and an ex-governor of Georgia. The red-haired May had been a reporter for the *Anderson Independent* before joining the *Observer* and knew his way around South Carolina. At the time of his appointment, he was also a celebrity. His story of brutality among moonshine distillers in western North Carolina had been featured on "The Big Story," a national TV series based on real-life newspaper stories.

In December 1957, May left the Columbia bureau for a job in public relations, and McKnight hired thirty-four-year-old Charles H. Wickenberg, Jr., executive secretary to South Carolina Gov. George Bell Timmerman and a man acquainted with most of South Carolina's political leaders. Wickenberg, also a redhead, was a Columbia native, had previously reported for the United Press and the Associated Press, and was married to a newspaper woman who had assisted

May in covering the South Carolina legislature. Wickenberg proved to be a highly resourceful correspondent whose stories often contained data not published elsewhere. If Wickenberg did not know the background himself, he knew where to get it. Wickenberg's work helped change the competitive climate in South Carolina. Other South Carolina papers soon established Columbia bureaus, and in September 1962, the morning paper in Columbia, the *State*, which had previously relied on wire-service coverage of the South Carolina legislature, hired him to direct its governmental coverage. Succeeding Wickenberg in Columbia was Fred Sheheen, who had established the *Observer*'s Rock Hill bureau and assisted Wickenberg when the South Carolina legislature was in session. Sheheen stayed through 1964, then went to Washington as an aide to ex-governor Donald Russell, who was appointed to the United States Senate.

As a Knight paper, the *Observer* began to receive daily reports from the group's Washington bureau headed by Edwin A. Lahey of Chicago, a crusty ex–crime and labor reporter renowned for trenchant lead sentences. After witnessing the first explosion of a hydrogen bomb by the United States, Lahey's story began, "Megatons, smegatons, it was a helluva blast." Soon the *Observer* was sending its own representatives to that bureau, first Don Oberdorfer, later Chuck Hauser and Jim Batten.

In a move to strengthen *Observer* ties to the region, McKnight opened news bureaus in Gastonia, Rock Hill, Wadesboro, Statesville, and Monroe. The effort paid off in wider coverage and increased circulation. When reporter Rolfe Neill opened the Gastonia bureau in 1957, daily *Observer* circulation in Gaston County was 2,786; by 1965, daily sales had risen to 13,959. When reporter Fred Sheheen opened the bureau in Rock Hill in 1959, *Observer* circulation in York County was 1,056; by 1965 it was 7,591.

While they were improving *Observer* reporting and editing, McKnight and Fesperman were also putting greater emphasis on photography. They had the photo lab moved out of the rude, converted restroom on the second floor and into stainless-steel facilities on the third floor. They also hired a succession of gifted cameramen, among them Don Sturkey, Charles Kelly, Maurie Rosen, Michael Mauney, Declaun Haun, Bruce Roberts, Tom Walters, David Nance, and David Cupp. Year after year those men dominated Carolinas, Southern, and occasionally national photo exhibits. Sturkey was "National Newspaper Photographer of the Year" in 1960 and Mike Mauney was "Southern Photographer of the Year" an unprecedented four years in a row.

The photographers also introduced dramatic changes in photo technology. They abandoned the bulky sheet-film cameras, which required an array of flashbulb and strobe-light equipment, in favor of simpler reflex cameras and later 35mm lenses that allowed the use of high-speed film. The advances changed the nature of press photography. Instead of posed pictures of people shaking hands or pretending to converse, the new, smaller cameras allowed photographers to work unobtrusively and shoot candid photos in available light. News photography lost its stiff artificiality and began to reflect real life.

While recruiting and training new talent, McKnight and Fesperman were also molding Kays Gary into a columnist of remarkable appeal and impact. Actually, little molding was needed, for Gary, then in his mid-thirties, was already an exceptional writer. In the fall of 1955, McKnight's secretary Ellen Crosby entered four of his best human-interest stories in a national contest named for Ernie Pyle, a World War II war correspondent famed for reporting the human side of combat. Four weeks later, the surprised Gary was named winner of the $1,000 first prize. Thereafter Gary was relieved of reporting chores and became a full-time columnist.

At the urging of McKnight and Fesperman, Gary widened his range and varied his subject matter. He learned to strike a balance between columns about people and pets and columns about political and economic issues in which he had an impassioned interest. Gary also learned to draw on his own experience and upbringing in writing insightful essays on the lives and times of people in the Carolinas. His presence on the newspaper's second-front page ensured that few readers could mistake the *Observer* for a "northern" newspaper.

Perhaps the best illustration of his influence was a series of columns and stories about the wife and daughter of Pvt. James McRacken, a young Red Springs, North Carolina, soldier who in World War II gave his life to save a bridge that kept the ninth-century town of Mayenne, France, from being reduced to rubble. As German troops fled the American army across Normandy, they sought to make a stand at Mayenne by blowing up the bridge leading into the town. But McRacken rushed to the center of the span and, in a hail of small-arms fire, defused the explosives, saving the bridge and allowing the Americans to continue their pursuit. McRacken died, but Mayenne was spared the bombardment that would have wrecked it.

In tribute to McRacken's heroism, the 18,000 residents of Mayenne named the bridge for him and each August 5, on the anniversary of his death, held a memorial service at the spot where he fell. For sixteen years, they invited his widow and daughter to join them for the ceremony, but Mae McRacken and her eighteen-year-old daughter could not afford such a trip. Mrs. McRacken was working in the gift shop at Manger Motor Inn on North Tryon Street when Gary heard her story. Gary informed *Observer* readers of her situation and within two days they contributed enough money to send the McRackens to Mayenne in style.

Gary's moving account of the town's reception of the McRackens raised an ache of both joy and sadness. The people of Mayenne lined both sides of the 500-yard street leading to the bridge and both sides of the bridge leading to the McRacken Memorial. As Mae McRacken and her daughter walked through those solemn lines, the townspeople on each side whispered "merci" at their every step, thanking the widow and orphan for their sacrifice. Gary described it as a chorus that began as a whisper and became a hymn: "Merci, . . . merci, . . . merci, . . . merci." By the time the McRackens reached the monument, tears streamed down the faces of men and women alike. Gathering her strength, Mae McRacken stood erect and proud as the band played the "The Star-Spangled Banner" and then the "Marseillaise."

The story was an example of a sensitive newspaper reporter's power to inspire in people and nations a stronger appreciation of their common bond. The story gave new meaning to James McRacken's short life. It also gave new meaning and purpose to the lives of his widow and daughter, who could take renewed pride in their husband and father and in themselves. Mrs. McRacken emerged from the experience with a new poise and grace. She learned to make public appearances and to speak easily before groups, and she got a better job.

McKnight and Fesperman also put new emphasis on the sports pages of the *Observer*. I rejoined the paper about then and felt the mounting excitement. As a high school boy and later as a college student, I had been an *Observer* sports correspondent and was completing a two-year army stint in the fall of 1955 just as Whitey Kelley arrived to rev up the paper's sports coverage. With the encouragement of sportswriters Dick Pierce and Herman Helms, I convinced him that while completing my studies at Chapel Hill, I could fill an *Observer* need for live sports copy from North Carolina's "Big Four" campuses, Duke, UNC, North Carolina State, and Wake Forest. Because it was 75 to 150 miles from those institutions, the *Observer* suffered a disadvantage against competitors in Raleigh, Greensboro, Winston-Salem, and Durham. Live "Big Four" copy would also give the *Observer* an edge over the sports pages of the *Charlotte News.*

Kelley agreed to try me out and after a month made the arrangement permanent. For two years I wrote daily sports stories from the Durham–Chapel Hill–Raleigh area. I covered the 1957 UNC basketball team as it rolled through an unbeaten season and won the national championship. That team's success inflamed basketball passions in the area and gave rise to a network that began televising regular season Atlantic Coast Conference basketball games for the first time.

Afterward, the *Observer* made the "Big Four" job a permanent slot in its sports department and filled it with a series of talented student writers, among them Buzz Merritt, Jr.; Wayne Thompson, who became managing editor of the *Portland Oregonian*; Jerry Stokes, later the assistant dean of the University of Virginia Law School; Curry Kirkpatrick, who went on to be a writer for *Sports Illustrated*; and Ford Worthy, who was to join the staff of *Fortune* magazine.

The breezy, cigar-chewing Whitey Kelley overcame the initial resentment toward him and built a strong department. He trained several men who moved into the news and editorial side of journalism, including Larry Tarleton, who became managing editor of the *Dallas Times Herald*; Allan Sloan, later a writer for *Forbes* magazine; Sam Fulwood, the first black hired as a full-time sportswriter, later South Africa correspondent for the *Baltimore Sun*; Jerry Shinn, who moved on to be editor of the *Observer* editorial pages; and Frank Barrows, who later took over as the *Observer*'s executive sports editor.

When the occasion demanded, Kelley himself could be a hard-nosed reporter. After a gambling scandal killed the Dixie Classic holiday basketball tournament in 1961, he led the *Observer* sports staff, which included Buzz Merritt and columnist George Cunningham, in compiling an exhaustive report that traced the scandal's origins and its academic, legal, and political implications. In the mid-1960s, his digging broke the story of the University of South Carolina's efforts to recruit a basketball star whose scores on college entrance exams were too low. The two stories did not win Kelley or the *Observer* many friends among basketball fans, but they reinforced the paper's reputation for unflinching honesty and helped prod sports coverage beyond hero worship to explore the legal, financial, and ethical side of amateur and professional athletics. In the early 1970s, Frank Barrows pushed the *Observer* further in that direction by revealing that

Howard Porter of Villanova University and Jim McDaniels of Western Kentucky had accepted bonuses from professional teams while playing college basketball. As a consequence, Villanova had to give back the trophy and revenues it won in the NCAA basketball finals in 1971.

McKnight and Fesperman also hired more women than the *Observer* had previously employed. They came and went as reporters and writers and occasionally broke into the male-dominated editing echelon. One of the first hired was Bunny Harris, a digger who broke several stories by studying public records that other reporters ignored. One story was about a secret $350,000 surplus in the treasury of the Parks and Recreation Commission. Another was Eudora Garrison, Curtis Johnson's former secretary, who blossomed as a food editor and Sunday columnist. Her mother wit and down-home charm shone through everything she wrote. Another was Dorothy Ridings, a West Virginian from Northwestern University who came to the *Observer* with ambitions of reporting on race, labor and industrial developments in the South. First she had to write fashion news, then moved into public affairs. She later became national president of the League of Women Voters, hosting presidential debates.

A fourth woman was Luisita Lopez, a petite Latin with a sharp eye, a tough mind, and a soft writing touch. Tenaciously she worked her way up the editing ladder to assistant managing editor, the highest rank achieved by a woman in the *Observer* newsroom. She later moved to the *Philadelphia Inquirer*. Another exceptional woman was Susan Jetton, a strawberry blonde from Tennessee and the University of Missouri, who, in addition to introducing the newsroom to miniskirts, developed into a versatile writer and became the *Observer*'s first female city hall reporter before moving to the *San Diego Union*.

Three women became *Observer* columnists. One was the poet Harriet Doar, a resourceful reporter who started in the women's department and then created one of the state's most respected book pages. Before retiring, she wrote a pithy editorial-page commentary. Another was Dot Jackson, a slip of a mountain girl who as a proofreader complained so often about poor headlines and bad grammar that Tom Fesperman finally said, "If you can do better, come and show us." She did and became a second-front columnist. Finally, there was Polly Paddock, a Queens College graduate whom Pete McKnight hired because he thought her name would make a wonderful byline. She started as a clerk, advanced to reporting, and helped cover the volatile school-busing controversy in the early

1970s. She worked in the Washington bureau and on the editorial page before writing a second-front column.

One casualty of the constant shuffle of young people coming and going was a knowledge of the territory. Occasionally a story was mangled by reporters and editors who lacked a feel for the relative importance of various public figures and institutions in the Carolinas. Instances of that might have been more numerous had McKnight and Fesperman not installed Carlos Kumpe as night news editor. As the last person to see the copy before it went to the print shop, Kumpe was the arbiter of accuracy, quality, and taste. He knew the territory and had the grit to hold a check rein on the young colts who were reporting and editing. A short-spoken ex-marine, he got little argument when he said, "No," to a questionable headline or story.

Kumpe was also one of the fastest workers in the newsroom. One winter when a flu outbreak struck the editing desks, Kumpe was left to edit most of the copy and write the headlines. He did so for two days with little lapse in quality. The third day McKnight stopped by the desk and said, "Mess it up a little tonight, Kump. I don't want Jim Knight to think we can get along permanently with one copy editor."

On Saturday nights and Sundays, Kumpe's news editor responsibilities were handed over to the veteran Hayti Thompson, who was Sunday editor, and, later, to Earl Heffner. Both had learned newspapering under Ernest Hunter and were well acquainted with Carolinas geography and people.

To assist young reporters and writers in knowing who was who in the Carolinas, McKnight and Randolph Norton expanded the *Observer*'s library. They moved it into much larger quarters on the third floor (in space that had been the auditorium), and gave it professional direction, first under Anita Green, who learned library methods in American military and diplomatic missions in Europe, then under Florence Bramhall, and finally under Joy Walker of Hickory, a World War II Wave who learned systems management in the navy and oversaw the library's development until 1980.

The one area of the paper that gave McKnight the least satisfaction was the editorial page, perhaps because he expected so much of it. He turned the page in a more positive direction, aroused its conscience, and gave it the vigor to define public issues, but it rarely achieved the sparkle that met McKnight's standard or that of the Knights. The flaw was not in its content, but in its style and tone. Initially, McKnight worked with two inherited associate editors who did not share his editorial outlook. The senior associate, Rupert Gillett, stayed until September 1957, then retired after twenty-eight years on the paper to write anticommunist editorials for WBT and WBTV. The more moderate Hal Tribble remained an associate editor until October 1960, when he left to edit the *Asheville Citizen*. For several years, McKnight leavened their influence on the page with the talents of J. Simmons Fentress, whom he hired from the Raleigh *News and Observer*. Fentress brought to the page a welcome background in state affairs, but did not stay long enough to infuse it with his personality. He left in 1961 to join *Time* magazine and at his death in 1981 he was *Time*'s chief political correspondent.

In August 1961, McKnight went outside the staff to hire thirty-nine-year-old David E. Gillespie, a Gastonia native then editing the *Shelby Star*. Gillespie came with the title associate editor, but remained all but anonymous. Though he led the editorial pages for ten crucial years, and gave them their character and moral force, he never enjoyed the prestige of being listed on the masthead as a member of the management. If there was an unsung hero in the *Observer*'s struggle to define the searing social and political issues of the 1960s, it was Gillespie.

The son of a Presbyterian minister, he grew up within the shadow of Gastonia textile mills and was a competitor in mill athletics. He led his high school class, played varsity sports, but never went to college. A lack of money, his love of sports, and a chance to edit the *Gastonia Gazette* sports pages intervened. After that came World War II (in which he won a Silver Star for gallantry) and a family to support. By 1948, he was managing editor of the *Gazette*, by 1951 a member of the Gastonia City Council, and by 1957 editor of the *Shelby Star*.

He came to the *Observer* just after the editorial page had suffered its first major disappointment at the hands of the Knight organization. Under Pete McKnight, the *Observer* began reviewing and recommending candidates in all elections, local, state, and national, something it had not done since Joseph Caldwell's days. Not only did it endorse candidates but it also sought to define the issues against which candidates were held accountable, a practice that sharpened local debate but offended some readers, who were used to a passive election commentary. Noting that the paper had endorsed Eisenhower in 1952 and 1956, McKnight weighed the alternatives for 1960 and suggested an endorsement of John F. Kennedy for president. When Jim Knight strongly discouraged that idea, McKnight reluctantly brought the *Observer* out for Nixon, but the endorsement was so tepid that one reader suggested, "Mr. Nixon should demand a retraction."

Gillespie arrived shortly afterward, at a time when *Observer* editorial pages were being criticized within the Knight organization for a preoccupation with race, poverty, and social justice. But Gillespie had grown up as a battler and did not back off. With McKnight's consent, he continued to express enlightened views on freedom-riders, the desegregation of Clemson, the Birmingham bombings, the March on Washington, the Civil Rights Act of 1964, women's rights, reapportionment, and, in wake of the political assassinations of the sixties, on gun controls. With McKnight's encouragement, he also supported the desegregation of Charlotte-Mecklenburg schools and the voluntary integration of local restaurants, movie houses, and swimming pools. His advocacy helped Mecklenburg County win the right to levy a local sales tax (later adopted statewide) that was essential to expanding local services. It also helped Charlotte College become a branch of the University of North Carolina, a movement that McKnight personally led.

Perhaps the paper's most crucial contribution to local progress in those years was the identification of urban redevelopment as the critical issue in the 1961 city council election. McKnight and Gillespie saw that tool as essential to Charlotte's effort to rebuild the inner city, but one the previous council was reluctant to use. On its editorial pages, the *Observer* cited the issue's importance, identified incumbents who opposed the process, and urged their defeat. Accepting the paper's recommendations, the voters elected a council that got on with clearing Brooklyn's slums, building a civic center, and rebuilding Independence Square's Block No. 1 (later the site of NCNB and the Radisson Plaza).

During the early 1960s, Pete McKnight was president of the North Carolina Fund, an experimental antipoverty agency whose organization and methods were used as a model for President Lyndon Johnson's antipoverty program. McKnight's leadership of that agency helped make the *Observer* even more sensitive to the struggle for economic as well as social equality.

While the paper's "liberal" views on race and poverty might have been ahead of some readers, they were not ahead of Charlotte's business and civic leadership. Businessmen like Mayor Stan Brookshire, financier J. Ed Burnside, banker Addison Reese, and influential ministers like Carlyle Marney and Warner Hall often touched base with McKnight and the *Observer*. Recognizing the social challenges that lay ahead, they welcomed the paper's stands in preparing the community to accept change. As a result, Charlotte managed to avoid many of the racial confrontations that left other communities bloody and divided.

The Knights' infusion of new management and talent paid big dividends in raising the *Observer*'s journalistic standards. For years the paper had barely scratched in the North Carolina Press Association's writing contests. Under McKnight, it began to dominate the competition, winning six awards in 1955 and at least four every year for the next ten years. It won six again in 1958 and 1963, five in 1961, and seven in 1964 and 1965. Several times, its writers also claimed national prizes: Roy Covington, for the coverage of religion; Don Seaver, for a moving series on the plight of disturbed children; Dwayne Walls and Jim Batten, for a series on the Ku Klux Klan and for another on rural poverty.

Circulation that was stagnant for five years before the Knight's purchase began to rise. It climbed from 135,000 in December 1954 to 155,000 in March 1959. The paper's lead over the *Charlotte News* in local circulation rose from 1,300 papers in 1954 to 13,000 in 1959. Though *News* people were competing furiously, they were outmanned and being driven to the wall.

In April 1959, after searching the country for new capital, *News* publisher Thomas L. Robinson summoned Charlotte business leaders to a meeting in the old City Club (then at Fourth and South Tryon streets) and announced that he was selling his paper to the Knights. He reminded the businessmen that he had been to each of them for investments needed to fend off the *Observer*, but they, like sixty-four financiers elsewhere in the country, had found the venture too risky. To continue operating independently, the *News* had to have a new press—its 1928 model, known affectionately as "the Old Lady," was breaking down every other day. It also would need a new plant to house the press, plus other modern equipment. Altogether, its capital needs totaled $2 million. But *News* earnings would not support such an outlay. "Last year . . . we failed by a wide margin to earn enough to meet even the payments on our mortgage," Robinson said. In twelve years, *News* profits had averaged $65,000 a year, a "fair" return on a $1 million investment, according to Robinson, but hardly enough to justify an additional $2 million. Only the Knights could afford to buy the paper, he said, because they already owned a modern press and printing plant. He noted that the *News*'s predicament was not unusual. In the Carolinas, nearly all papers in two-paper cities had merged, except in Charlotte.

The Knights were not eager to buy the *News*, but they faced a dilemma. Either they buy it and be accused of enjoying a monopoly, or they let it die and be accused of driving it out of business in order to enjoy a monopoly. In a similar situation in Akron, the Knights saw the competing paper go under—and the *Beacon-Journal* pressured to perform onerous chores because it was "the only paper in town." In dealing with Robinson, they were led to believe that if they did not buy the *News* they would be accused of killing it. So, for about $1 million, they purchased the *News* and crowded it onto the third floor of the Observer Building, filling up what had been regarded as the *Observer*'s expansion space. The next day, as the *News* was being published on the *Observer*'s big twelve-unit presses, only about eighty copies had been printed before the press's folding pins broke, causing a long delay and teeth-gnashing embarrassment among *Observer* officials. It was an omen. Though the *Observer* was healthy, its 1927 plant and 1950 press were hardly adequate for one newspaper, much less for two, a fact that rapidly became painfully apparent to employees of both the *News* and the *Observer*.

CHAPTER 12

OUT OF ANGST, A NEW BEGINNING
1965–1975

By the mid-1960s, the excitement of the early years of the Knight-McKnight decade had begun to wane. In both its editorial offices and its print shop, the *Observer* was running out of room to grow. The purchase of the *Charlotte News* precluded a simple expansion; now a whole new complex was needed, with room for more offices, more printing facilities, and more parking. A bold proposal to build downtown rather than on cheaper land in the suburbs helped spur redevelopment in the inner city, but for the *Observer* it meant more than five years of hold-the-line operations until the new plant could be occupied. In the meantime, the paper lost talent and momentum.

Compounding the frustrations were other difficulties. The textile industry entered a five-year recession, laying off employees and causing a slump in *Observer* circulation. On a trip to Russia, Pete McKnight suffered an eye inflammation that left him nearly blind for a year and a half. Unable to read the paper or participate in editorial conferences, he became increasingly fretful and isolated from the staff. In that interim, his responsibilities fell heavily on managing editor Tom Fesperman, whose own work load was wearying. Under the double burden, Fesperman's nerves frayed and his sunny outlook gave way to frowns. The paper's involvement in three volatile issues, including a fierce battle over busing to desegregate schools, aroused waves of angry protests. As a result, much of the staff developed a siege mentality, and the paper seemed to lose touch with the community. When time came to occupy the new building, younger management was brought in to reorganize the paper, rebuild its staff, and brighten its outlook.

In the turmoil were several consolations. Editorial cartoonist Gene Payne won the paper's first Pulitzer Prize. Almost as soon as Pete

McKnight regained his sight, he was elected president of the American Society of Newspaper Editors, an honor previously accorded only two other Knight editors, John S. Knight and Lee Hills. Jim Batten, the *Observer*'s Washington correspondent, was dispatched to Israel to cover what proved to be the lightning Six-Day War between Israel and Egypt. Batten's crisp reporting won national exposure and gave the paper a welcome sense of pride. The *Observer* also launched a successful TV magazine and installed one of the nation's first electronic editing systems.

Another consolation was that the decade between 1965 and 1975 was a time of upheaval for other institutions also. In Charlotte, the racial revolution raised sensitivities between police and black citizens. So did desegregation in housing, which gave rise to block-busting that changed the racial makeup of neighborhoods from white to black almost overnight. The continued decay of downtown encouraged commercial development in older neighborhoods ringing the inner city, threatening the residential fabric of Dilworth and Myers Park until neighborhood organizations rose to restore stability. Optimism that greeted the unveiling of a master plan for downtown redevelopment faded when voters rejected the first bond issue for a civic center that was the plan's centerpiece.

In North Carolina, debate continued over an embarrassing "speaker ban law" that was finally declared unconstitutional. The state government struggled to reorganize 200 independent agencies into only twenty-five. A fight over a medical school for East Carolina University brought on the restructuring of sixteen colleges and universities under one board of governors. Gov. Bob Scott and legislators battled over levying the state's first tax on tobacco products. With Democrats deeply divided, North Carolina elected the first Republican governor in more than seventy-two years, an event in which the *Observer* played a decisive role.

Nationally, the ten years were marked by continued unrest over the war in Vietnam, by the assassinations of Robert Kennedy and Martin Luther King, Jr., by America's successful landing of men on the moon, by the step-by-step unfolding of the Watergate scandal that strained citizen credulity and ultimately discredited President Nixon, and by congressional action opening national debate on an Equal Rights Amendment.

As the divisive decade opened, *Observer* editors and production managers were chafing under printing limitations that were requiring a ruinous change in production schedules. To get the last copy of the paper off the press by 4:00 a.m., in time for before-breakfast delivery in Charlotte, the *Observer* was having to print more of its 170,000 daily papers (nearly 200,000 on Sundays) before eleven o'clock the night before. That meant that on many mornings, major communities such as Lenoir, Morganton, Rutherfordton, and Hickory, traditionally strong circulation points for the *Observer*, were getting the ten o'clock edition, which contained few late-breaking news stories or night sports scores. Each time that happened, readers in those communities threatened to cancel their subscriptions. In time, many did.

Earlier, the paper had planned to expand its production capacity by adding a second line of presses next to the existing twelve units. But with the purchase of the *News*, that stop-gap plan was no longer prudent. A new plant had to be built.

General manager Bill Dowd appointed controller Frank Trull and production superintendent Frank White to survey departmental space needs for the next ten years and recommend the size building the company should construct. They were encouraged by publisher Jim Knight to be liberal in their estimates. Having watched the *Miami Herald* outgrow its facilities, Knight told Trull and White, "Figure out what you think you need and double it." When the Trull-White surveys showed a need for about 300,000 square feet, Jim Knight suggested the addition of another 50,000 square feet, to assure a balanced building and room to grow.

While those surveys were being made, Bill Dowd was looking at possible sites. He had test borings made on urban redevelopment land then being cleared on South McDowell Street (later the site of the Adam's Mark Hotel). But that location lacked a rail siding for unloading newsprint. He also looked at suburban tracts off Interstate 85, but both Dowd and Jim Knight wanted the newspapers to remain downtown if possible. In the ten years since the first suburban shopping center had opened, street life on Charlotte's Tryon and Trade streets had suffered a steep decline. Most of the shops and offices that once brought people thronging to the inner city had moved to the suburbs. The six movie houses that gave the city life after dark had dwindled to only one. Sidewalks were crowded at noon and 5:00 p.m., but thereafter were all but deserted. Dowd feared that the newspapers' move to the suburbs at that juncture would cripple downtown. Jim Knight had seen what a stimulus the new *Herald* complex had been for downtown Miami and wanted to strike a similar spark in Charlotte.

Real estate man Louis Rose was commissioned to put together a tract large enough to let the company expand at its Stonewall and

Tryon street site. Even though adjacent properties were held by thirty-eight separate owners, Rose quietly made headway, thanks in part to a land swap allowing City Chevrolet Company to move to East Independence Boulevard and give up Hill Street land that was key to the Knight expansion. In time, Rose assembled the entire four-acre tract bounded by Stonewall, Tryon, Hill, and Church streets, and a 2.7-acre tract across South Church for a newsprint warehouse and parking garage.

In December 1965, Bill Dowd announced, "We are particularly pleased that our newspapers are to remain in downtown Charlotte, and we are hopeful that the development we have in mind will be an enhancement of downtown and a stimulus to plans for revitalizing the central business district." Dowd predicted construction of the new plant would start in early 1967 and be completed by April 1969. The newspapers' commitment to the inner city had the desired effect. Over the next fifteen years a series of real estate developments added a new generation of towers to the Charlotte skyline, eclipsing those built in the 1920s.

Unfortunately, Bill Dowd was not around to witness any of those events. Even as he made his announcement, he knew he had lung cancer. He died on March 12, 1966, at age sixty-six. His passing was mourned by colleagues throughout the Carolinas. The *News and Observer* in Raleigh called him "a journalist this state could not easily spare." Said the *Greensboro Daily News*, "[His] influence on the North Carolina press . . . was generous, responsible and constructive."

Dowd's death ended ten years of stability in the management of the Knight Publishing Company. After him came a distracting succession of general managers, advertising directors, circulation managers, and production superintendents. Dowd's immediate replacement was sixty-seven-year-old Brodie S. Griffith, who had guided the *Charlotte News* since the mid-1920s. Griffith was general manager from March 1966 to June 1968; he then gave way to John S. Prescott, Jr., who served until January 1970. Next came Beverly R. Carter, who served until June 1973, and Erwin R. Potts, who served until September 1975.

Each of the general managers made lasting contributions to the two newspapers. John Prescott installed a plant-wide budgeting system that tightened accountability and improved planning. Carter introduced computers and launched initiatives that ultimately eliminated the plant's labor unions by raising salaries, improving working conditions, and strengthening worker-manager trust. He also brought to the paper Roberto Suarez, a Cuban-born banker-accountant who became the paper's controller and later its president. Potts carried the computer program forward but had the misfortune to be in charge during the 1973 recession, when tight money forced the company to abandon the Christmas bonuses that had been paid for twenty-eight years. For that he became "the man who killed Santa Claus."

Most of the departing general managers went to work elsewhere in Knight Newspapers' rapidly expanding corporation. Since selling the *Chicago Daily News* and buying the *Charlotte News* in 1959, the Knights had acquired eleven more newspapers, including the *Philadelphia Inquirer* and the tabloid *Philadelphia Daily News*, bringing their total to sixteen. In 1974, the Knight group joined Ridder Newspapers in forming Knight-Ridder Newspapers, the nation's largest newspaper conglomerate, with thirty-five papers and a combined circulation of 3.6 million copies a day. Those acquisitions contributed to the destabilization of the *Charlotte Observer* and the *Charlotte News* by making personnel transfers within the corporation more common.

Construction of the new plant did not meet Bill Dowd's optimistic schedule. The building's design was delayed by uncertainty over the route of I-277 (later named the John Belk Expressway), which skirts the site's southern edge, and by disagreement over the number and placement of windows. Initial plans called for no windows in the news and editorial offices on the top floor and for big windows exposing the pressroom on the bottom floor. Protests from editors and reporters got windows added to editorial offices; riots that followed the assassination of Martin Luther King, Jr., eliminated the pressroom windows as a security risk. Planning the building's interior layout and appointments dragged on for months, creating another distraction for *Observer* editors and managers.

As a result, construction that was expected to start early in 1967 did not get under way until March 1968, and the completion that was expected in April 1969 did not occur until the fall of 1971. In the meantime, both the *Observer* and *News* squirmed in cramped facilities, first in the old *Observer* building and later, for sixteen miserable months, in makeshift offices in the old Elks Club, a three-story, yellow-brick building on the northeast corner of Tryon and Stonewall. While in the Elks Club, the *Observer* staff watched with some sense of loss as its old building, the narrow, three-story structure that Curtis Johnson built in 1926, went under the wrecking ball on Labor Day in 1970.

For most of those years, the *Observer* could not expand its staff or operations because there was no space in its newsroom for another desk or telephone. Reporters joked that they were so closely clustered that four of them could smoke the same cigarette without knowing it. Window sills were filled with file cabinets. At one point editors studied a proposal for stacking teletype machines, one on top of the other, to free up space for another editing desk. But the stacking plan proved to be unwieldy. Over and over, the editors' response to complaints about crowding was "Wait 'til we get into the new building."

Pressure for space became so great that *Observer* editorial writers gave their third-floor office to the women's department and moved a block and a half south into the old City Chevrolet building. They were joined by people from the promotion, public service, and circulation departments. Associate editor David Gillespie and his staff had to walk back and forth to the old building to use the library, confer with reporters, or read proof on pages. One day a lady stopped in the office with a piece of paper she found on the sidewalk. "Does this belong to you?" she asked. It was the lead editorial for the next day's paper, lost on the way to the print shop.

Not only did the size of the news staff remain static, but so did most salaries and expenses. Pete McKnight complained that the *Charlotte News* was a drain on *Observer* resources and a distraction to overall management. *Observer* salaries and costs were pegged to those of the *News*, which had less than half the circulation. Under those restraints, the *Observer* staff began to develop lethargy and a sense of drift. The bright prospects the paper offered ten years earlier had disappeared. Some of the most talented writers and editors left. Columnist Kays Gary, whose *Observer* salary was less than $12,000 a year, took a job with a mountain development company that gave him a $10,000 raise. Other departures included Jay Jenkins, Joe Doster, Bob Rosenblatt, Bob Lipper, Buzz Merritt, Mike Mauney, David Cupp, and Dwayne Walls. In all, more than forty-five staff members left between 1966 and 1971, about twice the normal turnover. In addition to the departures, news editor Carlos Kumpe, the most experienced member of the editing staff, was pulled out of day-to-day operations to become the newsroom budget officer, a by-the-numbers post that wasted his best talents.

Pressure to hold down salaries made finding replacements difficult. The nation's journalism schools were still turning out highly qualified graduates, but competition from major metropolitan dailies priced most of those prospects beyond the *Observer*'s reach. For several years when it could no longer attract journalism graduates, the *Observer* resorted to recruiting people from other vocations: a former insurance salesman, a former glass salesman, the driver of a laundry truck, a foreign service officer from the United States State Department. All proved to be good newsmen, but on the whole, the talent recruited in the second decade of the Knight-McKnight era fell short of what had been hired earlier.

There were many exceptions, of course. One was Edward L. Cody, a modest but bright Oregonian who had studied in Europe and yearned to become a foreign correspondent. He arrived at the *Observer* in the late 1960s, covered public schools for about a year, and then left for a job with the Associated Press. He learned Arabic and a few years later was assigned to Beirut, then one of the world's newsiest capitals. Another exception was Bradley K. Martin, a big, fun-loving, Peace Corps veteran with a Fu Manchu mustache. He stayed with the *Observer* through the early 1970s, then took a job with the *Baltimore Sun*, and wound up in Tokyo with the Asian edition of the *Wall Street Journal*. Another was Ron Alridge, a Gastonia native who graduated from UNC-Charlotte, joined the *Observer* as a police and courts reporter, was assigned to cover radio and television, and went on to become TV critic for the *Chicago Tribune*. A fourth exception was Richard Maschal, who came from the *Journal-Herald* in Dayton, Ohio, and stayed to become the music, art, and architecture critic. Perhaps the most notable exception of all was Jack Bass, a dark-eyed, dark-haired, native of North, South Carolina, who completed a Nieman fellowship at Harvard in 1966 and joined the *Observer* as its Columbia bureau chief. For the next seven years, his reporting on South Carolina politics and racial affairs made him one of the South's most respected journalists.

In this period the *Observer* hired its first black reporter. It had tried to recruit blacks from the big journalism schools, but with every major news agency in the country bidding for them, blacks with training were reluctant to go South. In July 1966, Jacob E. ("Jake") Simms walked in and asked for a job. A tall, athletic Winston-Salem native with a master's degree in education, Simms was teaching English and journalism at all-black Second Ward High School. When he applied for an *Observer* job, the receptionist assumed he wanted a carrier's route and told him none were open. When he said he wanted a reporting job, she summoned personnel manager John Schweitzer, who asked, "Who sent you? The NAACP?"

Simms completed an application, passed the personnel tests, and, after some delay, met Tom Fesperman, who asked him to write an essay on what he could offer the *Observer*. Glancing over the essay, the pleased Fesperman observed (as he did for applicants white or black), "You can spell!" Simms was uncertain whether to be pleased or insulted. Simms and Fesperman agreed he should start slowly, working a few hours a week on the copy desk where he could edit stories, write headlines, and learn newspapering from the inside out.

The work was often frustrating, but Simms learned fast and gradually increased his working hours. After ten months he quit teaching to work full time for the paper. Returning from dinner one night he found a packet of Ku Klux Klan pamphlets in his chair. Attached was a note: "For Your Nigger-Loving Friends." It was a gift from composing room workers upset at seeing a black in the newsroom.

Simms did not stay long. Within less than two years, he won a *Time* magazine fellowship to the Columbia School of Journalism and, afterward, joined the *Time* bureau in Chicago. Later he taught journalism and became city editor of the *Post-Tribune* in Gary, Indiana. Before leaving, Simms recruited the first black woman hired by the *Observer*. She was Shirley Johnson, a Rowan County native and Livingstone College graduate who also taught at Second Ward. When Simms left for Columbia, he urged her to apply for his job. She followed the Simms training pattern and gradually worked her way into editing and reporting. She stayed four years, and later became a communications specialist for the public school system.

During the frustrations of the late 1960s, one event momentarily brightened the staff's outlook. In May 1968, Gene Payne won a Pulitzer Prize for editorial cartoons. The announcement came only a few days after he had received the Sigma Delta Chi award for the best cartoon of 1967—a drawing of President Lyndon Johnson boarding a bus with a squalling infant labeled Vietnam War and being told by the driver, Dr. Martin Luther King, Jr., to "Please Move to the Back of the Bus." The cartoon dramatized the clash of issues competing for national attention—the black quest for civil rights and the escalating war in Vietnam. Payne entered that cartoon and nine others in the Pulitzer competition.

Then forty-nine years old, Payne had grown up in a South Tryon Street neighborhood three blocks south of the *Observer*'s offices. He attended Charlotte schools, Fishburne Military Academy, and Syracuse University, where he studied art. During World War II, he was a B-29 pilot. After the war he joined Foremost Dairies and was the local sales manager in 1957 when he began submitting three cartoons a week to Pete McKnight on a free-lance basis. Within a year he was hired as the newsroom artist, retouching photos, drawing maps, and turning out editorial cartoons. In 1959 he went to the *Birmingham News* but returned a year later.

When associate editor David Gillespie arrived in 1961, he and Payne became an effective team. Payne was quiet and low-key, with a sly sense of humor; Gillespie was quick, impassioned, and given to outrageous puns. They would meet each morning, talk over cartoon subjects, laugh at each other's jokes, and generally stimulate each other's thinking. Payne would go to the drawing board, sketch out three or four ideas that illustrated *Observer* editorials, and take those back to Gillespie, who would choose one—or perhaps parts of several—which Payne would then execute in finished form.

Payne's style was clean, smooth, and light. He was a fast worker and preferred cartoons that made people laugh. His specialties were jowly politicians with large hats, string ties, big feet, and fat cigars. Rarely did his work make people angry, though he was frequently betrayed by a casual approach to spelling. He spelled words according to sound, and often had to redraw a cartoon at the last minute to correct an error. He once referred to North Carolina Gov. Dan K. Moore as "Dam Moore." He mislabeled the British Isles as "Great Britian," and got a prim complaint from the British ambassador. Payne's response to such grievances was usually "To hell with a fellow who can't spell a word but one way."

A few days before the Pulitzer awards, word had leaked that the *Observer* was a finalist in the competition, along with two other Knight newspapers. In addition to Payne's cartoons, the *Observer* had submitted a series of stories by medical writer Bob Conn, exposing the injustice of state laws on epilepsy and the limited privileges accorded epilepsy victims. The series had prompted legislative reforms. As the teletype began to clatter with a story from New York about the Pulitzer winners, people in the newsroom gathered around, waiting expectantly. They shouted joyously as the machine hesitantly spelled it out, "For editorial cartoons, Eugene Gray Payne, *The Charlotte Observer . . .* " Sitting at his easel maybe eight feet away, Payne was suddenly hugged, pummeled, and clasped by squealing colleagues. The placid cartoonist's reaction was "Well, what do you know about that?" It was the first Pulitzer awarded a North Carolina newspaper since 1952, when the *News Reporter* of Whiteville and the *Tribune* in Tabor City shared the public service prize for a revealing series on the Ku Klux Klan.

The other Knight winners in 1968 were John S. Knight for his weekly "Editor's Notebook," in which he opposed the Vietnam War, and the staff of the *Detroit Free Press* for its report on the 1967 urban riots and their causes. It was the first time in the fifty-two-year history of the Pulitzer awards that one newspaper group had won three prizes. Gene Payne's cartoon the next day was a drawing of a doorknob from which was hanging a big sign that said, "Out to Celebrate."

The euphoria did not last. In July 1971, while the *Observer* was cramped in the Elks Club, Payne joined the staff exodus by becoming a cartoonist for WSOC-TV. It was a matter of money, he said. His salary at the time he won the Pulitzer was less than $10,000 a year, and was not increased much afterward.

In the three years between Gene Payne's Pulitzer and his departure, the *Observer* took stands on three highly controversial issues that provoked furious debate in the community and made the newspaper the object of intense public anger. The most heated was a series of federal court orders requiring the busing of schoolchildren to desegregate Charlotte-Mecklenburg schools.

United States District Judge James B. McMillan's first ruling in *Swann* v. *Mecklenburg* came in April 1969, when he found the city-county school board had been operating a segregated system and ordered it to submit a plan for desegregating all schools. When the board repeatedly failed to draft such a plan, the judge ordered it to implement a busing plan drawn by expert witnesses for the black plaintiffs. The plan called for every school to have a racial makeup approximating the county population, which was 70 percent white and 30 percent black. That required busing many children to schools that might be on the other side of town.

Though southern communities had used buses for generations to keep schools segregated, the court requirement that buses be used to desegregate them seemed outrageous to many Mecklenburg residents. White parents argued that in buying homes they had chosen neighborhoods on the basis of the schools their children would attend. To bus children out of those neighborhoods was unfair and a threat to real estate values, they said. Judge McMillan responded that under the Constitution schools had to be equal, that there could no longer be white schools or black schools but just schools.

From the opening order, the *Observer* supported Judge McMillan—and for several years was the only local institution to do so. The Chamber of Commerce, the Parent-Teacher Association, and the local clergy organization were silent on the issue. The city's two television stations opposed the court order, and the editorially independent *Charlotte News* criticized both the court and the *Observer*, often in jeering terms. Political figures found that attacking the *Ob-*

server was a popular sport. Each day's mail brought stacks of angry letters. The telephone rang insistently with calls from readers who wanted to argue with the editorial writers.

Also critical was John S. Knight. At a cocktail party during a national meeting of newspaper editors, he asked *Observer* associate editor Dave Gillespie why he expected Charlotte to do what Detroit or Chicago or other metropolitan communities could not do. Gillespie replied that he did not know what those cities were capable of, but if by busing schoolchildren Charlotte could become one community and avoid the hostility and alienation that had caused urban decay and riots elsewhere, why should Charlotte not be encouraged to do that? Jack Knight said he would have to think about that.

To help readers understand the narrow options open to the district court, the *Observer* ran texts of Judge McMillan's orders. It accompanied them with editorials and other commentary explaining the precedents upon which the judge had based his decisions. Fifteen years after the Supreme Court's famous "all deliberate speed" edict of 1955, the high court and other appellate courts were urging less deliberation and more speed in school desegregation.

But readers were listening to other spokesmen who urged that Judge McMillan's opinions be defied or appealed. An angry group, called the Concerned Parents Association, was organized and elected three antibusing members to the school board and assisted the board in opposing the court orders. The association held neighborhood meetings throughout the county to raise money for legal fees. *Observer* reporters covering those meetings were usually identified and hissed, and sometimes surrounded by angry parents. Speakers at the meetings urged audiences to cancel their subscriptions to the *Observer*. At the peak of public outrage—the year 1970–71, when Judge McMillan's busing order was first implemented—daily circulation of the *Observer* fell from 175,604 to 170,228. Much of the loss was attributed to the paper's support of desegregation. From the outside, the *Observer* may have seemed arrogant, self-righteous, and dictatorial, but on the inside, among members of its staff, it seemed vulnerable, lonely, and besieged.

The uproar over school desegregation poisoned the atmosphere for other ventures undertaken by the community and supported by the *Observer*. One was an effort to write a charter for replacing the city and county governments with a new, single government. The goal was to create a representative body that could better coordinate the rapid growth under way in the community and to assure the timely delivery of public services throughout the county. Just as it had in the 1920s when city-county consolidation first arose as an issue, the *Observer* became a strong advocate for the merger. L. M. Wright, Jr., an *Observer* editorial writer and former city editor, took a leave of absence to head the staff that helped a citizens commission draft a charter for the new government. His presence, plus a steady stream of supporting editorials and feature stories, strongly identified the *Observer* with the charter effort.

As drafting of the charter proceeded, controversy erupted over a provision for district representation on the proposed county council, replacing the at-large system in effect since the early 1940s. District representation would give blacks and other minorities a chance to win seats; the at-large system favored wealthy whites who lived in the city's southeast quadrant and dominated the government. Many citizens associated district representation with the "by the numbers" desegregation of public schools and wanted nothing to do with it.

Again, while the *Observer* was supporting those reforms, the *Charlotte News* was dubious about them. By the time the charter was submitted to the voters in a March 1971 referendum, its two-to-one defeat was all but assured—in part because of the reformist character of the charter proposals and in part because of the hostile climate created by court-ordered busing.

While the *Observer* was taking its lumps for supporting desegregation and the charter, another event stirred community emotions. Early on the morning of October 17, 1970, just as the deadline approached for the *Observer's* final edition, the police radio crackled with excited voices. Two policemen had been shot and several civilians injured in a police raid on a gambling house in the 1300 block of East Fourth Street. *Observer* reporter Howard Maniloff and state editor Bill Fuller hurried to the scene, arriving just in time to see ambulances picking up two injured officers. Other police were arriving in squad cars. The air was heavy with the smell of gun powder and the shouts of enraged officers dragging men from the rear of the gambling house. The two reporters returned to the paper and hastily wrote a story that said one officer, Ronald L. McGraw of the county police, had been killed and another, Buster Tanner of the Alcoholic Beverage Control squad, had been wounded. The story also described police kicking, beating, and cursing the handcuffed men who were being arrested.

The story made the front page in time for distribution to most Charlotte readers. It enraged police and provoked a furious response from public officials, who charged that it was unfair, inaccurate, and exaggerated. An *Observer* editorial the next day explained that there was no time for getting the police perspective into the story. The apologetic editorial did no good; police wives picketed the *Observer* building several days, carrying signs saying the paper was more sympathetic to criminals than to policemen killed in the line of duty. Police Chief J. C. Goodman, Jr., commended the police for their conduct and complained about the *Observer's* raid coverage. Later he exchanged angry letters with Pete McKnight on the *Observer's* front page. Again, the paper seemed to be under attack from all quarters.

In time the *Observer* was vindicated in all three controversies. In April 1971, the United States Supreme Court unanimously upheld Judge McMillan in the school-busing case, citing arguments the judge and the *Observer* had laid out earlier. The *Observer's* support proved to be crucial. Before the circuit court and twice before the Supreme Court, judges asked whether anyone in Charlotte agreed with the busing order. Both times NAACP lawyer Julius Chambers cited *Observer* editorials. A few years later, Charlotte won national acclaim for successfully desegregating its schools. Though the city-county charter was defeated, several of its provisions, including district representation, which most voters came to regard as fair, were later implemented. When defendants in the gambling-house raid got a fair trial, the *Observer's* initial story was corroborated. The judge accused the police of breaking more laws than the misdemeanants they captured.

But vindication came too late to repair the *Observer's* scarred image. In its finest hour of service to Charlotte, the paper had lost respect within the community, within the Knight organization, and within its own staff. Strain was evident throughout the news and editorial ranks. Even the return of columnist Kays Gary in February 1971 did not lift sagging morale.

The five-year exodus had left the paper with a newsroom full of green reporters and few experienced desk hands. Copy chief Jim Hardin supervised a copy-editing staff made up entirely of women, most of whom worked for lower salaries than their male counterparts. His colleagues called it "Hardin's Harem." The most seasoned reporter, the prize-winning Roy Covington, was appointed city editor, a post that wasted his best skills and one in which his gentleness was not an asset.

After fifteen years of heavy responsibility and intense pressure, McKnight and Fesperman were vexed and weary. Like Joseph Caldwell and D. A. Tompkins, their work had been their lives, and they were burning out. Neither had a hobby or a regular exercise program. Communication and trust broke down between the two of them and between them and their subordinates, especially associate editor David Gillespie. McKnight blamed Gillespie for having involved the paper too deeply in controversy by entering the trenches as a combatant instead of remaining above the strife and commenting on it. Yet, against waves of angry opposition, Gillespie had held firm and rallied the paper through the battle.

One day in July 1971, Gillespie reported for work and found in his typewriter a note from McKnight saying he had decided to make a change. A month later Gillespie was moved to the newsroom to do special-assignment reporting, and Reese Cleghorn was named editor of the editorial page. Cleghorn, forty-one, was an elegant Georgian, raised in a small town, educated at Emory University, and trained on the *Atlanta Journal*. He came to the *Observer* from the Southern Regional Council, where he had edited a magazine devoted to southern social and educational issues. A graceful writer, Cleghorn was even more gifted as an editor. He could put a pencil to a piece of copy and quickly improve it. His appointment did not change the substance of *Observer* editorials. The paper was as committed as ever to education, civil rights, and southern uplift. But in place of Gillespie's moral combat came Cleghorn with a quieter passion and more measured tone, drawn from an even deeper knowledge of southern history and culture.

Four weeks after Cleghorn's arrival, while workmen were still painting door frames and completing other finishing touches, employees of the *Observer* and the *News* gathered up their files and notebooks and moved across Tryon Street into the boxy, block-long new building, a structure that Tom Fesperman had nicknamed "the Taj," as in Taj Mahal. The *Observer* occupied one-half of the fifth floor; the *Charlotte News* the other half.

The building contained twenty-seven press units (most of them bought used from the *Miami News*), doubling the press capacity of the old building and ending the *Observer*'s need to send early editions to nearby counties. It also contained new desks, new chairs, new file cabinets, and room to work in comfort. Somebody said the new furniture and putty-colored walls looked like the claims office of a huge insurance company. After the crowded Elks Club, it looked like a palace—and bore a palace price tag. Initially expected to cost $10 million, the new building was completed and furnished at a cost of $19.7 million. That, too, contributed to the *Observer*'s image problems. Raised on a pedestal, set back from the street, and surrounded by a "moat" of grass and shrubs, the building reinforced the public impression that the *Observer* was rich, powerful, insular, and aloof.

Contrary to earlier hopes, the new building had not made everything all right. While offices and furnishings were new and spacious, staff salaries, attitudes, and expectations were not. The *Observer* was still a troubled newspaper, suffering from an excess of ideology and lack of leadership. Among its young reporters and editors, low morale was giving way to rising discontent. A "newsroom association" was exploring possibilities of forming a union.

Unbeknownst to most staff members, moves were already under way to strengthen the paper's management. In Detroit, James K. Batten was preparing to return to Charlotte as executive editor, to give Pete McKnight and Tom Fesperman needed relief and the *Observer*'s news coverage a fresh perspective. Planning toward that end had been going on since midsummer. Quietly, Batten had been in and out of town several times, comparing notes with *Observer* editors and managers.

McKnight had decided at least ten years earlier that when the time came for him to step aside his successor would be Jim Batten. He made that choice when Batten returned to the *Observer* in 1962 after two years of graduate study at Princeton. He told Lee Hills about Batten's potential and began exposing him to a wide variety of reporting assignments. In 1965, Batten was transferred to the Washington bureau and from there was dispatched to the Six-Day War in the Middle East.

During Batten's fourth year in Washington, Lee Hills invited him to dinner one evening and inquired about his career goals. Then thirty-three years old, Batten said he loved reporting but figured that it was probably time he learned something about editing. When Hills asked what future opportunities interested him, Batten said his "most sublime ambition" was to be editor of the *Charlotte Observer*. Hills indicated such an assignment was not entirely out of the question.

A year later, at the suggestion of Hills, Batten was assigned to the *Detroit Free Press* where he would get a variety of editing assignments. Batten learned fast and in a year and a half demonstrated the mental toughness and emotional stamina to excel as an editor. He showed he could adapt to another style of newspapering, outside the politics-education-poverty mainstream he had known at the *Observer*. In the highly competitive Detroit market, the *Free Press* strived to make itself essential to readers, and that meant providing consumer services as well as being a political watchdog.

By the summer of 1971, when it was obvious to Knight executives that the *Observer* needed immediate help, his training was accelerated. Hills asked him to look over recent editions of the *Observer* and recommend improvements. In a long memo, Batten described the *Observer*'s troubles as an overemphasis on government and politics and a dearth of people-oriented stories that would make the paper appealing to everyday readers. He suggested a number of reforms: personalizing the news, providing more profiles of interesting people, spotlighting heroes and heroines, providing useful tips about upcoming cultural and entertainment events, doing a better job of informing readers about TV, providing travel tips, restaurant reviews, tidbits about behind-the-scenes developments. Mostly, he said, the *Observer* needed a friendlier attitude, professional polish, and the leadership to break out of its we-versus-them mentality.

About the time Batten submitted his memo to Hills, *Observer* reporters were again discomfiting Charlotte business and political leaders by standing up for principle. When Mayor John Belk summoned city council members to the Mayor's Office at City Hall to discuss a parking proposal, *Observer* reporter Bill Arthur joined the gathering. The mayor asked him to leave, saying the meeting was private. Arthur pointed out that the state's open-meetings law made it illegal for elected officials to conduct public business in private. When the mayor ignored that warning and banished Arthur from the meeting, the reporter sued on behalf of the Charlotte chapter of Sigma Delta Chi, the national journalism fraternity.

The fact that the *Observer* did not file the suit or pay Arthur's legal fees made little difference in community perception. To many readers, it was another example of the newspaper's self-righteousness. When the suit came to trial, the judge held that Mayor Belk and the city council had indeed violated the state law and ordered them to stop holding private meetings. But reporter Arthur's assertion of the public interest went unappreciated by the average reader. Sigma Delta Chi spent more than a year holding attic sales and peddling "Do It in the Open" T-shirts to raise money to pay its legal fees. Many *Observer* staff members thought the paper should have paid, because Arthur was acting in the line of duty. The paper's failure to exert that leadership increased staff disillusionment.

In that charged atmosphere, Jim Batten's return to the *Observer* was announced. On January 25, 1972, the paper carried a front-page story saying Batten would become executive editor on March 1 with full authority over news and editorial operations under editor Pete McKnight's supervision. Managing editor Tom Fesperman, editorial page editor Reese Cleghorn, and other supervising editors would continue in their positions. Many *Observer* staff members interpreted the appointment as a vote of no confidence, as evidence that the Knights thought the *Observer* had failed. Morale was at a low ebb.

Overnight, Batten took charge. Though he was southern in speech and habit and Princetonian in dress and manner, Batten was Detroit tough in execution. He expanded the staff, hiked salaries, and raised expectations. He led reporters and editors to think that the *Observer* was on the move again, that it was expanding its news and feature coverage and was destined to become one of the great newspapers of the South. In group meetings and one-on-one conferences he instilled in reporters and editors a sense of journalism as a high calling, as the first draft of history, and he encouraged them to write and edit with a historian's responsibility for objectivity and accuracy.

In evaluating the staff, Batten was alarmed at its relative inexperience and at the number of non-Carolinians and nonsoutherners. He set out to hire people with more seasoning and with a greater knowledge of the region. He brought back reporters Jerry Shinn, Marion Ellis, and John York, each of whom had resigned earlier to take jobs in business. He hired southerners Mark Ethridge III, son of a famous Louisville newspaper family; Frye Gaillard, an Alabamian from the Race Relations Reporter in Nashville (the agency Pete McKnight founded in 1954 as the Southern Education Reporting Service); and Lew Powell from Mississippi, a wit with an eye for comic comparisons. He also hired Bob Hodierne and Marilyn Mather from the *News-Journal* in Wilmington, Delaware, and Mary Bishop of Richmond, Virginia, a religion writer who later produced a biography of evangelist Billy Graham.

To tighten control over the paper's news and feature content, Batten restructured the editing system and made it more central and metropolitan instead of dispersed and regional. In a controversial move, he closed news bureaus in surrounding counties or reduced their size, weakening *Observer* ties to the region. He hired more experienced editors to run the news desks. From Toronto, he brought in Bob De Piante, formerly of the *Miami Herald*, to be the graphics editor. Roy Covington went back to writing about business, his first love. Larry Tarleton was brought home from Miami as executive sports editor, relieving Whitey Kelley in the same way Whitey Kelley had earlier relieved Wilton Garrison. A second echelon was added to the editing structure with the appointment of assistant editors to

deal directly with reporters. Slowly, the *Observer* became less of a reporter's paper and more of an editor's paper.

Gradually, the *Observer* began to disengage itself from ongoing
stories. A good example was the school-busing story, which remained an explosive issue. In turning the assignment over to Frye
Gaillard and Polly Paddock, Batten encouraged them to stand back
from day-to-day events and make more sense of overall developments.
As a result, *Observer* coverage began to reflect a change in issues
being discussed in the neighborhoods, among them the busing
plan's fairness. Residents of northern and western sectors of the
county thought they were bearing a greater share of the busing burden than those in the east and south. Out of that came a Citizens
Advisory Group that drafted a more balanced busing plan, which
won greater public support. When the court accepted that plan, attitudes in Charlotte and Mecklenburg County began to change, and
people began to take pride in the fact that their community had made
busing a success. Their pride increased as that accomplishment attracted national attention.

Elsewhere in the paper, Batten was adding more reader services:
restaurant reviews, a livelier book page, a reader-service column
called "Tell-It Line," calendars of upcoming events, and a number of
"insider" features, including one called "Inside the Observer," in
which editors and writers discussed how and why the paper does
what it does. The goal was to make the *Observer* seem more open and
personable.

In the reorganization, the work of managing editor Tom Fesperman was sharply reduced. Assigned to oversee the sports and wom-
en's departments, he got a chance to relax a little, and in relaxing realized he was unhappy and had been unhappy for several years. He
made trips to nearby cities and towns and began writing a column
called "Visiting Around." That revived an old ambition to write a syndicated column. Could he travel the country and produce a readable
column about people and the pace and taste of national life? In 1973,
he resigned from the *Observer* and set out to try. After five years, he
lit briefly at Hilton Head, South Carolina, to edit the *Island Packet*,
and then went west to Santa Barbara, California, to edit the editorial
page of the *News-Press*.

On the *Observer*'s editorial page, Reese Cleghorn was making
changes. He replaced the departed Gene Payne with twenty-two-
year-old Douglas N. Marlette, a cartoonist from Florida with roots in
North Carolina and Mississippi. Marlette was born in Greensboro
and lived in Durham until he was twelve. His first cartoon, pub-

lished on January 2, 1972, was about the Christmas bombing of Vietnam. One of its elements was a bomb with a smiling, female face, similar to those of stewardesses in airline ads. The bomb said, "I'm Napalm . . . Fly Me." Under the bomb was the caption, "Fly Napalm to Quang Binh—She Has Great Connections North of the DMZ."

The style was dramatically different from what *Observer* readers were used to. Gene Payne liked to sneak up on subjects; Marlette went right for the jugular. Payne's cartoons were light and appealed to the funny bone; Marlette's were heavy and stirred emotions. A Payne cartoon could be laughed at and forgotten; Marlette cartoons usually got under readers' skins.

Over the next few years, Marlette's drawings provoked constant controversy. His hard-hitting style forced people to examine their prejudices and guilt. Perhaps his most controversial cartoon, one the *Observer* at first refused to publish, was an anti–capital-punishment drawing done for Easter Sunday. It showed Jesus carrying an electric chair up the hill at Calvary. When the cartoon was published, many people resented it; they did not like seeing modern capital punishment equated with the crucifixion.

Among those who objected to Marlette's work was John S. Knight, who repeatedly complained to Pete McKnight that Marlette cartoons were crude, not funny, and tended to overpower *Observer* editorials. McKnight counseled with Marlette, occasionally rejected one of his cartoons, but defended him to Knight, arguing that Marlette was popular with young readers the *Observer* sought to attract. At one point, Knight suggested that Marlette be fired, but later accepted a compromise that moved him off the editorial page, where it was assumed he spoke for the *Observer*, to the Viewpoint page, where he could speak for himself, along with a variety of other cartoonists and syndicated columnists. Marlette's popularity spread, and by 1975 King Features Syndicate was distributing his drawings to more than seventy-five other newspapers, including the conservative *Chicago Tribune* and the liberal *Washington Post*. He was often reprinted in *Time*, *Newsweek*, *Rolling Stone*, and the British humor magazine *Punch*.

Under Cleghorn, *Observer* editorial writers put greater emphasis on the paper's political endorsements, a service that helped readers sort out the candidates at election time. Editorial writers interviewed candidates for office, reviewed their backgrounds, compared notes with people who knew them, and made recommendations to Charlotte and Mecklenburg voters on the basis of tightly reasoned arguments. For a number of years, *Observer* endorsements had been significant factors in local elections. In 1967, for instance, the paper's endorsement of Stan Brookshire probably meant the difference in his forty-four-vote victory over banker John A. ("Jack") Tate, Jr. In 1969, the paper's preference for John Belk over Gibson Smith probably decided that election, which Belk won by only 367 votes. Under Cleghorn, the paper's endorsement made a crucial difference in the 1972 election of a North Carolina governor.

On a Sunday morning ten days before Election Day, the *Observer* endorsed Republican James E. Holshouser, Jr., of Boone, because it thought he would "clear out some of the cobwebs" left by seventy years of Democratic domination of state government and because Holshouser promised to lead the North Carolina Republican party toward a moderate progressivism. The next day, news that the state's largest newspaper, previously Democratic in state and local elections, had endorsed a Republican for governor made headlines in afternoon papers across North Carolina. No Tar Heel Republican had won the governor's office since Daniel Russell in 1896, but the *Observer* endorsement portrayed Holshouser as electable. Overnight, voters began to reassess his candidacy. His supporters went to work with extra zeal, while the campaign of Democrat Hargrove ("Skipper") Bowles of Greensboro, who had not united his party after a bitter spring primary, went downhill. On Election Day, Holshouser won by 38,000 votes out of 1.4 million cast. He owed his election to the coattails of President Richard Nixon, but the *Observer*'s endorsement was still a significant factor in Holshouser's victory.

In that same election, the *Observer* made no recommendation in the race for president. It found neither Democrat George McGovern nor Republican Richard Nixon fit for the job. The editorial supporting that conclusion filled an entire editorial page and remains one of the more remarkable in *Observer* history. In reviewing the candidates' records, it found McGovern speaking over the heads of the people he sought to govern, and Nixon appealing too often to the voters' baser instincts. To the dismay of many readers, the *Observer* had run every *Washington Post* story about the unfolding Watergate scandal, and in reviewing the Nixon record in that light, the editorial found that Nixon had "demeaned the office of the presidency." In saying so, the editorial presaged the drama that would soon drive the president from the White House.

Later that fall, in an another effort to soften the *Observer*'s image and identify it more closely with Charlotte and local issues, Reese Cleghorn encouraged me, as a Charlotte native, to start writing a Saturday morning editorial page column called "This Time and

Place," in which a contemporary event was looked at in historical terms. The first installment, on the day of the Shrine Bowl football game between high school stars from North Carolina and South Carolina, was about the building of American Legion Memorial Stadium, which had made the annual charity game possible. The idea behind the feature was to let people know that the *Observer*, unlike its gleaming new building at Tryon and Stonewall streets, had been in Charlotte many years and knew the city's past. The feature generated a favorable response and has been continued since.

Cleghorn's other major addition to the editorial page was Edwin N. Williams, fresh from a year as a Nieman Fellow at Harvard. Born in a small town in Missouri, Williams had attended the University of Mississippi, edited the campus newspaper, and served as capital correspondent for Hodding Carter's *Delta Democrat-Times* in Greenville, Mississippi, one of the South's most admired newspapers. Arriving in the fall of 1973, Williams brought to the *Observer* a mischievous humor, a keen insight into southern politics and history, and a hard-headed logic. Though he had never written editorials, in his first year at the *Observer* he won first place in the North Carolina Press Association's annual writing contest.

During its coverage of the 1972 elections, the *Observer* was pioneering an electronic system that often produced anguish among its editing staff but in time greatly increased the newspaper's efficiency. The *Observer* was one of two newspapers in the country (the *Detroit News* was the other) to introduce computers to the newsroom. It installed an editing system designed by the Hendrix Company of Manchester, New Hampshire, for the Associated Press. When the computer boxes and video terminals arrived on hand trucks, *Observer* editors greeted them with anxiety and suspicion. They were ordered by managers of the production system, and few people in the news and editorial departments knew how they worked.

The first system consisted of a computer box, seven connecting video display terminals and a machine that could read and punch perforated tape. Essentially, the system received telegraph stories from the Associated Press and converted them to perforated tape that could be read and edited on video display terminals. The edited versions of those tapes could be fed into a Linotype machine that would set the stories into type. The process eliminated several steps from the traditional editing-typesetting routine, saving time and money.

But the computers often broke down, and Jim Hardin, an assistant telegraph editor who sat nearest the computer box, grew weary of summoning technicians to fix whatever was wrong. A Shelby native who had trained at UNC, Hardin brought a canny Scotch-Irish industry to his practice of journalism. Quick and feisty, with a stumpy, compact build and a boyish, dimpled grin, he set out to learn how to repair the computers himself. He went to the public library and read a book about computer theory, then another about the applications of computer theory, and a third on computer programming. In the process he realized that the *Observer*'s computer had been designed to fit production needs, not editing needs. It required copy editors to make their work conform to computer technology. Hardin asked, "Why not adapt computer technology to the work of copy editors?"

Technicians insisted that could not be done until they discovered Hardin knew enough about computer technology to argue otherwise. With Hardin's help they began to reprogram the computer system to accommodate more editing functions. Soon, Hardin was flying back and forth to Hendrix headquarters in New Hampshire, helping the company make its electronic editing-typesetting equipment more useful to newsrooms.

In late 1973, again on the initiative of production managers, the *Observer*'s computer system was expanded from seven video display terminals to twenty-one. When Hardin saw the plan for installing the fourteen new terminals, he winced. Only one was going where it was most needed; the others were being scattered over the newsroom. Hardin thought that was a waste of resources. A newspaper operates like a funnel: reporters are at the wide end, writing stories; supervising editors are at the midpoint, reading and evaluating stories and assigning them to space in the newspaper; copy editors are at the funnel's neck, reading stories, checking accuracy, writing headlines, and relaying everything to the print shop. If computer terminals were used for editing, the greatest number was needed at the copy desk, where the most editorial matter was processed.

Encountering Pete McKnight in the company cafeteria, Hardin asked if he understood that his terminals were about to be put in the wrong places. When McKnight seemed uncertain, Hardin grew bolder. He said computers were going to create the greatest change in newspaper production in McKnight's lifetime, one more revolutionary than the Linotype in the 1880s. Typesetting that was once done in composing rooms was about to be done in newsrooms, and McKnight ought to understand the implications of that. The next day, McKnight and Jim Batten called in Hardin, heard him explain where the new terminals should be placed, and asked him to become the newsroom expert in computer operations.

Soon after the fourteen new terminals were in place, Hardin learned that the company was proposing to buy electric typewriters and scanners that would further commit the newsroom to electronic editing. To him, that seemed like a backward step. Under the proposal, reporters would write stories on electric typewriters and feed them into a scanner that would send them to a computer. The computer would display the stories on a video terminal, where they could be edited, headlined, and converted to perforated tape, then fed to a Linotype machine. Hardin said a better approach would be to buy enough terminals to let reporters write directly on the computer, skipping the cumbersome electric typewriters and scanners.

Hardin convinced *Observer* managers that his alternative was more efficient and less expensive, but met stiff opposition from Knight-Ridder executives in Miami because his plan challenged prevailing opinion about newspaper production. Hardin flew to Miami with David Orbaugh, the *Observer*'s new advanced systems manager, taking along charts and graphs that in time swung Knight-Ridder executives to their point of view. The executives agreed to let the *Observer* expand its computer system to eighty-four terminals at a cost of $900,000. When that expansion proved successful, the word went forth that from now on the Charlotte system was to be a model for other Knight-Ridder newspapers. In May 1975, the electronic system allowed the *Observer* to shift to larger text type and a six-column page, making the paper easier to read. It was the first departure from the eight-column page since Curtis Johnson and Walter Sullivan introduced the format in 1920.

Jim Hardin had won his point and, like "Uncle Bill" Sandlin twenty years earlier, had given the newsroom control over the paper's production system. In time, computers let newspapers abandon perforated tape for light-sensitive film, eliminating the need for Linotype machines in 1982. Type was literally being set in the newsroom, and the traditional ratio of newspaper manpower was turned upside down. From the founding of the 1869 *Observer* by four unemployed printers until the 1972 *Observer*'s introduction of computer terminals, the newspaper employed more people in production than it did in reporting and editing. When the *Observer* occupied its new building in 1971, it employed about 200 people in its print shop and about 100 in the newsroom. A decade after the expansion to eighty-four computer terminals, that ratio was reversed: the newsroom employed twice as many people as the print shop. The daily stock market report, which once took eight hours to set in type, was being set by computer in four minutes. The difference allowed the newspaper to hire more reporters, more editors, and more news specialists. It also eliminated all the labor unions.

With the changes Batten made in salary, editing, personnel, and professionalism, the *Observer* began to regain some of the circulation lost during the busing controversy; but then came the 1973 Arab oil embargo, creating gasoline shortages, sharply raising gas prices, and forcing an increase in *Observer* subscription rates that sent circulation into another tailspin. By March 1975, it had fallen to 167,477, its lowest level since 1964.

During that decline, Batten was offered a job in Knight-Ridder's executive offices in Miami. He agonized over the choices. The opportunity to represent the editorial side of the newspaper business among executives who had come up through the business side had a strong appeal. But so did Charlotte and Batten's obligation to the people he had brought to the *Observer*. On his arrival three years earlier, he stated his intention to spend the rest of his life at the *Observer*. He discussed the job offer with his wife Jean and friends and decided to turn it down. Then he talked it over again with Pete McKnight. McKnight later said it was "the hardest day's work I've ever done" but he persuaded Batten that the offer was the chance of a lifetime. Batten went home, took a long walk through Latta Park, and weighed the options. Reluctantly, he decided to take the appointment. His job was to oversee news operations on a number of small and medium-sized Knight-Ridder newspapers, mostly in the West. Within a year, he was made vice-president for news operations of all Knight-Ridder papers, large and small. Within six years he was president of the corporation.

Batten's departure threw the *Observer* newsroom into trauma. He had given the staff a new appreciation of its own potential and led everyone to believe that the paper was on the way to doing great things. The editing team he put together was just beginning to function smoothly. Now it had to adjust to Batten's successor, quick, tireless, aggressive David Lawrence, Jr., a thirty-three-year-old New Yorker with a Florida education. He had worked in St. Petersburg and West Palm Beach before joining the *Washington Post* and later being managing editor of the tabloid *Philadelphia Daily News*. His appointment as *Observer* executive editor under Pete McKnight was announced on July 9, 1975, and he arrived in early August.

The rumpled Lawrence provided a striking contrast to the buttoned-down Batten. In place of oxford shirts and black wingtip shoes, Lawrence appeared in rump-sprung suits, battered loafers, and a shirt-tail that constantly climbed over his belt. He walked fast, talked fast, and was quick with a quip. He also smoked three packs of cigarettes a day, a habit he successfully broke during his Charlotte tenure. As if to make up for the staff's disappointment over Batten's departure, Lawrence worked hard to know everybody in the building on a first-name basis, and went out of his way to meet people in the Charlotte community. He was forever organizing tours of this or that plant or institution, to help make people on the *Observer* more aware of their surroundings.

For at least two staff members, Lawrence's appointment was foreboding. Metropolitan editor Walker Lundy and Carolinas editor Bill Fuller had been his rivals since undergraduate days at the University of Florida where they clashed for the honor of editing the campus newspaper. Even before Lawrence arrived, the old poison was at work. Though the three tried to coexist, they found they could not. First Fuller, then Lundy left for jobs elsewhere.

Early in Lawrence's tenure, the *Observer* issued its first quarto-sized weekly television guide, *TV Week*, which had been planned under Batten. The paper had been publishing a tabloid-sized TV weekly since 1970, when Pete McKnight and Tom Fesperman commissioned ex-photographer Jimmy Dumbell to design one. It was successful, but the paper needed something handier that would stay around the house all week and compete with the national *TV Guide*. A local counterpart to *TV Guide* was expected to boost the *Observer*'s Sunday circulation. Electronic typesetting made such a publication possible; the dozens of complex TV schedules could be composed and edited on a computer terminal. On Sunday, October 4, 1975, under the editing of Gerry Leland, the magazine's first issue appeared. It was an immediate success and helped increase Sunday sales of the paper by 5,000 to 6,000 copies.

The second important appointment at the *Observer* that fall was in the business office, where Erwin Potts, a Charlotte native and former *Charlotte News* reporter, resigned as general manager. His departure weakened the paper's official ties to the Carolinas and the Charlotte community, especially with a New Yorker as executive editor. In Miami, Lee Hills and Alvah Chapman, president of Knight-Ridder, looked for a successor who had not only the right background and accent but the skills and personal force to pull together what had become a fractured organization. They found one in forty-two-year-old Rolfe Neill.

Neill, then editor of the *Philadelphia Daily News*—the paper David Lawrence had just left—was vacationing with his family that August on the lonely beaches of Salter Path, near Morehead City, North Carolina. Coming in from the ocean one afternoon he found pinned to his cottage door a note asking him to "Call Mr. Hills in

Miami." The note was dated two days earlier, indicating it had taken awhile to reach him. Neill could not imagine what the trouble might be, but went immediately to a pay phone—*the* pay phone at Salter Path—and placed a long-distance call. Hills said he and Alvah Chapman wanted Neill to come to Miami to talk about a job change.

Neill spent the last days of his vacation trying to anticipate the change. He had a hunch it might be Wichita, where Knight-Ridder owned the *Eagle-Beacon*. Once back in Philadelphia, he got down the encyclopedias and read everything he could about Wichita, which seemed a long way off.

When he arrived in Miami a week later, he learned that Hills and Chapman wanted him to return to Charlotte as president and publisher, uniting operations of both the *Observer* and the *News* under one executive. Hills remembered Neill's success as an *Observer* business writer in the late 1950s and early 1960s, when he won friends among business leaders who were still upset over the paper's sale to the Knights. Hills might also have known that during one of Jim Knight's visits to Charlotte in the early 1960s, Knight and Pete McKnight were talking over lunch about the need to interest young journalists in the business side of newspapering. McKnight said he had a reporter on the *Observer* who showed such interests, a newsman who might make a publisher one day. When they got back to the office, he introduced Knight to Rolfe Neill.

Hills told Neill that the *Observer* and the *News* needed someone who knew the territory, could talk the language, and could respond to regional and community concerns, someone who could repair the damage done by a divided management. The *Observer* had many relationships that needed restoring: with blacks, with people in surrounding communities, and with advertisers. In appointing Neill president and publisher, the company assured him expert financial assistance by promoting controller Roberto Suarez to vice-president and business manager. Neill was pleased at the prospects but also a little concerned: could he really go home again? He was about to find out. His appointment was announced on September 12, and he reported for work November 1, 1975.

CHAPTER 13

NEILL, OPPEL BRING STABILITY, GROWTH
1976–1986

For several years after Rolfe Neill's arrival, the *Observer* continued to shudder and lurch. The times were still contentious, Charlotte remained a divided community, and editors and reporters continued to come and go in the newsroom. Gradually, as the new publisher and his managers arrived at a common vision of the newspaper's role and relationship to its readers, the *Observer* settled on a steady course that soon brought stability and renewed growth. During the decade, the paper got a new editor who restored and expanded its regional emphasis. It won a long and potentially disastrous libel suit brought by the city police chief. It won six national awards for reporting, including a Pulitzer Prize gold medal for public service. It absorbed the staff of the *Charlotte News*, and two years later saw the *News* cease publication. By March 1986, as it celebrated its centennial, the paper hit a circulation peak of 216,000 daily to become the nation's thirty-second largest morning newspaper in the forty-eighth largest city.

The decade also marked the end of Pete McKnight's tenure in the newsroom. On September 30, 1976, a few days after *Time* magazine had listed the *Observer* as one of the five best newspapers in the South, editor McKnight packed up twenty-one years of memories and moved downstairs to become associate publisher, following a precedent set by Ernest B. Hunter in 1955 and Brodie S. Griffith in 1968. The shift left David Lawrence, Jr., as editor outright, prompting a shuffle in editorial page supervision, and signaling an important transition in the character and status of *Observer* editors.

Other changes included an end of "women's pages" in favor of a "Carolina Living" section, which implied a more varied content and a less sexist presentation; the introduction of a Friday morning magazine section called "Extra," offering guides to weekend entertainment; and the loss of two popular writers, business editor Roy Covington and sports columnist Bob Quincy, both of whom died of cancer.

During those ten years, the South returned to the political mainstream with the election of Jimmy Carter as the first truly southern president since Zachary Taylor in 1848, and the election of Ronald Reagan, whose political base was a tier of states that included the South and the Southwest. The South also joined the economic mainstream as industries from the "Frostbelt" of the East and Midwest moved to the "Sunbelt" of the South and Southwest. For the first time in more than a century, more people moved into the South than moved out. As the nation opened its doors to a flood of refugees from Southeast Asia, Cuba, and Central America, many of the immigrants settled in the South.

The impact of those events was felt in North Carolina, where James B. Hunt, Jr., was amending the state constitution to become the first governor since Reconstruction to serve successive terms. In his eight years in office, the value of new industry entering the state each year rose from millions of dollars to billions of dollars. New plants and parking lots sprang up on old cotton lands, many of them in the Research Triangle between Raleigh, Durham, and Chapel Hill, and in University Research Park outside Charlotte. Instead of Winston-Salem and Greensboro, its former rivals for economic and commercial prestige, Charlotte found itself competing with burgeoning Raleigh.

Rolfe Neill need not have worried about coming home again. The Charlotte that welcomed him as a publisher in the fall of 1975 was a different city from the one he left as a business reporter in March 1961. Most of the firms he covered then were locally owned, often by the men or families that had founded them; now most were part of large national or multinational corporations. Then most of the banks were locally controlled and managed; now most were headquarters or branches of statewide organizations. The downtown that had been the focus of community activity and leadership had lost its glamour to a ring of suburban shopping centers and was gathering momentum for a comeback. Development in the county's southeastern quadrant that stopped at Cameron Morrison's Morrocroft Farms in the early 1960s had since spawned SouthPark and miles of subdivisions beyond, stretching to Carmel Road and N.C. 51.

When Neill left in 1961, the Chamber of Commerce was running Charlotte. Now it was struggling to regain its influence in a political spectrum crowded with rival groups. The city was about to vote on district representation for the city council, a move that would further dilute the chamber's influence. The chamber was pushing for legalized sales of liquor by the drink that would improve the city's convention, hotel, and travel accommodations. It was also plumping for a bond issue for a new airport terminal.

But perhaps the greatest change in the area was the presence and increasing influence of the University of North Carolina at Charlotte, which did not exist when Neill was a reporter. Now UNCC and the 40,000-student Central Piedmont Community College were enrichments to the city's cultural and political life and important elements in the city's campaign to attract new business and industry. People from UNCC were among the leaders in the campaign for district representation.

The years had changed Rolfe Neill, too. The boyish reporter had become a stylish executive. When he left Charlotte as a twenty-eight-year-old, he wore his brown hair in a bristling crew cut; when he returned at age forty-two, it was silver and casually tousled. Just before leaving Philadelphia, a magazine there had named him one of the town's ten "sexiest" men. The director of Philadelphia's CBS affiliate wanted to hire him as its television news anchor at double his newspaper salary.

Though born in Mt. Airy, the son of a dairy manager, Neill grew up in Columbus, Georgia, where he wrote sports for his high school newspaper, won a portable typewriter, and got a summer job on the morning *Columbus Enquirer*. He also won a Navy ROTC scholarship to the University of North Carolina at Chapel Hill, and then lost it by devoting most of his study hours to managing the *Daily Tar Heel*, which he later edited. By the time he was a college boy, Neill had developed a maturity and disarming boldness that made him seem older than his years. He addressed elders by their first names and often startled them by asking brash, direct questions. He also had a knack for remembering people's names and an unerring sense of how they perceived themselves, two qualities that gave him a commanding presence.

After college, he did a two-year stint in the army as an editor for *Stars and Stripes* in Tokyo. Afterward, despite attractive offers from major North Carolina dailies, he took a fifty-five-dollar-a-week job on the tiny *Franklin Press*, a Macon County weekly edited by Weimar Jones, who had taught a course in country journalism during Neill's undergraduate days at Chapel Hill. After a year, the idealism of country newspapering lost much of its appeal, and Neill accepted Pete McKnight's offer of $100 a week to open an *Observer* bureau in Gastonia. There he crossed paths and swapped newspaper lore with two old *Observer* hands. One was James W. Atkins, editor and publisher of the *Gastonia Gazette*, who had been a copy editor on the *Observer* under Joseph Caldwell. The other was Fred W. Hunter, who had been an *Observer* carrier in 1911 and a city and state circulation agent under M. H. ("Mooch") Brandon in the 1920s. The experience of reporting on Gaston County affairs helped teach Neill the importance of local news in the *Observer*'s success as a regional newspaper.

Thirteen months later, he was transferred to Charlotte to become the *Observer*'s business reporter, a beat where his aggressiveness and engaging personality won him many friends. The profiles of business leaders he wrote in the Sunday business section were widely admired and did much to help the *Observer* regain the respect of business people.

In March 1961, after winning the William T. Polk Award for business writing, he left the *Observer* to edit the failing *Coral Gables Times*, a weekly owned by Knight Newspapers. After putting that paper in the black, Neill went on to edit the *Miami Beach Sun*. In 1965, he was hired as assistant to the publisher of the *New York Daily News*. Four years later, he returned to the Knight organization as editor of the *Philadelphia Daily News*, a post he held for six years before returning to the *Observer* as resident publisher.

Neill's appointment was no balm to a newsroom still smarting over the loss of Jim Batten. To some staff members, Neill was the ex-editor of what they regarded as a sleazy tabloid unworthy of comparison with the *Observer*. Others regarded him as a friend of bankers and industrialists, sent in to placate Charlotte's business establishment. The fact that he was made publisher bothered many staff members, who asked, "Who the hell is he to tell us what to put in the newspaper?" David Lawrence and others argued that Neill was a newsman first and a business manager second, but could not persuade their colleagues that he would be a friend of the newsroom. Neill would have to earn their respect.

At that moment, Neill's larger concern was restoring public respect for the newspaper. Judge James B. McMillan had just filed his final order in the school-busing case, and Charlotte-Mecklenburg schools were beginning to regain lost enrollment, but many readers still resented the *Observer*'s support of the judge. The role of the press in unraveling the Watergate scandal had made newsmen seem more self-righteous than ever, and *Observer* editors were constantly courting public favor and inviting reader participation in the newspaper to help soften that image. One product of those efforts was the paper's sponsorship of the *Charlotte Observer* Marathon, beginning in December 1977.

That sensitivity about the paper's image and objectivity was evident in the October 1975 firing of Jerry Simpson, a popular book editor and restaurant reviewer, for privately advising restaurant owners about what paintings to hang, what wines to list, and how to train waiters. When he gave a restaurant that followed his advice a favorable review, editors termed it "a serious breach of ethics" and dismissed him. David Lawrence wrote a personal column, explaining, "We live in a time when many institutions (including newspapers) are being reassessed and individuals' integrity is being questioned. . . . We must make sure that we at *The Observer* avoid any conflicts and even the appearance of potential conflict," he said.

The explanation was one of many attempts by *Observer* editors to let readers see the inside of newspaper operations and invite their trust. When editors decided the feminist movement had made "For and About Women" an inappropriate heading for "women's pages," they invited readers to suggest an alternative. The result was a unisex "Carolina Living" section. When Dannye Romine succeeded Jerry Simpson as book editor and Richard Maschal and Allen Oren took over from the retiring Dick Banks as reviewers of music and movies, the editorial staff wrote columns explaining what *Observer* critics are hired to do and why the paper publishes their critiques. In the spring of 1976, before another round of political endorsements, editors wrote columns about how the newspaper reviews political candidates and why it makes recommendations to readers. The explanations did not prevent an uproar when the paper passed over Charlotte businessman Ed O'Herron in endorsing Jim Hunt of Wilson in the Democratic primary for governor. Many Charlotteans thought that the paper should have supported the local candidate, no matter what it thought of his qualifications. The *Observer* considered O'Herron out of date; apparently, so did voters.

While the paper was being whipsawed by critics inside and outside its newsroom, it was winning high praise from sources within the journalism establishment. In its issue for September 27, 1976, *Time* magazine surveyed "Dixie's Best Dailies" and ranked the *Observer* as one of the five best, along with the *Miami Herald*, the *St. Petersburg Times*, the *Commercial Appeal* in Memphis, and the *Dallas Times Herald*. According to *Time*:

> The *Charlotte Observer* (circ. 169,969), owned by the Knight-Ridder chain, sends four editions across the Carolinas every

morning, and more than 60% of its readers live outside Charlotte. Editor C. A. McKnight covers a lot of ground with only 38 reporters, but does not slight long-term investigative projects. One example: *Observer* reporters spent 21 months digging through expense vouchers at the Southern Bell Telephone Co.; so far, eleven executives have been indicted for cheating the utility. The paper's support of school busing has not pleased many readers, but Editor Reese Cleghorn's sensitive editorials rarely offend. That editorial-page task is left to Doug Marlette, 26, whose tough cartoons are syndicated to 80 dailies. Lately, Executive Editor David Lawrence has invited local businessmen to sit in on editorial meetings. "We're not afraid of criticism," he says. "I want this paper to reflect the ideas of the people who live here."

Several days after the *Time* survey appeared on newsstands, the man most responsible for the paper's climb to such a status was relieved of his duties as editor. Though he was only sixty, Pete McKnight appeared to be tired and dispirited, broken by his constant battle with daily pressures, failing eyesight, and an assortment of other ailments. He had lost touch with the paper and was so isolated from day-to-day operations that it was no longer possible to maintain the fiction that he was in charge. Clearly David Lawrence, the high-energy executive editor, was running the newspaper, and bringing McKnight into the daily decision-making process was awkward and often embarrassing. Several times newsroom dissenters tried to work through an inattentive McKnight to countermand decisions that had Lawrence's backing. Painfully Neill came to the conclusion that the kindest thing to do was to end the charade, honor McKnight for what he had accomplished, and turn the paper's news and editorial management over to Lawrence alone.

On Sunday, September 26, 1976, a front-page story said that effective October 1, David Lawrence, Jr., would be editor of the *Observer* and Pete McKnight would become associate publisher, assisting Neill in all phases of the *Observer*'s operations. A few days later, McKnight moved out of the newsroom to a new office on the third floor, between Rolfe Neill and business manager Roberto Suarez.

On the afternoon of October 1, a reluctant McKnight made a brief appearance in the newsroom to acknowledge the applause of staff members and accept a small farewell gift. They gathered around him in the center of the room and gave him engraved copies of the first masthead listing him as editor, dated July 7, 1955, and of the last one, dated September 30, 1976. The two engravings marked a span of twenty-one years and eighty-five days, the longest term of any *Observer* editor except Wade H. Harris, who served twenty-three years and six months. In making the presentation, the staff recalled that four years before McKnight became editor, *Time* magazine had dismissed the *Observer* as a newspaper with the "editorial voice [of] a whisper." After twenty-one years under McKnight's leadership, the same newspaper was ranked by *Time* as one of the South's five best. McKnight accepted the tribute with teary eyes and trembling hands, and in response uttered an almost inaudible "Thanks. You kids have meant a lot to me." And with that, he left. (A year later, he was one of the first five inductees in the North Carolina Journalism Hall of Fame at UNC, the only non–UNC alumnus to be so honored. Two years later, he became the only newspaper editor given a lifetime membership in the American Society of Newspaper Editors. Three years later, his friends endowed a scholarship in his name at the UNC School of Journalism.)

McKnight's departure was one of a series of major changes that churned personal relations in the *Observer* newsroom over the next several months. Stuart Dim, forty, a New Yorker who was the paper's first male woman's editor—it was he who led the move to reorient the section toward "Carolina Living"—was promoted to managing editor, a long-hours, high-pressure responsibility he later decided he did not want. South Carolinian Carl Stepp came home from the Washington bureau to become assistant national editor, then national editor, and was replaced in the capital by Jerry Shinn. But Shinn and his family had deep roots in the Carolinas and were happy to return ten months later, when he became government editor. With McKnight's departure, Reese Cleghorn left the editorial pages to go to the *Detroit Free Press* and was succeeded by Ed Williams. Metropolitan editor Walker Lundy resigned to go to the *Tallahassee Democrat* and was replaced by Mike Lewis from the *Sentinel-Star* in Orlando, Florida. Lewis lasted only a few months before being replaced by ex–government editor Joe Distelheim, who was transferred from the sports department.

While those and other unsettling shifts were taking place, investigative reporters Bill Bancroft and Marion Ellis were asking questions and getting answers that would involve the paper in a long and bitter controversy leading to a $13 million libel suit. The questions had to do with alleged wiretapping by Charlotte police. After eight weeks of painstaking interviews, Bancroft and Ellis reported in a front-page story on March 6, 1977, that Police Chief J. C. ("Jake")

Goodman, Jr., had "illegally ordered evidence of unlawful police wire-tapping destroyed after a patrolman threatened to expose the wire-tapping." The story, which relied heavily on information from un-named sources, infuriated police officials, whose relations with the newspaper had been testy since the gambling-house-raid incident in 1970. Four weeks later, an attorney for Chief Goodman served the *Observer* with a letter formally demanding an apology and a retrac-tion. The *Observer* did not retract, and two months later the chief filed a lawsuit, demanding $11.5 million from the *Observer* and re-porters Bancroft and Ellis and $2 million from Allan L. McCoy, a for-mer policeman who was the source of much of the newspaper's story.

While the wiretapping controversy was coming to a rapid boil, the *Observer* stirred rage from another quarter: the religious right. In a series of features on Charlotte-born evangelist Billy Graham and his organization, *Observer* reporters Bob Hodierne and Mary Bishop disclosed the existence of a seven-year-old, $22.9 million fund, com-posed mostly of land, stocks, bonds, and cash, credited to Graham's World Evangelism and Christian Education Fund but not reported among Graham finances. Their story pointed out that the fund was perfectly legal and was "normal, good money management." Graham said the fund was kept secret because he did not want to be inun-dated with requests for charity. He said the money was being saved to build a Bible-study institute for laymen in the North Carolina mountains, already the site of many religious retreats.

The story caused a furor among Christian groups. Some were crit-ical of the Graham organization for not revealing the fund's exis-tence to its two million contributors, whose annual gifts averaged about ten dollars apiece. Others were critical of the *Observer* for rais-ing an issue about the fund. One of the harshest critics was WBTV, which said, "The *Observer* is practically alone in trying to make something immoral out of the fund. . . . We don't know why it is so urgent, in the first place, to have all the funds with which Billy Graham is connected spread out for public view." Billy Graham and *Observer* officials, including publisher Rolfe Neill, had several dis-cussions about the paper's policies in reporting on the fund. The in-cident was forgotten after Graham, in a luncheon address to the Na-tional Press Club in Washington, D.C.—with reporter Bob Hodierne sitting in the audience—cited the *Observer*'s story as an example of responsible newspapering. He said the story taught him that in so-liciting public funds religious groups have a duty to be scrupulous and accountable in the handling and disclosure of their finances. That was not the reaction of Jim Bakker, leader of the PTL television ministry, who later accused the *Observer* of "doing the the devil's work" in repeatedly reporting PTL's financial troubles.

Though the Graham brouhaha soon died, the wiretapping controversy waxed and waned for four and a half years. Various investigations were made without decisive results until December 1978, when the Charlotte City Council hired attorney David Sentelle (later a federal judge) to investigate the charges. His report to the council included findings that police wiretapping was widespread in the early 1970s. The council later issued a report detailing wiretapping incidents and concluding that they were mishandled by high-ranking police officers. But the council recommended no disciplinary action.

Many of the divisions within the *Observer* newsroom were healed in the spring of 1978 when the staff confronted a personal tragedy. In early April business writer Roy Covington, then forty-nine years old, learned that he had an inoperable cancer. His only hope for survival, doctors said, was the chemical therapy available at M. D. Anderson Hospital in Houston, Texas. Publisher Neill, editor Lawrence, and others encouraged Covington to take the therapy and arranged to have colleague Jimmy Dumbell accompany him to Texas.

The next day Lawrence summoned the staff to the auditorium and announced the nature of Covington's illness and treatment. He asked for suggestions about what response the paper might make. A colleague recalled hearing Covington say that he planned to spend his summer vacation painting his house. Could the staff do the painting for him? The suggestion was enthusiastically accepted, and the next weekend, while Covington was in Houston, *Observer* reporters and editors painted his house inside and out. They also repaired plumbing and plaster, trimmed trees and shrubs, replaced a rotting rear deck, and repaired a boat dock. Rolfe Neill, Bob Suarez, and David Lawrence were among the painters. So was Jim Batten, who flew in from Miami. Food editors Eudora Garrison and Helen Moore laid out a picnic lunch. When the work could not be completed in one weekend, it was carried over to a second. The effort, much like an old-fashioned barn-raising, comforted the staff in its concern for Covington and united it like nothing else had since Batten's departure. Nearly a year later Covington died, but the memory of his life was all the sweeter after those warm April outings at his home.

Staff morale also improved after David Lawrence rehired cartoonist Eugene Payne. The headline on the July 6, 1978, story announcing his return said, "Welcome Back, Gene!" reflecting the newsroom's general satisfaction. Payne's return also salved an old wound to *Observer* pride. "Gene Payne is one of our profession's greatest craftsmen with a special feel for this region and people," Lawrence said. "I'm very excited about his return." Said Payne, "I've enjoyed my seven years at WSOC, but I've come to the conclusion that the best medium for cartooning is newspapers." Payne rejoined the newsroom's art department and began turning out four cartoons a week on the paper's feature page, under the heading, "Gene Payne's View."

The March 1978 audit of circulation raised hopes that the *Observer* at last might be regaining its stride. Average daily sales showed a gain for the second year in a row, and the 171,477 total was the paper's best in four years. But any hopes of stability were dashed in October by a succession of events, beginning in Detroit where *Free Press* executive editor Kurt Luedtke resigned to try his hand at writing screenplays. (He wrote *Absence of Malice* and the screenplay for *Out of Africa*). Named to succeed him was David Lawrence, Jr., thirty-six-year-old editor of the *Observer*. Named to replace Lawrence was Richard Oppel, thirty-five, executive editor of the *Tallahassee Democrat*.

The news, first published in the *Detroit News*, afternoon rival of the *Free Press*, was announced to *Observer* editors at a meeting at Lawrence's Myers Park home. It was later announced to the staff at a hastily called meeting in the newsroom. At both places it brought tears and regret. In a breathless three years the popular Lawrence brought energy, toughness, accessibility, and a sense of immediacy and directness to the daily production of the newspaper. Publisher Neill cried in announcing his departure. The irrepressible Lawrence quipped, "I wasn't here long enough for it to be an era, so it's not the end of an era."

It was probably inevitable that David Lawrence's stay in Charlotte would be brief. He had a big-city style and ambition and found Charlotte, as much as he admired it, a trifle tame and too homogeneous. He hungered for big-city diversity, big-city intrigue, big-city sports events—and the excitement of big-city newspaper competition. All awaited him in Detroit, where the *Free Press*, the nation's eighth largest newspaper, was engaged in a daily war with the *Detroit News*, the nation's fifth largest newspaper.

Yet his tenure in Charlotte signaled a significant change in the role and status of *Observer* editors. Most previous *Observer* editors (James C. Hemphill and Ralph Nicholson the notable exceptions) had had strong ties to the Charlotte area. They had either grown up in the region or been educated and trained there. Indeed, most had apprenticed on the *Observer* or the *Charlotte News*. Furthermore, those editors, from Johnstone Jones in the 1870s to Pete McKnight in the 1970s, were thinkers and writers whose own vision and imagination were reflected in the newspaper; they gave the paper its standards and sense of direction and put the stamp of their personality on its news and editorial columns. Their names were familiar to most of the paper's readers.

David Lawrence was a departure from that tradition. He was more than an editor, in the conventional sense of the word; he was a manager, the chairman of a board of colleagues, someone who charged the atmosphere in which ideas were hatched, haggled over, and implemented. He worked long hours and busied himself with details major and minor. But while he was a dominant force in the newsroom, he did not impose his will and personality on the paper in the manner of Joseph Caldwell or Pete McKnight. He treated the paper more like an institution, a piece of the civic landscape that reflected community standards more than his own. Under Rich Oppel, that collegial and institutional approach would be even more pronounced.

Oppel got his first inkling of the Lawrence appointment while attending a meeting of Associated Press managing editors in Portland, Oregon, in October 1978. He ran into Jim Batten and learned that Kurt Luedtke was leaving the *Free Press*. Both Oppel and Batten previously had worked with Luedtke and admired his talent. Oppel speculated that David Lawrence was surely a contender for Luedtke's job, and Batten, then a Knight-Ridder vice-president overseeing news operations of metropolitan papers, agreed. Later that day, Oppel's wife, Carol, flew into Portland, and Oppel met her with the news that "Luedtke's leaving to write screenplays, and Dave Lawrence is going to Detroit." Without missing a beat, Carol Oppel added, " . . . And you're going to Charlotte."

A few days later, at another newspaper meeting, this time in Miami, Batten took Oppel to lunch and asked if he would be interested in editing the *Observer*. Immediately Oppel's answer was yes. Batten said, "I wondered how you would respond, but Kurt [Luedtke] said, 'He'll accept on the spot. He's ambitious as hell.'"

The final decision was up to *Observer* publisher Rolfe Neill, who sent Oppel a copy of the *Observer* to critique and invited him to Charlotte. Arriving on a Saturday at the old airport terminal off West Boulevard, Oppel was met by Neill and taken to lunch at Rogers Barbecue, a cinder-block, paper-plate and plastic-fork emporium on Atando Avenue, in the middle of an industrial park. Later they adjourned to Neill's third-floor office at the Knight Publishing Company building, which, on a weekend, was all but deserted. There they met for several hours in what Oppel recalled as a "grueling" interrogation about his views on newspapers and journalistic standards. Neill expressed the desire to see the *Observer* become a great newspaper and asked whether Oppel was capable of getting it there. Over and over, their discussions returned to matters of accuracy and fairness, topics that were to remain the central currency of Neill and Oppel's professional relationship. Oppel also spent some time visiting general manager Roberto Suarez.

After the session both Oppel and Neill went away uncertain about how to proceed. Neill considered Oppel unproven and a little unsure of himself. Oppel regarded Neill as a dominating personality who probably doubted Oppel's ability.

Born in New Jersey, raised in St. Petersburg, Florida, and an ex-marine, Oppel was, at thirty-five, only a few months younger than David Lawrence. Most of his experience—ten and a half years—had been as a political writer and bureau chief for the Associated Press, which was not quite like running a daily newspaper. For twenty-two months he had been executive editor of the *Tallahassee Democrat* and had led its switch from afternoon to morning publication, a move that increased both its circulation and public image. But editing a much larger, more established newspaper like the *Observer* represented a stiffer challenge.

That evening Oppel dined at the Radisson Plaza with David Lawrence and his wife Bobbie, and afterward flew home to Tallahassee. Within a few days, Neill called and invited him to become the *Observer*'s editor. Oppel accepted, and together they laid plans for coordinating the announcements, first Lawrence's transfer to Detroit, then Oppel's move to Charlotte. But by then too many people were involved, and the secret would not keep. Leaks forced the announcement nearly a week ahead of schedule, with Oppel notifying the staff he had recruited in Tallahassee, and then flying to Charlotte to be introduced at a stand-up staff meeting in the middle of the newsroom at the *Observer*. His name went on the masthead as editor on Sunday, November 19, 1978, the day the paper ran David Lawrence's farewell under the headline "Thanks, Charlotte, For Giving Us a Sense of Home."

From the outset, Oppel was perceived as less forceful than the hard-charging Lawrence. He was reputed to be a team player who liked to delegate to associates a large share of his authority. He listened a lot and encouraged a lot more give-and-take. When questioned about his management style, Oppel said, "I'm fortunate to have strong people working for me to assume a lot of the responsibility." Over the next three to four years, as he assembled an editing team he was comfortable with and felt he could trust, the newsroom went through another round of turnovers.

It was a dicey time, full of doubt, frustration, and office intrigue. Oppel was under insistent pressure from Neill, a publisher with an editor's instincts, to lower the paper's voice and make it friendlier and more accountable to readers. From the opposite direction, Oppel was being badgered by subordinates to stand up to the publisher and pursue the kind of investigative journalism that would win the paper regional and national prestige. His privacy and inability to mix comfortably with members of the staff limited his ability to lead. Several subordinates openly questioned his competence and commitment to excellence. Somehow—perhaps by reaching into his reserve of Marine Corps grit—Oppel survived the conflicts and gradually dispelled the doubts. He learned to look his critics in the eye, listen to their complaints, and respond in positive ways.

Assessing the strengths and weaknesses of the men and women around him, he carefully assembled a new editing team, one that functioned collegially. Shrewdly he chose people whose talents complemented his own. For managing editor, for instance, he chose Mark Ethridge III, the son and grandson of former newspaper editors. A young man (age thirty) with high energy and a keen eye for seeing holes in news stories, Ethridge was one of the best hands-on editors in the newsroom. Oppel appointed a series of assistant managing editors, Bob Ashley for features and sports, Gil Thelen for news and business, Bob De Piante for administration, and, later, Dennis Sodomka for South Carolina coverage. When Ed Williams sought relief as editor of the editorial pages, Oppel moved Jerry Shinn from the metropolitan desk to serve as Williams's assistant and then to take over. Shinn was forty-three, a native of Gaffney, South Carolina, and a Phi Beta Kappa graduate of UNC. He knew the territory, was a smooth writer and editor, and had a talent for cool diplomacy. With Shinn in charge of editorials, Williams was asked to improve the selection of columns and to strengthen Sunday Perspective fronts.

Steadily, Oppel won the newsroom's respect and confidence—and, in time, its admiration—but only after enduring many humbling moments. His associates, including Rolfe Neill, marveled at his tolerance, his resilience, and his growth. By 1982, with a new editing team in place, he was clearly in command, the undisputed leader of the newsroom and an effective spokesman for the news and editorial department among other executives of the Knight Publishing Company.

Also helping to raise Oppel's confidence was a series of prize-winning projects, to which he was deeply committed. The first, which he initiated, was a sobering look at North Carolina's tobacco industry and the hazards of smoking. "Our Tobacco Dilemma," published in March 1979, won first place for public service in the North Carolina Press Association contest and was a national finalist for the Associated Press Managing Editor's award. Two months later, in marking the twenty-fifth anniversary of the Supreme Court's May 1954 decision outlawing school segregation, the paper produced a special section, "Black and White," reviewing the local and regional reforms flowing from that decree. The section won the Charles Stuart Mott Award and the national Education Writers Award. In February 1980, in another look at a North Carolina industry, the paper hit even closer to home with "Brown Lung: A Case of Deadly Neglect," which focused on the deleterious effects of cotton dust produced in textile mills surrounding Charlotte. It too won first place in the state press contest and five national prizes: the George Polk Award for best regional reporting, the Clarion Award from Women in Communications, the Roy W. Howard Public Service Award, the Robert F. Kennedy Award for reporting on the plight of the disadvantaged, and the Pulitzer Prize for public service.

The "Brown Lung" series had taken seventeen staff members four and a half months to produce. It included twenty-two stories, eight editorials, and forty photographs. It charged that state industrial inspectors had been derelict in protecting the lives of workers from cotton dust. It also charged that many textile industry executives were resisting efforts to clean up dirty mills.

The idea for the series originated in reporter Howard Covington's investigation of state worker-compensation claims. Hearing more and more about unpaid claims for brown lung, he suggested that the paper take a hard look at the issue. Joining the effort were investigative reporter Marion Ellis, labor writer Bob Dennis, medical writer Robert Conn, Washington correspondent Robert Hodierne, general assignment reporter Robert Drogin, photographers Phil Drake and Bill Billings, and copy editor Barbara Mathews. The project was coordinated by managing editor Mark Ethridge and twenty-nine-year-old projects editor Laura Sessions Stepp.

Word that the *Observer* was a winner in the Pulitzer competition leaked a few days before the prizes were announced. Pete McKnight got a call from a friend on the Pulitzer jury and alerted Oppel to be prepared. The day before the announcement, as they were taking their daily noontime run down East Morehead Street, Oppel informed managing editor Mark Ethridge that they had won a Pulitzer. "What?" shouted Ethridge, who was running a few steps behind. "Yeah," said Oppel. "We won!" Ethridge caught up and the two sweating runners, dressed in shorts and running shoes, paused in the middle of the Morehead and Kenilworth intersection, whooped and embraced joyfully, and then continued their run. Later that day, Oppel stopped at a store, bought two cases of champagne and quietly had them stashed—on ice—in his office, violating a company rule against bringing alcohol to the newsroom. The instant that word of the award became official, Oppel climbed atop a desk in the middle of the newsroom and shouted to the assembled staff, "It's the gold medal in public service. We won the big one!" And out came the champagne.

One by one, members of the team that produced the series climbed to the desk top with him and were ceremonially drenched in wine. On the newsroom floor, the champagne was being consumed by cheering onlookers. Peering into the ice chest, and seeing only two bottles left, newsroom clerk Linwood Sawyer walked over to Rolfe Neill and, in a wonderfully nasal twang, accused him of being "too cheap" to pay for a decent celebration on the day his newspaper won the Pulitzer. Neill reached into his pocket, pulled out seventy-five dollars, and sent Sawyer for more champagne.

Oppel's confidence was further strengthened in the fall of 1981, when the *Observer* won the libel suit brought by Police Chief Jake Goodman. The story that provoked the suit was then four years old, and Goodman had retired as police chief. Yet the case was still a serious challenge to the credibility and prestige of the *Observer*. The trial lasted seven days, with *Observer* reporters Ellis and Bancroft and ex-chief Goodman spending hours on the witness stand. The central issue was the accuracy of the *Observer*'s story. In the end, after fifty minutes of deliberation, the jury decided the story was essentially true. When Ellis and Bancroft returned to the *Observer* newsroom that afternoon, they were greeted by spontaneous applause from their colleagues. It was a rare gesture and more than a tribute to a job well done; it also expressed the staff's sense of relief.

Another big plus for Oppel was the paper's return to regional reporting. The turnaround had begun under Lawrence, but the mere restoration of news bureaus in nearby communities did not bring a commensurate increase in circulation. It remained for the regional tabloids to do that. The "tabs" were the outgrowth of a City Club luncheon between Oppel and general manager Roberto Suarez. Oppel described the type of hometown news he wanted to get before *Observer* readers in surrounding cities and towns. He had in mind church notes, school news, features on local heroes and heroines, schedules of upcoming events. Suarez asked why that could not be put in a special tabloid that would accompany the *Observer* and be delivered only in a given community, something the *Miami Herald* had been doing for years. The tabs would let the *Observer* continue to offer the broad overview of state and national news, yet still cover newsworthy events in the many communities it served. They would make the *Observer* seem more responsive and less remote. They also would allow community advertisers to purchase space in the tabs at prices far below run-of-paper rates.

The concept was fleshed out, money was budgeted for a trial run, and the first target was York County, just across the state line in South Carolina, traditionally a strong *Observer* market where circulation was static. The first twice-a-week *York Observer* was published in May 1981, with a staff of five—an editor, two reporters, a photographer, and a clerk. The editor was Al Johnson, a thirty-three-year-old black from High Point who had graduated from North Carolina A&T University and apprenticed on the *News-Leader* in Richmond, Virginia. An immediate success, the tab was soon being published three times a week, and similar tabloids were produced for Union County (June 1981), Gaston County (November 1981), Catawba County (April 1983), Iredell County (October 1983), and Cabarrus County (February 1984). In a three-year period, the number of people working on the regional tabloids, which became known in the office as "Little O's," went from five to thirty-three, all under the general supervision of Al Johnson, a protégé of Rich Oppel who eventually became assistant to the editor. With the tabloids came a steady rise in circulation. From March 1982, when the paper implemented its last price increase, average daily sales climbed from 168,276 to 171,226 in 1983, to 180,782 in 1984, and to 186,528 in 1985. In the same period, Sunday circulation went from 240,202 to 259,161.

Contrary to some newsroom fears, the emphasis on regional news did not diminish the paper's commitment to investigative journalism. A series on air pollution won first place in public service in the North Carolina Press Association contest in 1983, and another on patient neglect in South Carolina mental hospitals won second place in 1985. In the six North Carolina contests dating back to 1980, the *Observer* won first place in public service three times and second place twice.

Oppel's third major achievement was an increased emphasis on business coverage made possible by the introduction of the "Business Monday" tabloid in February 1982. Borrowed from a successful concept pioneered on the *Miami Herald*, the "Business Monday" tab earned revenues to support an expansion of the business-news staff from four people to nine, strengthening business coverage all week, not just on Mondays. The enlargement allowed the *Observer* to look beyond Mecklenburg County and cover business throughout the region, in much the same manner that the paper had done in the days of Caldwell and Tompkins. Planning for "Business Monday" was done by assistant managing editor Luisita Lopez and business editor Henry Scott in late 1981 and early 1982. Shortly after the section's introduction, Scott resigned and was succeeded by Ken Gepfert, a former Associated Press hand who knew Rich Oppel from his AP days in Florida. Gepfert came to Charlotte from the *Los Angeles Times* in April 1982 and gradually increased the business staff to fourteen people.

By June 1983, Oppel's performance had the full confidence of publisher Neill and many others, as evidenced by Knight Publishing Company's plans to merge the ailing *Charlotte News* into the *Observer* under Oppel's overall supervision. Despite staff improvement, promotion, and various sales campaigns, *News* circulation continued to fall as it had every year since hitting a 69,409 peak in 1972. In the audit of 1982 it stood at 44,956, not enough to offset production costs. A ten-member task force from throughout the company spent months studying *News* options and then recommended that its staff be merged into the *Observer* to cut costs and save jobs. For two years, the *Observer* and *News* staffs jointly produced both newspapers from the same newsroom. The walls dividing the *Observer* newsroom from that of the *News* were knocked down, creating an L-shaped expanse nearly 100 yards long. The room was redecorated, outfitted with new carpeting and furnishings, and equipped with a new, $3 million computer system with a greater memory and a wider range of typesetting options. Ronald Green, the *News*'s prize-winning sports columnist, began writing stories for both papers, as did other *News* writers and columnists, such as John Vaughan and Allen Norwood.

While the *Observer* was absorbing those *Charlotte News* personalities, it was sadly watching the demise of one of its own. In the fall of 1983, sports columnist Bob Quincy began taking radiation treatments for cancer of the throat. A West Virginia native and former World War II bomber pilot, Quincy came to Charlotte from UNC and Rocky Mount in the late 1940s as a sports writer and later sports columnist for the *News*. He headed a department that included Sandy Grady, Ronald Green, Julian Scheer, and Bob Saunders, perhaps the most talented sports staff ever assembled in North Carolina. The thick, broad-shouldered Quincy wore the menacing look of a professional wrestler and wrote in a sinewy style that befit his physique. You could hear the thud and crunch and grunt of straining athletes in his prose. He also had a low boiling point and once smashed a recalcitrant typewriter. But below the toughness, Quincy was a romantic soul and often wrote with surprising insight and sensitivity.

As the talent on his once-able staff departed, the restless Quincy left the *News* for a fling as sports publicist for UNC, and then returned to Charlotte to try his hand at sportscasting over television and radio. But Quincy was a shy, taciturn man, and standing in front of cameras and microphones was not his style. In 1971, Jim Batten persuaded him to join the *Observer* as a sports columnist. He still wrote splendidly, but was a generation older than the rest of the sports staff and remained an enigma to his younger colleagues. He came and went and did his job, but relations with co-workers were rarely close.

Then the cancer struck, and Quincy began showing up for work with fiery red blotches on his cheek and neck from the radiation therapy. Over passing weeks and months his voice got raspy. Quincy never said a word about his illness, never let on that he felt discomfort. But people in the newsroom looked on with awe and admiration at his courage. After a while, his columns became shorter, then disappeared altogether. Quincy could not come to the office anymore. On February 9, 1984, he died at age sixty. The next day, atop his cluttered desk near the center of the newsroom, someone had placed a single red rose.

In a similar way, the *Observer* staff watched the inexorable decline of the *Charlotte News*. Even as the staff merger was made in 1983, Knight Publishing Company officials knew that chances for a recovery were slim. Through no fault of their own, afternoon newspapers in morning-paper markets were in dire trouble throughout the country. Suburban living, television, and advertising trends clearly favored morning newspapers. By the fall of 1985, when average daily sales had fallen to 34,000, the decision was made to pull the plug and give the ninety-seven-year-old *News* a decent burial. The announcement brought tears, even among some *Observer* people who admired the *News*'s tradition and liked having an afternoon paper to compete against. The final edition, on November 2, 1985, containing profiles of ex-*News* greats and reminiscences by such people as Charles Kuralt, Sandy Grady, Tom Fesperman, and Emery Wister, sold 76,000 copies of an 80,000 press run. Then the *News* was no more.

Events since the Knight purchase in 1959 indicated that the expensive effort to save the *News*, while perhaps unavoidable, was at bottom a lost cause. Even at the time of the Knight purchase, the outlook for afternoon newspapers in morning markets was unpromising. The *News* lived comfortably—often at the expense of the *Observer* in terms of resources, management attention, and public favor—but could not regain the momentum it once enjoyed.

It accomplished many good things in those twenty-five borrowed years. It spurred community interest in various causes and projects. It enlivened competition with the *Observer*—and was often among the *Observer*'s most vigorous editorial critics. Its talented staff won many prizes for journalistic excellence. But, like afternoon newspapers elsewhere, it could not hold an audience and lost circulation in eighteen of its final twenty-five years. Its death was inevitable.

Once relieved of responsibility for the *Charlotte News*, the *Observer* surged to new circulation heights. Between March 1985 and March 1986, it increased its average daily sales from 186,528 to 216,024, an increase of 29,496, the largest single-year gain in the paper's history. Of that increase, only about 13,000 came from *Charlotte News* subscribers who switched to the *Observer* (half the subscribers to the *News* were already buying the *Observer*). One of the reasons for the gain was the introduction of *Mecklenburg Neighbors*, a twice-a-week tabloid like the regional tabs in surrounding counties.

While Rich Oppel was assembling a collegial editing team in the *Observer* newsroom, Rolfe Neill and Roberto Suarez were building a similar management structure for the entire company. The ten-year turnover in department heads stopped after Neill's arrival in 1975. He worked to break down barriers between departments, to end the turf-guarding that had too often barbed interdepartmental relations. He encouraged the sharing of ideas and a group approach to priority setting. In the process he achieved a stability that the company had not enjoyed since Bill Dowd's days. Gene Williams was in his tenth year as director of advertising. Ed Younghans was in his fifth year in production and his second as director since succeeding Otis Cox who retired. John Luby was in his sixth year as circulation manager; Dan Shaver, in his ninth as personnel manager; Dave Orbaugh, in his eleventh as advance systems director; and John Koslick, in his eighth year as director of research. Tim Breiding was in his twelfth year in marketing; Charles Daul, in his twelfth year in accounting and eighth as controller.

Presiding over that team was Roberto Suarez, truly an American success story. The Cuban-born Suarez went to high school with Fidel Castro and, as a banker and accountant, supported the revolution until Castro turned toward communism. He fled Cuba in 1961 and got a job in Miami bundling newspapers for the *Miami Herald*. When his skills became obvious to *Herald* managers, he was given larger responsibilities and ultimately was transferred to Charlotte as *Observer* controller in September 1972. He became business manager in 1975, general manager in 1978, and, at age fifty-seven, president of the Knight Publishing Company in January 1986.

In assembling a flexible, cooperative management team, Neill was following the dictates of modern corporate reality. To attract and maintain high-quality people, he had to share his authority and discretion with subordinates. A century earlier, when printers ran newspapers, nobody had to worry about management structures— there was little newspaper to manage. Later, when newspapers were run by editors such as Joseph Caldwell, the editors did the managing, with the help of assistants for business or advertising or circulation. Later, in the age of publishers, men like Curtis Johnson sat at the head of a patriarchal system, in which orders and directives emanated from the top to subordinates who were given narrow functions and little discretion. Even then, newspapers, while complex in their operations, were relatively simple to manage—the bottom line was always to cut costs. But in a corporate world, where there is less loyalty to an individual, a place, or a company, and the newspaper is part of a larger operation whose parts are nearly interchangeable, opportunities for management initiative, discretion, and growth must be broad, or the unhappy, unfulfilled manager will go to work elsewhere.

That need for shared responsibility and flexibility became even greater as the *Observer* diversified the products and services it offered the public. In addition to the daily newspaper, it was producing eight tabloids and also marketing many of the services that were once performed for the newspaper alone. The photo lab was in business as KPC Photography and as KPC Audio/Visuals. In addition to delivering the newspaper, the circulation department was in business as KPC Distribution. While serving the needs of the daily newspaper, the marketing department was in business as KPC Typeset-ting. In addition to doing polling and market studies for the newspaper, the research staff was in business as KPC Research. In effect, the concept introduced by Curtis Johnson in creating the Ob-server Transportation Company was being applied across the board, generating additional revenues by selling the redundant service and production capacity of various newspaper departments.

But the daily newspaper remained the heart of the operation. Its quality and prestige made it the bellwether for all the auxiliary ser-vices. The photos appearing in the daily *Observer* were a guide to the quality a client could expect from KPC Photography. The accuracy of the public opinion polling reported in the newspaper provided an in-dex to the reliability of market studies available from KPC Research. The community standing of the newspaper was crucial to the mar-ket potential of any of its subsidiaries.

After Neill's success in integrating the Charlotte company, similar moves were made to restructure the management systems of other Knight-Ridder newspapers. Most other papers in the chain were given resident publishers. Most others also began publishing "Busi-ness Monday" tabloids and special tabs for specific communities in their circulation territory. The example set by the *Observer* had won it a new status within the Knight-Ridder organization. In terms of quality, leadership, and profits, it had moved from the second eche-lon of Knight-Ridder properties into the corporation's "major league."

It had been a long, hard climb since January 1869, when four Con-federate veterans launched the fragile, four-page newspaper that in-troduced the name *Observer* to readers in the Piedmont Carolinas. Somehow the name endured, even if the newspaper did not. It had been a long and tortuous climb since March 1886, when William S. Hemby founded the *Chronicle* as a political rival that put that first *Observer* out of business, then fell upon hard times of its own. It had even been a long and difficult climb since March 1892, when Joseph P. Caldwell and Daniel A. Tompkins rescued the *Chronicle*, renamed it the *Observer*, and dedicated it to a rising New South and the in-dustrial potential of the surrounding region.

It was Curtis Johnson who built the *Observer* into the largest newspaper in the Carolinas, expanding its staff and modernizing its equipment. Ralph Nicholson had revamped the paper's appear-ance, and Mrs. Curtis Johnson had given it the courage to welcome the racial revolution. It was the Knights and Pete McKnight who lifted it to national stature by raising standards, recruiting bright young people, and arousing its social conscience. Jim Batten gave it professional polish, David Lawrence gave it energy and imagination, and Rolfe Neill and Rich Oppel gave it unity and versatility and restored its regional outlook.

Over the years, the role and setting for the paper had undergone profound change. The *Observer* was no longer a thin little daily intended to promote the town and its commerce, but a voluminous journal of many parts reflecting the diversity of an entire region and its people. It could no longer be a newspaper of record, chronicling every occurrence within its realm; it had become a herald of the singular events, large and small, that gave meaning and dimension to everyday life. It was no longer the voice of a single editor or publisher, expounding a personal point of view; it was a collective of many voices and interests, with an obligation to express the opinion of others as well as its own. From a blind booster of the city, the region, and all business and industry, it had become a discerning auditor that tried to measure the good against the bad.

Charlotte had grown from a plain country crossroads opening onto farms and forests into the servant of a sprawling metropolitan area laced with highways, dotted with factories and schools, and covering many counties and municipalities. The *Observer* was no longer the only source of information within that region; it was part of a complex communications market that included television, radio, shopping guides, magazines, as well as rival newspapers, local and state. Indeed, to compete in such a market the *Observer* itself had become a collection of publications: six different editions each day, plus eight separate tabloids and a variety of occasional special editions. It was offering services that went beyond the dissemination of news and advertising.

Fittingly, by the afternoon of March 21, 1986, the last day of its 100th year of publication, the paper was enjoying one of its happiest, most stable hours. Circulation was up, advertising was up, morale was high. Charlotte and the metropolitan region, despite a transition from a textile economy to diversified manufacturing and services, were prospering. Although there would be future conflict and controversy, because that is the nature of the news and opinion business, for the moment the *Observer*'s internal and external divisions seemed to have been healed. In a cheerful mood, the paper's 1,350 employees, their managers, and retirees and associates from the Observer Transportation Company jammed the lobby of the newspaper office, engulfing a photographic exhibit marking the paper's centennial. There they filled colorful balloons with helium gas, and listened to a few brief speeches about the paper's past struggles and future promise. They sang a lusty "Happy Birthday," then went out on the lawn and released the balloons against a clear, azure sky.

INDEX